lub

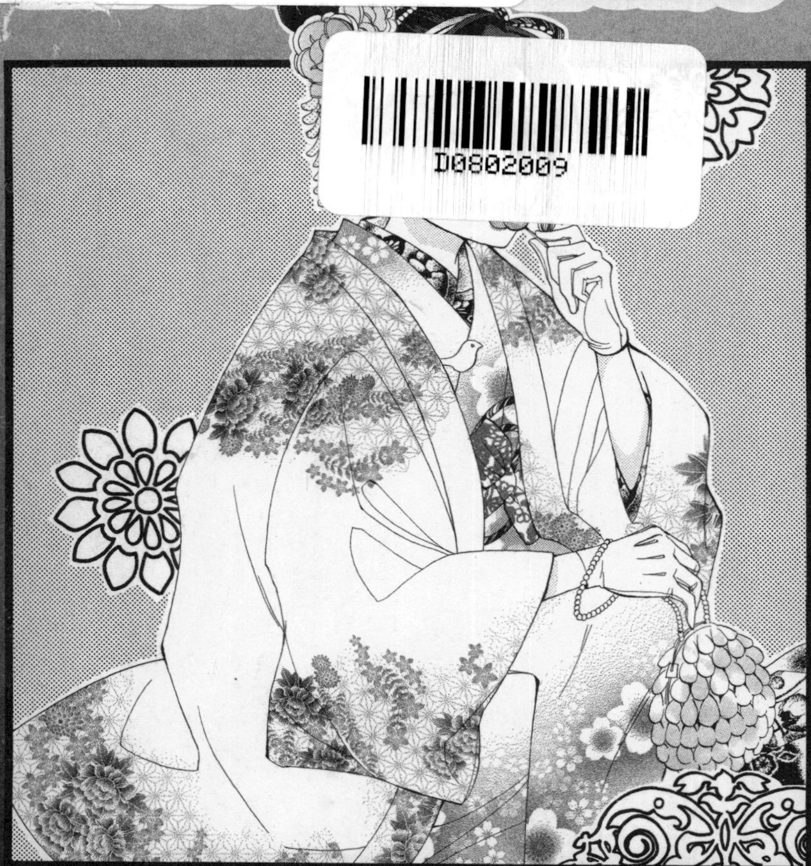

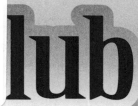

Vol. 11

Bisco Hatori

Ouran High School

Host Club

Vol. 11

CONTENTS

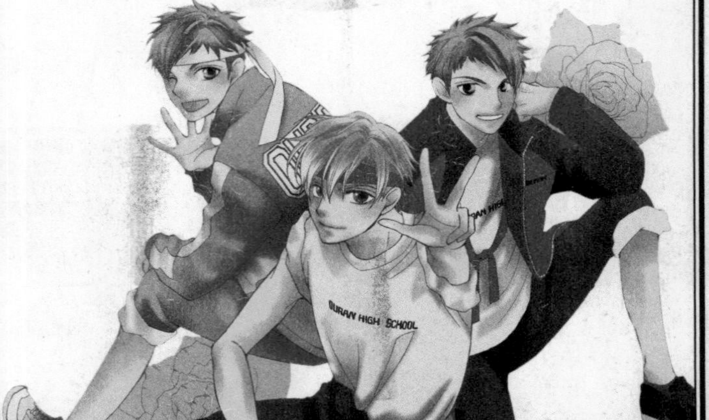
OURAN HIGH SCHOOL

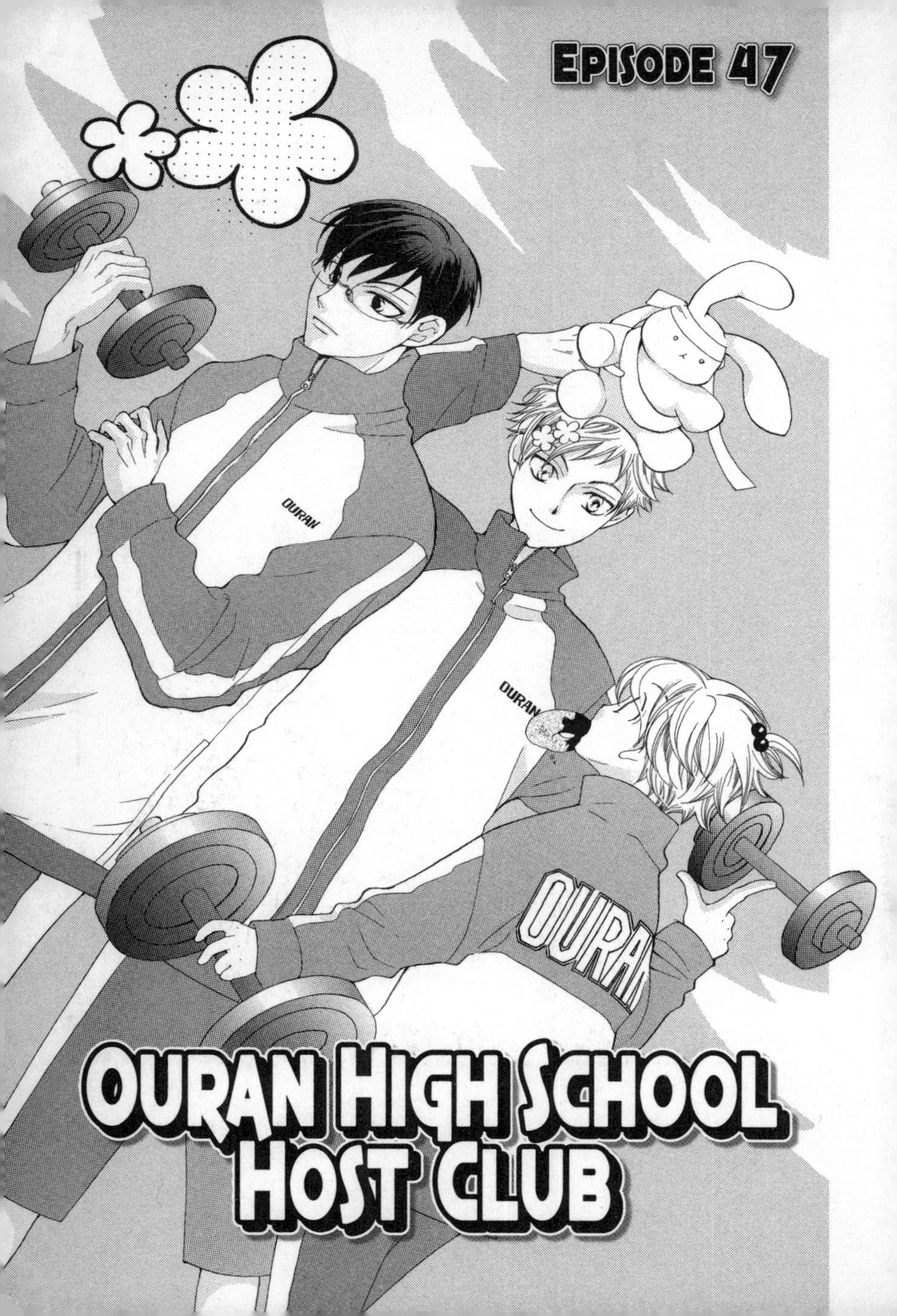
EPISODE 47
OURAN
OURAN
OURAN
OURAN HIGH SCHOOL HOST CLUB

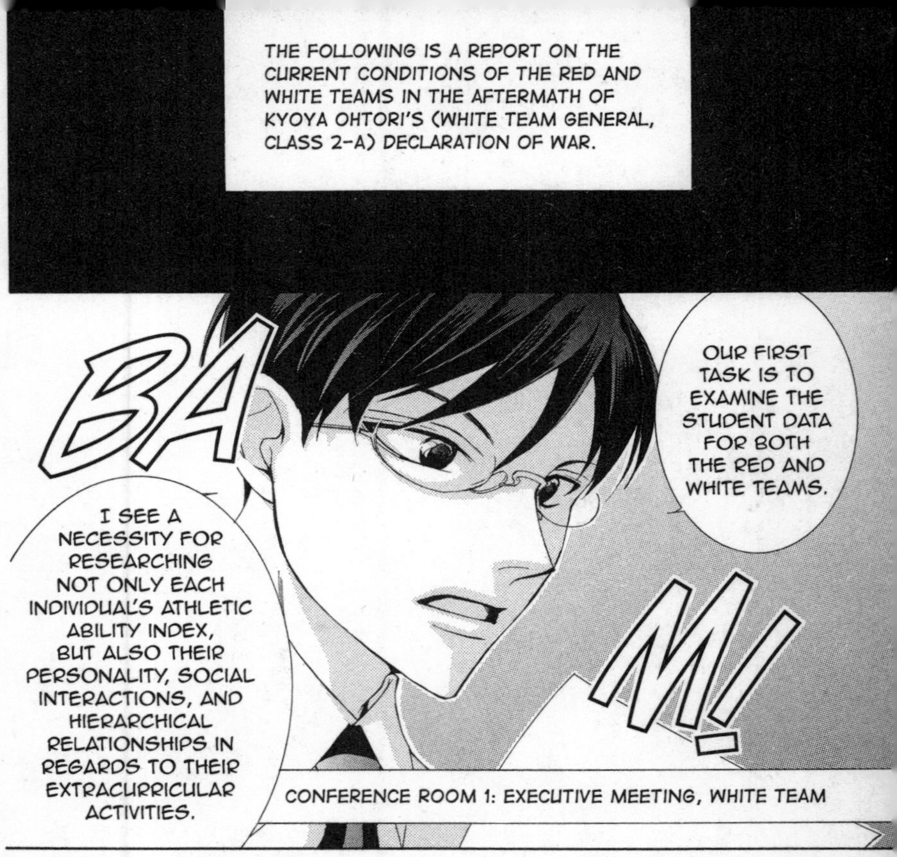
THE FOLLOWING IS A REPORT ON THE CURRENT CONDITIONS OF THE RED AND WHITE TEAMS IN THE AFTERMATH OF KYOYA OHTORI'S (WHITE TEAM GENERAL, CLASS 2-A) DECLARATION OF WAR.
OUR FIRST TASK IS TO EXAMINE THE STUDENT DATA FOR BOTH THE RED AND WHITE TEAMS.
BA
M!
I SEE A NECESSITY FOR RESEARCHING NOT ONLY EACH INDIVIDUAL'S ATHLETIC ABILITY INDEX, BUT ALSO THEIR PERSONALITY, SOCIAL INTERACTIONS, AND HIERARCHICAL RELATIONSHIPS IN REGARDS TO THEIR EXTRACURRICULAR ACTIVITIES.
CONFERENCE ROOM 1: EXECUTIVE MEETING, WHITE TEAM

✿ HATORI'S UNBIDDEN LIST OF FAVORITE ITEMS ✿

SINCE I'VE BEEN WEARING THIS AROUND MY NECK, MY NECK AND SHOULDER PAIN HAS DECREASED TO A THIRD OF WHAT IT WAS. I'M NEVER LETTING GO OF IT. I HIGHLY RECOMMEND IT! SOME PEOPLE MIGHT HAVE AN ALLERGIC REACTION TO THE MATERIAL, SO PLEASE USE CAUTION.

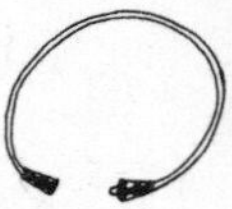

PIP MAGNET LOOP

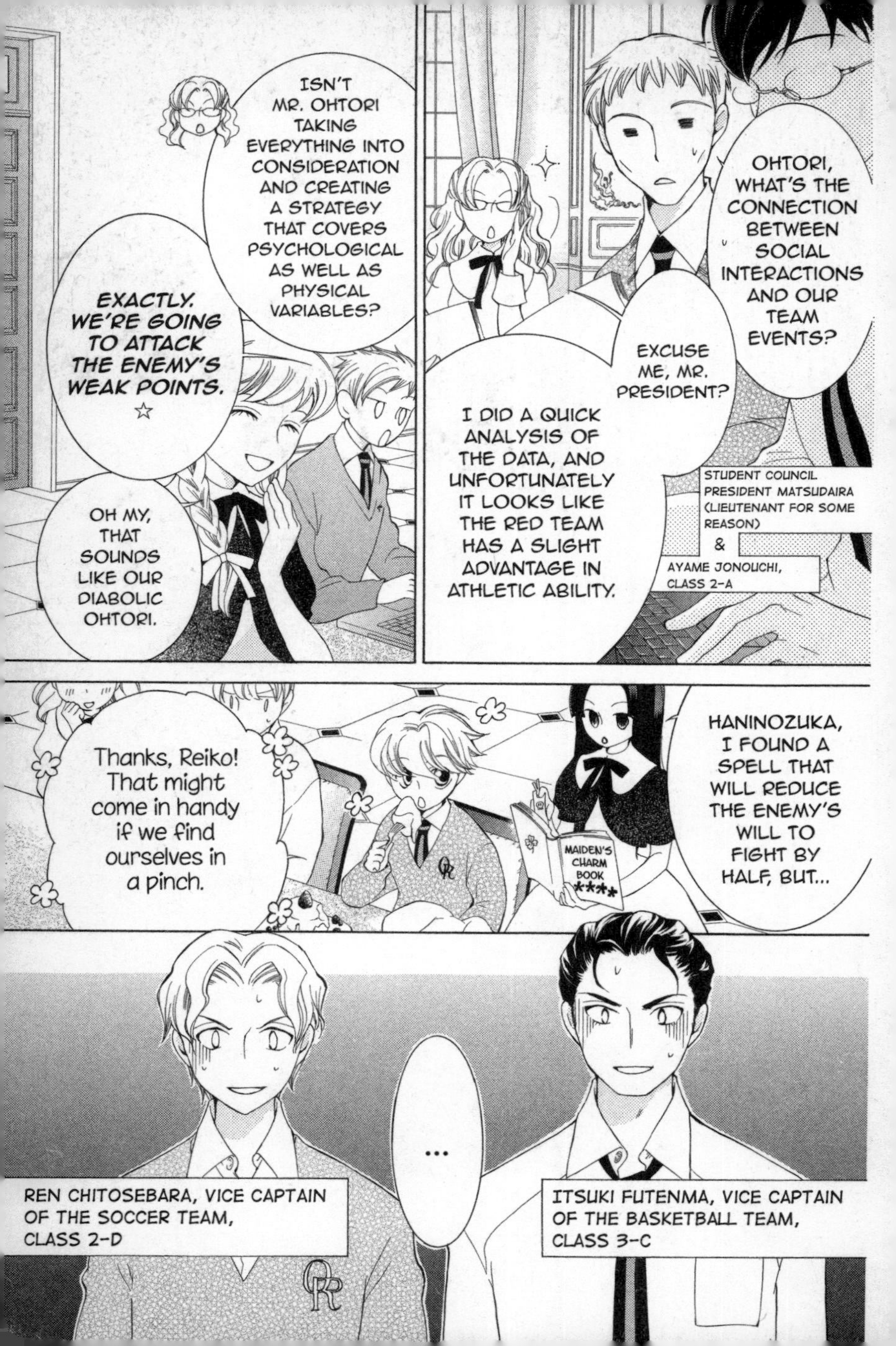
OHTORI, WHAT'S THE CONNECTION BETWEEN SOCIAL INTERACTIONS AND OUR TEAM EVENTS?
EXCUSE ME, MR. PRESIDENT?
I DID A QUICK ANALYSIS OF THE DATA, AND UNFORTUNATELY IT LOOKS LIKE THE RED TEAM HAS A SLIGHT ADVANTAGE IN ATHLETIC ABILITY.
STUDENT COUNCIL PRESIDENT MATSUDAIRA (LIEUTENANT FOR SOME REASON) & AYAME JONOUCHI, CLASS 2-A
ISN'T MR. OHTORI TAKING EVERYTHING INTO CONSIDERATION AND CREATING A STRATEGY THAT COVERS PSYCHOLOGICAL AS WELL AS PHYSICAL VARIABLES?
EXACTLY. WE'RE GOING TO ATTACK THE ENEMY'S WEAK POINTS. ☆
OH MY, THAT SOUNDS LIKE OUR DIABOLIC OHTORI.
HANINOZUKA, I FOUND A SPELL THAT WILL REDUCE THE ENEMY'S WILL TO FIGHT BY HALF, BUT...
MAIDEN'S CHARM BOOK
Thanks, Reiko! That might come in handy if we find ourselves in a pinch.
ITSUKI FUTENMA, VICE CAPTAIN OF THE BASKETBALL TEAM, CLASS 3-C
...
REN CHITOSEBARA, VICE CAPTAIN OF THE SOCCER TEAM, CLASS 2-D

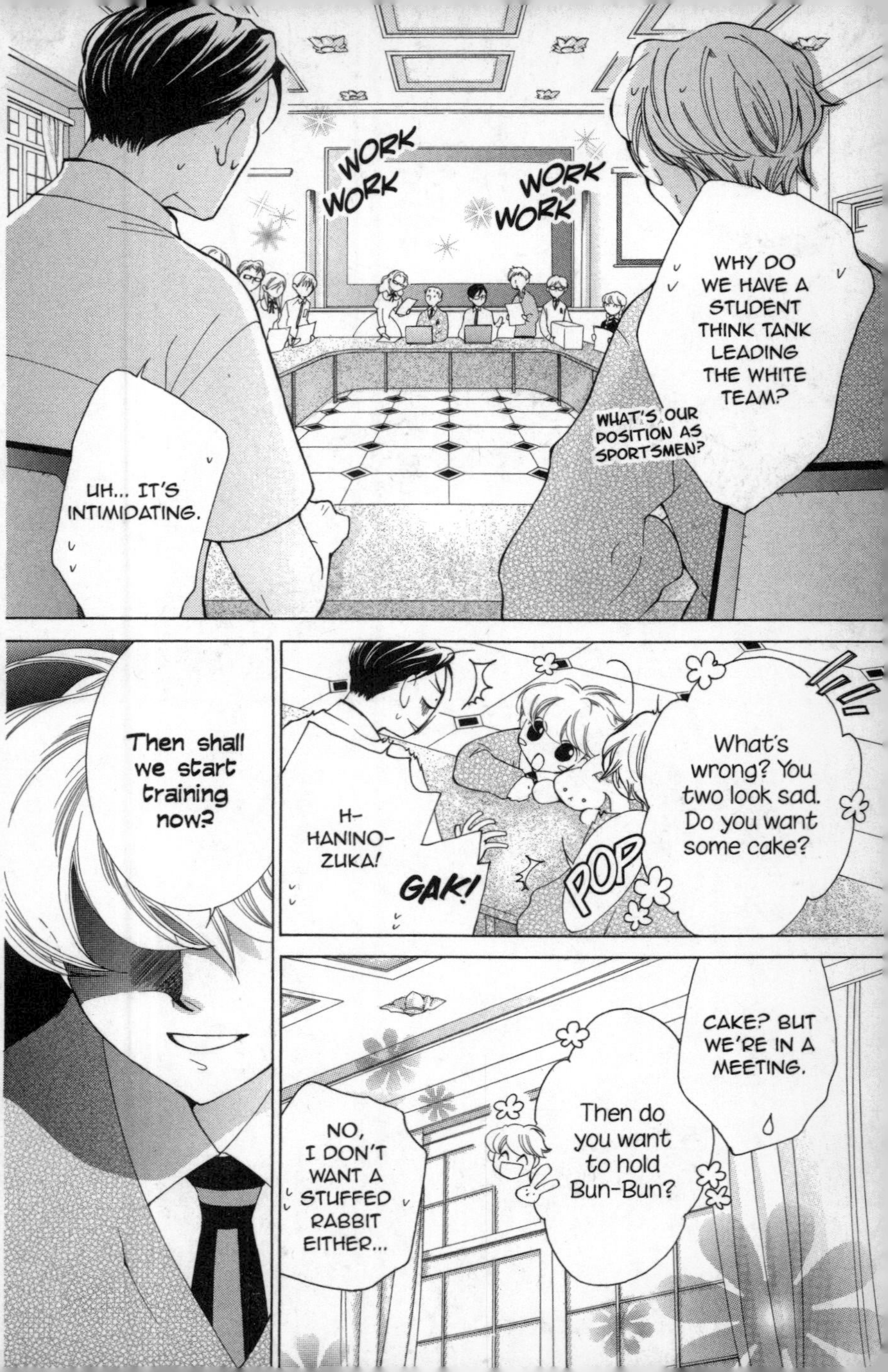
WHY DO WE HAVE A STUDENT THINK TANK LEADING THE WHITE TEAM?
WHAT'S OUR POSITION AS SPORTSMEN?
WORK WORK
WORK WORK
UH... IT'S INTIMIDATING.
What's wrong? You two look sad. Do you want some cake?
POP
GAK!
H-HANINOZUKA!
CAKE? BUT WE'RE IN A MEETING.
Then do you want to hold Bun-Bun?
NO, I DON'T WANT A STUFFED RABBIT EITHER...
Then shall we start training now?

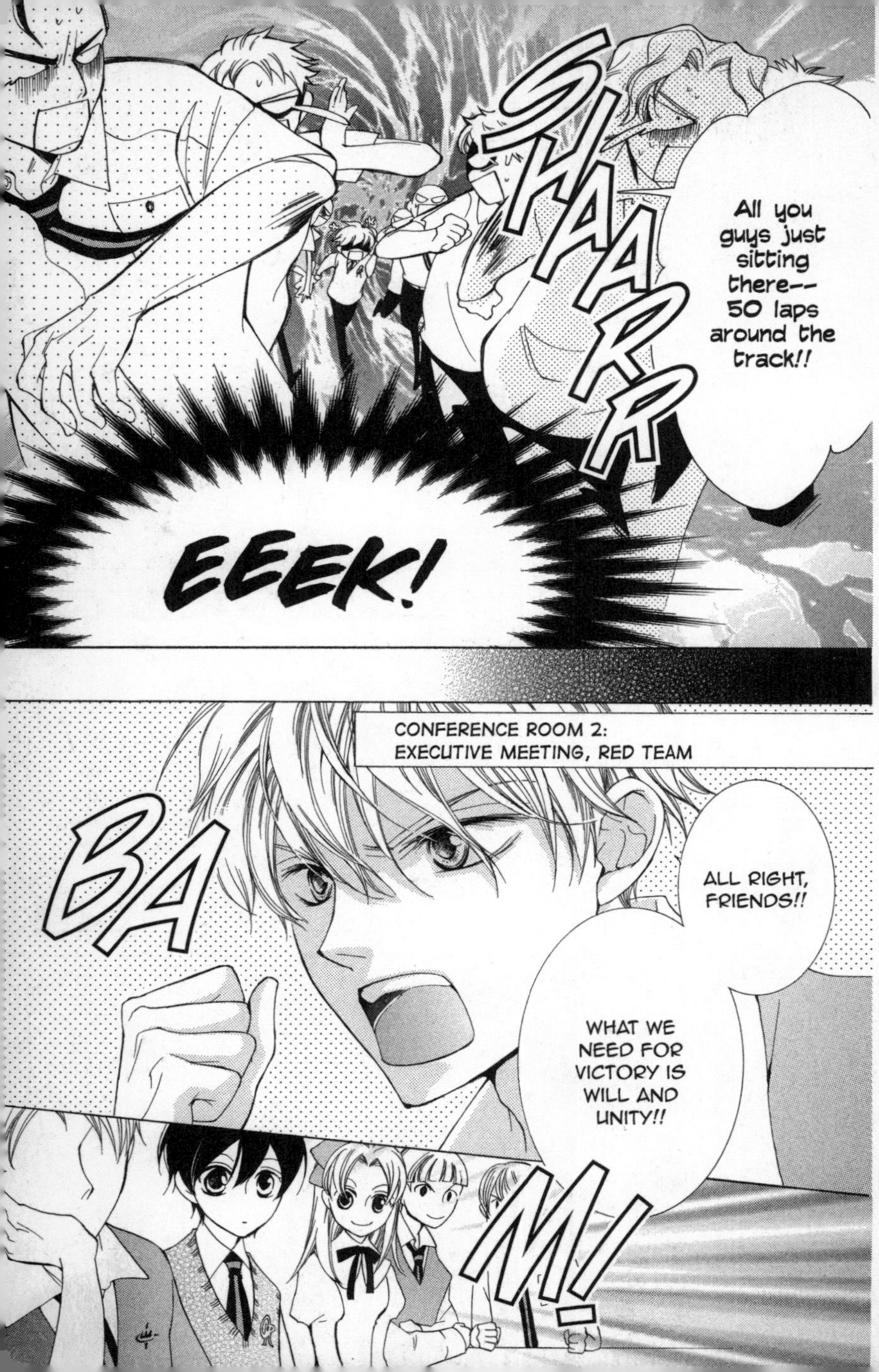
All you guys just sitting there--50 laps around the track!!
SHAARR
EEEK!
CONFERENCE ROOM 2: EXECUTIVE MEETING, RED TEAM
ALL RIGHT, FRIENDS!!
WHAT WE NEED FOR VICTORY IS WILL AND UNITY!!
BA
MI!

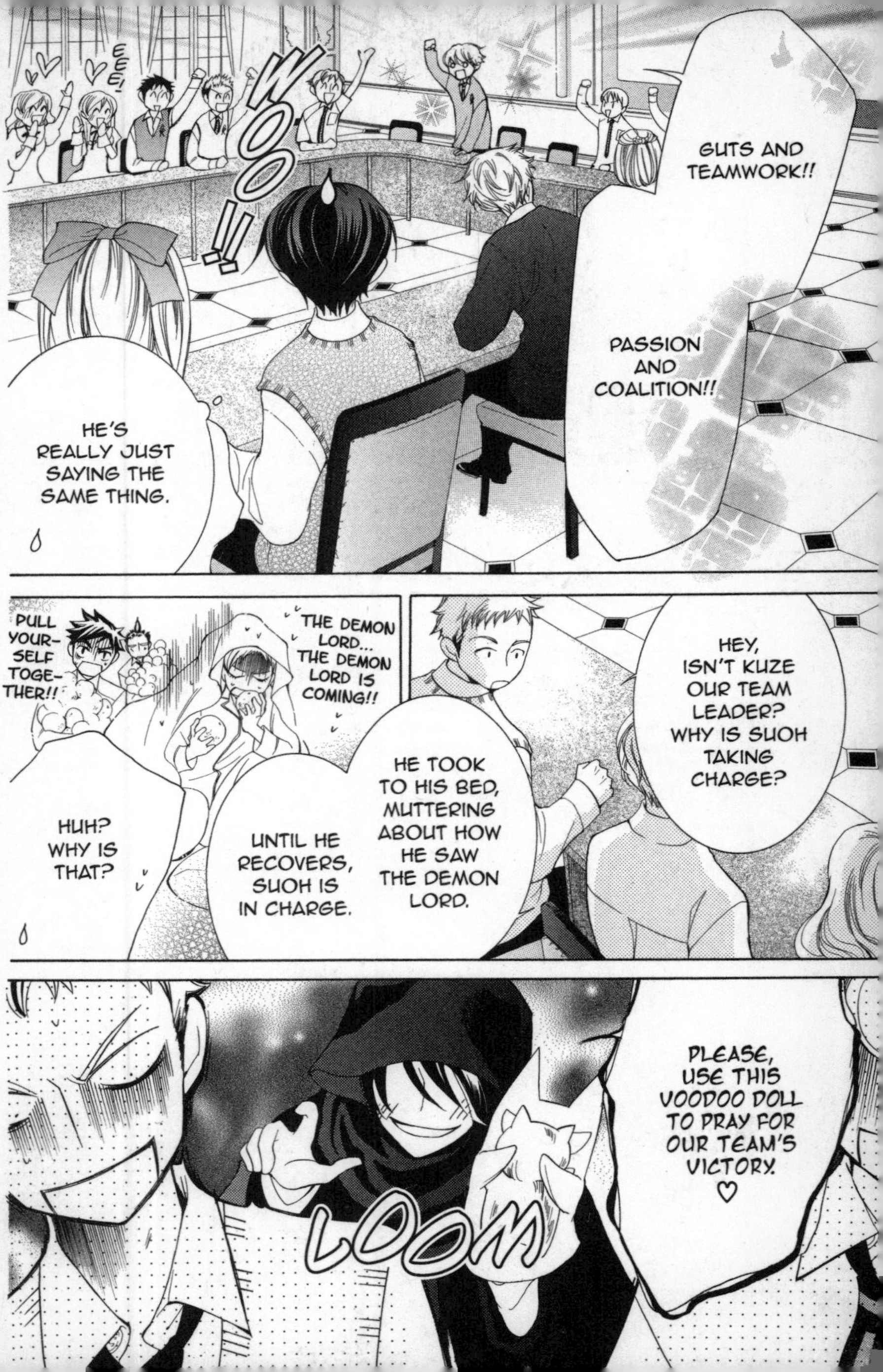

GUTS AND TEAMWORK!!
PASSION AND COALITION!!
WOOOO!!!
EEE!
HE'S REALLY JUST SAYING THE SAME THING.
HEY, ISN'T KUZE OUR TEAM LEADER? WHY IS SUOH TAKING CHARGE?
UNTIL HE RECOVERS, SUOH IS IN CHARGE.
HUH? WHY IS THAT?
HE TOOK TO HIS BED, MUTTERING ABOUT HOW HE SAW THE DEMON LORD.
THE DEMON LORD... THE DEMON LORD IS COMING!!
PULL YOURSELF TOGETHER!!
PLEASE, USE THIS VOODOO DOLL TO PRAY FOR OUR TEAM'S VICTORY. ♡
LOOM

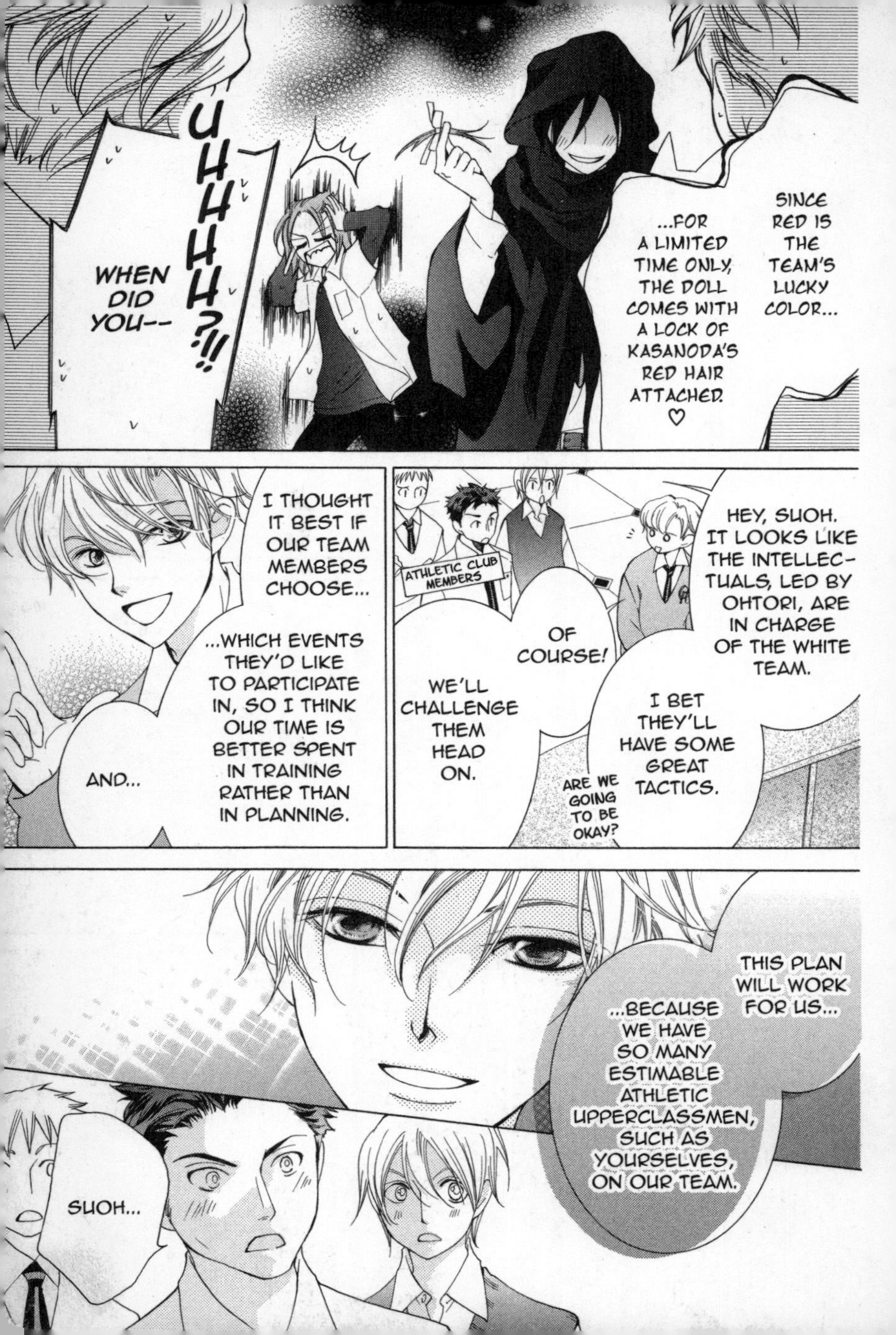
SINCE RED IS THE TEAM'S LUCKY COLOR...
...FOR A LIMITED TIME ONLY, THE DOLL COMES WITH A LOCK OF KASANODA'S RED HAIR ATTACHED. ♡
UHHHHH?!!
WHEN DID YOU--
HEY, SUOH. IT LOOKS LIKE THE INTELLECTUALS, LED BY OHTORI, ARE IN CHARGE OF THE WHITE TEAM.
I BET THEY'LL HAVE SOME GREAT TACTICS.
ARE WE GOING TO BE OKAY?
OF COURSE!
WE'LL CHALLENGE THEM HEAD ON.
ATHLETIC CLUB MEMBERS
I THOUGHT IT BEST IF OUR TEAM MEMBERS CHOOSE...
...WHICH EVENTS THEY'D LIKE TO PARTICIPATE IN, SO I THINK OUR TIME IS BETTER SPENT IN TRAINING RATHER THAN IN PLANNING.
AND...
THIS PLAN WILL WORK FOR US...
...BECAUSE WE HAVE SO MANY ESTIMABLE ATHLETIC UPPERCLASSMEN, SUCH AS YOURSELVES, ON OUR TEAM.
SUOH...

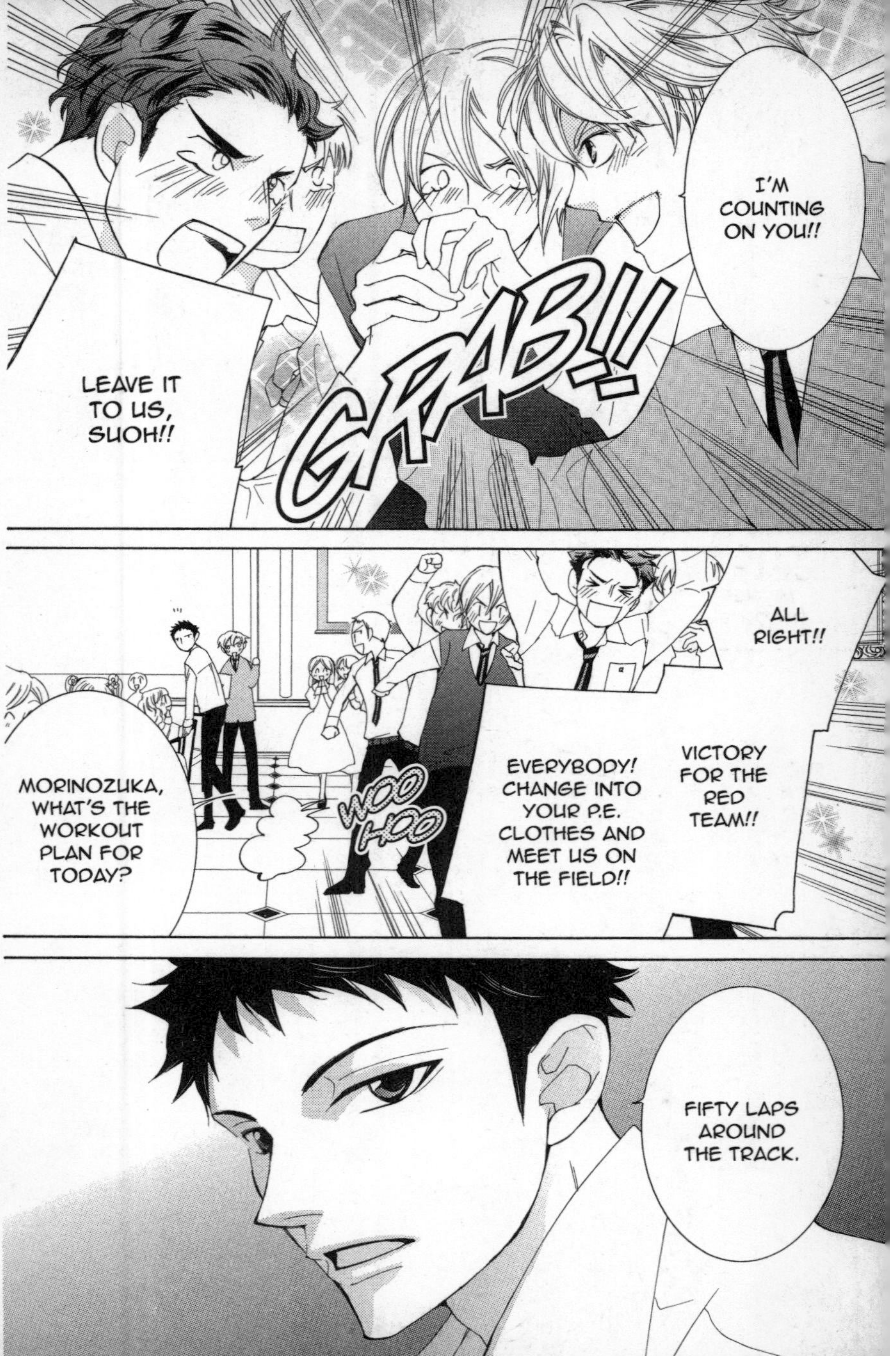
I'M COUNTING ON YOU!!
GRAB!!
LEAVE IT TO US, SUOH!!
ALL RIGHT!!
VICTORY FOR THE RED TEAM!!
EVERYBODY! CHANGE INTO YOUR P.E. CLOTHES AND MEET US ON THE FIELD!!
WOO HOO
MORINOZUKA, WHAT'S THE WORKOUT PLAN FOR TODAY?
FIFTY LAPS AROUND THE TRACK.

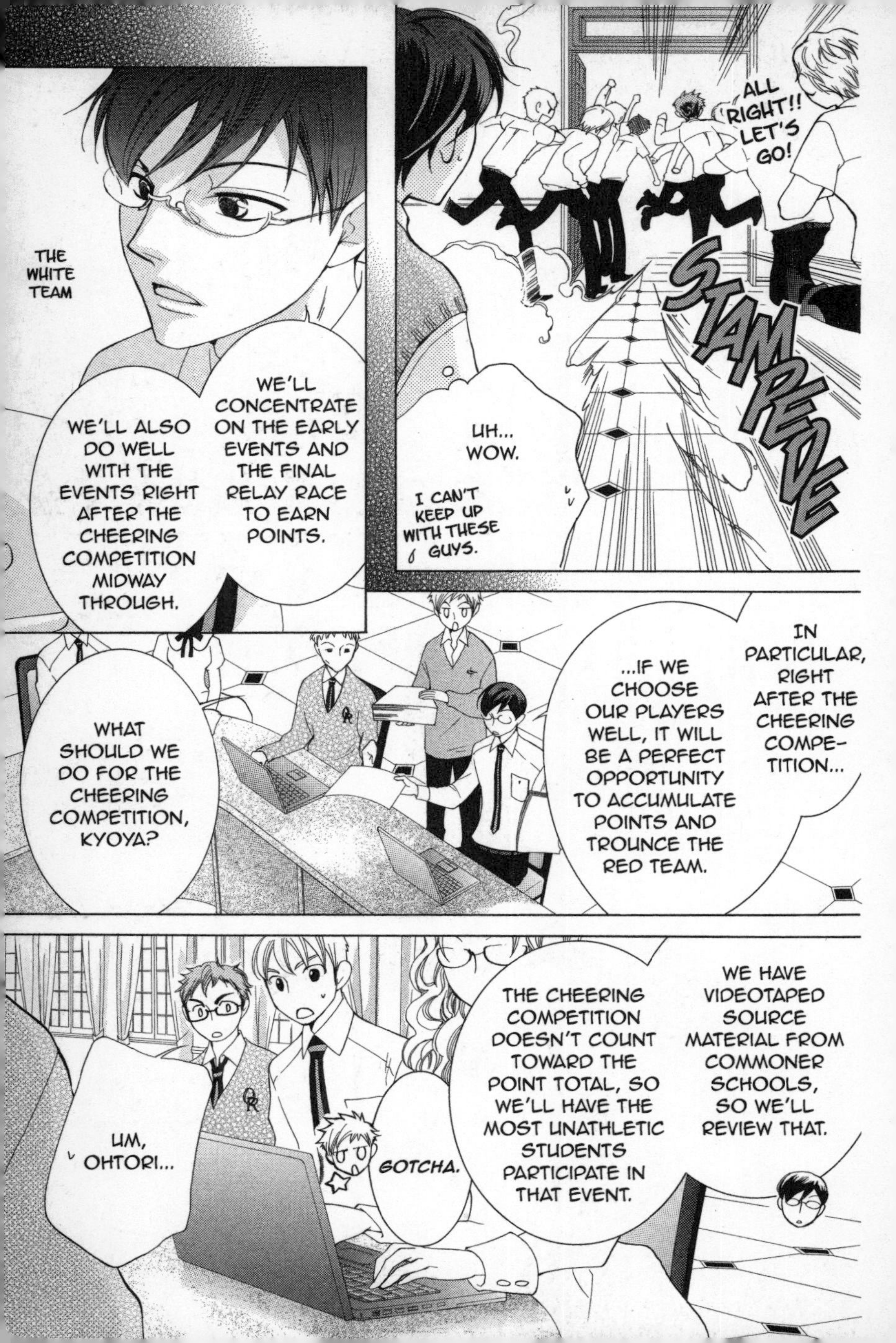
ALL RIGHT!! LET'S GO!
STAMPEDE
UH... WOW.
I CAN'T KEEP UP WITH THESE GUYS.
THE WHITE TEAM
WE'LL CONCENTRATE ON THE EARLY EVENTS AND THE FINAL RELAY RACE TO EARN POINTS.
WE'LL ALSO DO WELL WITH THE EVENTS RIGHT AFTER THE CHEERING COMPETITION MIDWAY THROUGH.
IN PARTICULAR, RIGHT AFTER THE CHEERING COMPE-TITION...
...IF WE CHOOSE OUR PLAYERS WELL, IT WILL BE A PERFECT OPPORTUNITY TO ACCUMULATE POINTS AND TROUNCE THE RED TEAM.
WHAT SHOULD WE DO FOR THE CHEERING COMPETITION, KYOYA?
WE HAVE VIDEOTAPED SOURCE MATERIAL FROM COMMONER SCHOOLS, SO WE'LL REVIEW THAT.
THE CHEERING COMPETITION DOESN'T COUNT TOWARD THE POINT TOTAL, SO WE'LL HAVE THE MOST UNATHLETIC STUDENTS PARTICIPATE IN THAT EVENT.
GOTCHA.
UM, OHTORI...

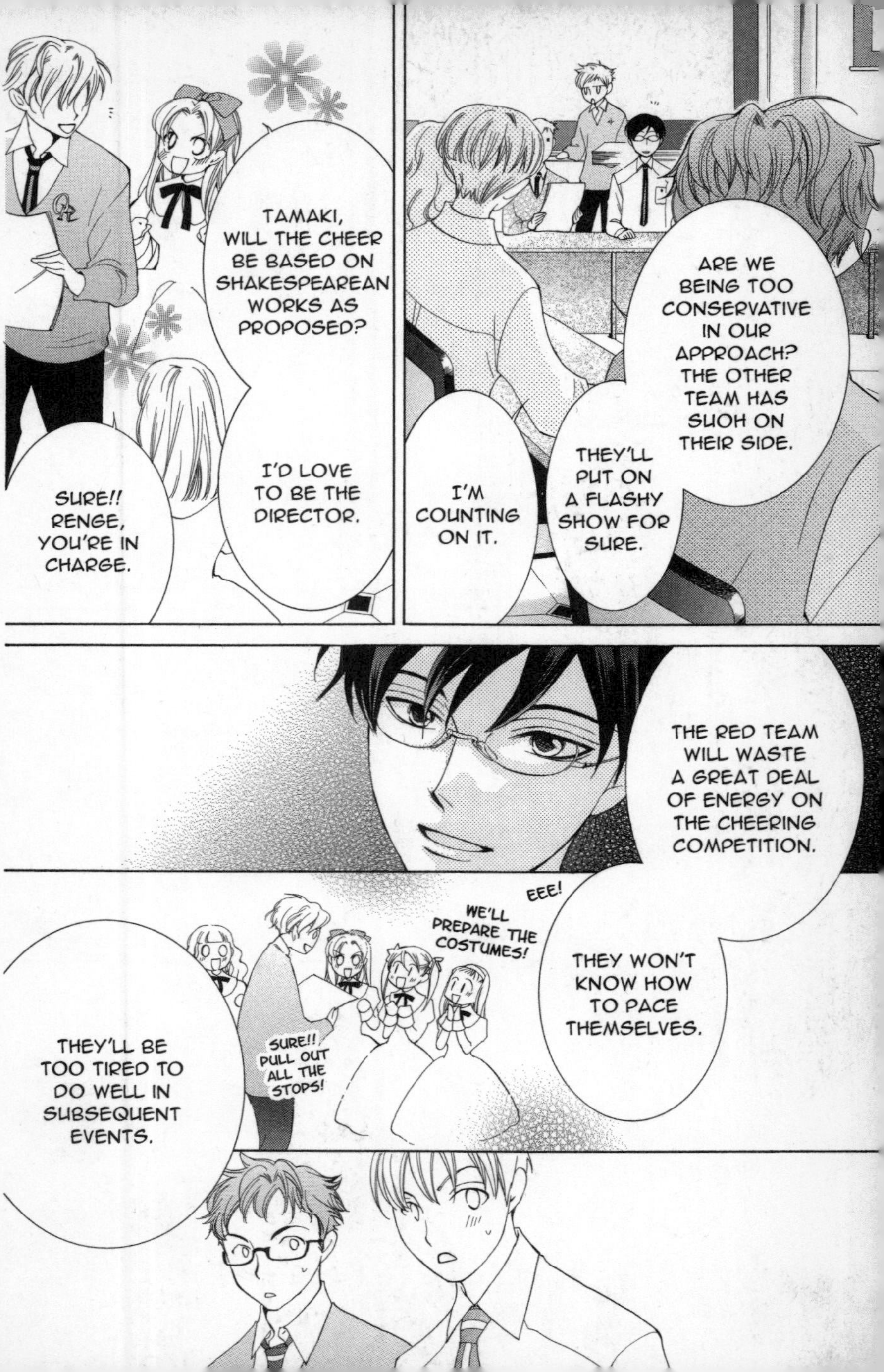
ARE WE BEING TOO CONSERVATIVE IN OUR APPROACH? THE OTHER TEAM HAS SUOH ON THEIR SIDE.
THEY'LL PUT ON A FLASHY SHOW FOR SURE.
I'M COUNTING ON IT.
TAMAKI, WILL THE CHEER BE BASED ON SHAKESPEAREAN WORKS AS PROPOSED?
I'D LOVE TO BE THE DIRECTOR.
SURE!! RENGE, YOU'RE IN CHARGE.
THE RED TEAM WILL WASTE A GREAT DEAL OF ENERGY ON THE CHEERING COMPETITION.
THEY WON'T KNOW HOW TO PACE THEMSELVES.
EEE!
WE'LL PREPARE THE COSTUMES!
SURE!! PULL OUT ALL THE STOPS!
THEY'LL BE TOO TIRED TO DO WELL IN SUBSEQUENT EVENTS.

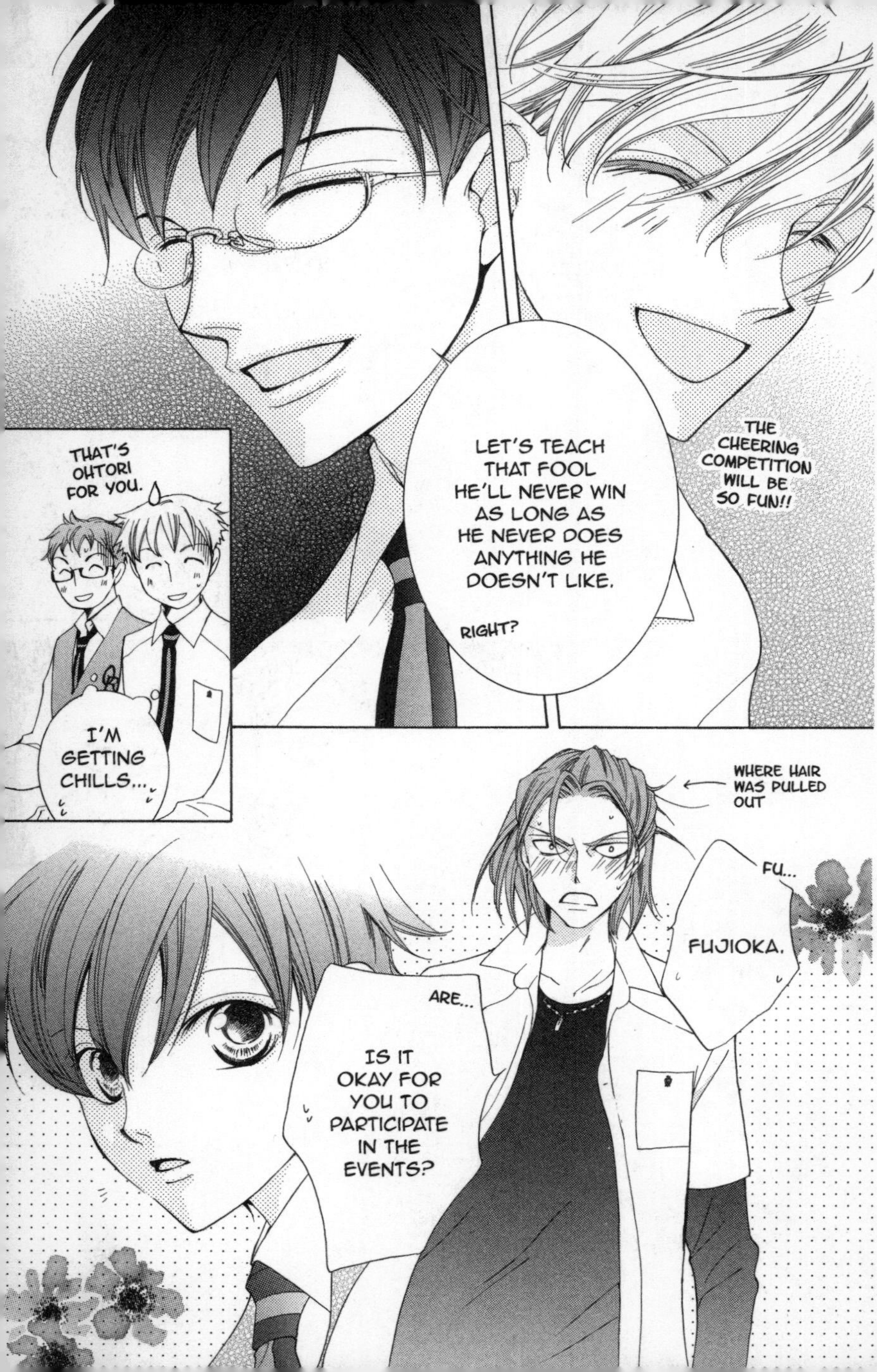
LET'S TEACH THAT FOOL HE'LL NEVER WIN AS LONG AS HE NEVER DOES ANYTHING HE DOESN'T LIKE.
RIGHT?
THE CHEERING COMPETITION WILL BE SO FUN!!
THAT'S OHTORI FOR YOU.
I'M GETTING CHILLS...
WHERE HAIR WAS PULLED OUT
FU...
FUJIOKA.
ARE...
IS IT OKAY FOR YOU TO PARTICIPATE IN THE EVENTS?

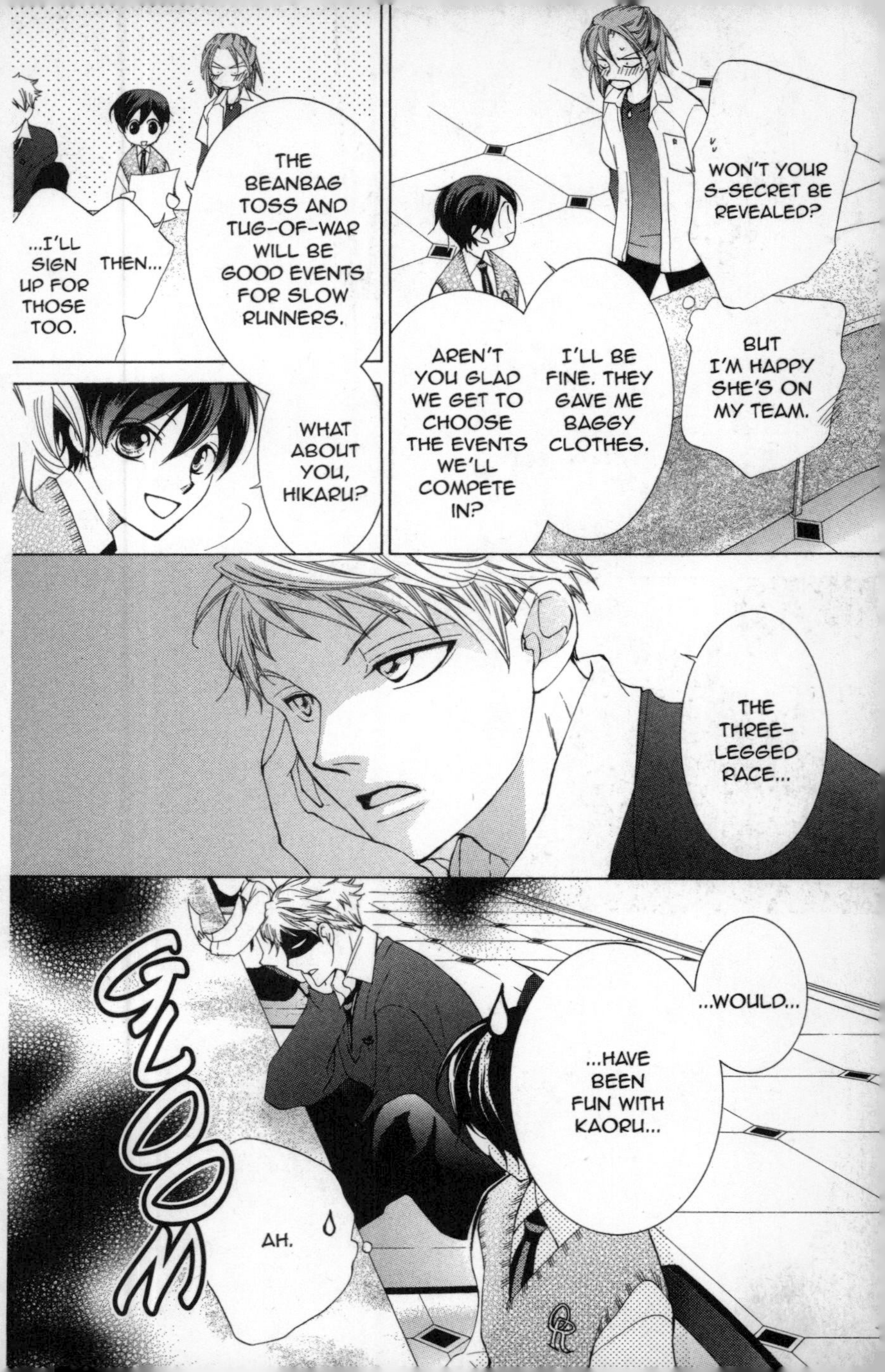
WON'T YOUR S-SECRET BE REVEALED?
I'LL BE FINE. THEY GAVE ME BAGGY CLOTHES.
BUT I'M HAPPY SHE'S ON MY TEAM.
AREN'T YOU GLAD WE GET TO CHOOSE THE EVENTS WE'LL COMPETE IN?
THE BEANBAG TOSS AND TUG-OF-WAR WILL BE GOOD EVENTS FOR SLOW RUNNERS.
THEN...
...I'LL SIGN UP FOR THOSE TOO.
WHAT ABOUT YOU, HIKARU?
THE THREE-LEGGED RACE...
...WOULD...
...HAVE BEEN FUN WITH KAORU...
GLOOM
AH.

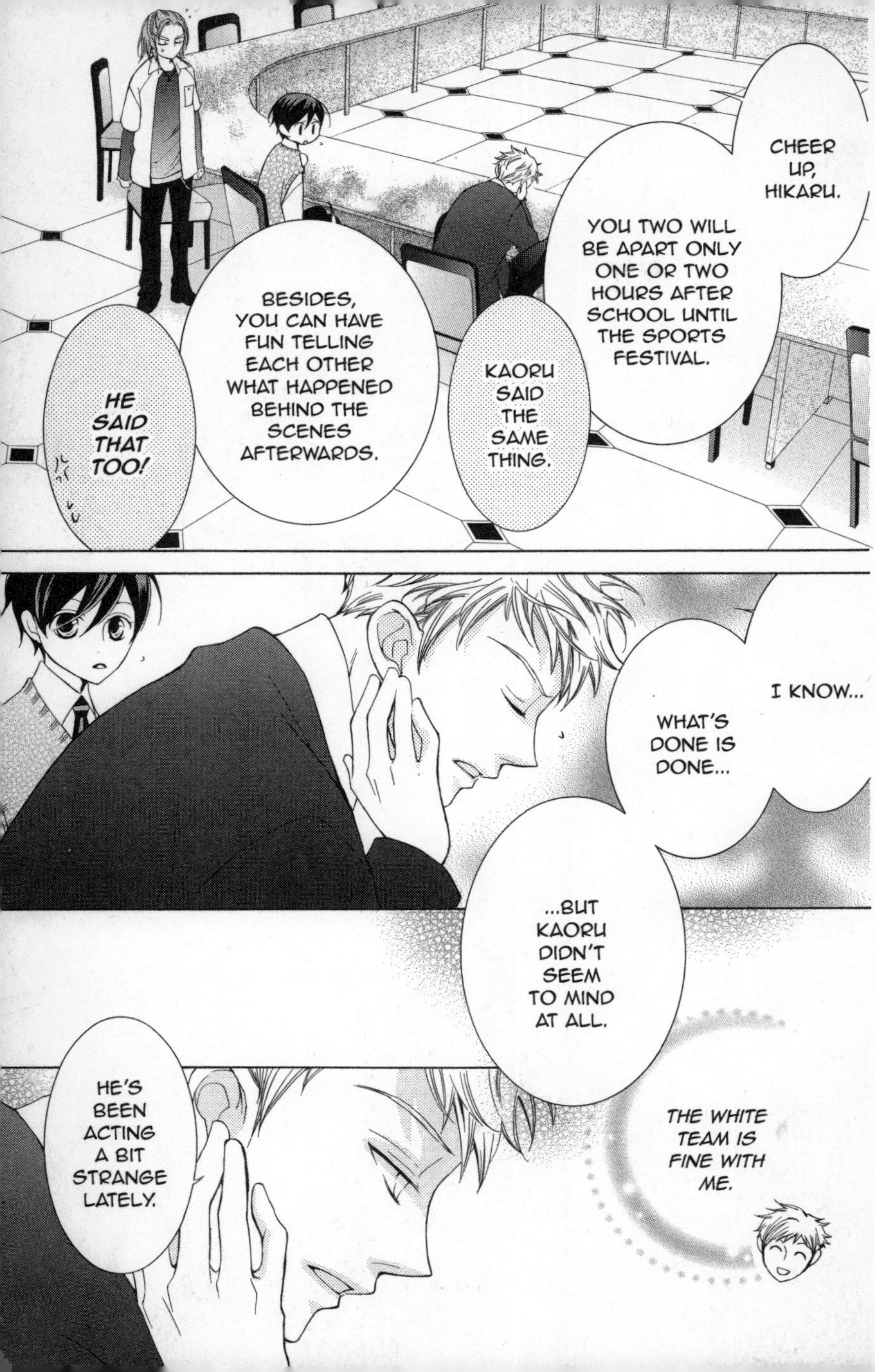
CHEER UP, HIKARU.
YOU TWO WILL BE APART ONLY ONE OR TWO HOURS AFTER SCHOOL UNTIL THE SPORTS FESTIVAL.
KAORU SAID THE SAME THING.
BESIDES, YOU CAN HAVE FUN TELLING EACH OTHER WHAT HAPPENED BEHIND THE SCENES AFTERWARDS.
HE SAID THAT TOO!
I KNOW...
WHAT'S DONE IS DONE...
...BUT KAORU DIDN'T SEEM TO MIND AT ALL.
THE WHITE TEAM IS FINE WITH ME.
HE'S BEEN ACTING A BIT STRANGE LATELY.

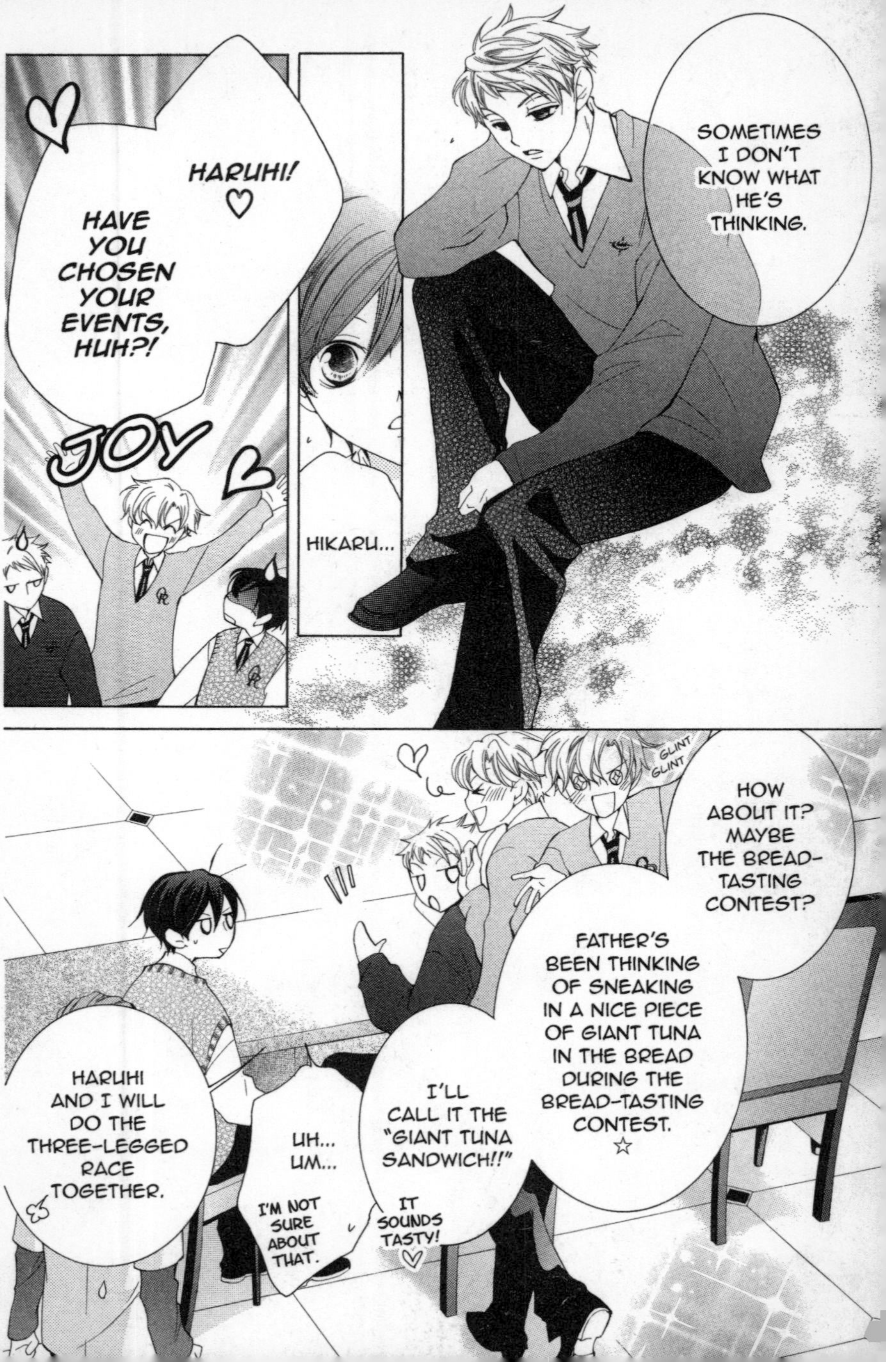
SOMETIMES I DON'T KNOW WHAT HE'S THINKING.
HIKARU...
HARUHI! ♡
HAVE YOU CHOSEN YOUR EVENTS, HUH?!
JOY
GLINT GLINT
HOW ABOUT IT? MAYBE THE BREAD-TASTING CONTEST?
FATHER'S BEEN THINKING OF SNEAKING IN A NICE PIECE OF GIANT TUNA IN THE BREAD DURING THE BREAD-TASTING CONTEST. ☆
I'LL CALL IT THE "GIANT TUNA SANDWICH!!"
IT SOUNDS TASTY! ♡
UH... UM...
I'M NOT SURE ABOUT THAT.
HARUHI AND I WILL DO THE THREE-LEGGED RACE TOGETHER.

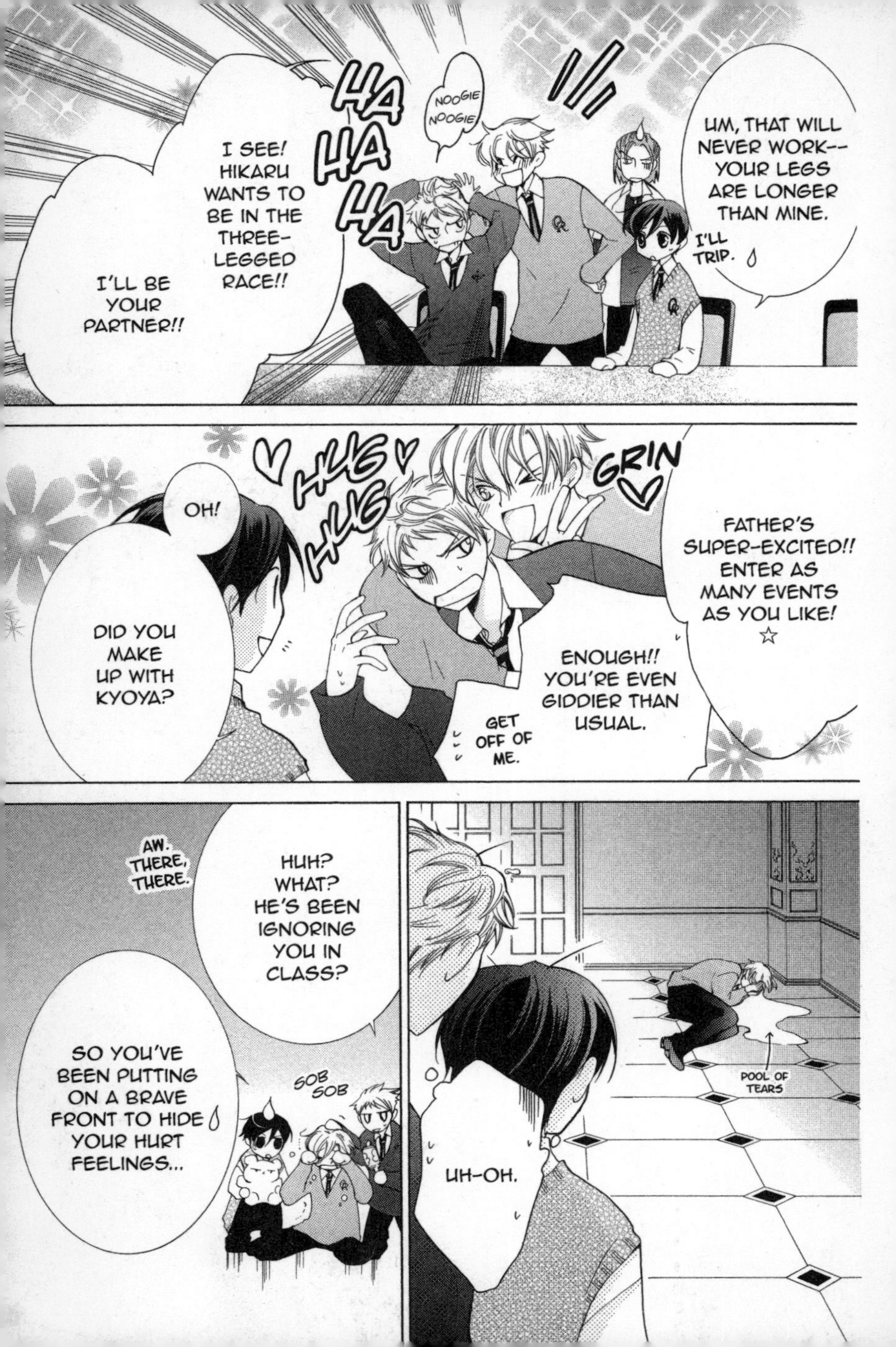
UM, THAT WILL NEVER WORK-- YOUR LEGS ARE LONGER THAN MINE.
I'LL TRIP.
NOOGIE NOOGIE
HA HA HA
I SEE! HIKARU WANTS TO BE IN THE THREE-LEGGED RACE!!
I'LL BE YOUR PARTNER!!
FATHER'S SUPER-EXCITED!! ENTER AS MANY EVENTS AS YOU LIKE! ☆
GRIN
HUG HUG
ENOUGH!! YOU'RE EVEN GIDDIER THAN USUAL.
GET OFF OF ME.
OH!
DID YOU MAKE UP WITH KYOYA?
POOL OF TEARS
UH-OH.
HUH? WHAT? HE'S BEEN IGNORING YOU IN CLASS?
AW. THERE, THERE.
SOB SOB
SO YOU'VE BEEN PUTTING ON A BRAVE FRONT TO HIDE YOUR HURT FEELINGS...

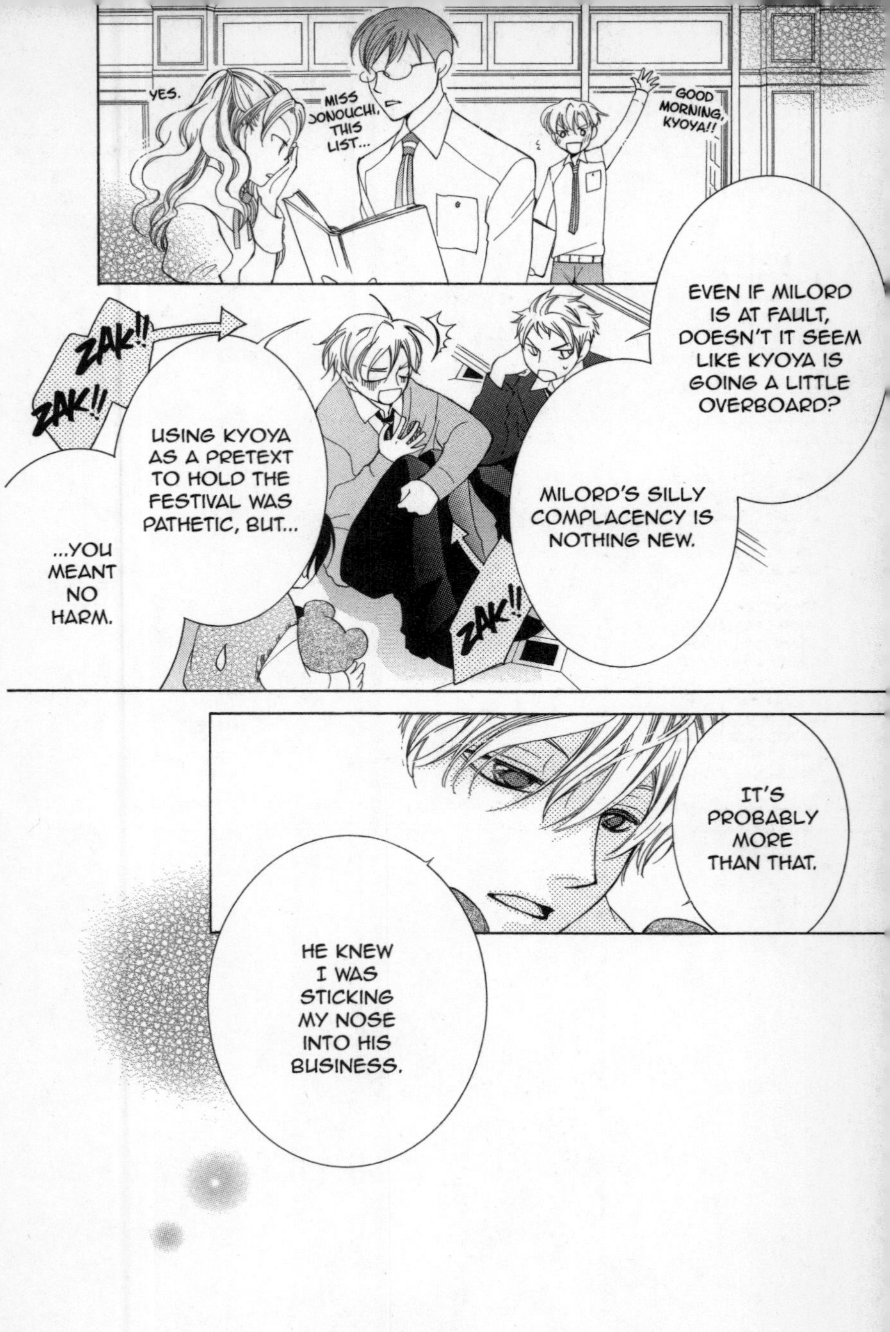
GOOD MORNING, KYOYA!!
MISS SONOUCHI, THIS LIST...
YES.
EVEN IF MILORD IS AT FAULT, DOESN'T IT SEEM LIKE KYOYA IS GOING A LITTLE OVERBOARD?
MILORD'S SILLY COMPLACENCY IS NOTHING NEW.
ZAK!!
USING KYOYA AS A PRETEXT TO HOLD THE FESTIVAL WAS PATHETIC, BUT...
ZAK!!
ZAK!!
...YOU MEANT NO HARM.
IT'S PROBABLY MORE THAN THAT.
HE KNEW I WAS STICKING MY NOSE INTO HIS BUSINESS.

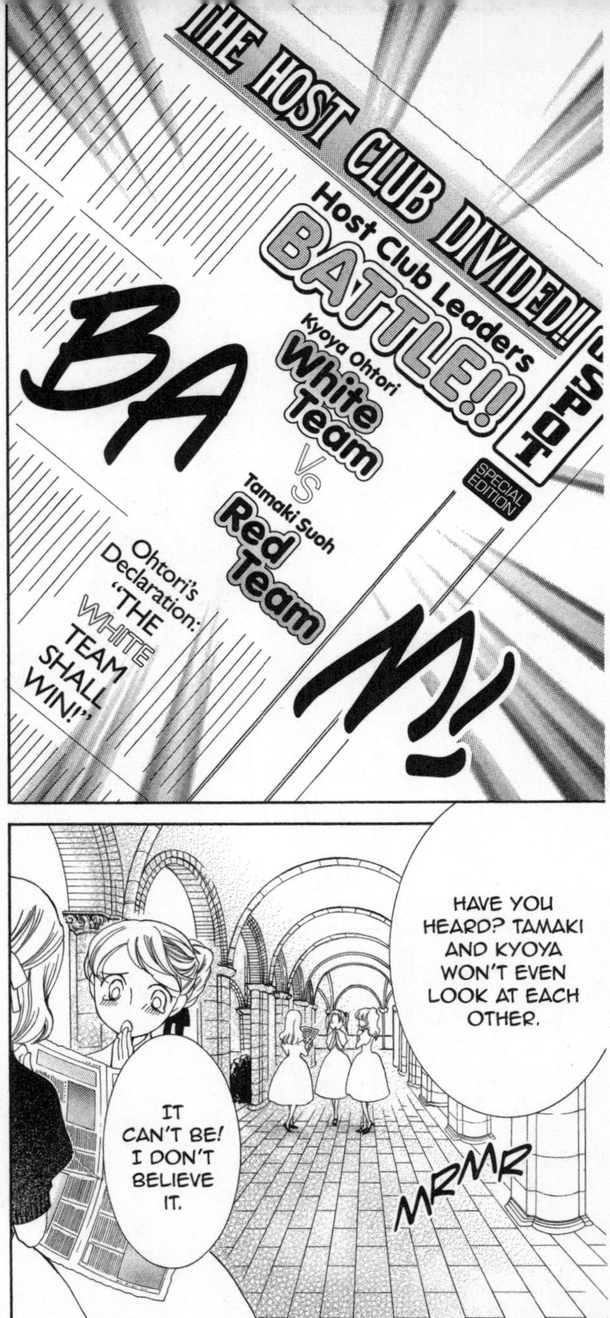
THE HOST CLUB DIVIDED!!
SPOT
SPECIAL EDITION
Host Club Leaders
BATTLE!!
Kyoya Ohtori
White Team
VS
Tamaki Suoh
Red Team
Ohtori's Declaration: "THE WHITE TEAM SHALL WIN!"
BAM!
HAVE YOU HEARD? TAMAKI AND KYOYA WON'T EVEN LOOK AT EACH OTHER.
IT CAN'T BE! I DON'T BELIEVE IT.
MRMR

1

GREETINGS!! HOW IS EVERYONE? SEASONS CHANGE IN THE REAL WORLD, BUT IT CONTINUES TO BE "FALL FOREVER!!" AT THE HOST CLUB.

WELL...I'M LEARNING THAT ALTHOUGH SYNCHRONIZING THE MANGA WITH THE REAL WORLD'S SEASONS IS DIFFICULT, THE OPPOSITE--COMPLETELY IGNORING THE REAL SEASONS AS I CREATE THE MANGA--CAN BE JUST AS CHALLENGING.

MY INTERNAL CALENDAR IS OFF, ESPECIALLY SINCE I'M HOLED UP INSIDE DRAWING MANGA.

I DO WORRY THAT READERS FOLLOWING THE SERIES MIGHT THINK, "WHY ARE THEY WEARING SCARVES IN SUMMER?"

PLEASE BEAR WITH ME AND CONTINUE READING THE SERIES.

I HOPE YOU ENJOY THIS VOLUME!

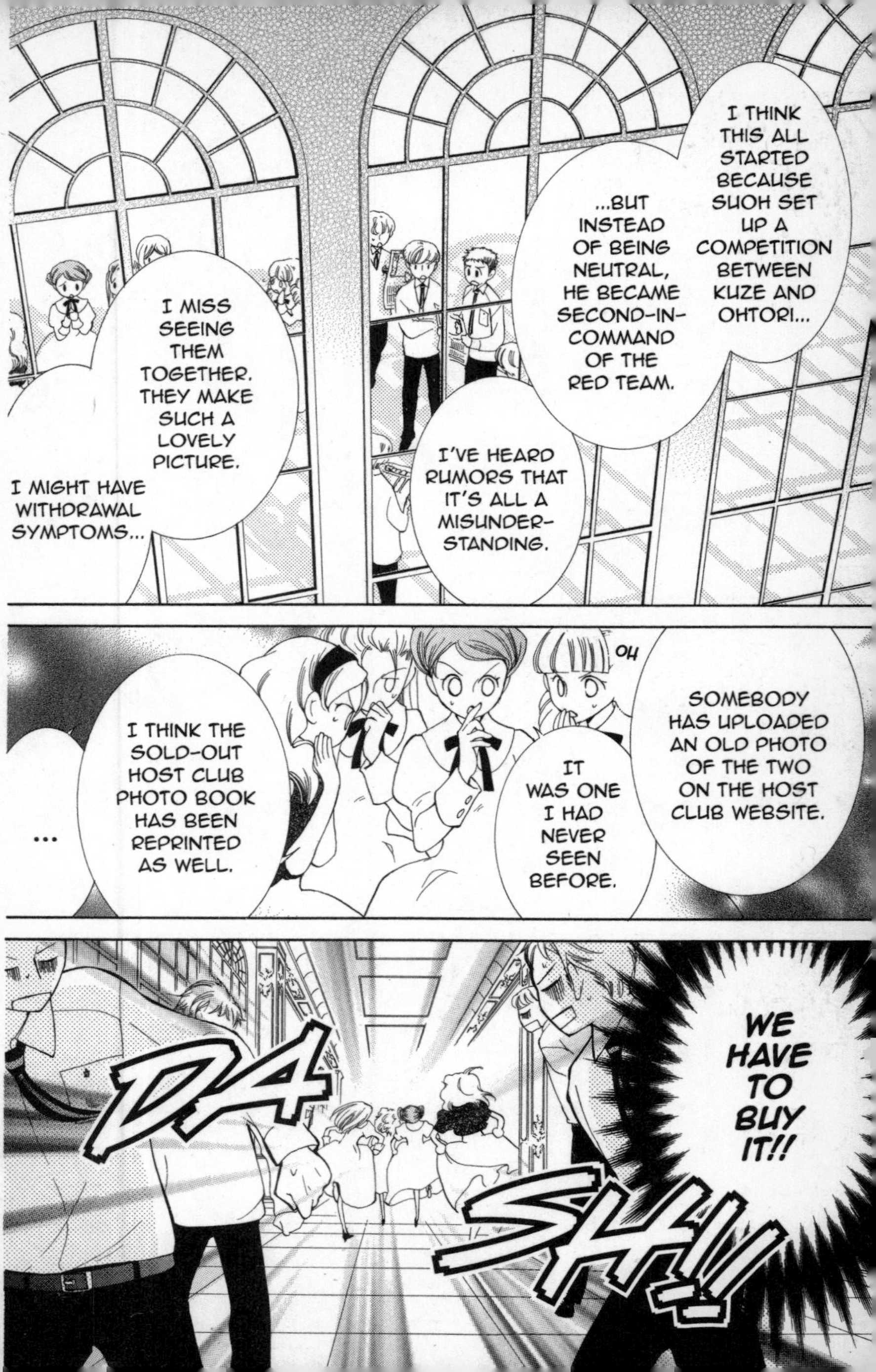
I THINK THIS ALL STARTED BECAUSE SUOH SET UP A COMPETITION BETWEEN KUZE AND OHTORI...
...BUT INSTEAD OF BEING NEUTRAL, HE BECAME SECOND-IN-COMMAND OF THE RED TEAM.
I'VE HEARD RUMORS THAT IT'S ALL A MISUNDERSTANDING.
I MISS SEEING THEM TOGETHER. THEY MAKE SUCH A LOVELY PICTURE.
I MIGHT HAVE WITHDRAWAL SYMPTOMS...
SOMEBODY HAS UPLOADED AN OLD PHOTO OF THE TWO ON THE HOST CLUB WEBSITE.
OH
IT WAS ONE I HAD NEVER SEEN BEFORE.
I THINK THE SOLD-OUT HOST CLUB PHOTO BOOK HAS BEEN REPRINTED AS WELL.
...
WE HAVE TO BUY IT!!
DA
SH!!

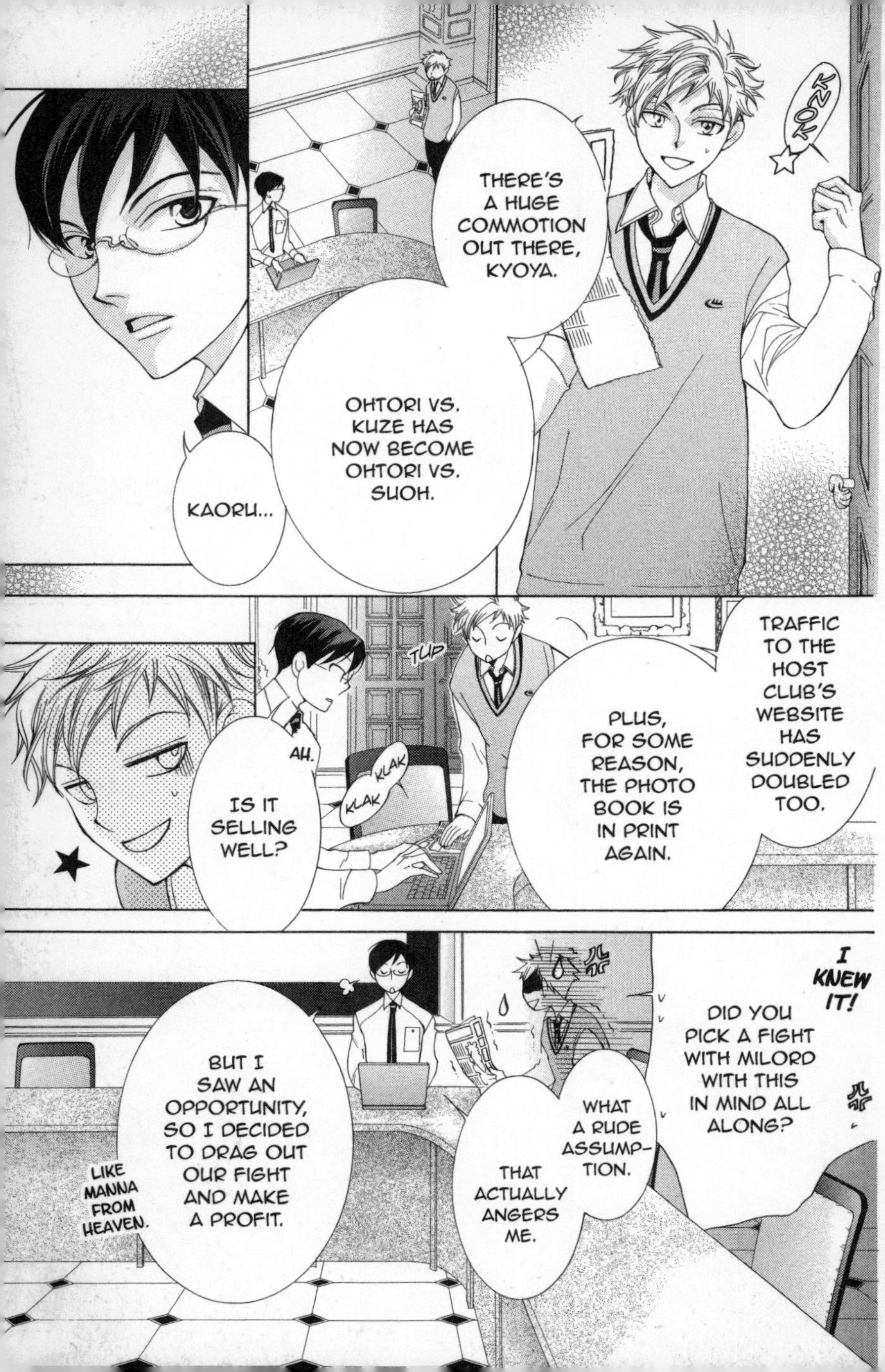
KNOK
THERE'S A HUGE COMMOTION OUT THERE, KYOYA.
OHTORI VS. KUZE HAS NOW BECOME OHTORI VS. SUOH.
KAORU...
TRAFFIC TO THE HOST CLUB'S WEBSITE HAS SUDDENLY DOUBLED TOO.
PLUS, FOR SOME REASON, THE PHOTO BOOK IS IN PRINT AGAIN.
TUP
AH.
KLAK KLAK
IS IT SELLING WELL?
I KNEW IT!
DID YOU PICK A FIGHT WITH MILORD WITH THIS IN MIND ALL ALONG?
WHAT A RUDE ASSUMPTION.
THAT ACTUALLY ANGERS ME.
BUT I SAW AN OPPORTUNITY, SO I DECIDED TO DRAG OUT OUR FIGHT AND MAKE A PROFIT.
LIKE MANNA FROM HEAVEN.

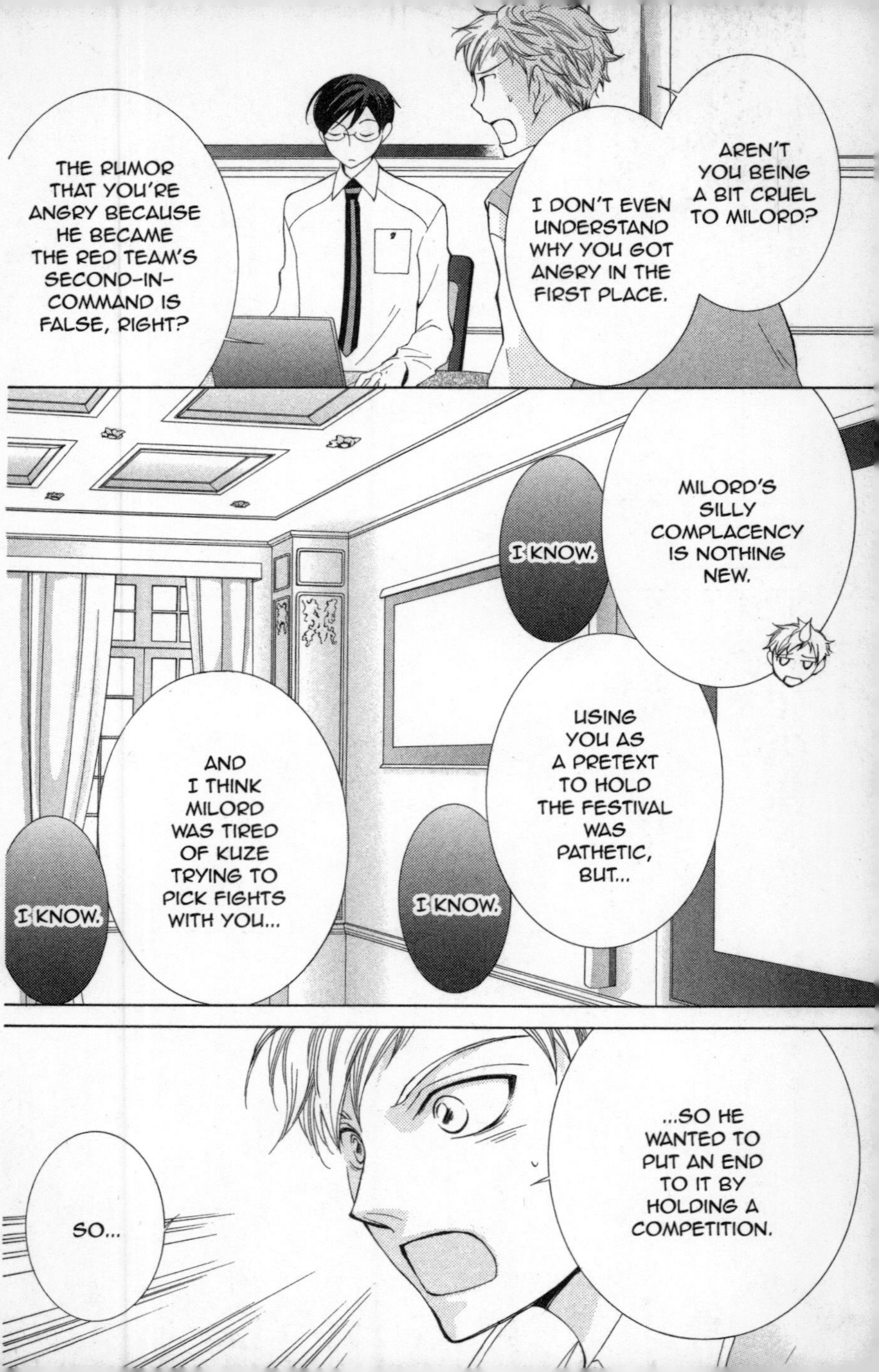
AREN'T YOU BEING A BIT CRUEL TO MILORD?
I DON'T EVEN UNDERSTAND WHY YOU GOT ANGRY IN THE FIRST PLACE.
THE RUMOR THAT YOU'RE ANGRY BECAUSE HE BECAME THE RED TEAM'S SECOND-IN-COMMAND IS FALSE, RIGHT?
MILORD'S SILLY COMPLACENCY IS NOTHING NEW.
I KNOW.
USING YOU AS A PRETEXT TO HOLD THE FESTIVAL WAS PATHETIC, BUT...
I KNOW.
AND I THINK MILORD WAS TIRED OF KUZE TRYING TO PICK FIGHTS WITH YOU...
I KNOW.
...SO HE WANTED TO PUT AN END TO IT BY HOLDING A COMPETITION.
SO...

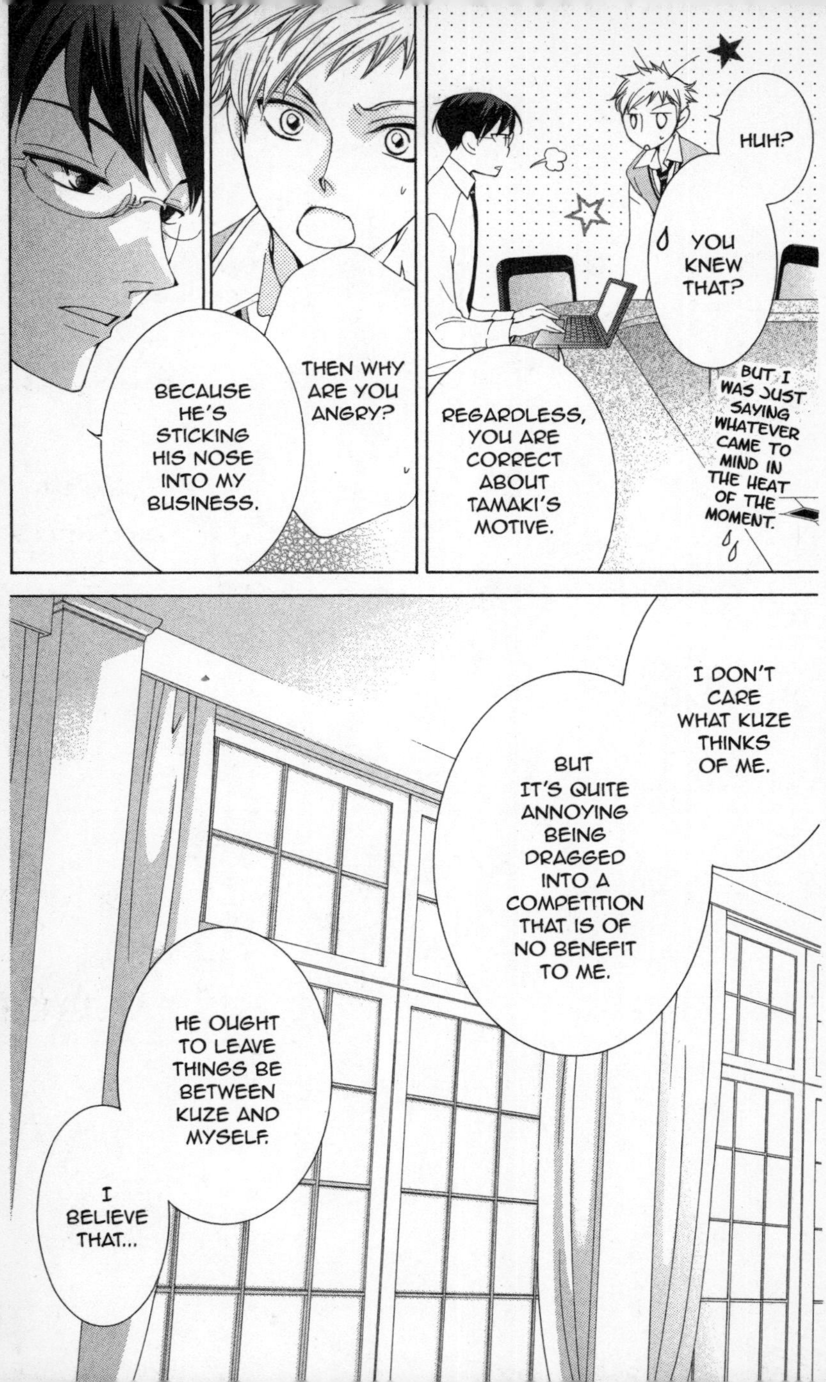
HUH?
YOU KNEW THAT?
BUT I WAS JUST SAYING WHATEVER CAME TO MIND IN THE HEAT OF THE MOMENT.
REGARDLESS, YOU ARE CORRECT ABOUT TAMAKI'S MOTIVE.
THEN WHY ARE YOU ANGRY?
BECAUSE HE'S STICKING HIS NOSE INTO MY BUSINESS.
I DON'T CARE WHAT KUZE THINKS OF ME.
BUT IT'S QUITE ANNOYING BEING DRAGGED INTO A COMPETITION THAT IS OF NO BENEFIT TO ME.
HE OUGHT TO LEAVE THINGS BE BETWEEN KUZE AND MYSELF.
I BELIEVE THAT...

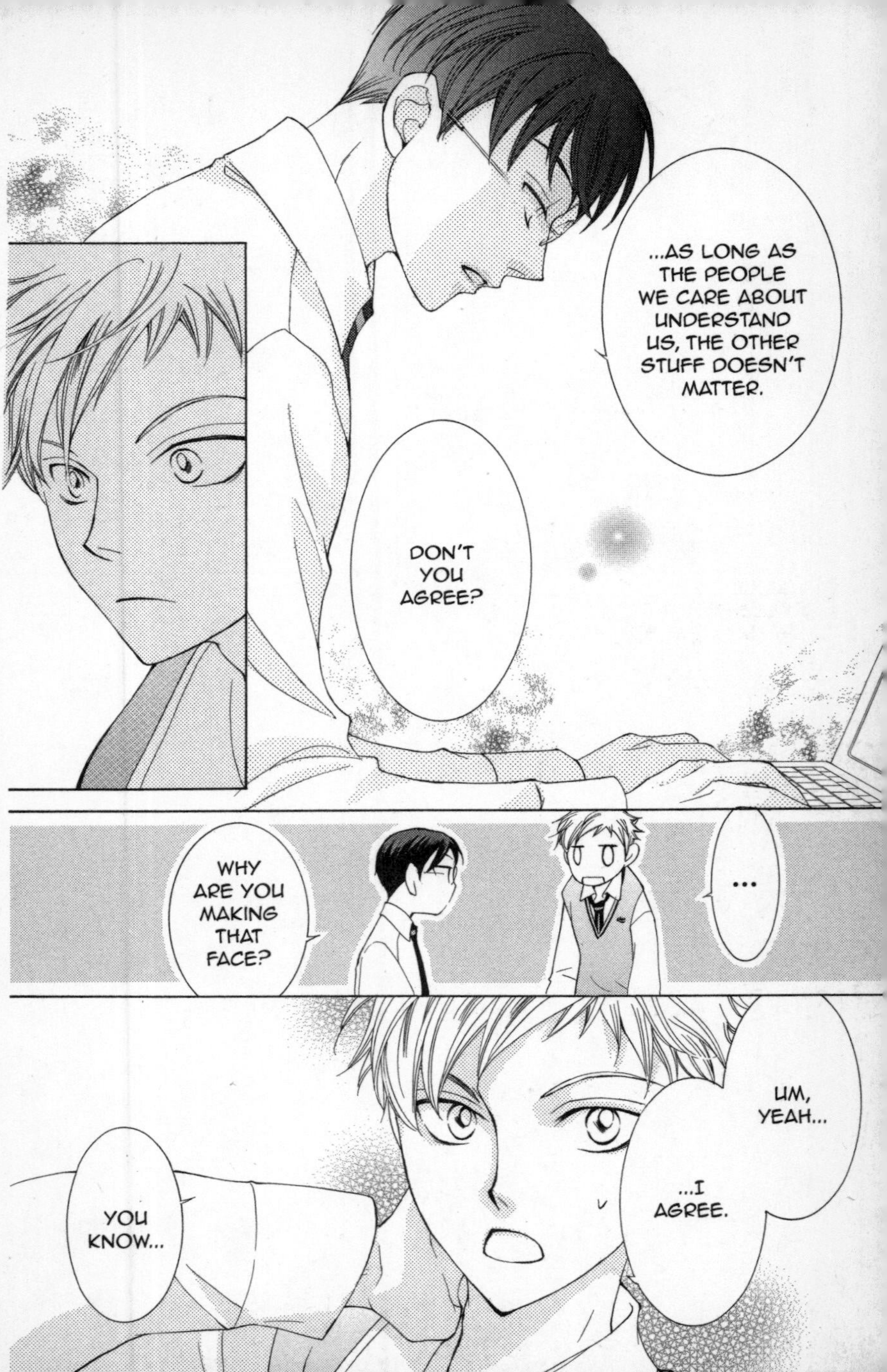
...AS LONG AS THE PEOPLE WE CARE ABOUT UNDERSTAND US, THE OTHER STUFF DOESN'T MATTER.
DON'T YOU AGREE?
...
WHY ARE YOU MAKING THAT FACE?
UM, YEAH...
...I AGREE.
YOU KNOW...

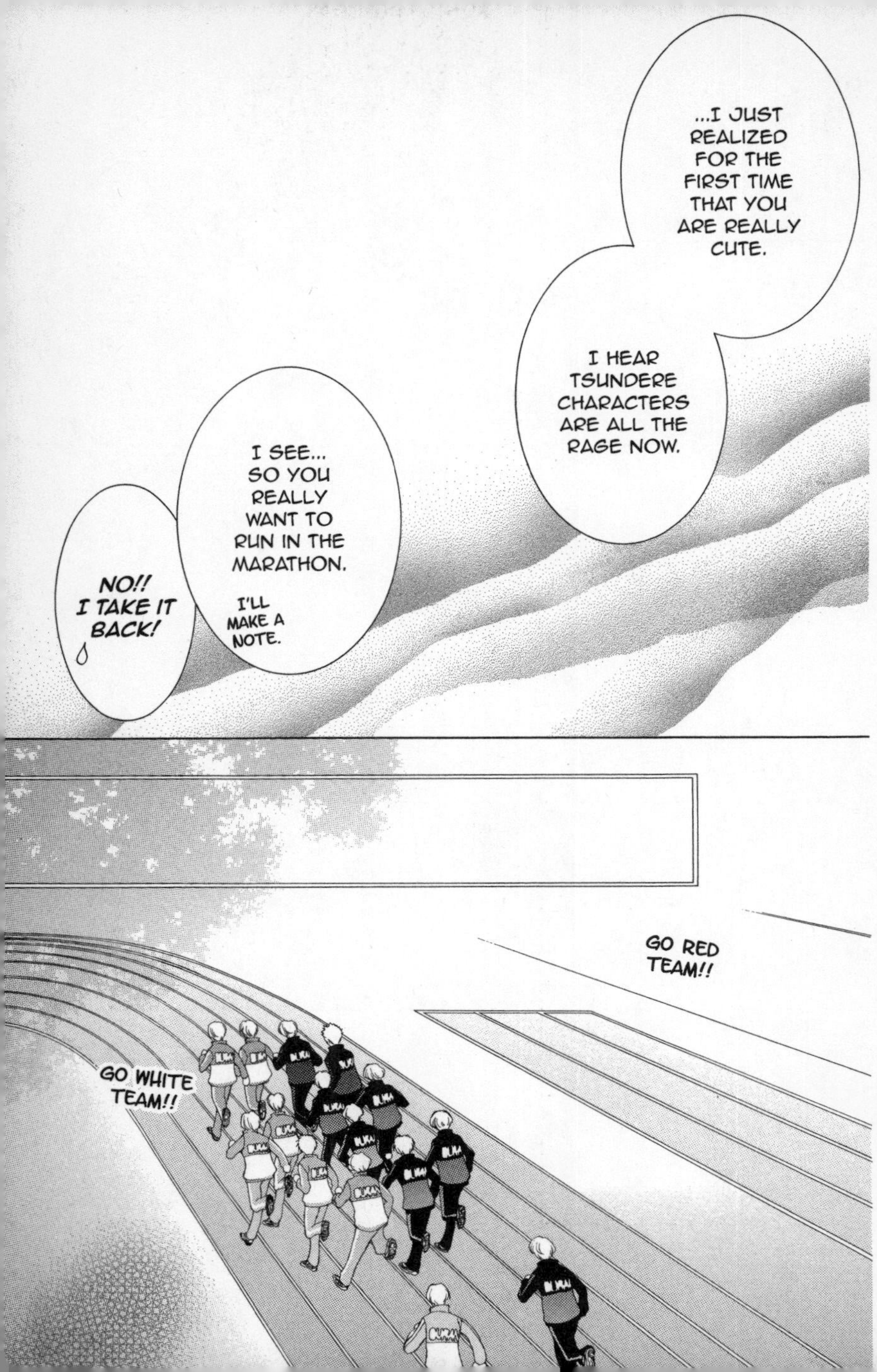
...I JUST REALIZED FOR THE FIRST TIME THAT YOU ARE REALLY CUTE.
I HEAR TSUNDERE CHARACTERS ARE ALL THE RAGE NOW.
I SEE... SO YOU REALLY WANT TO RUN IN THE MARATHON.
I'LL MAKE A NOTE.
NO!! I TAKE IT BACK!
GO RED TEAM!!
GO WHITE TEAM!!

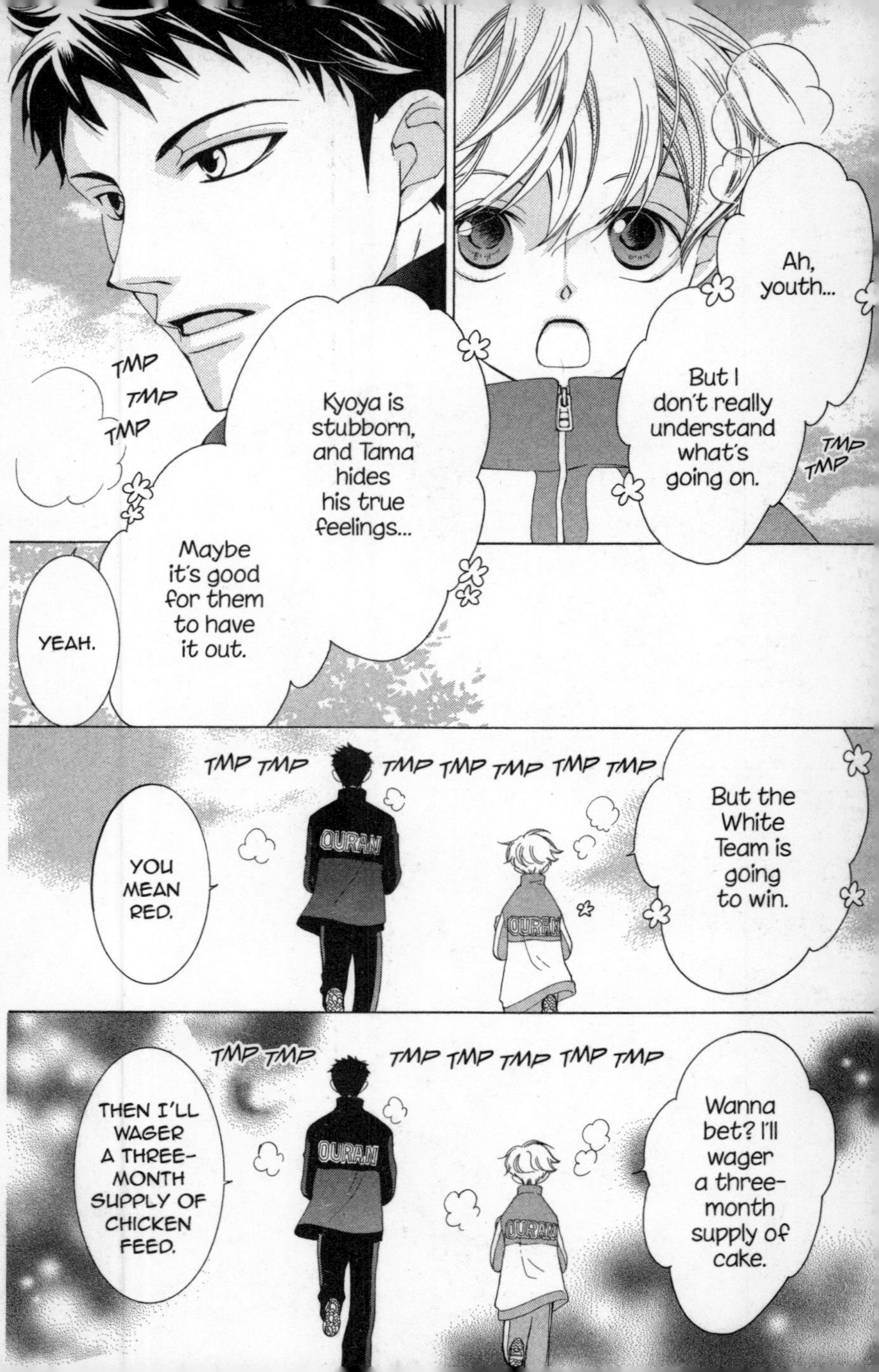
Ah, youth...
But I don't really understand what's going on.
TMP TMP
TMP TMP TMP
Kyoya is stubborn, and Tama hides his true feelings...
Maybe it's good for them to have it out.
YEAH.
TMP TMP TMP TMP TMP TMP TMP
But the White Team is going to win.
YOU MEAN RED.
TMP TMP TMP TMP TMP TMP TMP
Wanna bet? I'll wager a three-month supply of cake.
THEN I'LL WAGER A THREE-MONTH SUPPLY OF CHICKEN FEED.

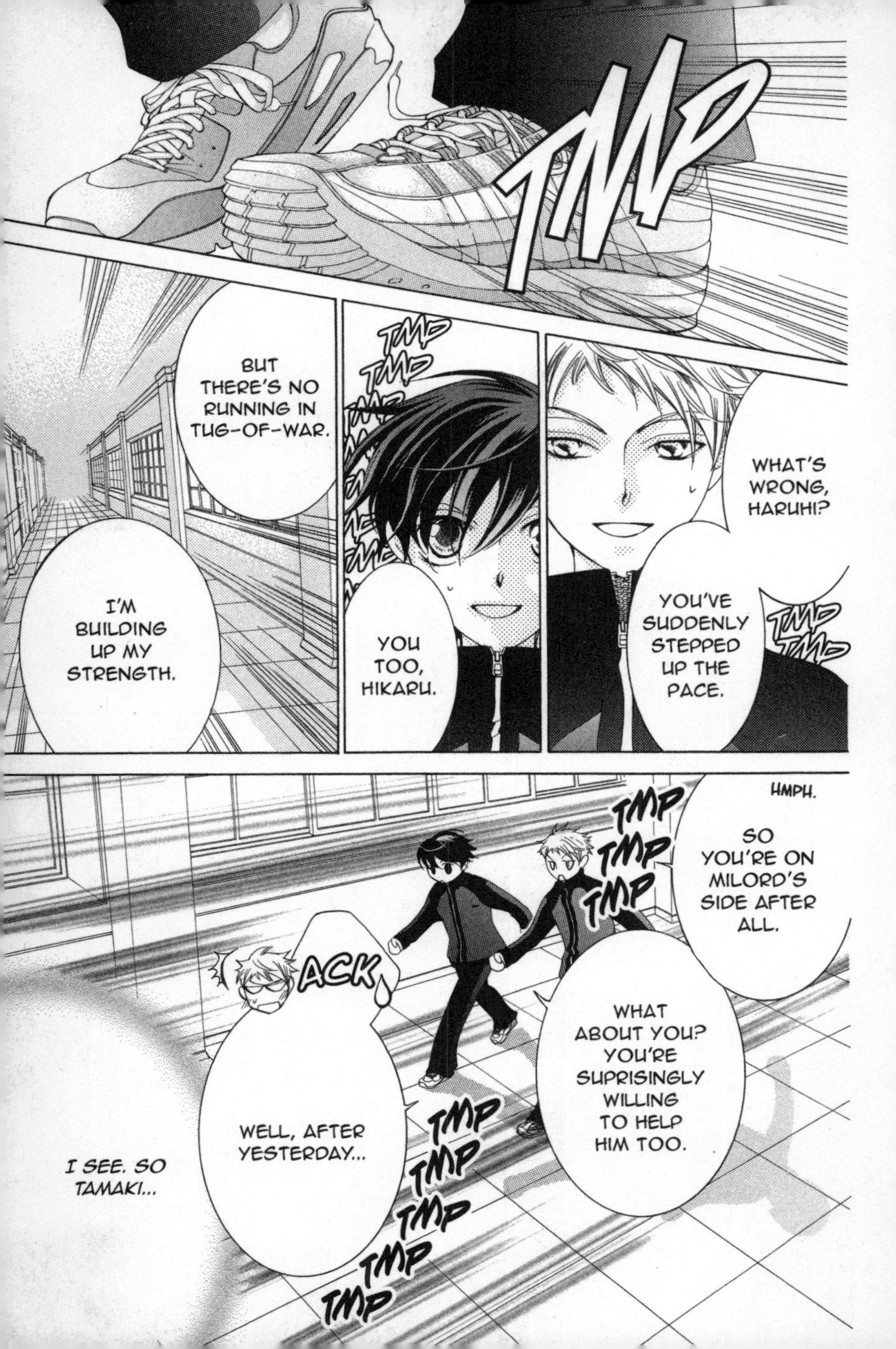
TMP
TMP
TMP
WHAT'S WRONG, HARUHI?
YOU'VE SUDDENLY STEPPED UP THE PACE.
TMP
TMP
YOU TOO, HIKARU.
BUT THERE'S NO RUNNING IN TUG-OF-WAR.
I'M BUILDING UP MY STRENGTH.
HMPH.
SO YOU'RE ON MILORD'S SIDE AFTER ALL.
TMP
TMP
TMP
WHAT ABOUT YOU? YOU'RE SUPRISINGLY WILLING TO HELP HIM TOO.
ACK
WELL, AFTER YESTERDAY...
TMP
TMP
TMP
TMP
TMP
I SEE. SO TAMAKI...

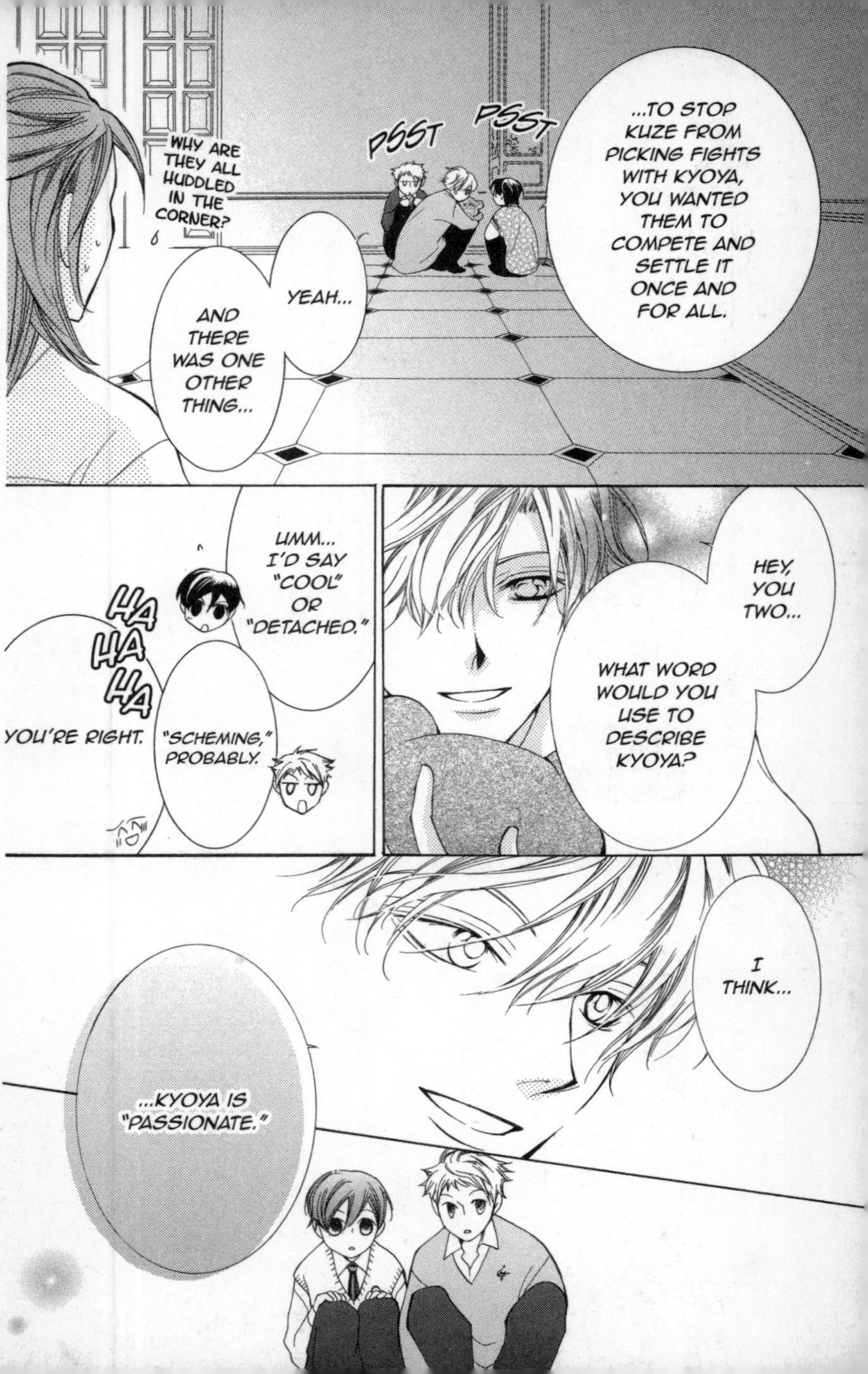
...TO STOP KUZE FROM PICKING FIGHTS WITH KYOYA, YOU WANTED THEM TO COMPETE AND SETTLE IT ONCE AND FOR ALL.
PSST PSST
YEAH...
AND THERE WAS ONE OTHER THING...
WHY ARE THEY ALL HUDDLED IN THE CORNER?
HEY, YOU TWO...
WHAT WORD WOULD YOU USE TO DESCRIBE KYOYA?
UMM... I'D SAY "COOL" OR "DETACHED."
"SCHEMING," PROBABLY.
HA HA HA
YOU'RE RIGHT.
I THINK...
...KYOYA IS "PASSIONATE."

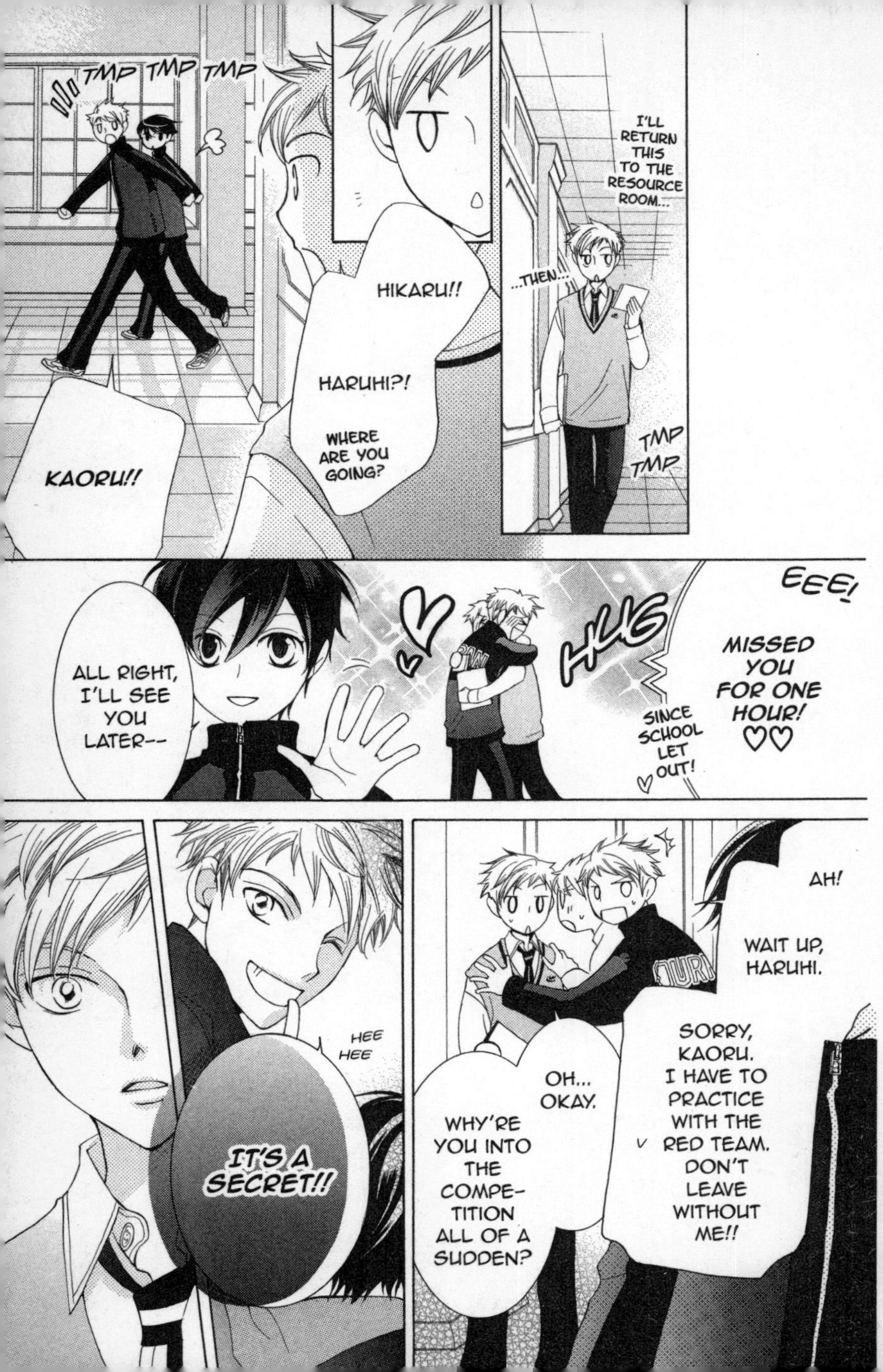
I'LL RETURN THIS TO THE RESOURCE ROOM...
...THEN...
TMP TMP
HIKARU!!
HARUHI?!
WHERE ARE YOU GOING?
TMP TMP TMP
KAORU!!
EEE!
MISSED YOU FOR ONE HOUR! ♡♡
SINCE SCHOOL LET OUT!
HUG
ALL RIGHT, I'LL SEE YOU LATER--
AH!
WAIT UP, HARUHI.
SORRY, KAORU. I HAVE TO PRACTICE WITH THE RED TEAM. DON'T LEAVE WITHOUT ME!!
OH... OKAY.
WHY'RE YOU INTO THE COMPETITION ALL OF A SUDDEN?
HEE HEE
IT'S A SECRET!!

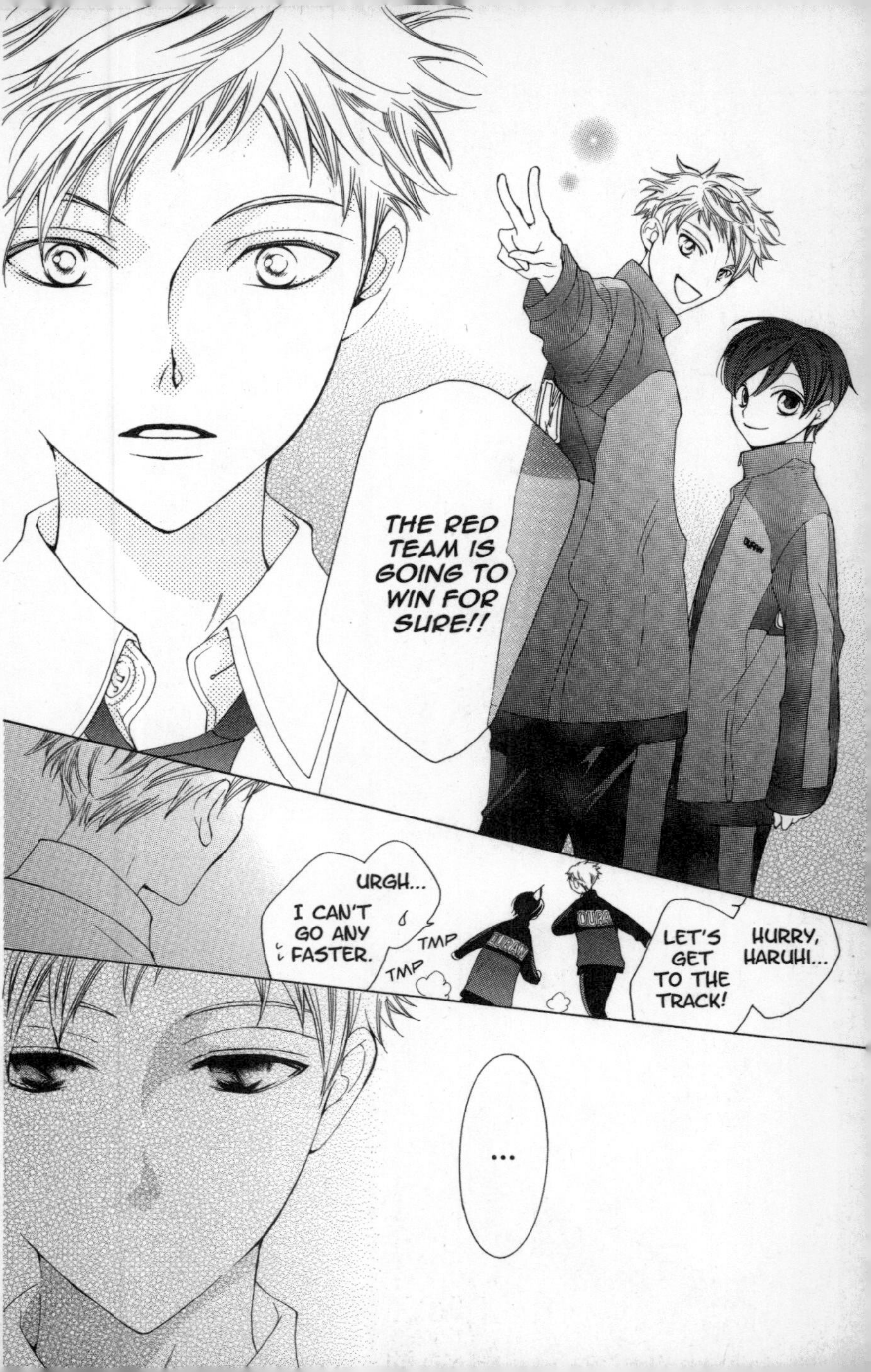
THE RED TEAM IS GOING TO WIN FOR SURE!!
HURRY, HARUHI...
LET'S GET TO THE TRACK!
TMP
TMP
URGH...
I CAN'T GO ANY FASTER.
...

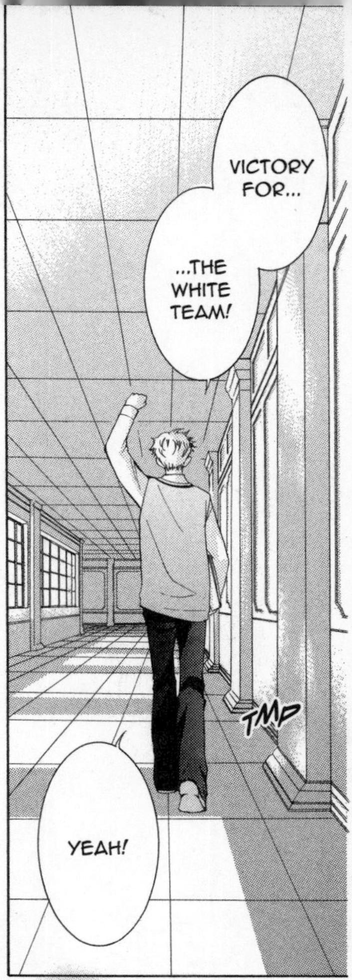
VICTORY FOR...
...THE WHITE TEAM!
TMP
YEAH!
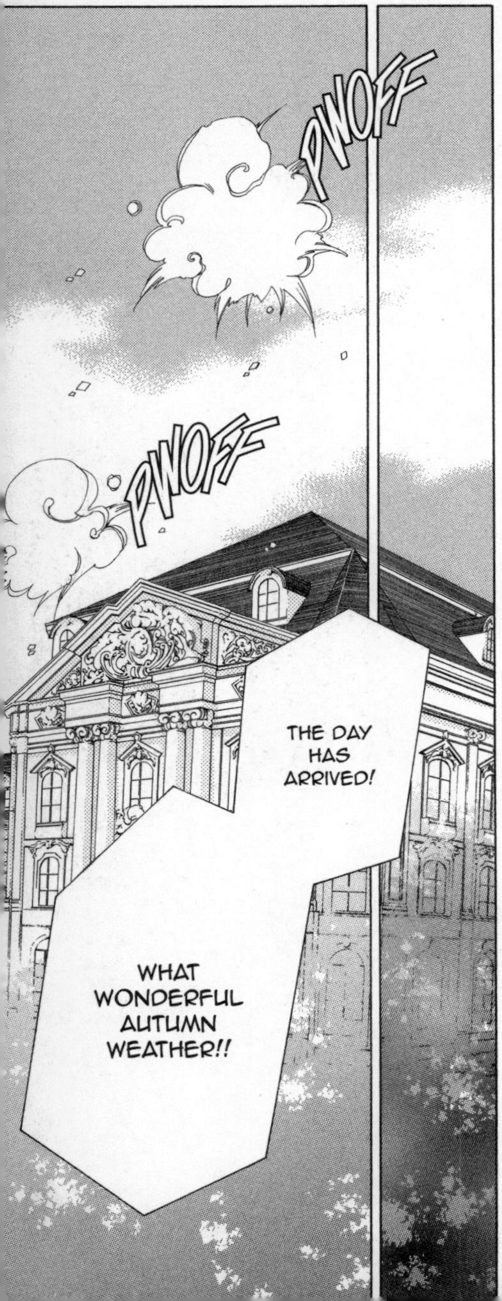
PWOFF
PWOFF
THE DAY HAS ARRIVED!
WHAT WONDERFUL AUTUMN WEATHER!!

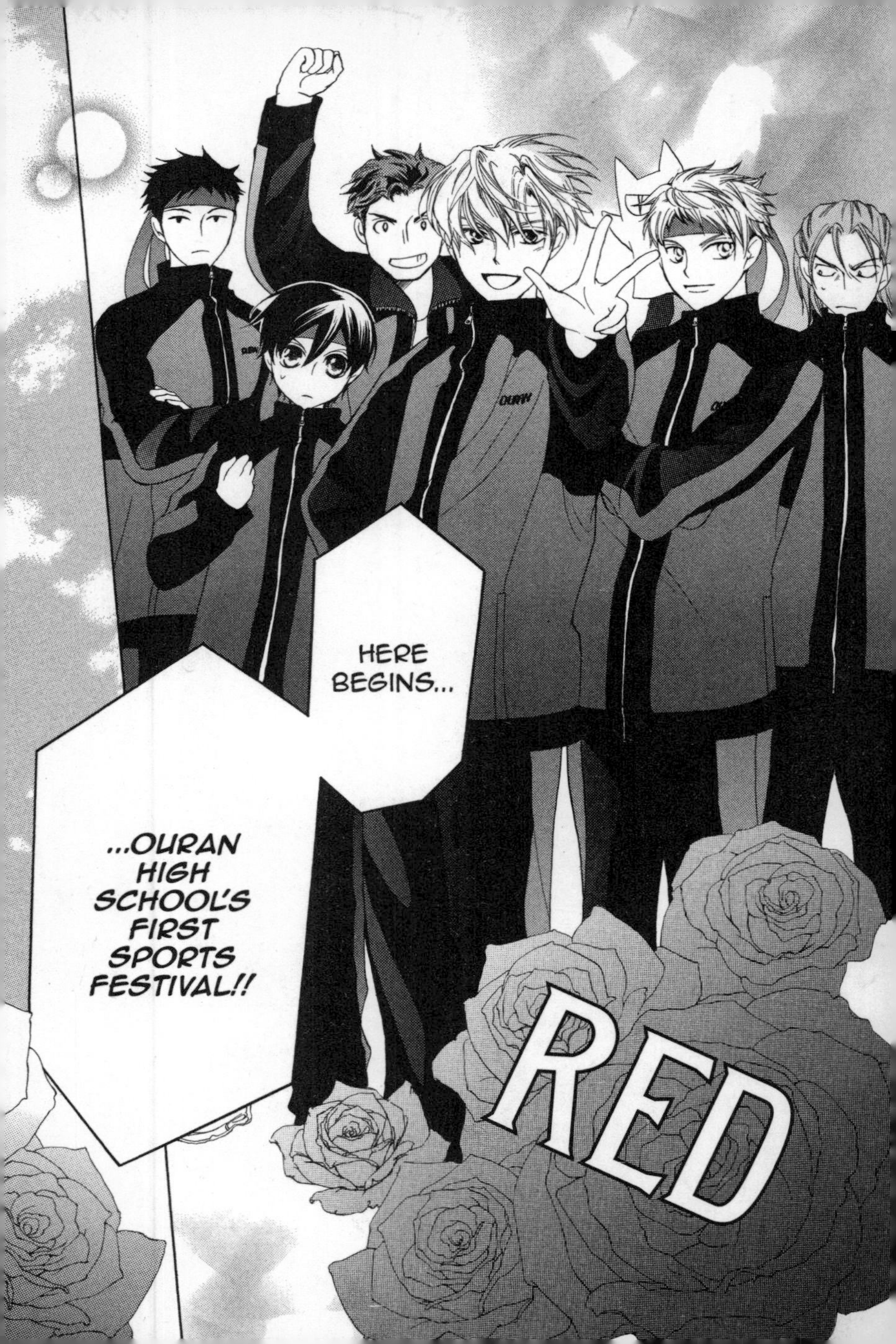
HERE BEGINS...
...OURAN HIGH SCHOOL'S FIRST SPORTS FESTIVAL!!
RED

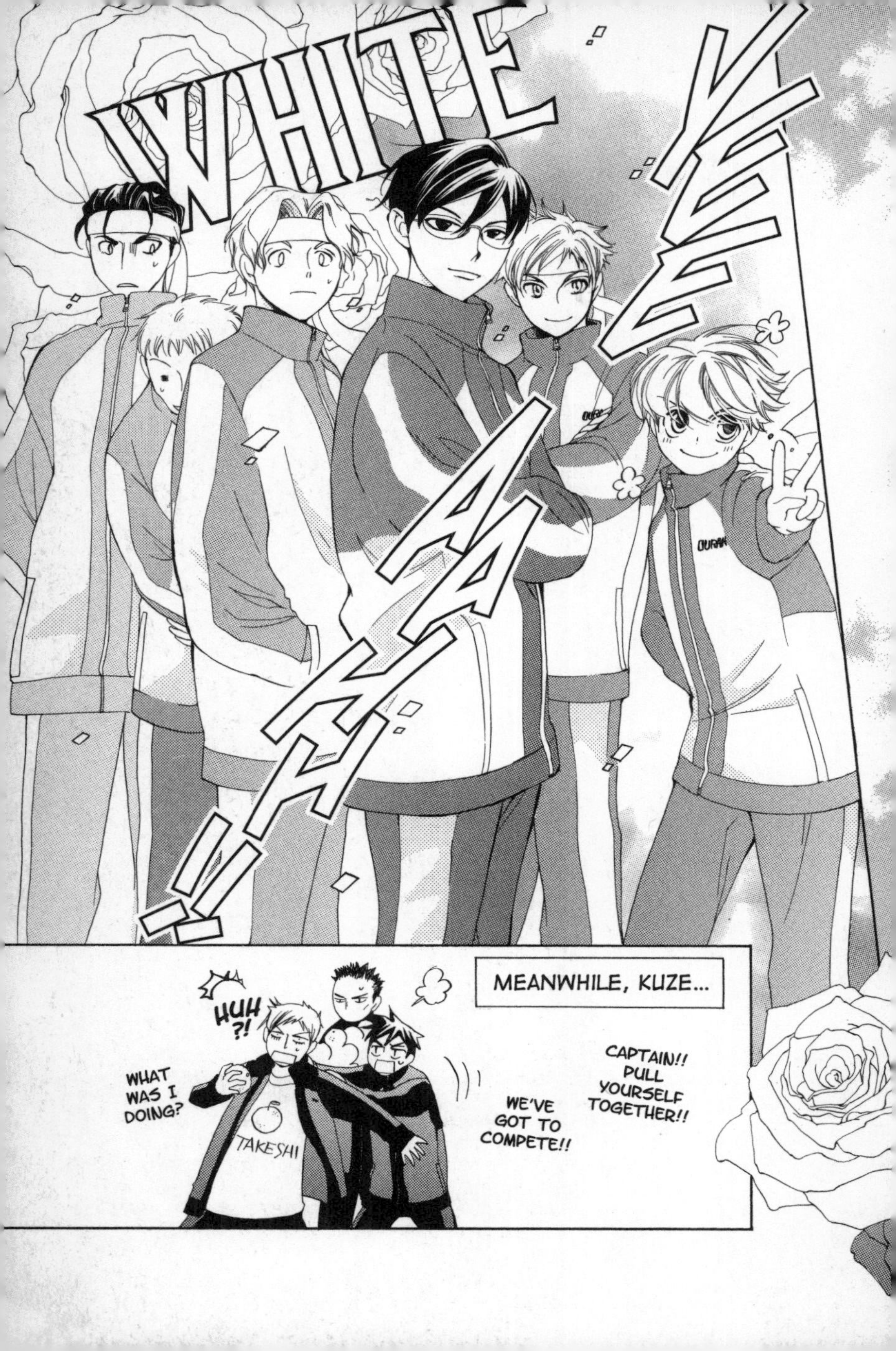
WHITE
MEANWHILE, KUZE...
CAPTAIN!! PULL YOURSELF TOGETHER!!
WE'VE GOT TO COMPETE!!
HUH ?!
WHAT WAS I DOING?
TAKESHI

GUEST ROOM: FAXES
SPECIAL THANKS TO YUKI KURE!!

SQUEEZE

PARDON MY DRAWING!! I APOLOGIZE TO ALL THE HUNNY AND MORI FANS. BUT I ENJOYED DRAWING THEM.

YUKI KURE

HUNNY AND MORI

SORRY, BUN-BUN! YOU DON'T GET TREATED LIKE THIS.

I RECEIVED AN ULTRA-BEAUTIFUL FAX FROM KURE-SAN, THE AUTHOR OF *LA CORDA D'ORO*!! IT STARTED WHEN SHE SAID HER MORI AND HUNNY WOULD BE LIKE CORDA'S TSUCHIURA AND SHIMIZU. WHEN I HEARD THAT, I SHOUTED OUT SHAMELESSLY, "BY ALL MEANS, PLEASE DO!! I DON'T MIND IF IT LOOKS LIKE TSUCHIYA AND SHIMIZU!" DESPITE HER BUSY SCHEDULE, SHE DREW THIS GREAT PICTURE. I'M VERY GRATEFUL. AND KURE-SAN, DON'T WORRY, BUN-BUN GETS TREATED QUITE A BIT WORSE THAN THIS!! (LAUGH) THANK YOU SO MUCH!!

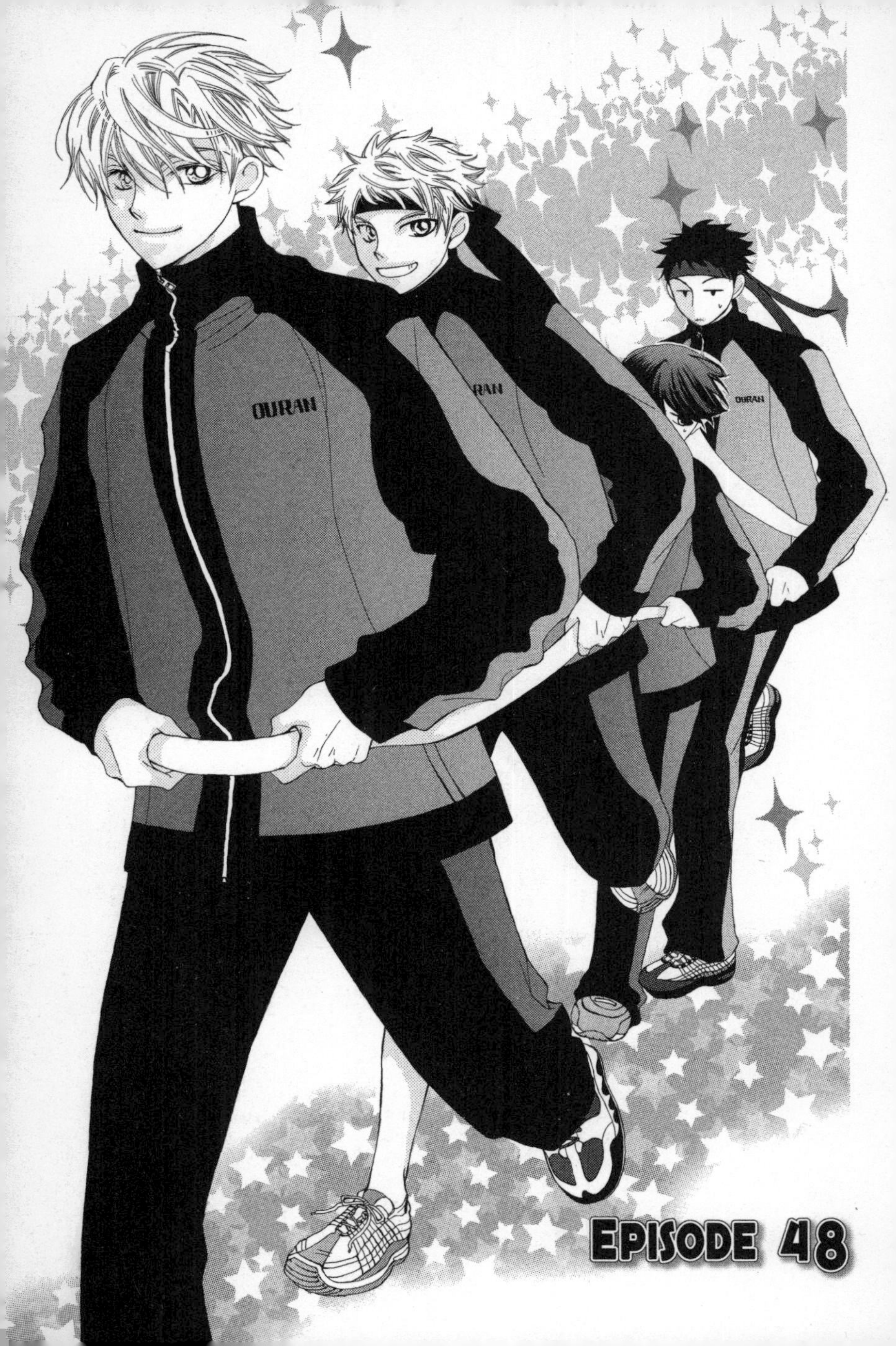
OURAN
RAN
OURAN
EPISODE 48

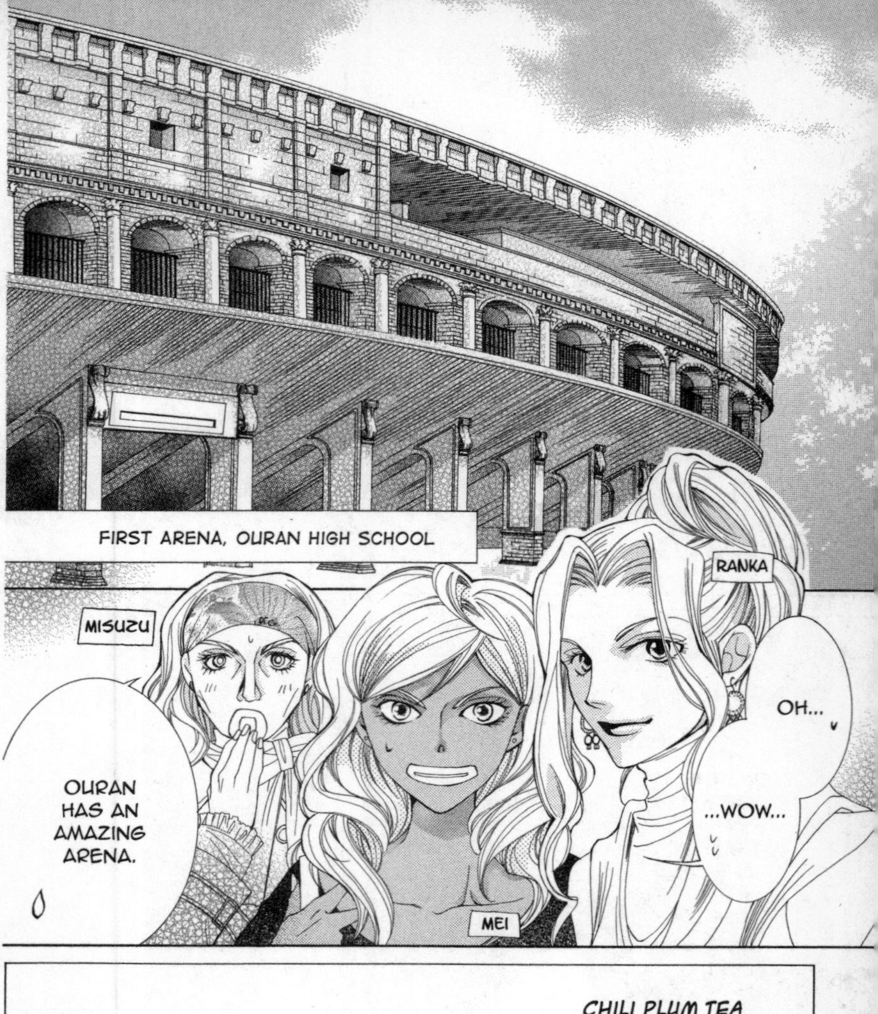
FIRST ARENA, OURAN HIGH SCHOOL
RANKA
OH... ...WOW...
MISUZU
OURAN HAS AN AMAZING ARENA.
MEI

CHILI PLUM TEA

I'VE BEEN HOOKED ON THIS SINCE I RECEIVED IT FROM THE STAFF AS A GIFT. IT WAKES YOU UP AND IS DELICIOUS TOO!!

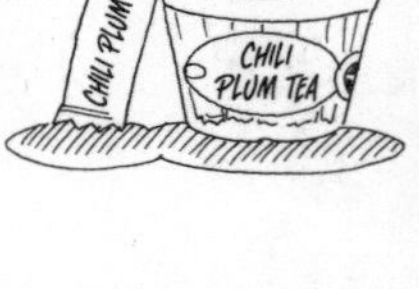
CHILI PLUM TEA
CHILI PLUM TEA

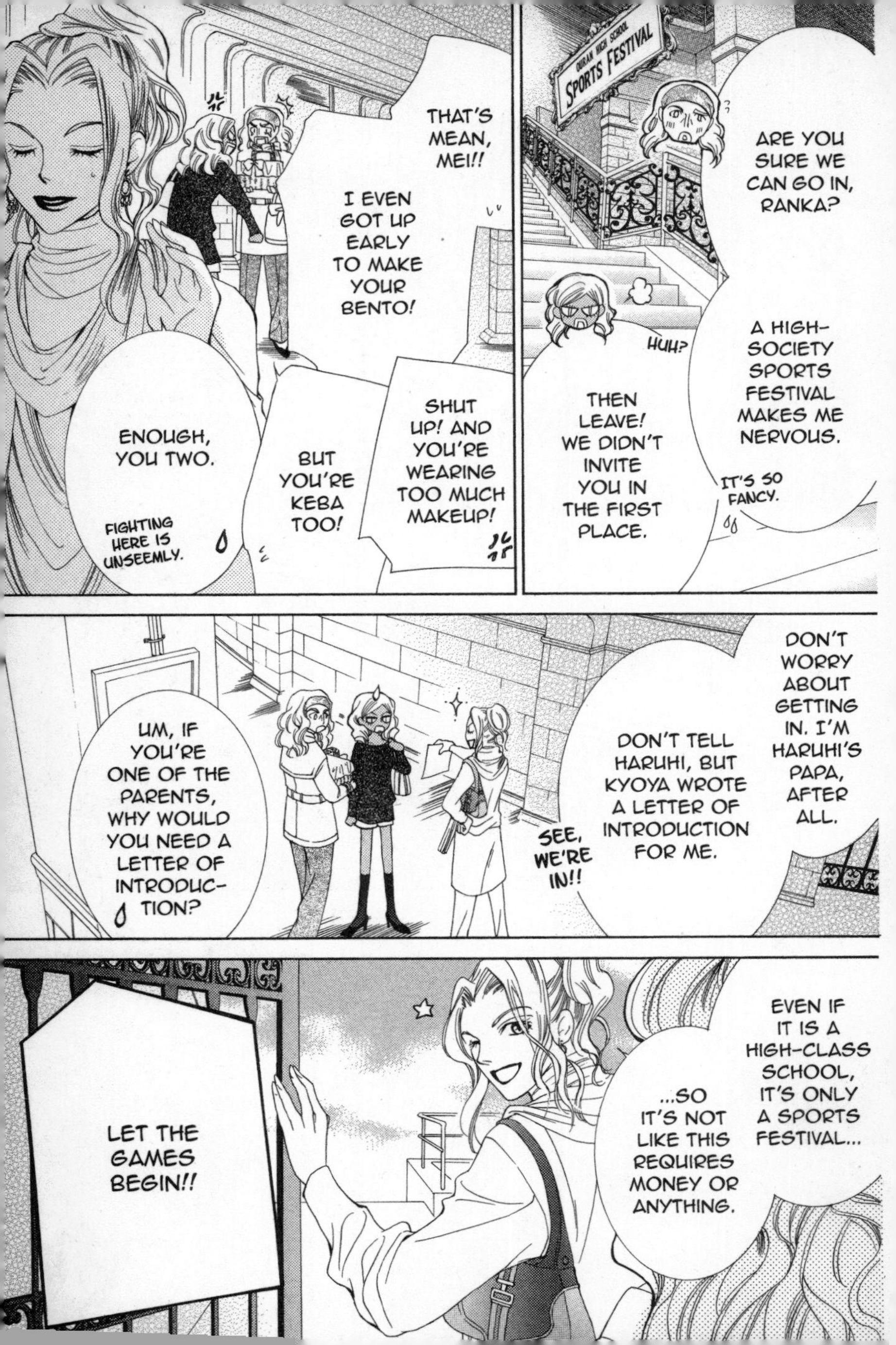
OURAN HIGH SCHOOL SPORTS FESTIVAL
ARE YOU SURE WE CAN GO IN, RANKA?
A HIGH-SOCIETY SPORTS FESTIVAL MAKES ME NERVOUS.
IT'S SO FANCY.
HUH?
THEN LEAVE! WE DIDN'T INVITE YOU IN THE FIRST PLACE.
THAT'S MEAN, MEI!!
I EVEN GOT UP EARLY TO MAKE YOUR BENTO!
SHUT UP! AND YOU'RE WEARING TOO MUCH MAKEUP!
BUT YOU'RE KEBA TOO!
ENOUGH, YOU TWO.
FIGHTING HERE IS UNSEEMLY.
DON'T WORRY ABOUT GETTING IN. I'M HARUHI'S PAPA, AFTER ALL.
DON'T TELL HARUHI, BUT KYOYA WROTE A LETTER OF INTRODUCTION FOR ME.
SEE, WE'RE IN!!
UM, IF YOU'RE ONE OF THE PARENTS, WHY WOULD YOU NEED A LETTER OF INTRODUCTION?
EVEN IF IT IS A HIGH-CLASS SCHOOL, IT'S ONLY A SPORTS FESTIVAL...
...SO IT'S NOT LIKE THIS REQUIRES MONEY OR ANYTHING.
LET THE GAMES BEGIN!!

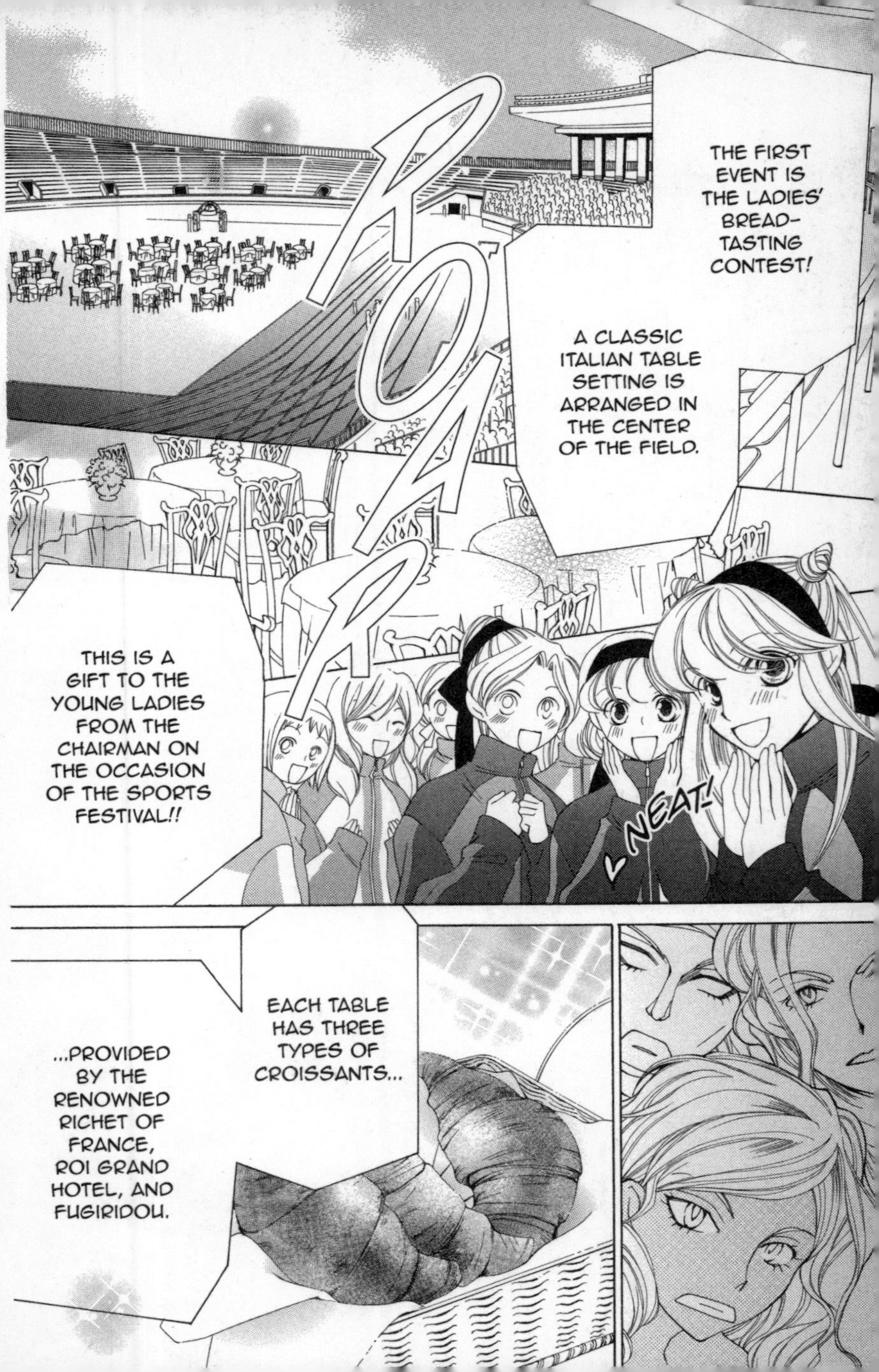

THE FIRST EVENT IS THE LADIES' BREAD-TASTING CONTEST!
A CLASSIC ITALIAN TABLE SETTING IS ARRANGED IN THE CENTER OF THE FIELD.
ROAR
THIS IS A GIFT TO THE YOUNG LADIES FROM THE CHAIRMAN ON THE OCCASION OF THE SPORTS FESTIVAL!!
NEAT!
EACH TABLE HAS THREE TYPES OF CROISSANTS...
...PROVIDED BY THE RENOWNED RICHET OF FRANCE, ROI GRAND HOTEL, AND FUGIRIDOU.

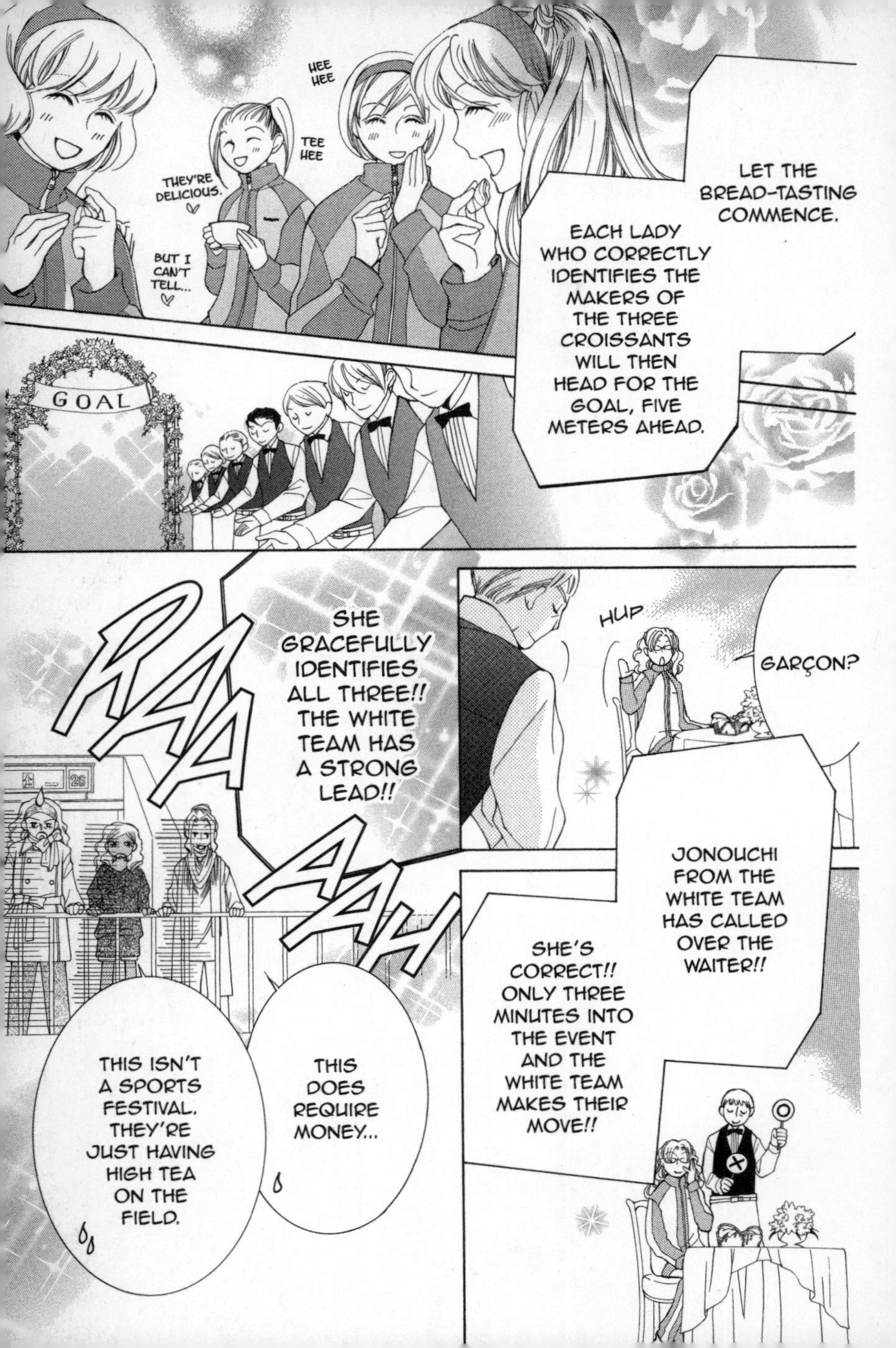
LET THE BREAD-TASTING COMMENCE.
HEE HEE
TEE HEE
THEY'RE DELICIOUS.
BUT I CAN'T TELL...
EACH LADY WHO CORRECTLY IDENTIFIES THE MAKERS OF THE THREE CROISSANTS WILL THEN HEAD FOR THE GOAL, FIVE METERS AHEAD.
GOAL
GARÇON?
HUP
JONOUCHI FROM THE WHITE TEAM HAS CALLED OVER THE WAITER!!
SHE'S CORRECT!! ONLY THREE MINUTES INTO THE EVENT AND THE WHITE TEAM MAKES THEIR MOVE!!
SHE GRACEFULLY IDENTIFIES ALL THREE!! THE WHITE TEAM HAS A STRONG LEAD!!
RAAAAAH
THIS DOES REQUIRE MONEY...
THIS ISN'T A SPORTS FESTIVAL. THEY'RE JUST HAVING HIGH TEA ON THE FIELD.

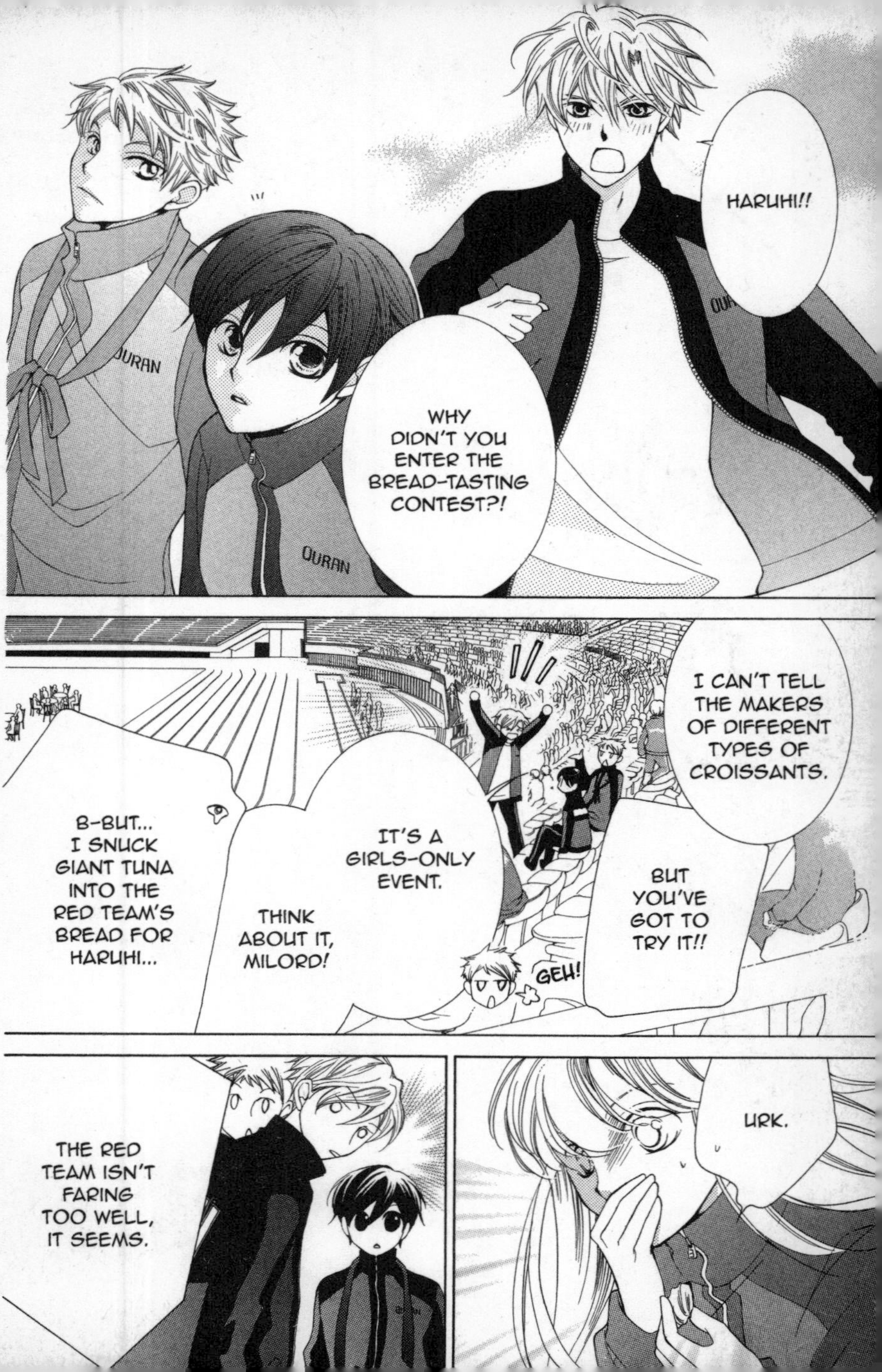
HARUHI!!
WHY DIDN'T YOU ENTER THE BREAD-TASTING CONTEST?!
I CAN'T TELL THE MAKERS OF DIFFERENT TYPES OF CROISSANTS.
BUT YOU'VE GOT TO TRY IT!!
GEH!
IT'S A GIRLS-ONLY EVENT.
THINK ABOUT IT, MILORD!
B-BUT... I SNUCK GIANT TUNA INTO THE RED TEAM'S BREAD FOR HARUHI...
URK.
THE RED TEAM ISN'T FARING TOO WELL, IT SEEMS.

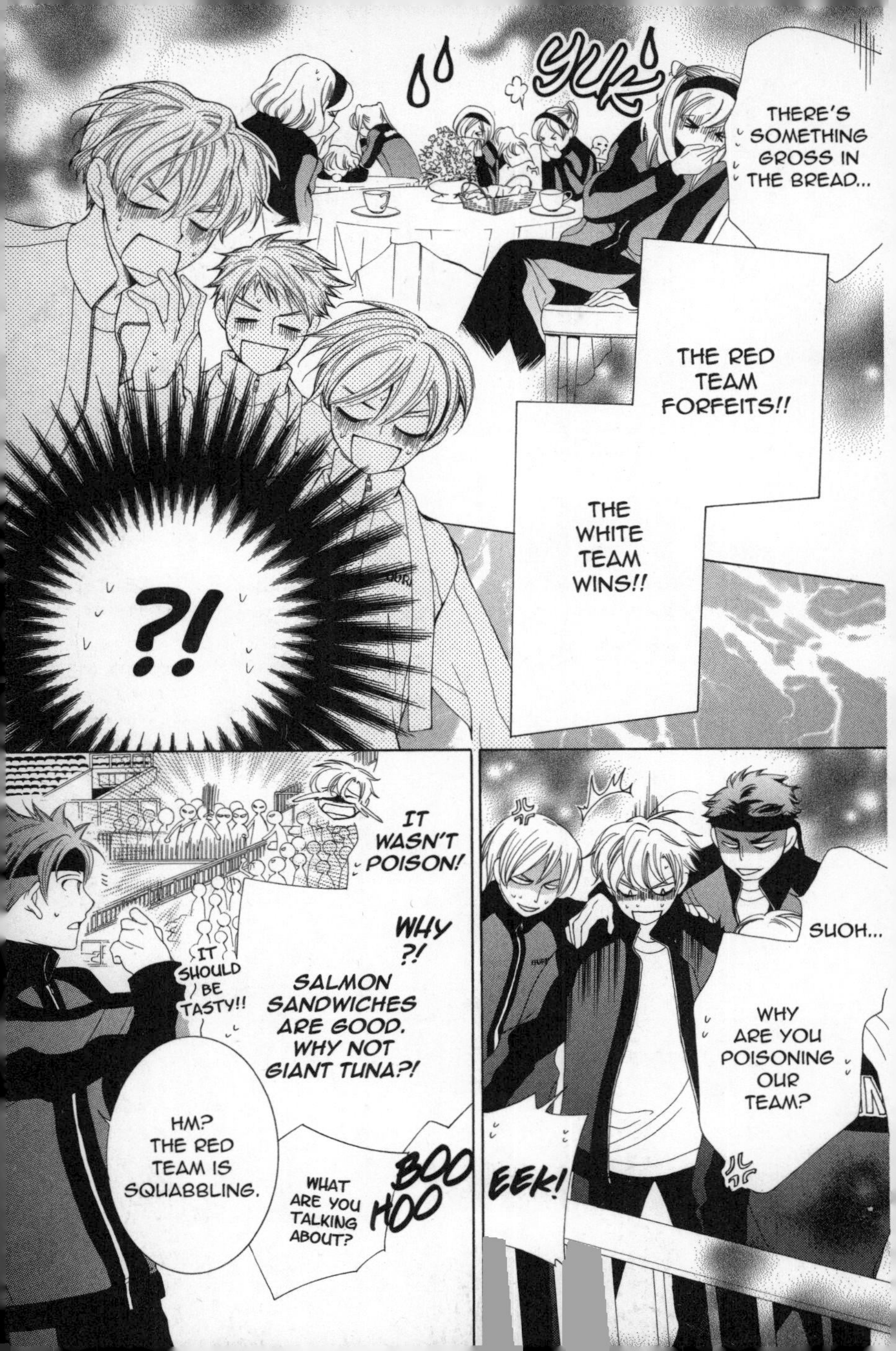
YUK
THERE'S SOMETHING GROSS IN THE BREAD...
THE RED TEAM FORFEITS!!
THE WHITE TEAM WINS!!
?!
SUOH...
WHY ARE YOU POISONING OUR TEAM?
EEK!
IT WASN'T POISON!
WHY ?!
SALMON SANDWICHES ARE GOOD. WHY NOT GIANT TUNA?!
IT SHOULD BE TASTY!!
BOO HOO
WHAT ARE YOU TALKING ABOUT?
HM? THE RED TEAM IS SQUABBLING.

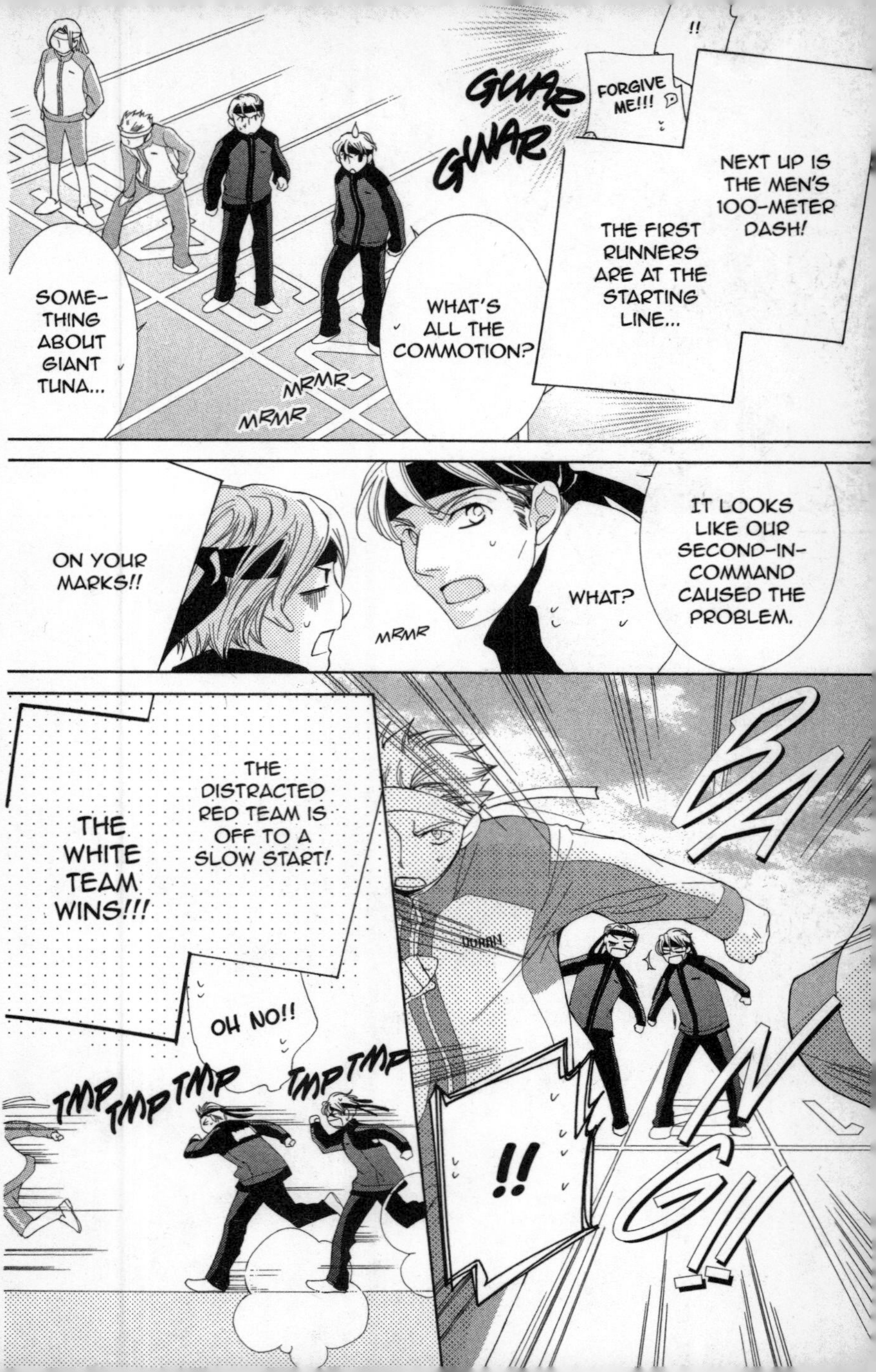
!!
FORGIVE ME!!!
GUAR
GUAR
NEXT UP IS THE MEN'S 100-METER DASH!
THE FIRST RUNNERS ARE AT THE STARTING LINE...
WHAT'S ALL THE COMMOTION?
SOME-THING ABOUT GIANT TUNA...
MRMR
MRMR
IT LOOKS LIKE OUR SECOND-IN-COMMAND CAUSED THE PROBLEM.
WHAT?
MRMR
ON YOUR MARKS!!
BANG!!
!!
OH NO!!
TMP TMP
TMP TMP TMP
THE DISTRACTED RED TEAM IS OFF TO A SLOW START!
THE WHITE TEAM WINS!!!

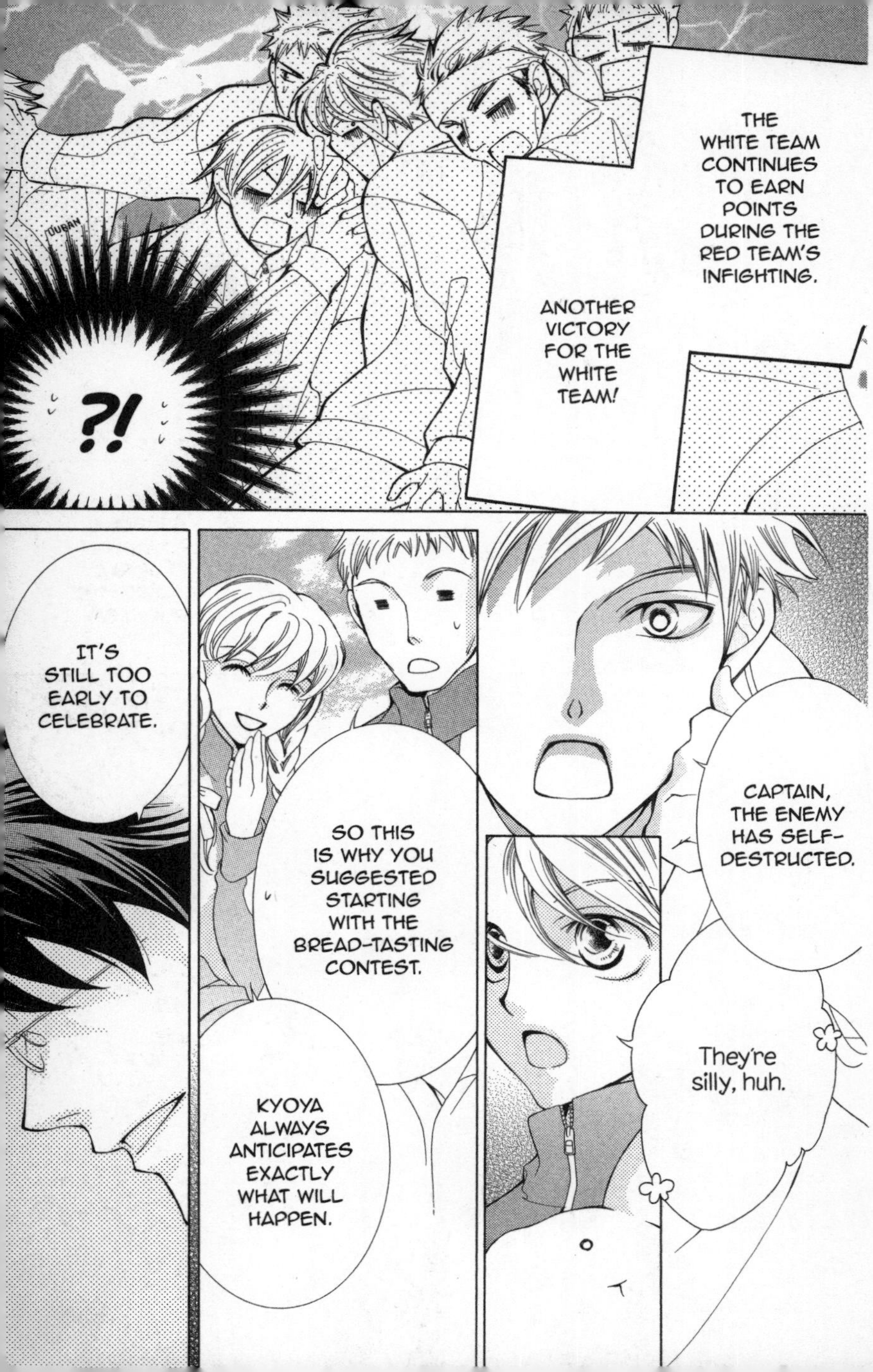
THE WHITE TEAM CONTINUES TO EARN POINTS DURING THE RED TEAM'S INFIGHTING.
ANOTHER VICTORY FOR THE WHITE TEAM!
?!
CAPTAIN, THE ENEMY HAS SELF-DESTRUCTED.
They're silly, huh.
SO THIS IS WHY YOU SUGGESTED STARTING WITH THE BREAD-TASTING CONTEST.
KYOYA ALWAYS ANTICIPATES EXACTLY WHAT WILL HAPPEN.
IT'S STILL TOO EARLY TO CELEBRATE.

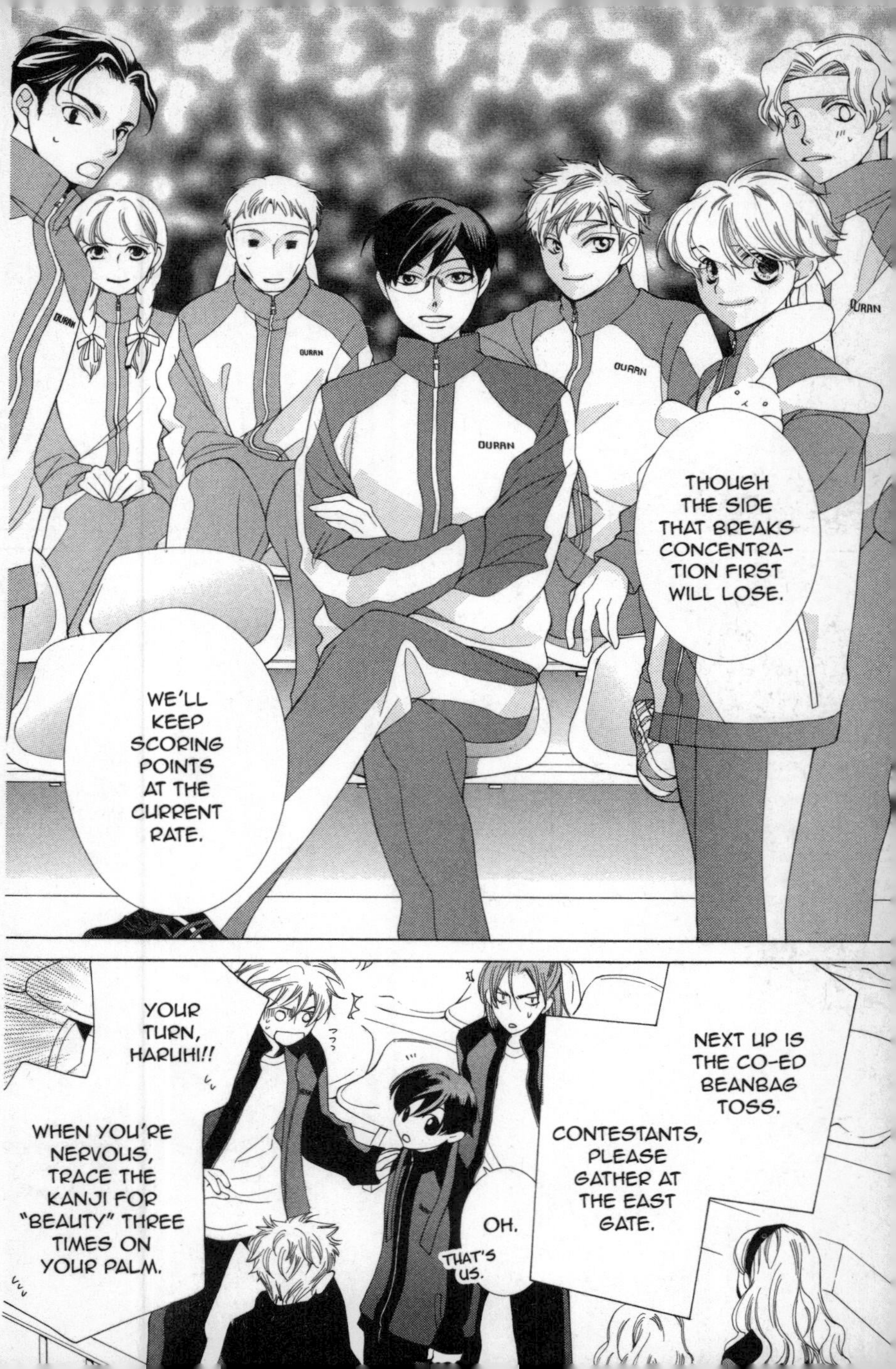
THOUGH THE SIDE THAT BREAKS CONCENTRATION FIRST WILL LOSE.
WE'LL KEEP SCORING POINTS AT THE CURRENT RATE.
NEXT UP IS THE CO-ED BEANBAG TOSS.
CONTESTANTS, PLEASE GATHER AT THE EAST GATE.
OH.
THAT'S US.
YOUR TURN, HARUHI!!
WHEN YOU'RE NERVOUS, TRACE THE KANJI FOR "BEAUTY" THREE TIMES ON YOUR PALM.

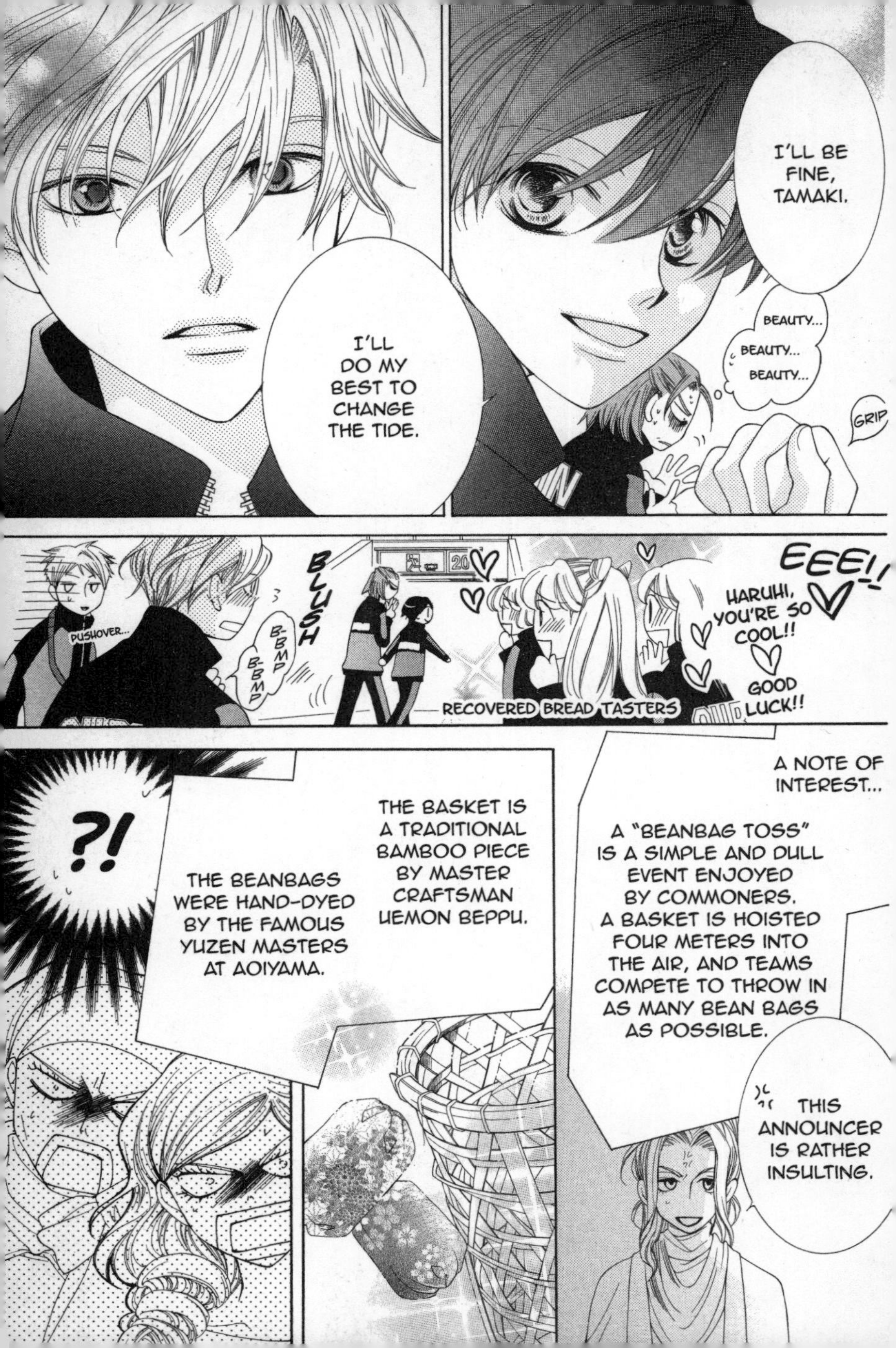
I'LL BE FINE, TAMAKI.
BEAUTY... BEAUTY... BEAUTY...
GRIP
I'LL DO MY BEST TO CHANGE THE TIDE.
EEE!!
HARUHI, YOU'RE SO COOL!!
GOOD LUCK!!
RECOVERED BREAD TASTERS
BLUSH
B-BMP B-BMP
PUSHOVER...
A NOTE OF INTEREST...
A "BEANBAG TOSS" IS A SIMPLE AND DULL EVENT ENJOYED BY COMMONERS. A BASKET IS HOISTED FOUR METERS INTO THE AIR, AND TEAMS COMPETE TO THROW IN AS MANY BEAN BAGS AS POSSIBLE.
THIS ANNOUNCER IS RATHER INSULTING.
THE BASKET IS A TRADITIONAL BAMBOO PIECE BY MASTER CRAFTSMAN UEMON BEPPU.
THE BEANBAGS WERE HAND-DYED BY THE FAMOUS YUZEN MASTERS AT AOIYAMA.
?!

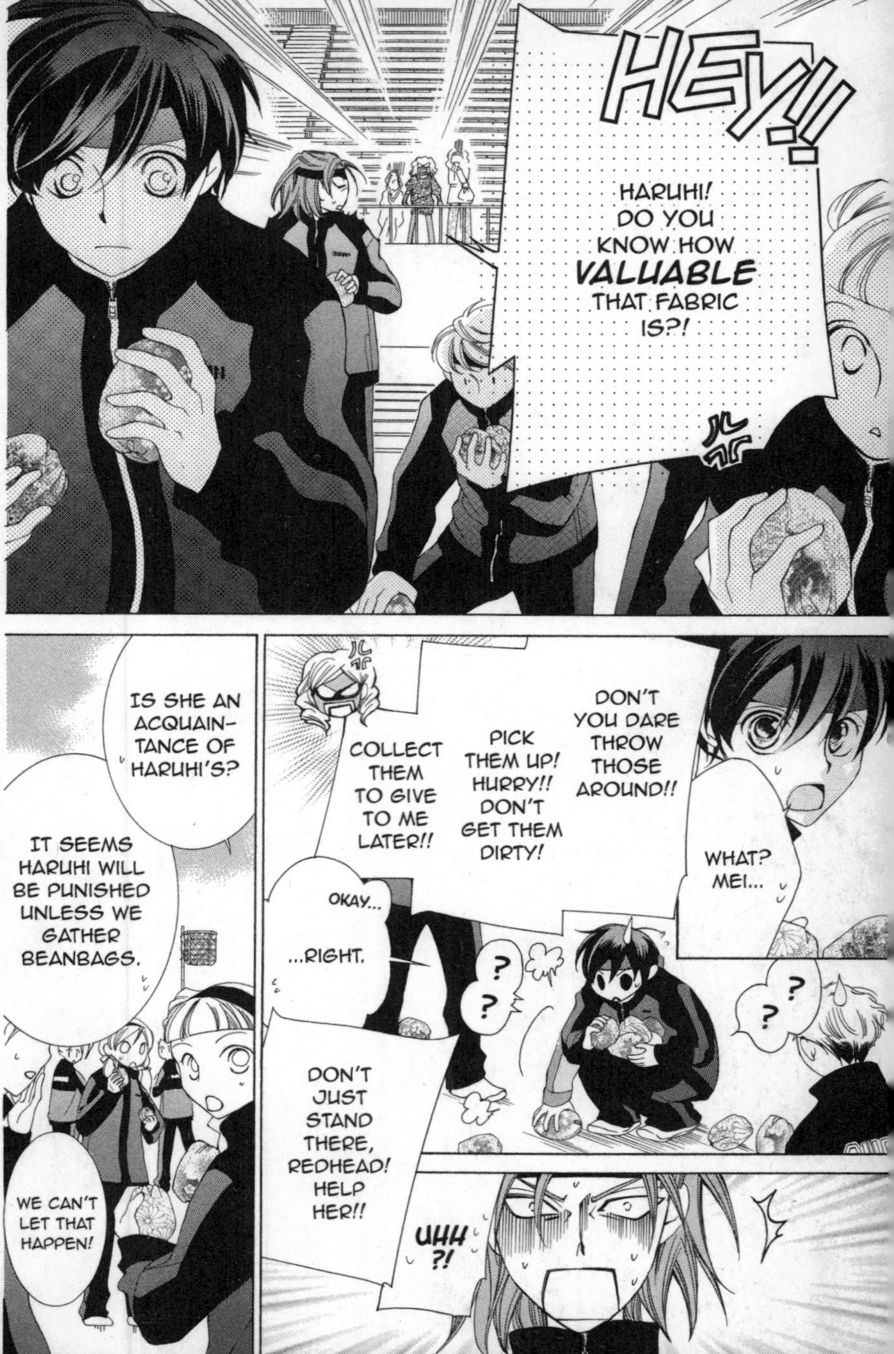
HEY!!
HARUHI! DO YOU KNOW HOW VALUABLE THAT FABRIC IS?!
WHAT? MEI...
DON'T YOU DARE THROW THOSE AROUND!!
PICK THEM UP! HURRY!! DON'T GET THEM DIRTY!
COLLECT THEM TO GIVE TO ME LATER!!
?
?
?
?
OKAY...
...RIGHT.
DON'T JUST STAND THERE, REDHEAD! HELP HER!!
UHH ?!
IS SHE AN ACQUAINTANCE OF HARUHI'S?
IT SEEMS HARUHI WILL BE PUNISHED UNLESS WE GATHER BEANBAGS.
WE CAN'T LET THAT HAPPEN!

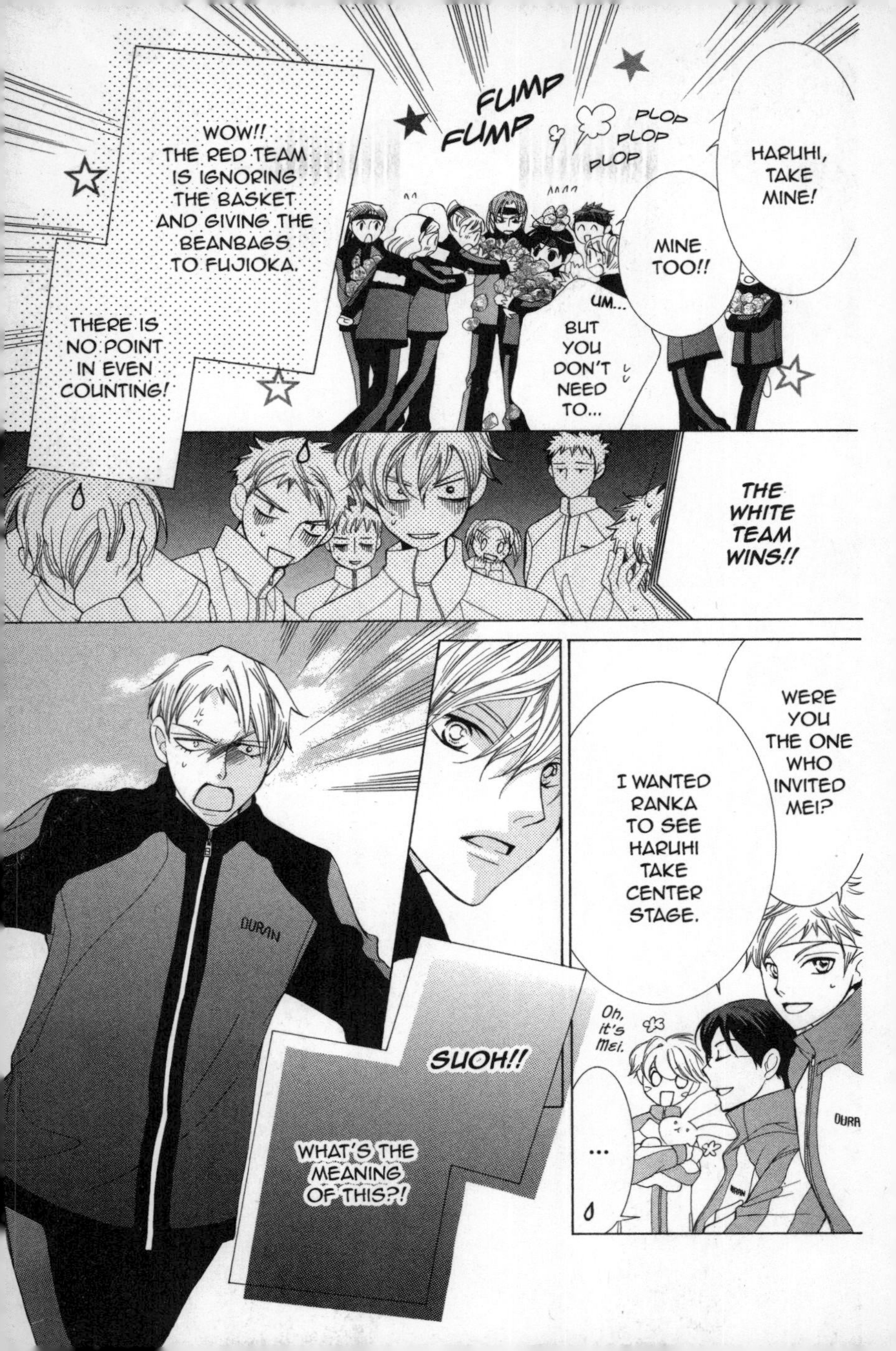
HARUHI, TAKE MINE!
FUMP FUMP
PLOP PLOP PLOP
MINE TOO!!
UM... BUT YOU DON'T NEED TO...
WOW!! THE RED TEAM IS IGNORING THE BASKET AND GIVING THE BEANBAGS TO FUJIOKA.
THERE IS NO POINT IN EVEN COUNTING!
THE WHITE TEAM WINS!!
WERE YOU THE ONE WHO INVITED MEI?
I WANTED RANKA TO SEE HARUHI TAKE CENTER STAGE.
Oh, it's Mei.
...
SUOH!!
WHAT'S THE MEANING OF THIS?!

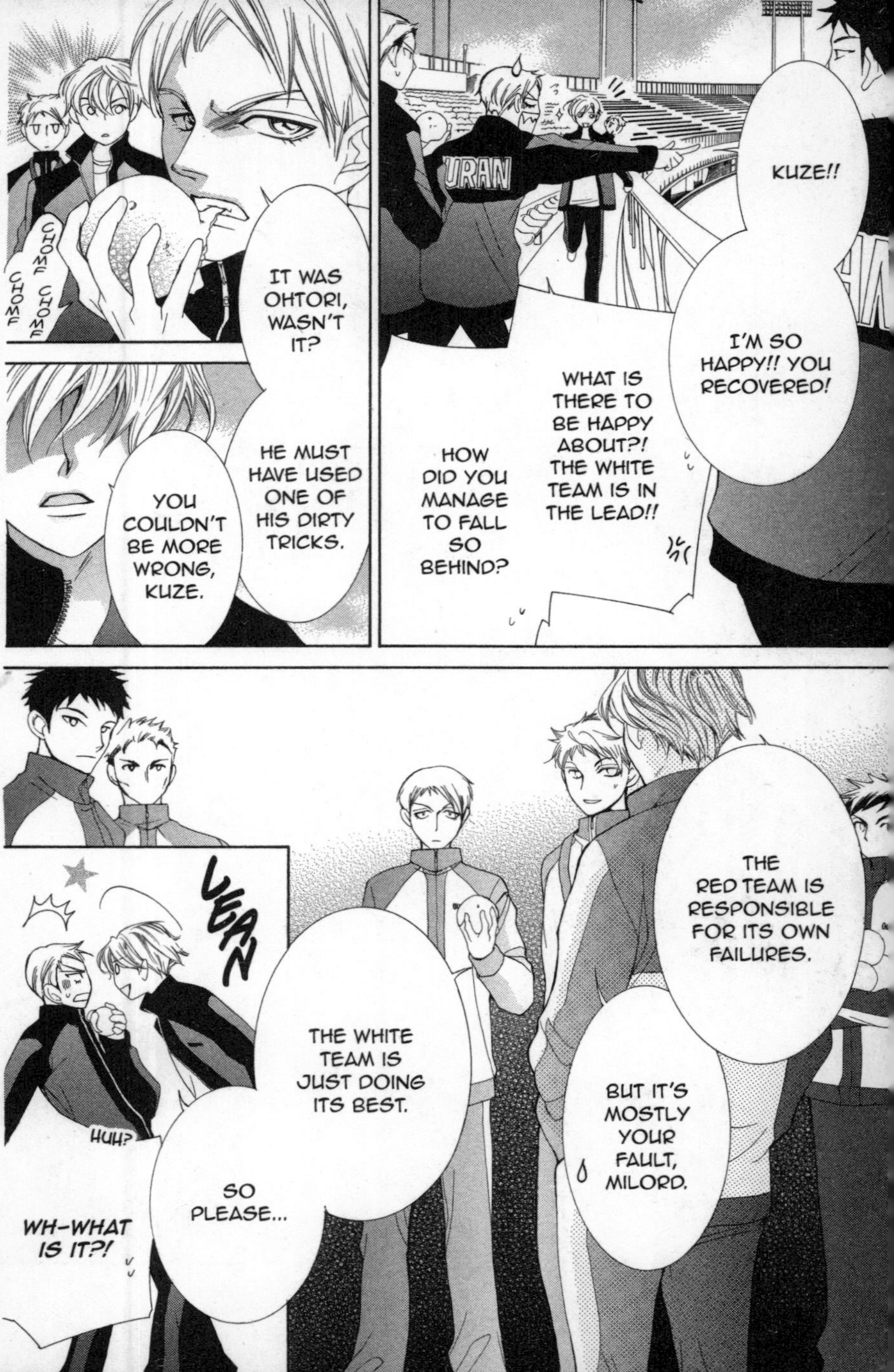
KUZE!!
I'M SO HAPPY!! YOU RECOVERED!
WHAT IS THERE TO BE HAPPY ABOUT?! THE WHITE TEAM IS IN THE LEAD!!
HOW DID YOU MANAGE TO FALL SO BEHIND?
CHOMF CHOMF
CHOMF CHOMF
IT WAS OHTORI, WASN'T IT?
HE MUST HAVE USED ONE OF HIS DIRTY TRICKS.
YOU COULDN'T BE MORE WRONG, KUZE.
THE RED TEAM IS RESPONSIBLE FOR ITS OWN FAILURES.
BUT IT'S MOSTLY YOUR FAULT, MILORD.
THE WHITE TEAM IS JUST DOING ITS BEST.
SO PLEASE...
LEAN
HUH?
WH-WHAT IS IT?!

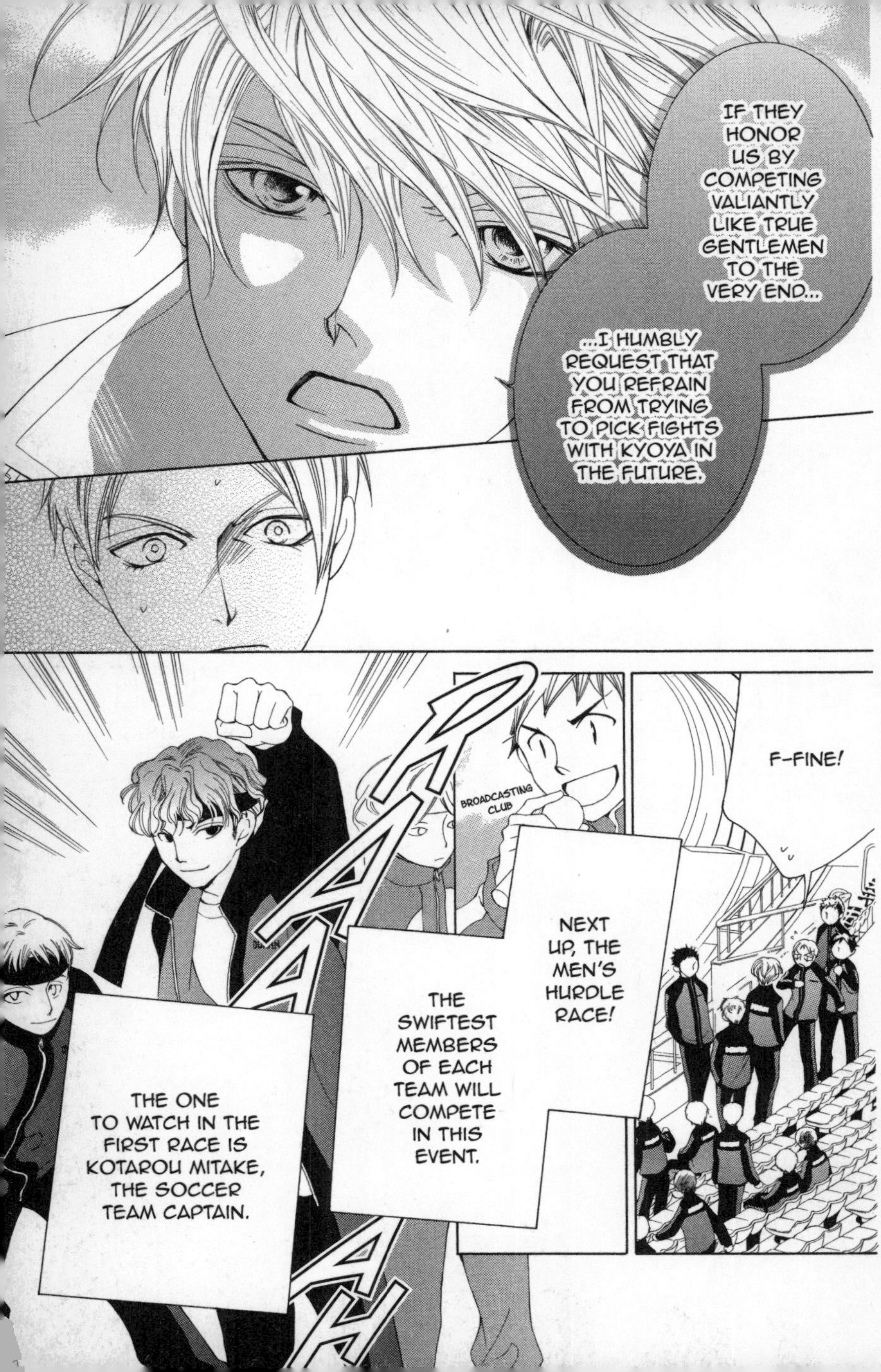
IF THEY HONOR US BY COMPETING VALIANTLY LIKE TRUE GENTLEMEN TO THE VERY END...
...I HUMBLY REQUEST THAT YOU REFRAIN FROM TRYING TO PICK FIGHTS WITH KYOYA IN THE FUTURE.
F-FINE!
BROADCASTING CLUB
NEXT UP, THE MEN'S HURDLE RACE!
THE SWIFTEST MEMBERS OF EACH TEAM WILL COMPETE IN THIS EVENT.
THE ONE TO WATCH IN THE FIRST RACE IS KOTAROU MITAKE, THE SOCCER TEAM CAPTAIN.

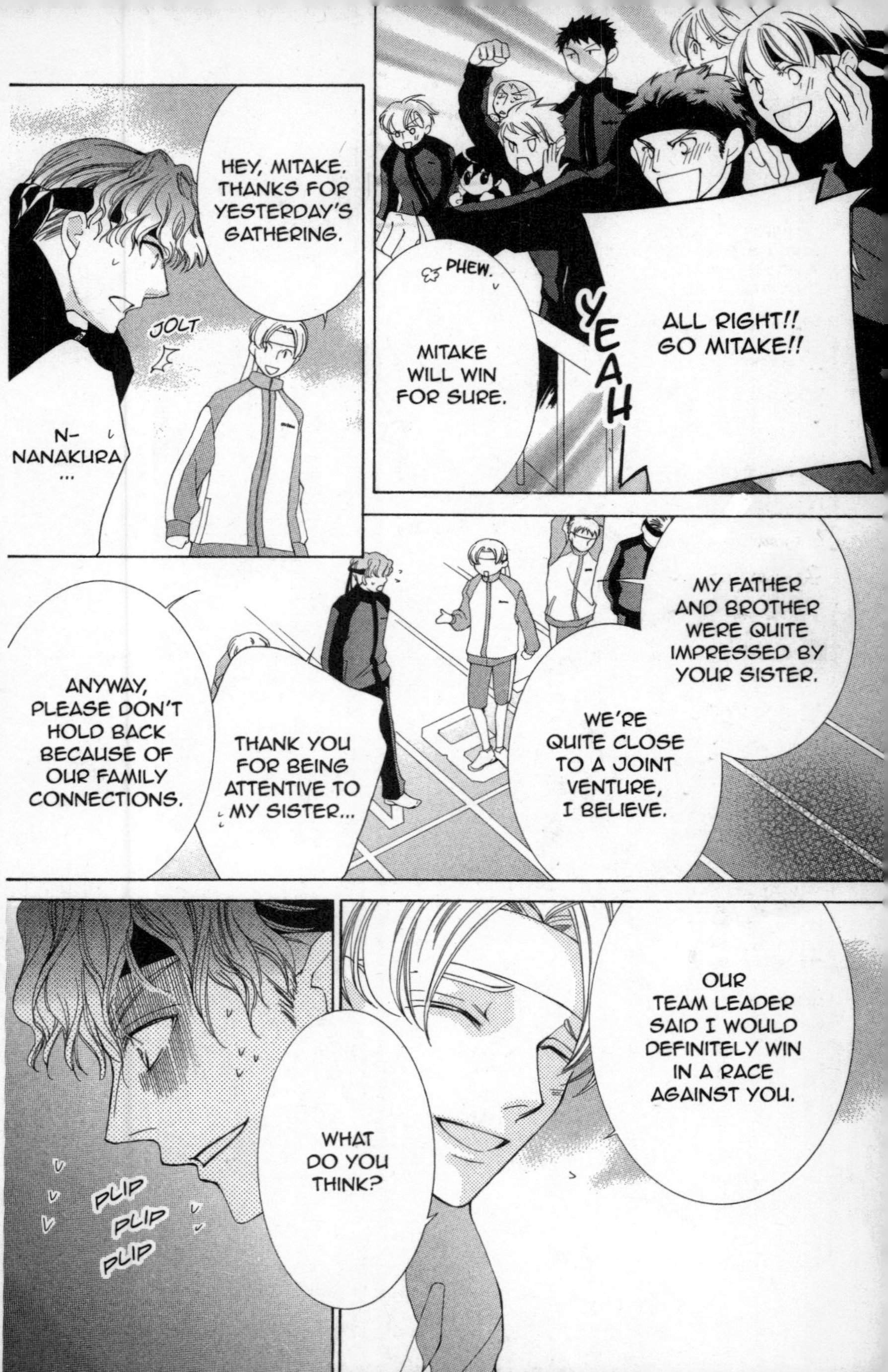
ALL RIGHT!! GO MITAKE!!
YEAH
MITAKE WILL WIN FOR SURE.
PHEW.
HEY, MITAKE. THANKS FOR YESTERDAY'S GATHERING.
JOLT
N- NANAKURA...
MY FATHER AND BROTHER WERE QUITE IMPRESSED BY YOUR SISTER.
WE'RE QUITE CLOSE TO A JOINT VENTURE, I BELIEVE.
THANK YOU FOR BEING ATTENTIVE TO MY SISTER...
ANYWAY, PLEASE DON'T HOLD BACK BECAUSE OF OUR FAMILY CONNECTIONS.
OUR TEAM LEADER SAID I WOULD DEFINITELY WIN IN A RACE AGAINST YOU.
WHAT DO YOU THINK?
PLIP
PLIP
PLIP

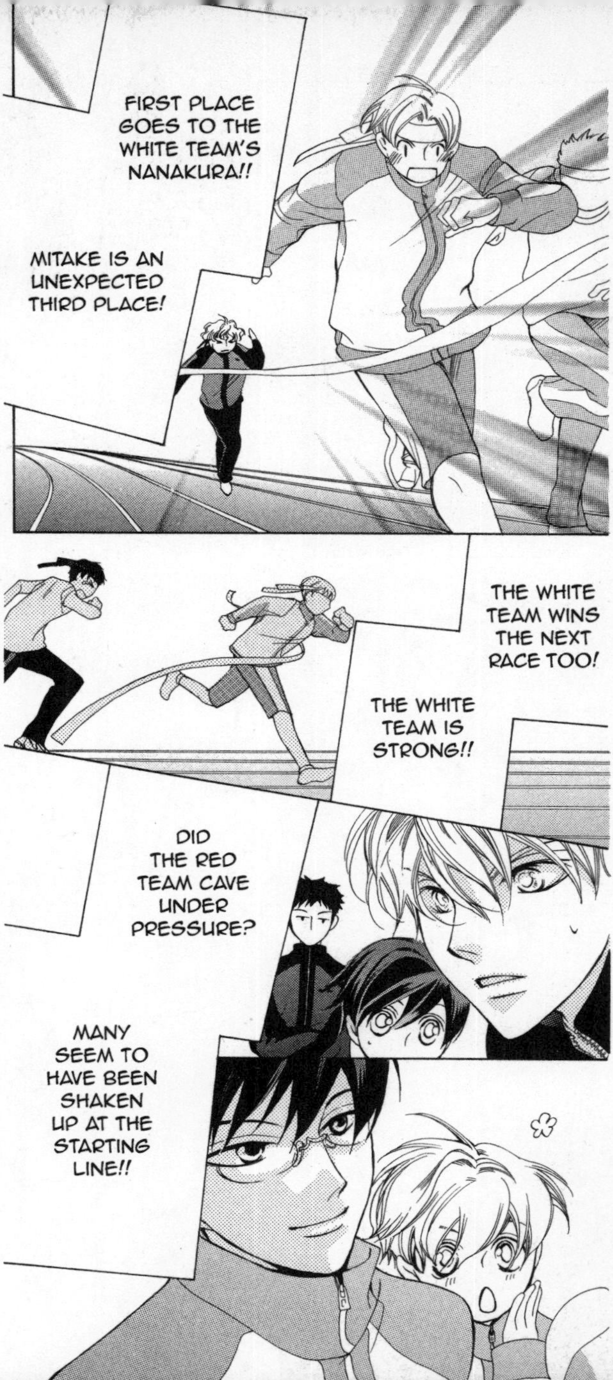
FIRST PLACE GOES TO THE WHITE TEAM'S NANAKURA!!
MITAKE IS AN UNEXPECTED THIRD PLACE!
THE WHITE TEAM WINS THE NEXT RACE TOO!
THE WHITE TEAM IS STRONG!!
DID THE RED TEAM CAVE UNDER PRESSURE?
MANY SEEM TO HAVE BEEN SHAKEN UP AT THE STARTING LINE!!

2

CHARACTER CONTEST RESULTS IN CELEBRATION OF THE 50TH EPISODE (P = POINTS)

1ST: HARUHI	1,512P
2ND: TAMAKI	1,413P
3RD: KYOYA	1,015P
4TH: KAORU	1,004P
5TH: HIKARU	887P
6TH: HUN	649P
7TH: MORI	619P
8TH: NEKOZAWA	120P
9TH: RENGE	62P
10TH: BEREZNOFF	48P

11TH: BOSSA NOVA
12TH: BUN-BUN
13TH: HARUHI'S FATHER
OTHERS: CHIKA, SATOSHI, TETSUYA, ET AL.

THANKS TO EVERYONE WHO PARTICIPATED!!

IN TRUTH, I DIDN'T THINK TAMAKI WOULD MAKE IT TO SECOND PLACE. LETTERS I RECEIVE USUALLY ASK ABOUT THE TWINS AND KYOYA.

(CONTINUED)

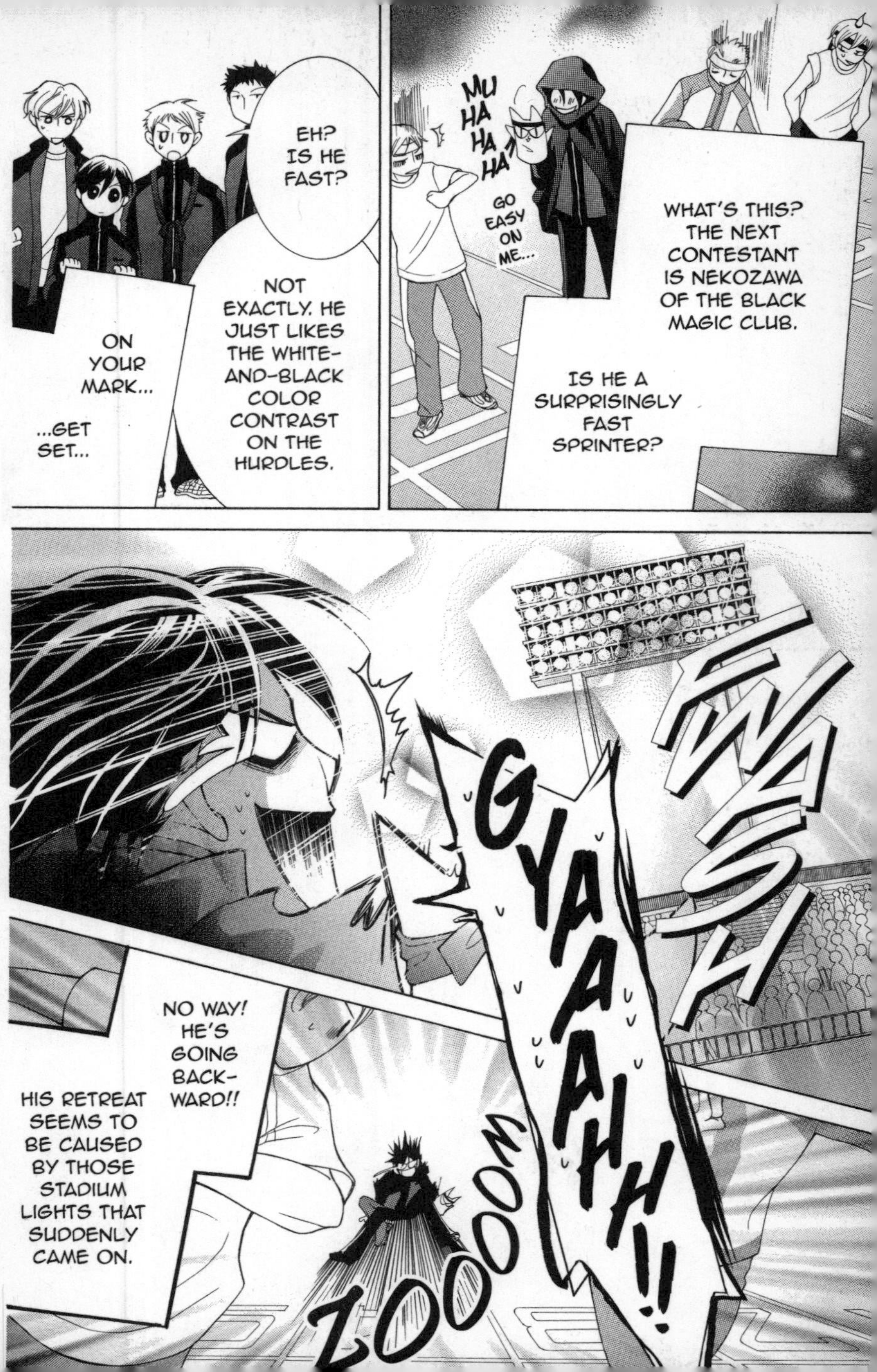
WHAT'S THIS? THE NEXT CONTESTANT IS NEKOZAWA OF THE BLACK MAGIC CLUB.
IS HE A SURPRISINGLY FAST SPRINTER?
MU HA HA HA
GO EASY ON ME...
EH? IS HE FAST?
NOT EXACTLY. HE JUST LIKES THE WHITE-AND-BLACK COLOR CONTRAST ON THE HURDLES.
ON YOUR MARK...
...GET SET...
FWASH
GYAAAHH!!
NO WAY! HE'S GOING BACKWARD!!
HIS RETREAT SEEMS TO BE CAUSED BY THOSE STADIUM LIGHTS THAT SUDDENLY CAME ON.
ZOOOOOM

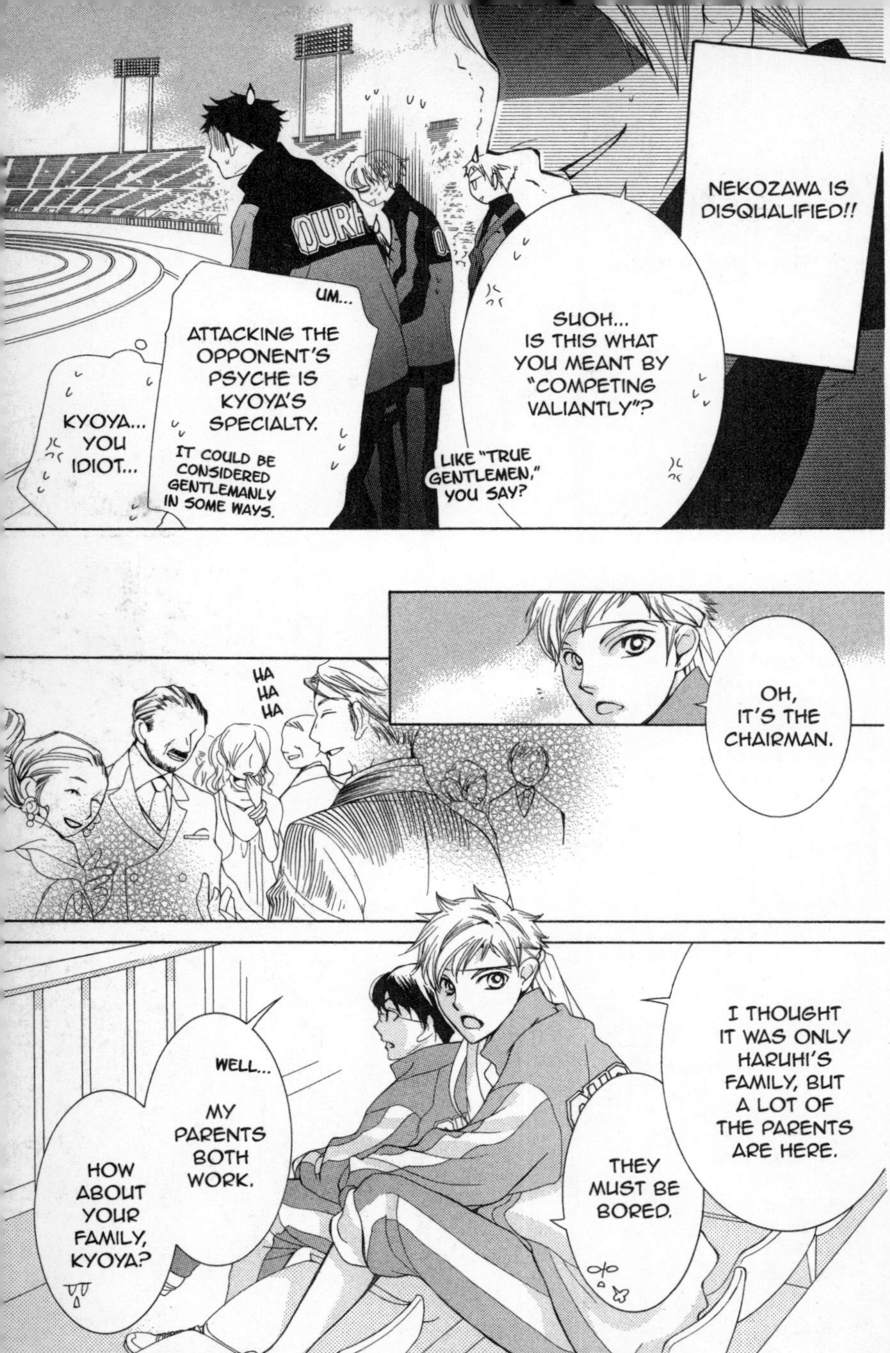
NEKOZAWA IS DISQUALIFIED!!
SUOH... IS THIS WHAT YOU MEANT BY "COMPETING VALIANTLY"?
LIKE "TRUE GENTLEMEN," YOU SAY?
UM...
ATTACKING THE OPPONENT'S PSYCHE IS KYOYA'S SPECIALTY.
IT COULD BE CONSIDERED GENTLEMANLY IN SOME WAYS.
KYOYA... YOU IDIOT...
OH, IT'S THE CHAIRMAN.
HA HA HA
I THOUGHT IT WAS ONLY HARUHI'S FAMILY, BUT A LOT OF THE PARENTS ARE HERE.
THEY MUST BE BORED.
WELL...
MY PARENTS BOTH WORK.
HOW ABOUT YOUR FAMILY, KYOYA?

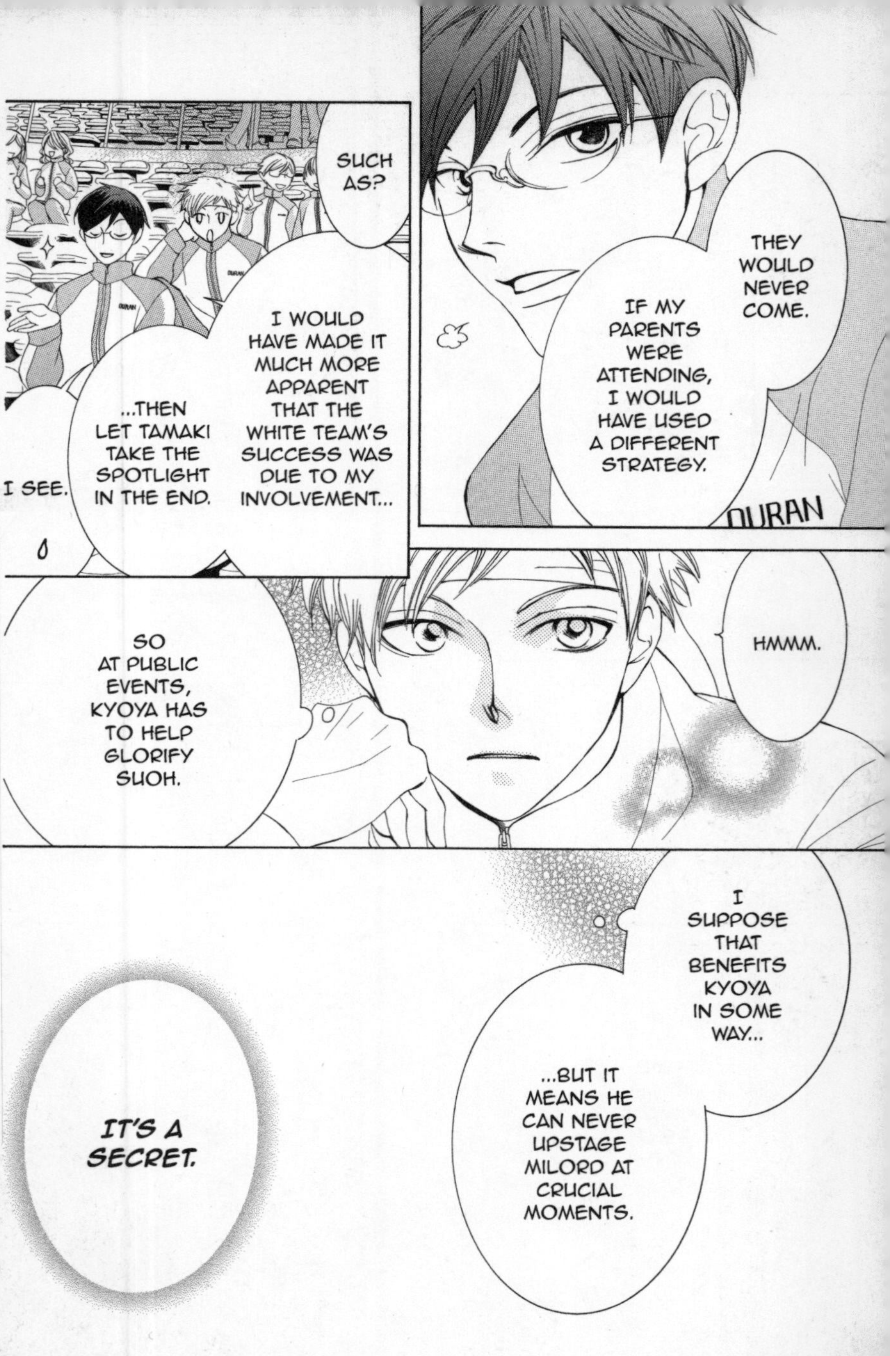
THEY WOULD NEVER COME.
IF MY PARENTS WERE ATTENDING, I WOULD HAVE USED A DIFFERENT STRATEGY.
DURAN
SUCH AS?
I WOULD HAVE MADE IT MUCH MORE APPARENT THAT THE WHITE TEAM'S SUCCESS WAS DUE TO MY INVOLVEMENT...
...THEN LET TAMAKI TAKE THE SPOTLIGHT IN THE END.
I SEE.
HMMM.
SO AT PUBLIC EVENTS, KYOYA HAS TO HELP GLORIFY SUOH.
I SUPPOSE THAT BENEFITS KYOYA IN SOME WAY...
...BUT IT MEANS HE CAN NEVER UPSTAGE MILORD AT CRUCIAL MOMENTS.
IT'S A SECRET.

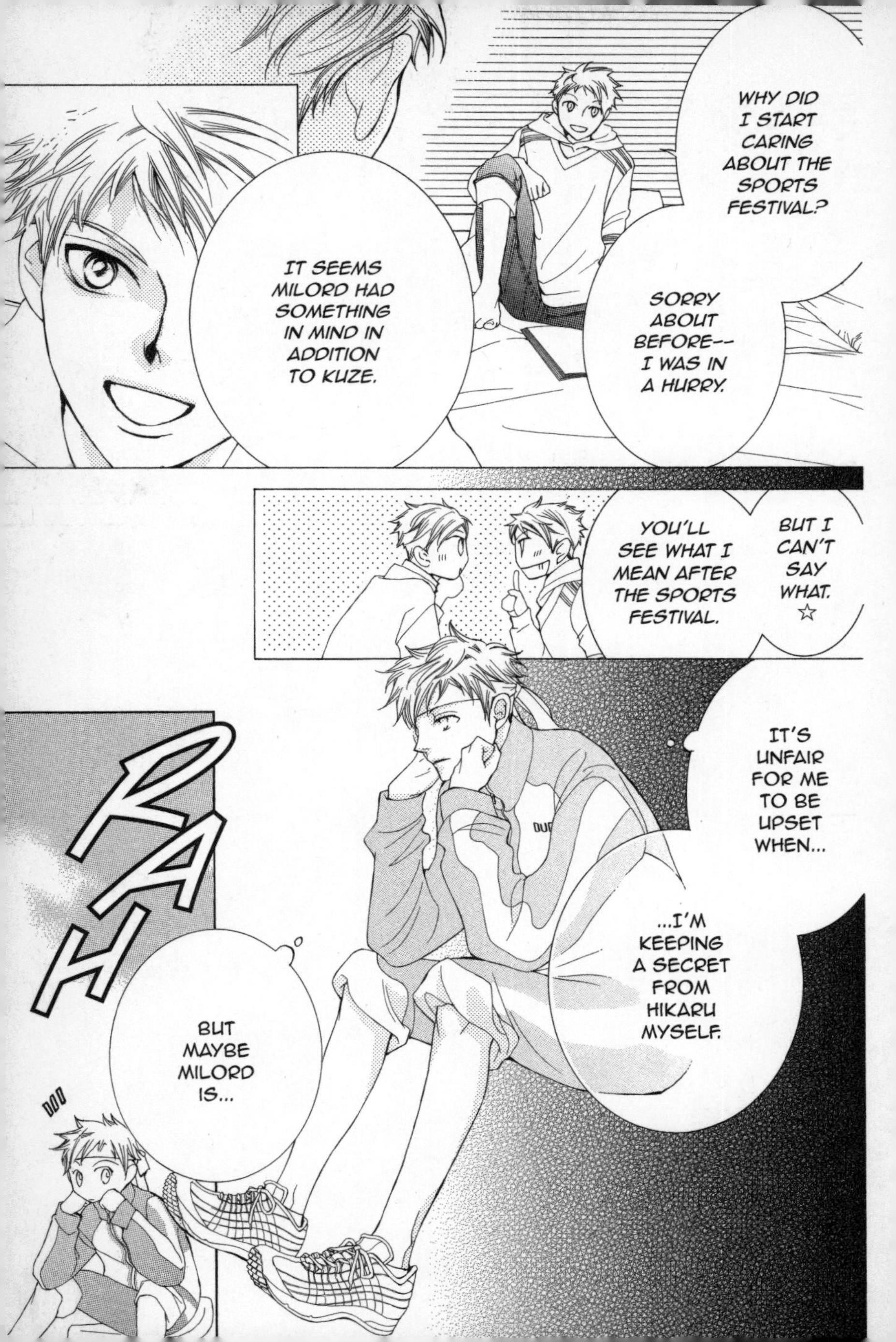
WHY DID I START CARING ABOUT THE SPORTS FESTIVAL?
SORRY ABOUT BEFORE-- I WAS IN A HURRY.
IT SEEMS MILORD HAD SOMETHING IN MIND IN ADDITION TO KUZE.
YOU'LL SEE WHAT I MEAN AFTER THE SPORTS FESTIVAL.
BUT I CAN'T SAY WHAT. ☆
IT'S UNFAIR FOR ME TO BE UPSET WHEN...
...I'M KEEPING A SECRET FROM HIKARU MYSELF.
RAH
BUT MAYBE MILORD IS...

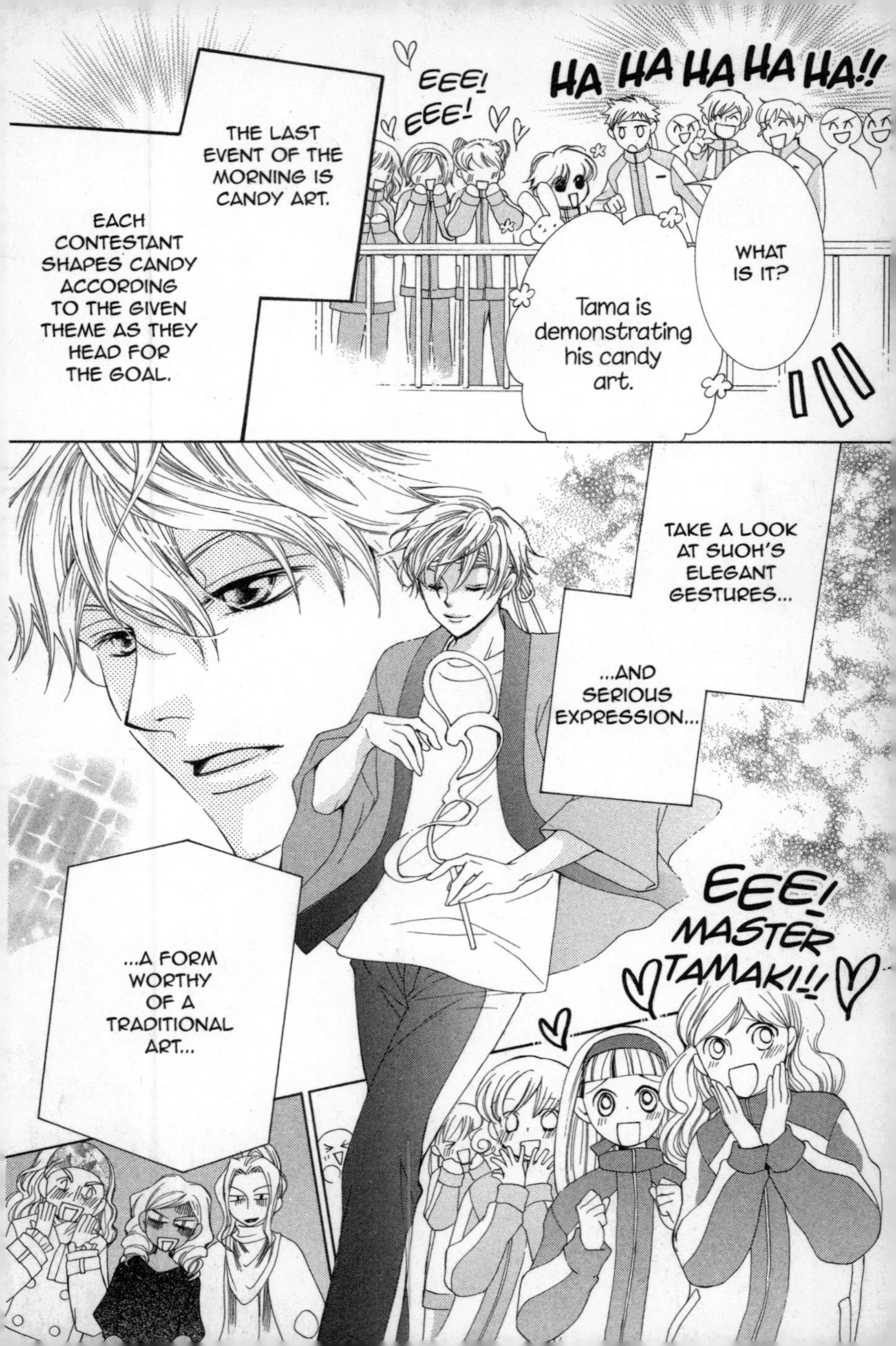
HA HA HA HA HA HA!!
EEE! EEE!
WHAT IS IT?
Tama is demonstrating his candy art.
THE LAST EVENT OF THE MORNING IS CANDY ART.
EACH CONTESTANT SHAPES CANDY ACCORDING TO THE GIVEN THEME AS THEY HEAD FOR THE GOAL.
TAKE A LOOK AT SUOH'S ELEGANT GESTURES...
...AND SERIOUS EXPRESSION...
...A FORM WORTHY OF A TRADITIONAL ART...
EEE! MASTER TAMAKI!!

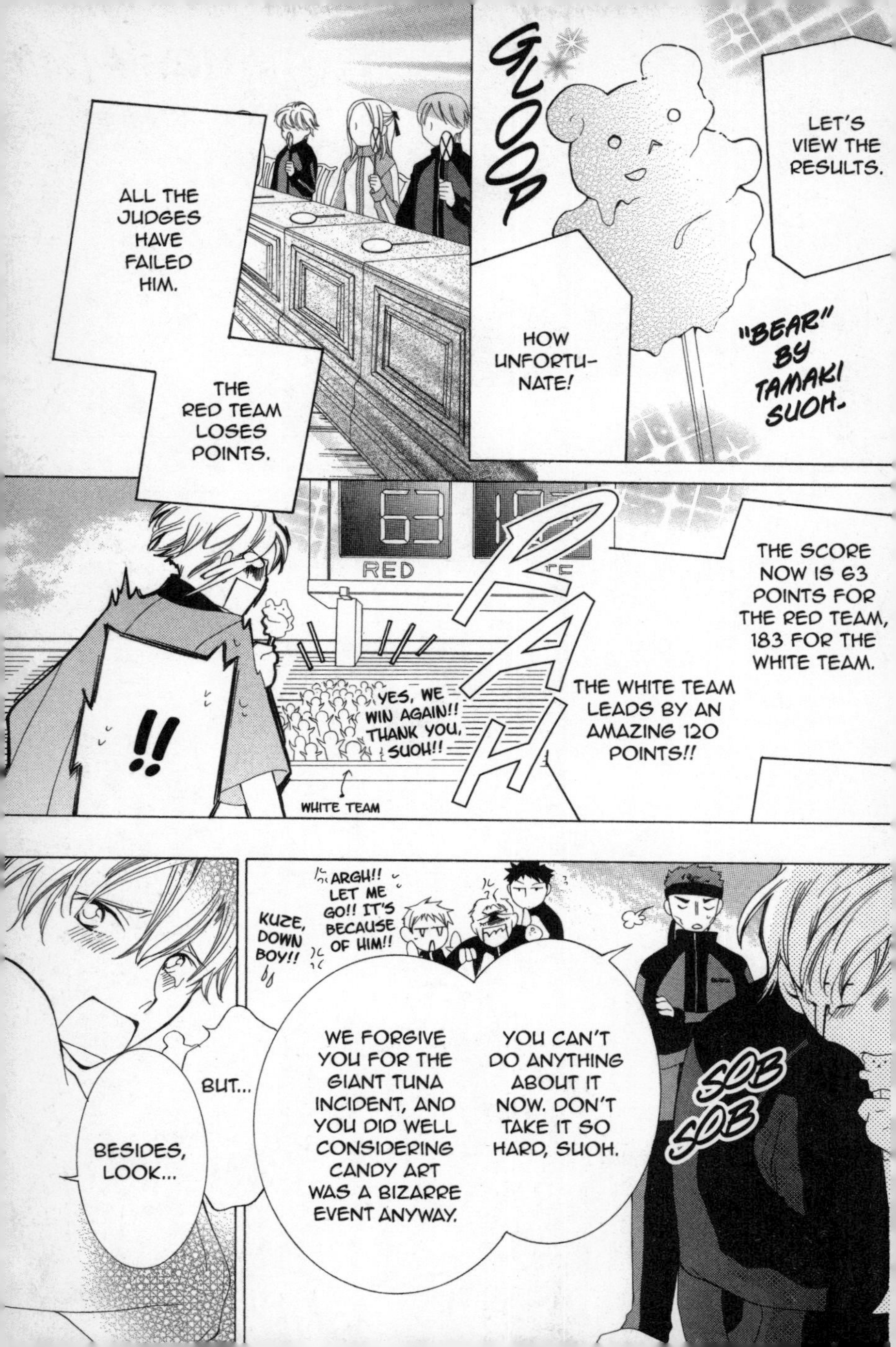
LET'S VIEW THE RESULTS.
GLOOOP
"BEAR" BY TAMAKI SUOH.
HOW UNFORTUNATE!
ALL THE JUDGES HAVE FAILED HIM.
THE RED TEAM LOSES POINTS.
THE SCORE NOW IS 63 POINTS FOR THE RED TEAM, 183 FOR THE WHITE TEAM.
THE WHITE TEAM LEADS BY AN AMAZING 120 POINTS!!
RAAH
63
RED
YES, WE WIN AGAIN!! THANK YOU, SUOH!!
WHITE TEAM
!!
SOB SOB
YOU CAN'T DO ANYTHING ABOUT IT NOW. DON'T TAKE IT SO HARD, SUOH.
WE FORGIVE YOU FOR THE GIANT TUNA INCIDENT, AND YOU DID WELL CONSIDERING CANDY ART WAS A BIZARRE EVENT ANYWAY.
ARGH!! LET ME GO!! IT'S BECAUSE OF HIM!!
KUZE, DOWN BOY!!
BUT...
BESIDES, LOOK...

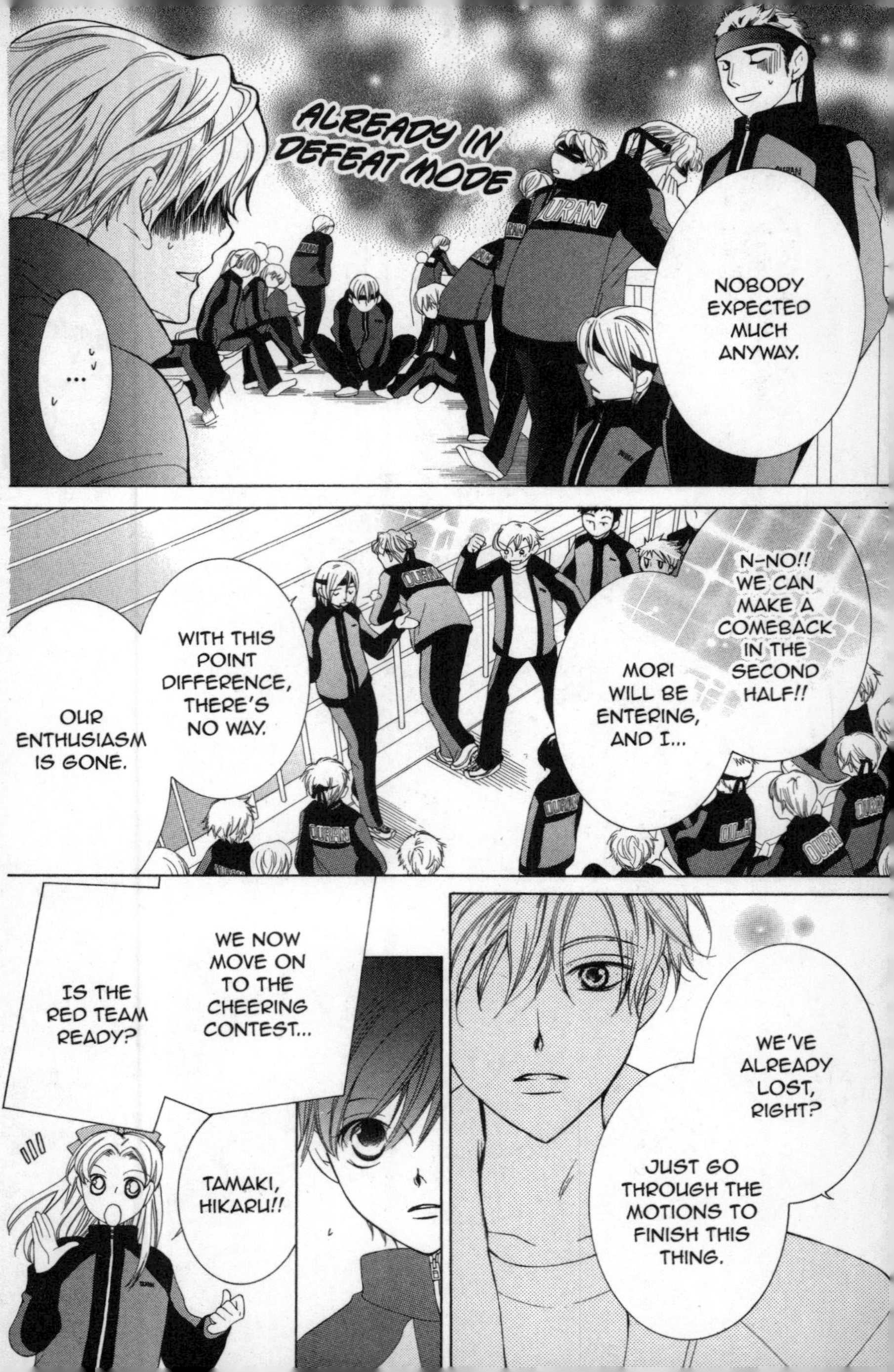
NOBODY EXPECTED MUCH ANYWAY.
ALREADY IN DEFEAT MODE
...
N-NO!! WE CAN MAKE A COMEBACK IN THE SECOND HALF!!
MORI WILL BE ENTERING, AND I...
WITH THIS POINT DIFFERENCE, THERE'S NO WAY.
OUR ENTHUSIASM IS GONE.
WE'VE ALREADY LOST, RIGHT?
JUST GO THROUGH THE MOTIONS TO FINISH THIS THING.
WE NOW MOVE ON TO THE CHEERING CONTEST...
IS THE RED TEAM READY?
TAMAKI, HIKARU!!

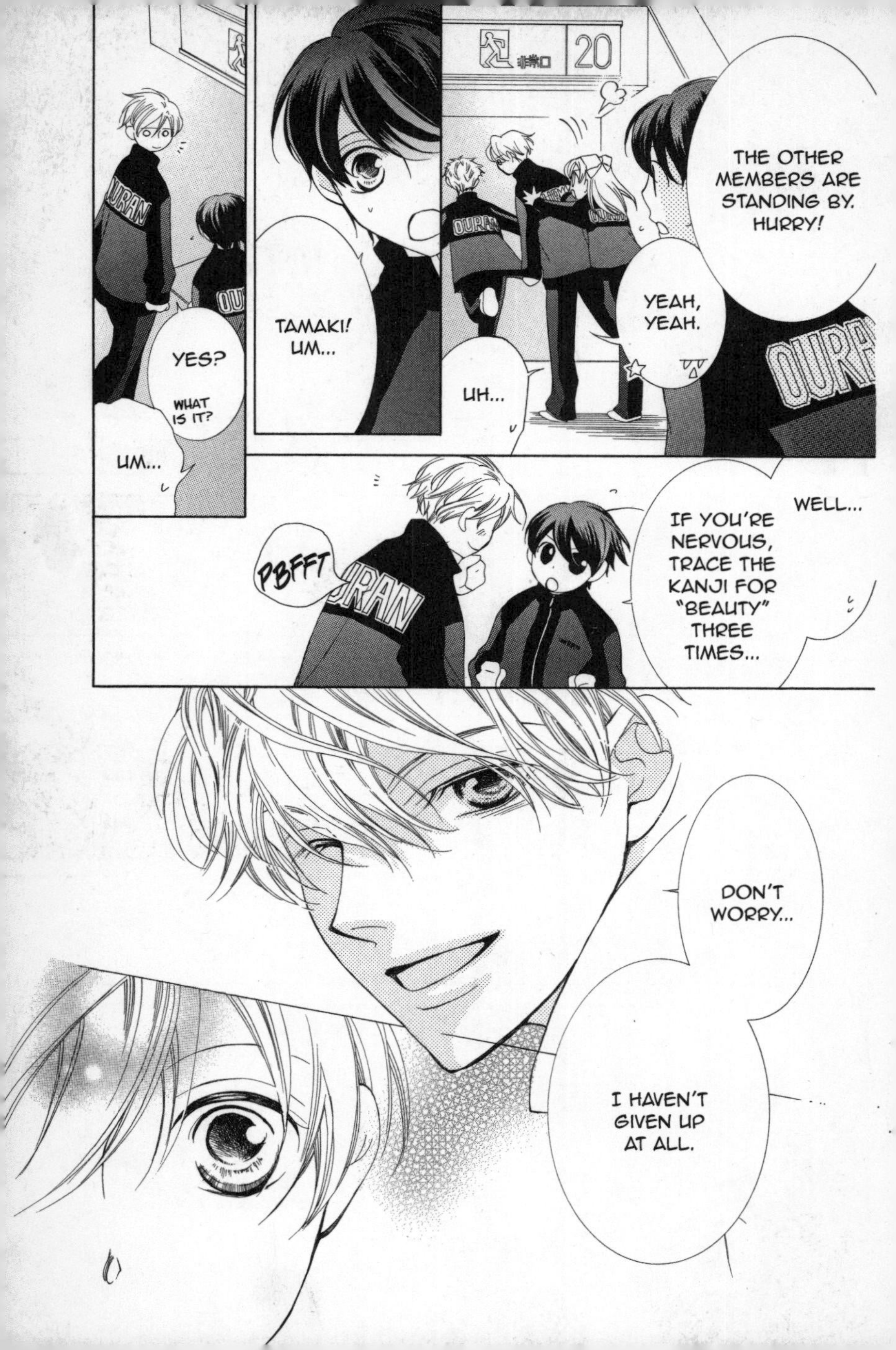
20
非常口
THE OTHER MEMBERS ARE STANDING BY. HURRY!
YEAH, YEAH.
UH...
TAMAKI! UM...
YES?
WHAT IS IT?
UM...
WELL...
IF YOU'RE NERVOUS, TRACE THE KANJI FOR "BEAUTY" THREE TIMES...
PBFFT
DON'T WORRY...
I HAVEN'T GIVEN UP AT ALL.

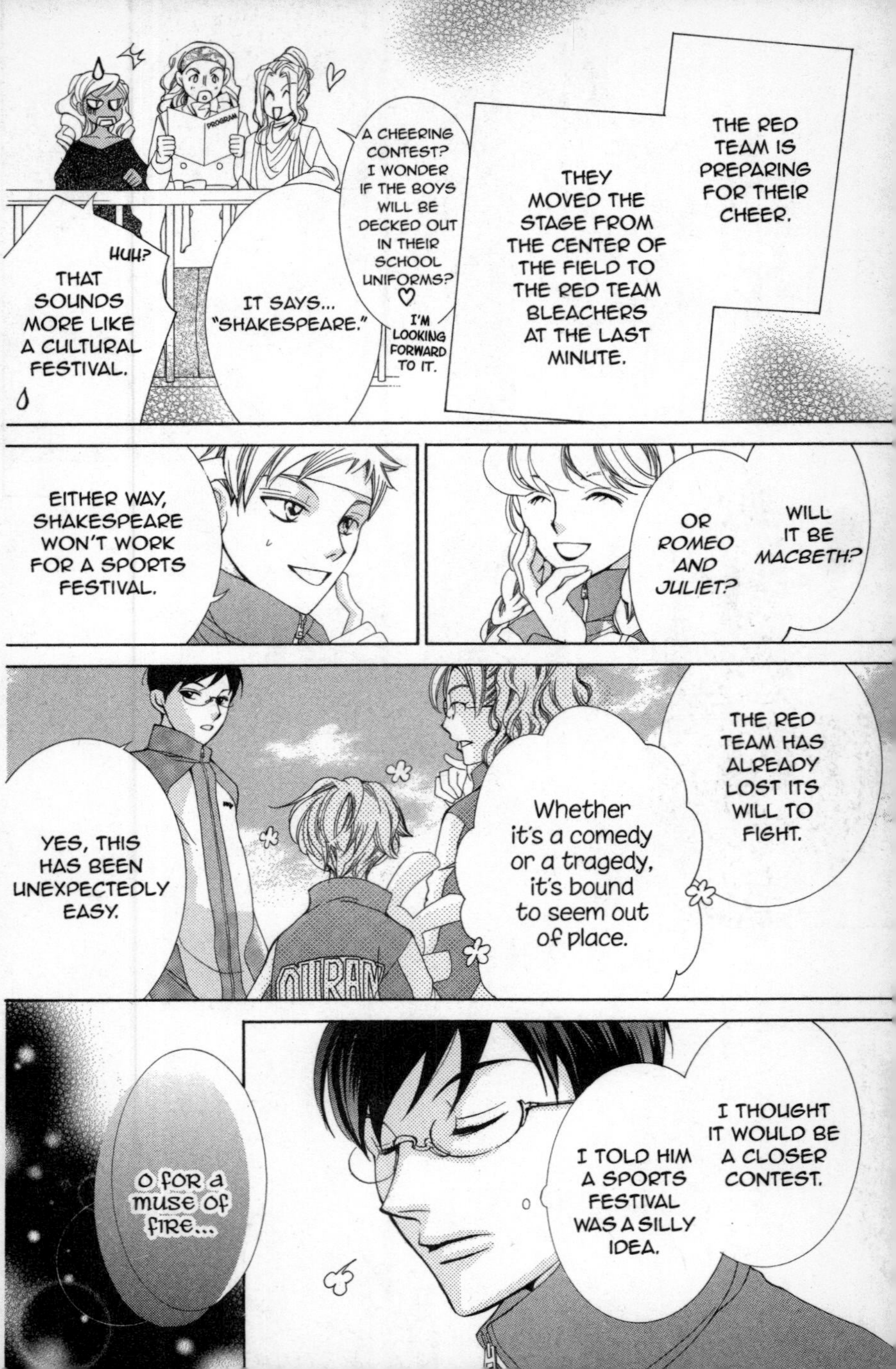
THE RED TEAM IS PREPARING FOR THEIR CHEER.
THEY MOVED THE STAGE FROM THE CENTER OF THE FIELD TO THE RED TEAM BLEACHERS AT THE LAST MINUTE.
A CHEERING CONTEST? I WONDER IF THE BOYS WILL BE DECKED OUT IN THEIR SCHOOL UNIFORMS? ♡
I'M LOOKING FORWARD TO IT.
PROGRAM
IT SAYS... "SHAKESPEARE."
HUH?
THAT SOUNDS MORE LIKE A CULTURAL FESTIVAL.
WILL IT BE MACBETH?
OR ROMEO AND JULIET?
EITHER WAY, SHAKESPEARE WON'T WORK FOR A SPORTS FESTIVAL.
THE RED TEAM HAS ALREADY LOST ITS WILL TO FIGHT.
Whether it's a comedy or a tragedy, it's bound to seem out of place.
OURAN
YES, THIS HAS BEEN UNEXPECTEDLY EASY.
I THOUGHT IT WOULD BE A CLOSER CONTEST.
I TOLD HIM A SPORTS FESTIVAL WAS A SILLY IDEA.
O for a muse of fire...

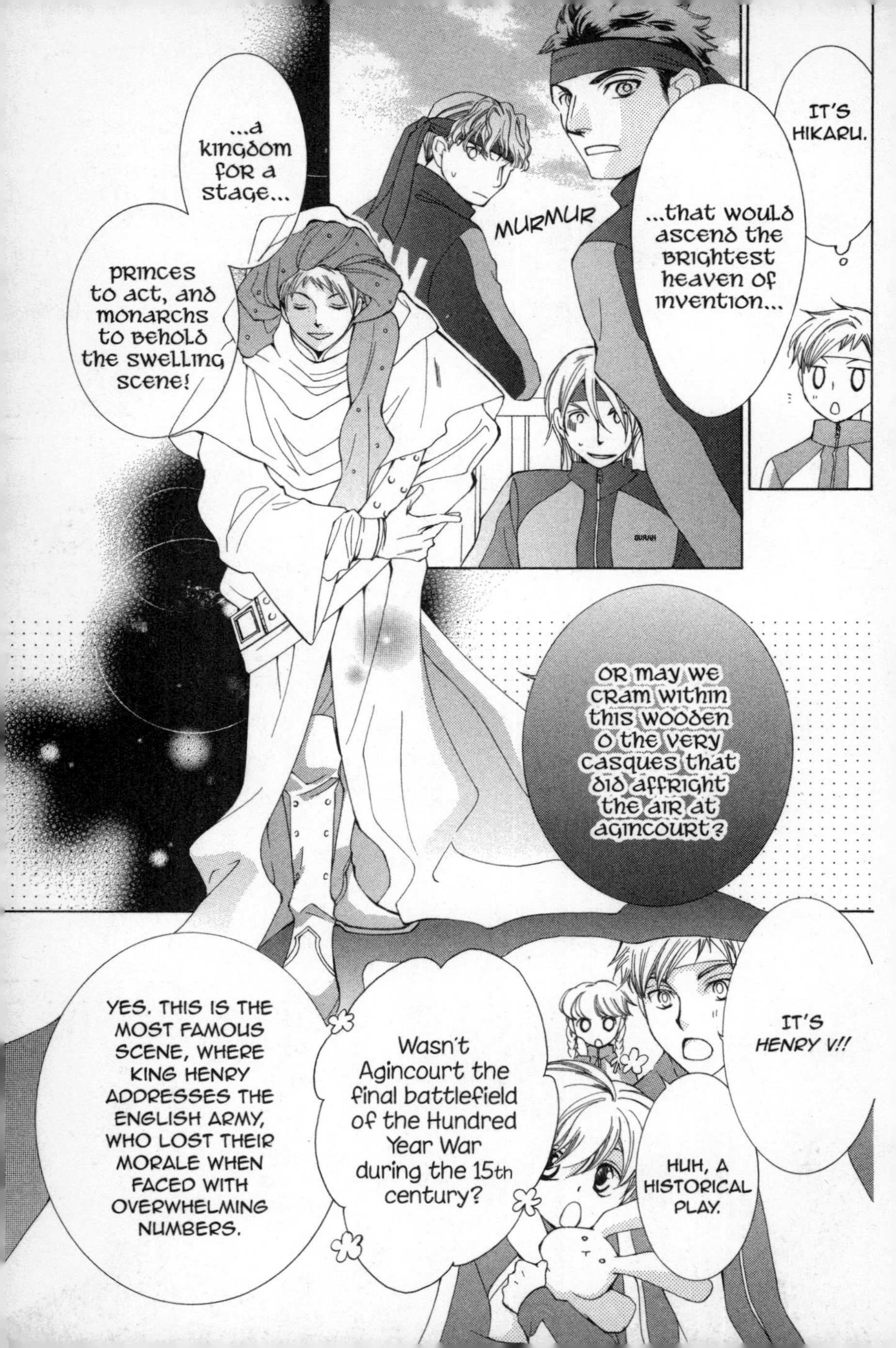
IT'S HIKARU.
...that would ascend the brightest heaven of invention...
MURMUR
...a kingdom for a stage...
princes to act, and monarchs to behold the swelling scene!
or may we cram within this wooden o the very casques that did affright the air at agincourt?
IT'S HENRY V!!
HUH, A HISTORICAL PLAY.
Wasn't Agincourt the final battlefield of the Hundred Year War during the 15th century?
YES. THIS IS THE MOST FAMOUS SCENE, WHERE KING HENRY ADDRESSES THE ENGLISH ARMY, WHO LOST THEIR MORALE WHEN FACED WITH OVERWHELMING NUMBERS.

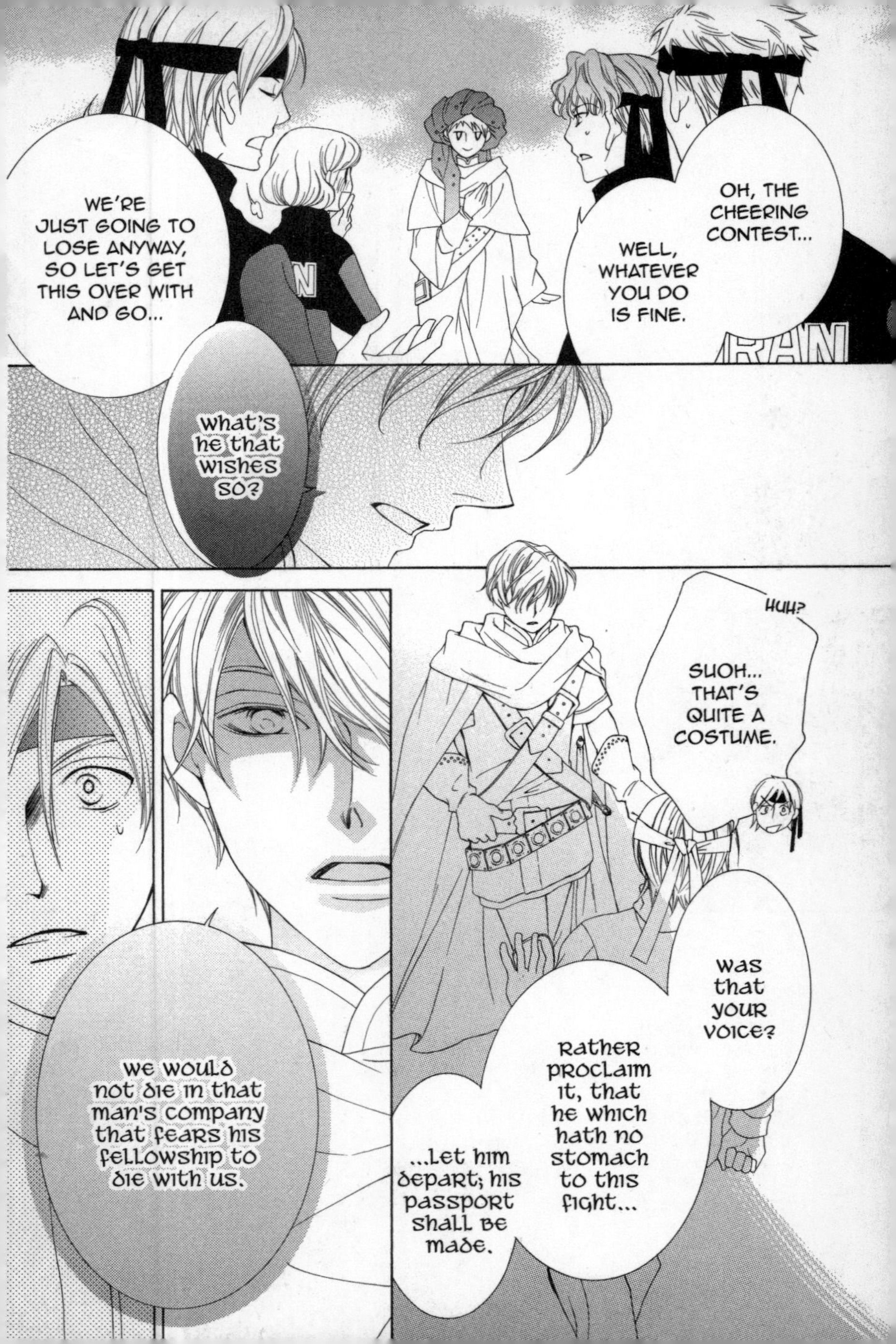
OH, THE CHEERING CONTEST...
WELL, WHATEVER YOU DO IS FINE.
RAN
WE'RE JUST GOING TO LOSE ANYWAY, SO LET'S GET THIS OVER WITH AND GO...
What's he that wishes so?
HUH?
SUOH... THAT'S QUITE A COSTUME.
Was that your voice?
Rather proclaim it, that he which hath no stomach to this fight...
...Let him depart; his passport shall be made.
We would not die in that man's company that fears his fellowship to die with us.

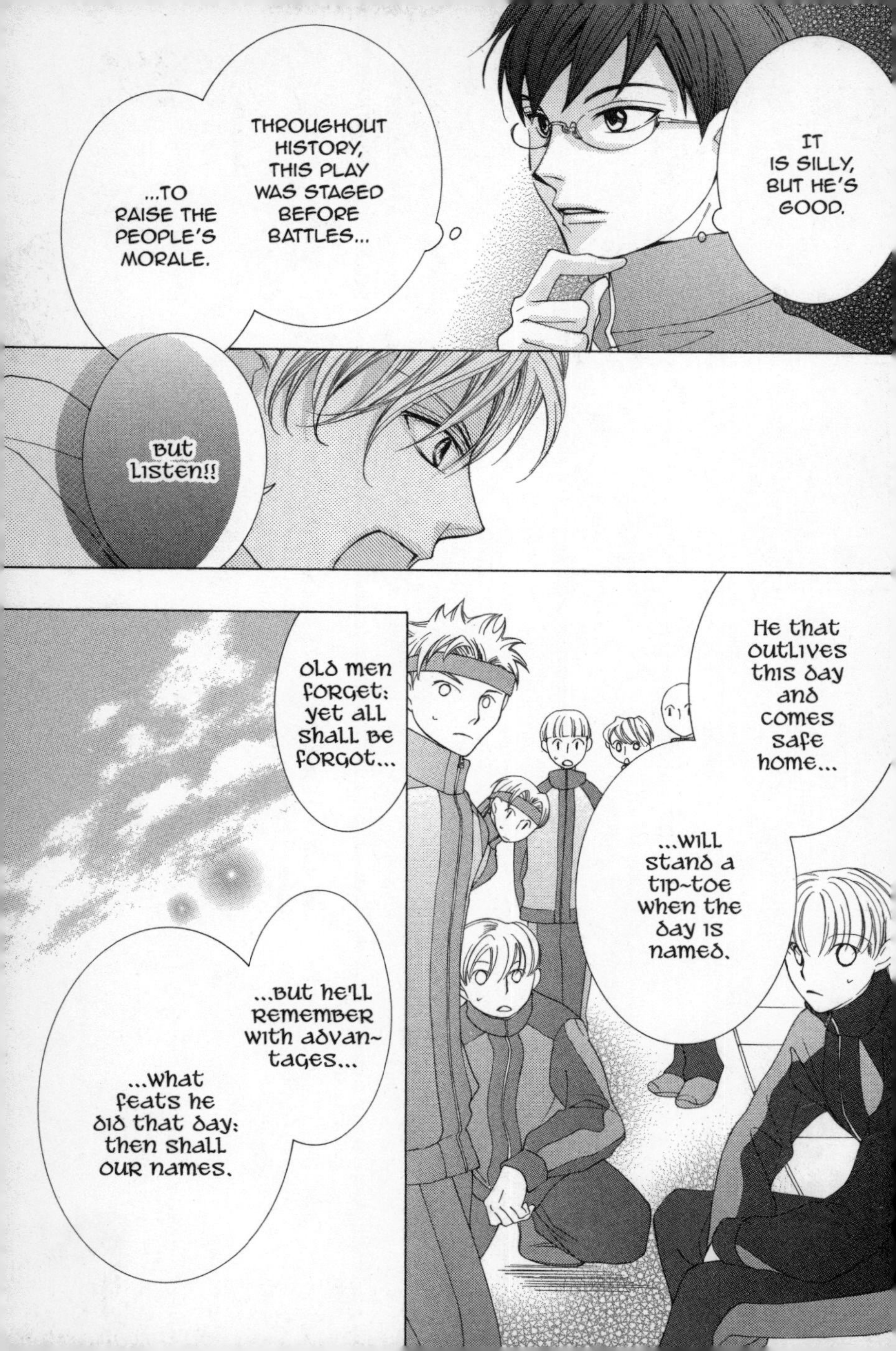
IT IS SILLY, BUT HE'S GOOD.
THROUGHOUT HISTORY, THIS PLAY WAS STAGED BEFORE BATTLES...
...TO RAISE THE PEOPLE'S MORALE.
But listen!!
He that outlives this day and comes safe home...
...will stand a tip-toe when the day is named.
Old men forget: yet all shall be forgot...
...but he'll remember with advan-tages...
...what feats he did that day: then shall our names.

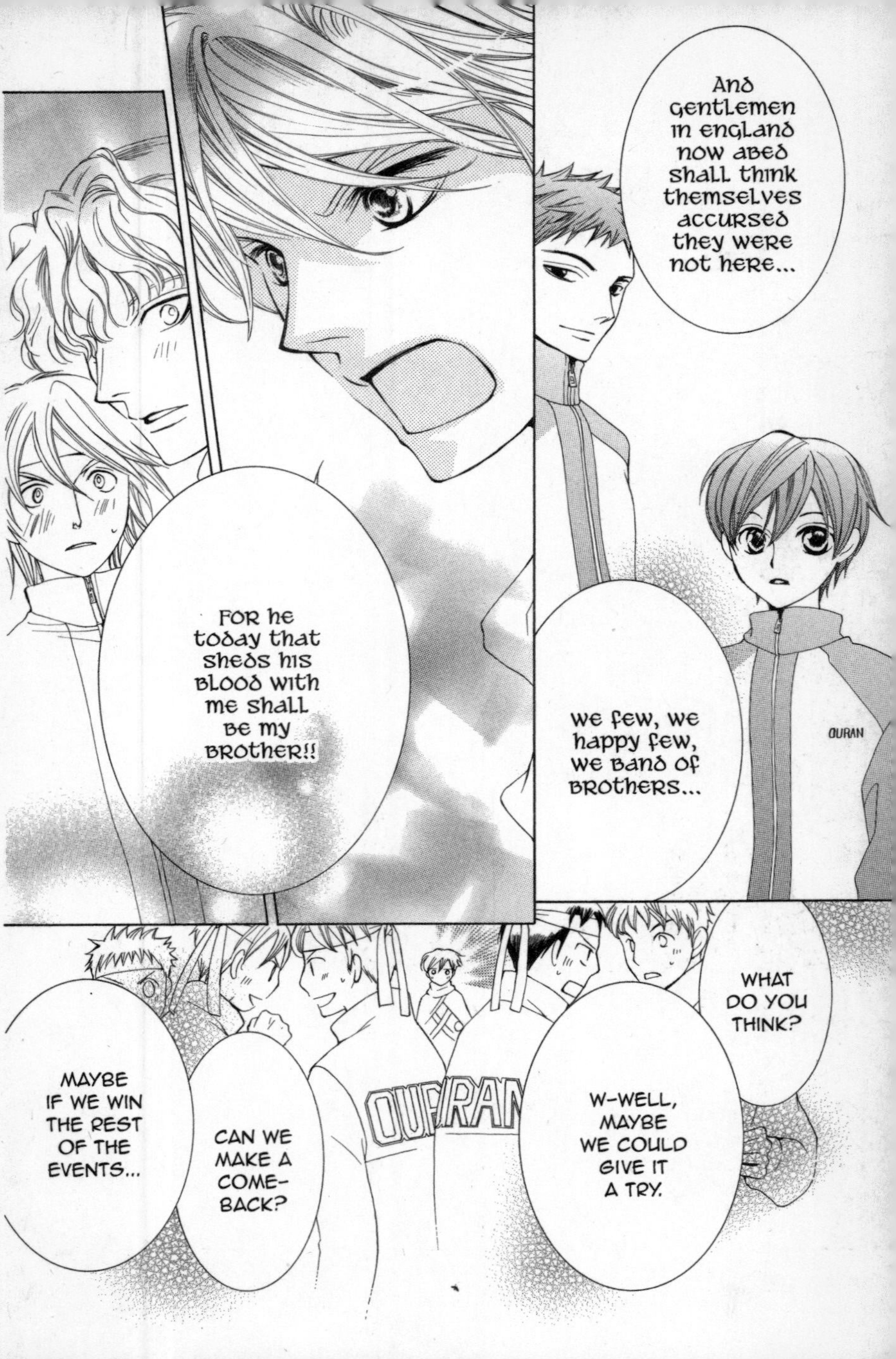
And gentlemen in england now abed shall think themselves accursed they were not here...
We few, we happy few, we band of brothers...
OURAN
For he today that sheds his blood with me shall be my brother!!
WHAT DO YOU THINK?
W-WELL, MAYBE WE COULD GIVE IT A TRY.
OURAN
CAN WE MAKE A COME-BACK?
MAYBE IF WE WIN THE REST OF THE EVENTS...

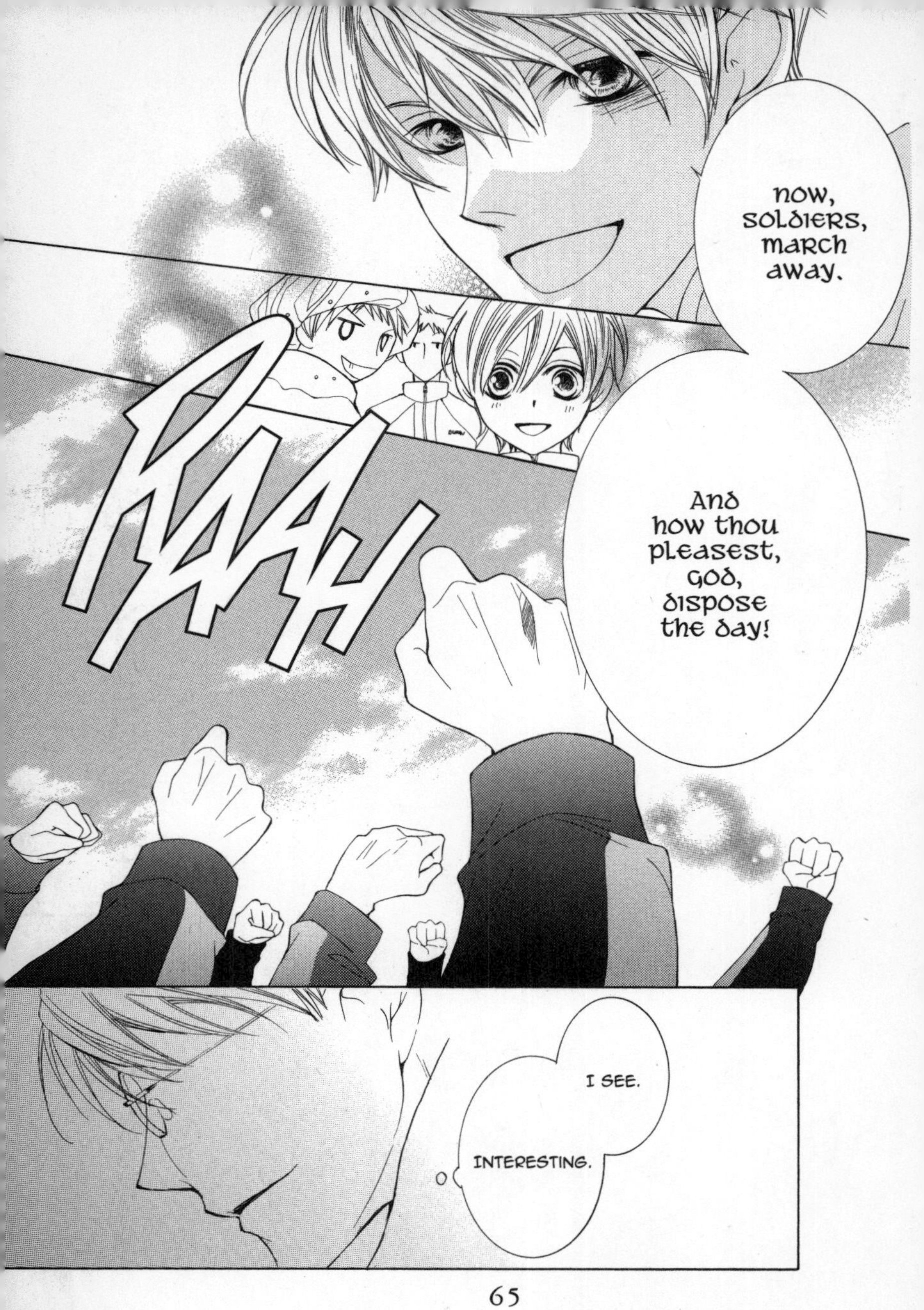
now, soldiers, march away.
And how thou pleasest, God, dispose the day!
RAAH
I SEE.
INTERESTING.

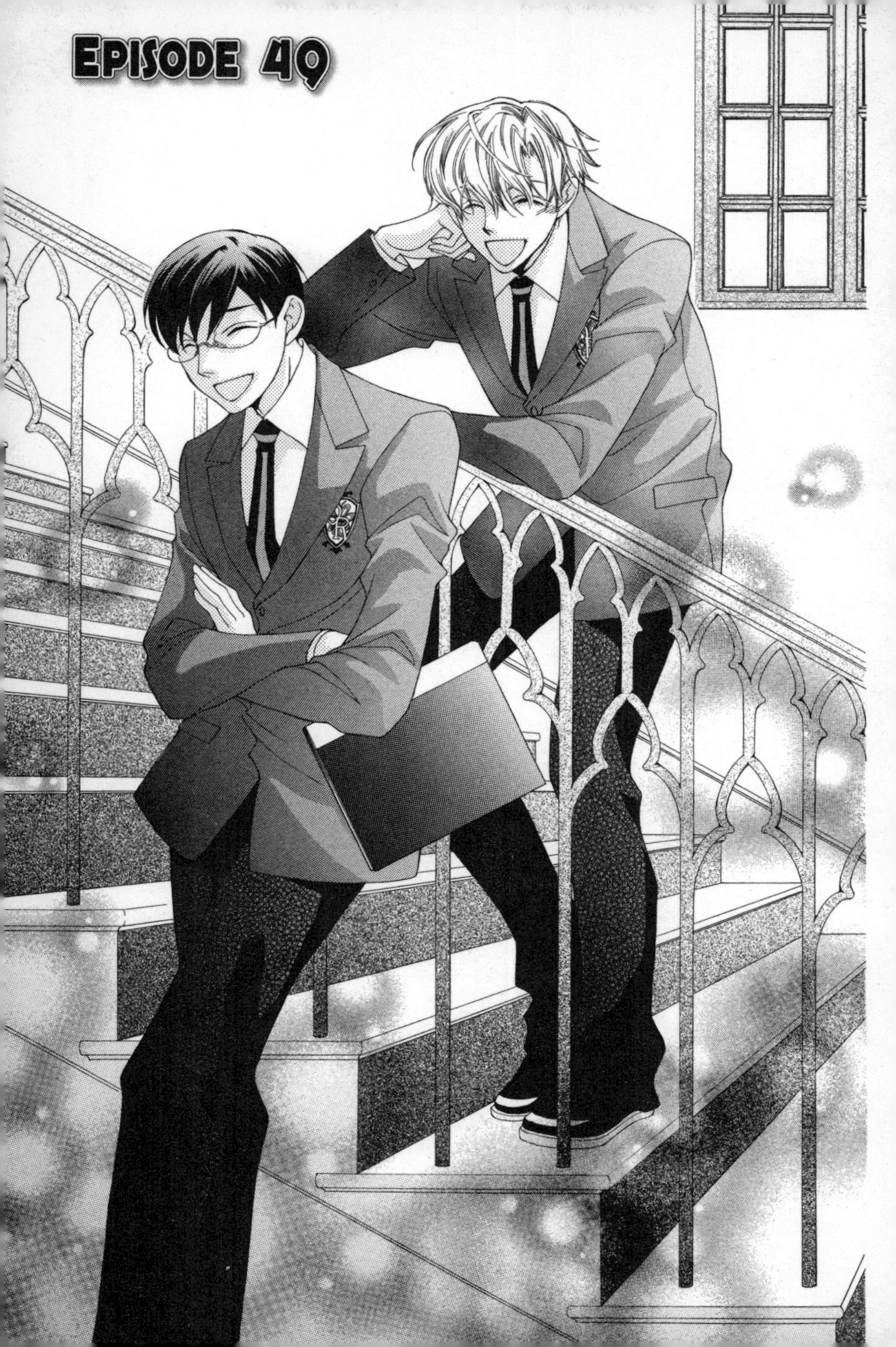
Episode 49

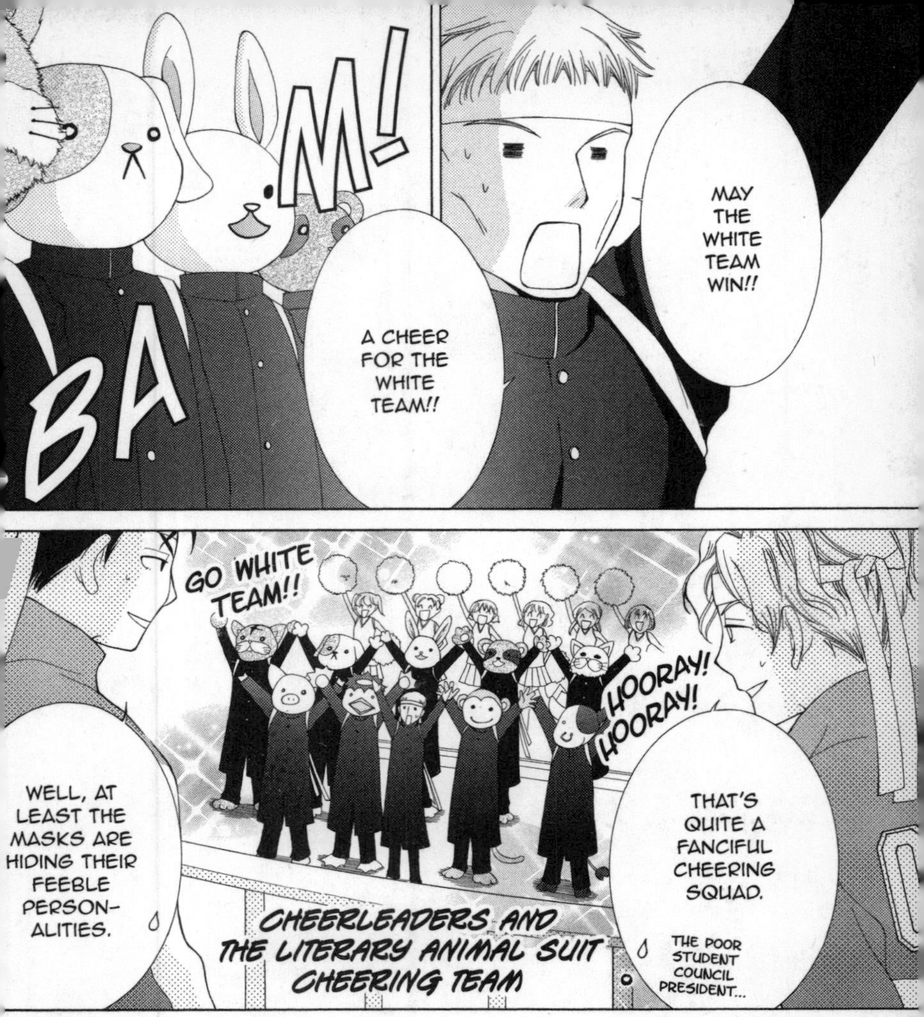
MAY THE WHITE TEAM WIN!!
A CHEER FOR THE WHITE TEAM!!
BAM!
THAT'S QUITE A FANCIFUL CHEERING SQUAD.
THE POOR STUDENT COUNCIL PRESIDENT...
HOORAY! HOORAY!
GO WHITE TEAM!!
CHEERLEADERS AND THE LITERARY ANIMAL SUIT CHEERING TEAM
WELL, AT LEAST THE MASKS ARE HIDING THEIR FEEBLE PERSON-ALITIES.

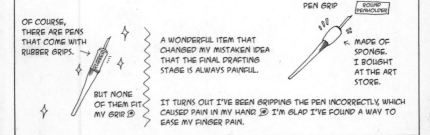

OF COURSE, THERE ARE PENS THAT COME WITH RUBBER GRIPS.

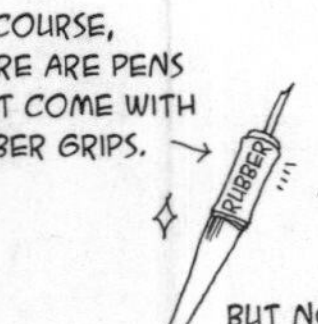
RUBBER

BUT NONE OF THEM FIT MY GRIP.

PEN GRIP

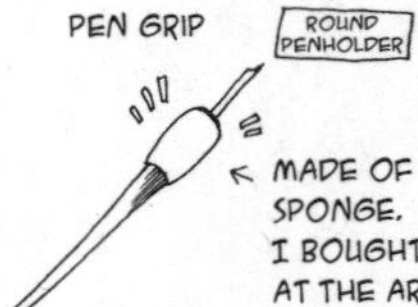
ROUND PENHOLDER

MADE OF SPONGE. I BOUGHT AT THE ART STORE.

A WONDERFUL ITEM THAT CHANGED MY MISTAKEN IDEA THAT THE FINAL DRAFTING STAGE IS ALWAYS PAINFUL.

IT TURNS OUT I'VE BEEN GRIPPING THE PEN INCORRECTLY, WHICH CAUSED PAIN IN MY HAND. I'M GLAD I'VE FOUND A WAY TO EASE MY FINGER PAIN.

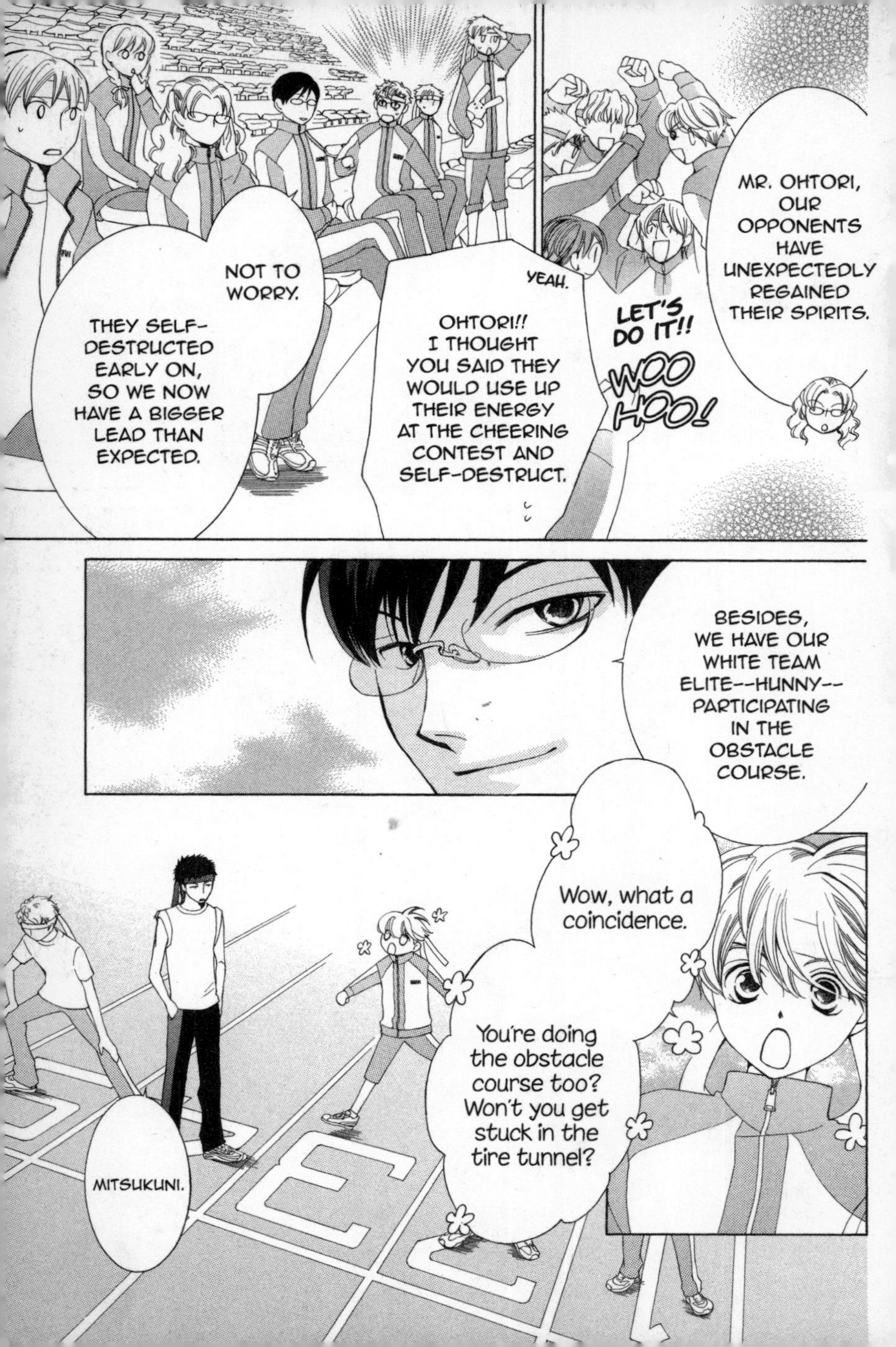

MR. OHTORI, OUR OPPONENTS HAVE UNEXPECTEDLY REGAINED THEIR SPIRITS.
LET'S DO IT!!
WOO HOO!
YEAH.
OHTORI!! I THOUGHT YOU SAID THEY WOULD USE UP THEIR ENERGY AT THE CHEERING CONTEST AND SELF-DESTRUCT.
NOT TO WORRY.
THEY SELF-DESTRUCTED EARLY ON, SO WE NOW HAVE A BIGGER LEAD THAN EXPECTED.
BESIDES, WE HAVE OUR WHITE TEAM ELITE--HUNNY--PARTICIPATING IN THE OBSTACLE COURSE.
Wow, what a coincidence.
You're doing the obstacle course too? Won't you get stuck in the tire tunnel?
MITSUKUNI.

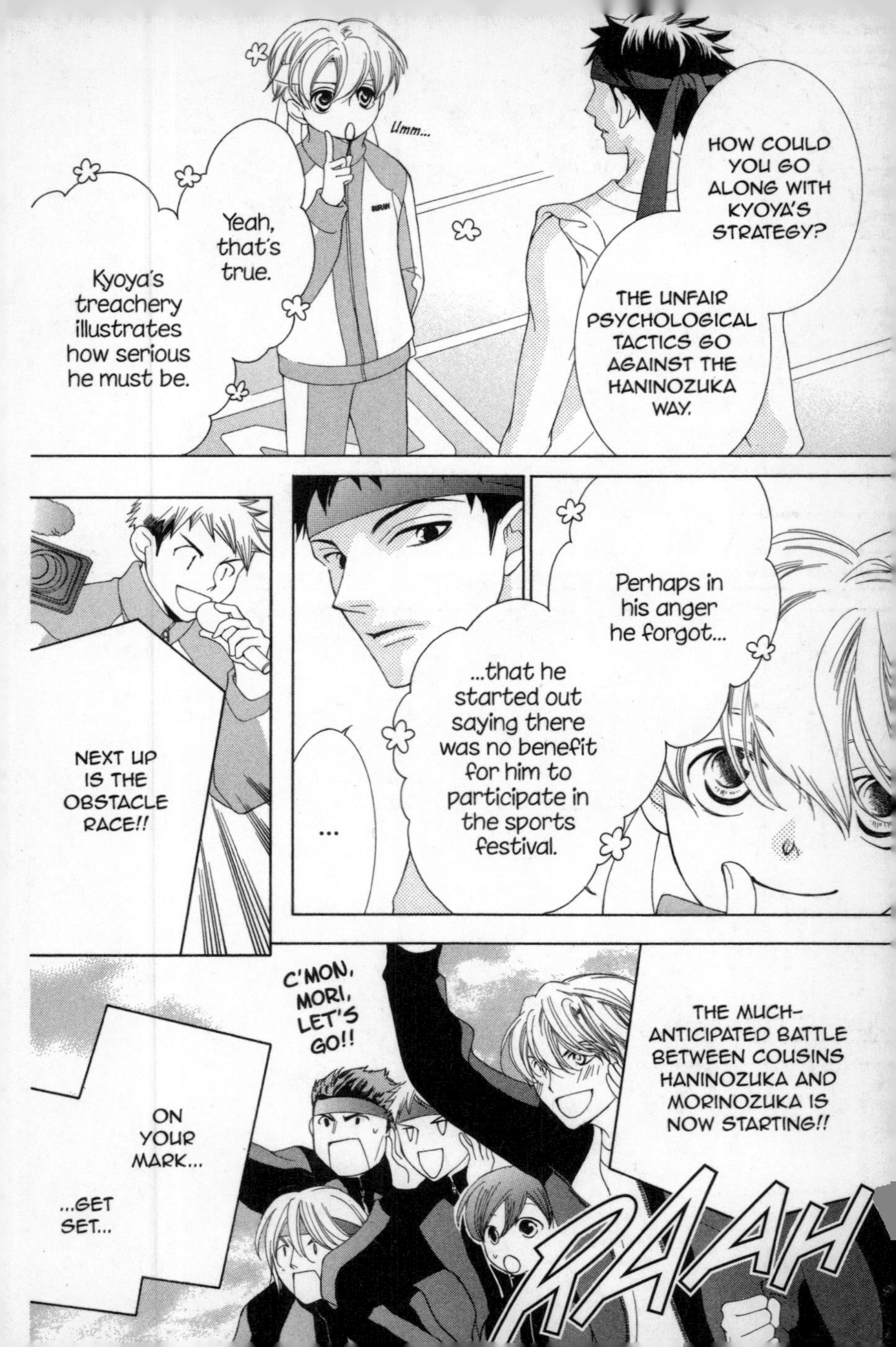
HOW COULD YOU GO ALONG WITH KYOYA'S STRATEGY?
THE UNFAIR PSYCHOLOGICAL TACTICS GO AGAINST THE HANINOZUKA WAY.
Umm...
Yeah, that's true.
Kyoya's treachery illustrates how serious he must be.
Perhaps in his anger he forgot...
...that he started out saying there was no benefit for him to participate in the sports festival.
...
NEXT UP IS THE OBSTACLE RACE!!
THE MUCH-ANTICIPATED BATTLE BETWEEN COUSINS HANINOZUKA AND MORINOZUKA IS NOW STARTING!!
C'MON, MORI, LET'S GO!!
ON YOUR MARK...
...GET SET...
RAAAH

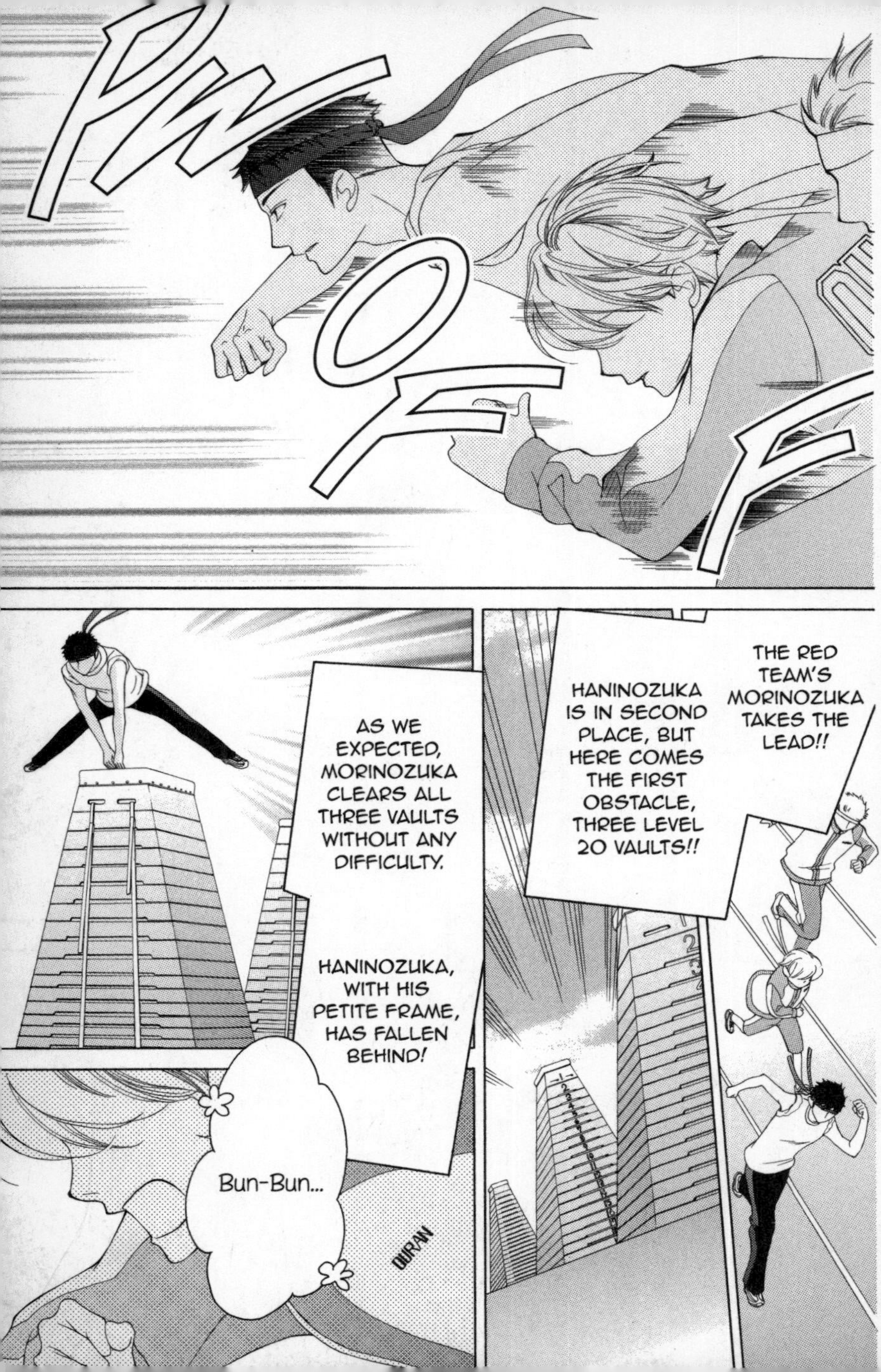
PWOFF
THE RED TEAM'S MORINOZUKA TAKES THE LEAD!!
HANINOZUKA IS IN SECOND PLACE, BUT HERE COMES THE FIRST OBSTACLE, THREE LEVEL 20 VAULTS!!
AS WE EXPECTED, MORINOZUKA CLEARS ALL THREE VAULTS WITHOUT ANY DIFFICULTY.
HANINOZUKA, WITH HIS PETITE FRAME, HAS FALLEN BEHIND!
Bun-Bun...
DURAN

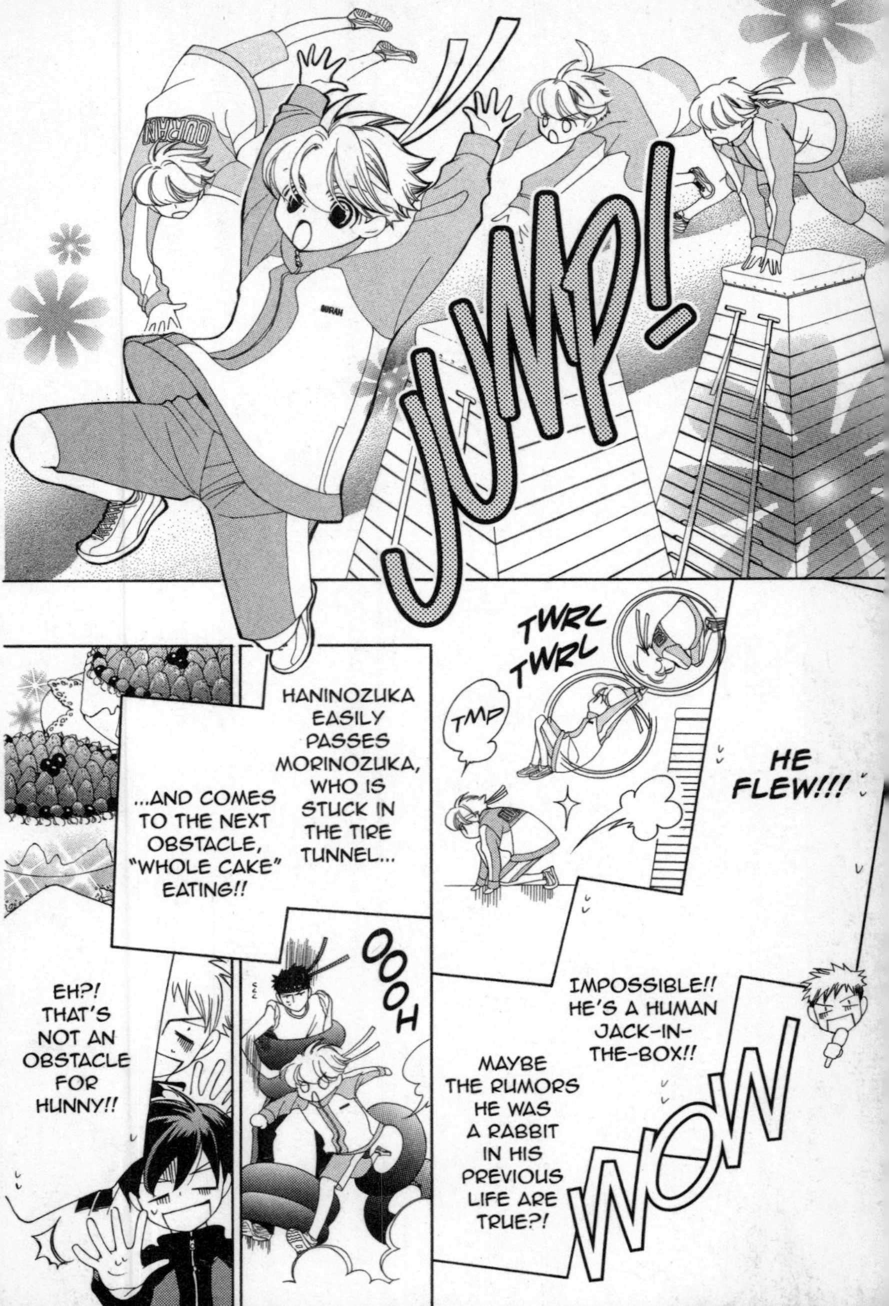
JUMP!
HE FLEW!!!
TWRL TWRL
TMP
HANINOZUKA EASILY PASSES MORINOZUKA, WHO IS STUCK IN THE TIRE TUNNEL...
...AND COMES TO THE NEXT OBSTACLE, "WHOLE CAKE" EATING!!
IMPOSSIBLE!! HE'S A HUMAN JACK-IN-THE-BOX!!
MAYBE THE RUMORS HE WAS A RABBIT IN HIS PREVIOUS LIFE ARE TRUE?!
WOW
OOOH
EH?! THAT'S NOT AN OBSTACLE FOR HUNNY!!

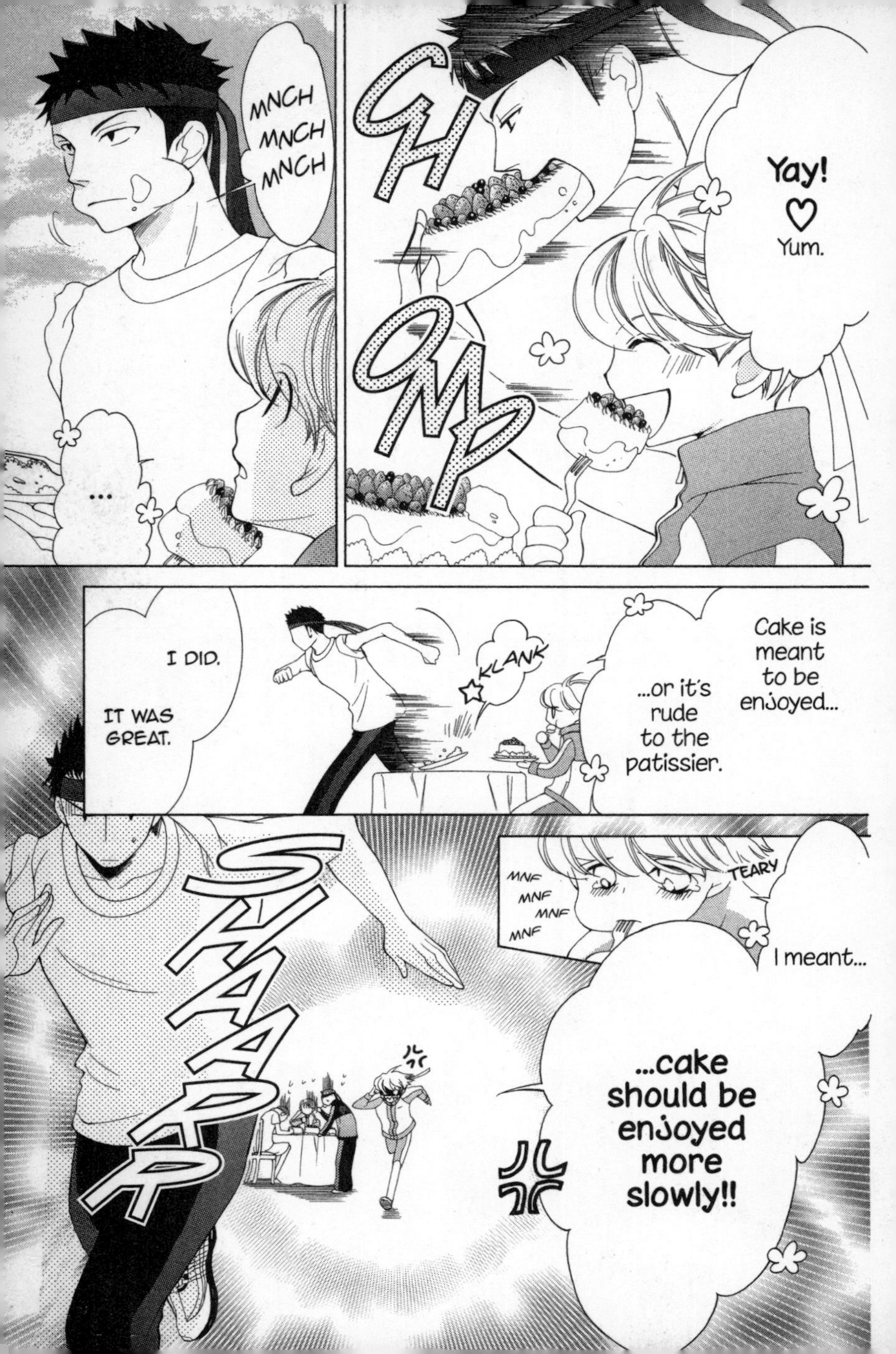
CHOMP
Yay! ♡ Yum.
MNCH MNCH MNCH
...
Cake is meant to be enjoyed...
...or it's rude to the patissier.
KLANK
I DID.
IT WAS GREAT.
TEARY
MNF MNF MNF MNF
I meant...
...cake should be enjoyed more slowly!!
SHAAPP

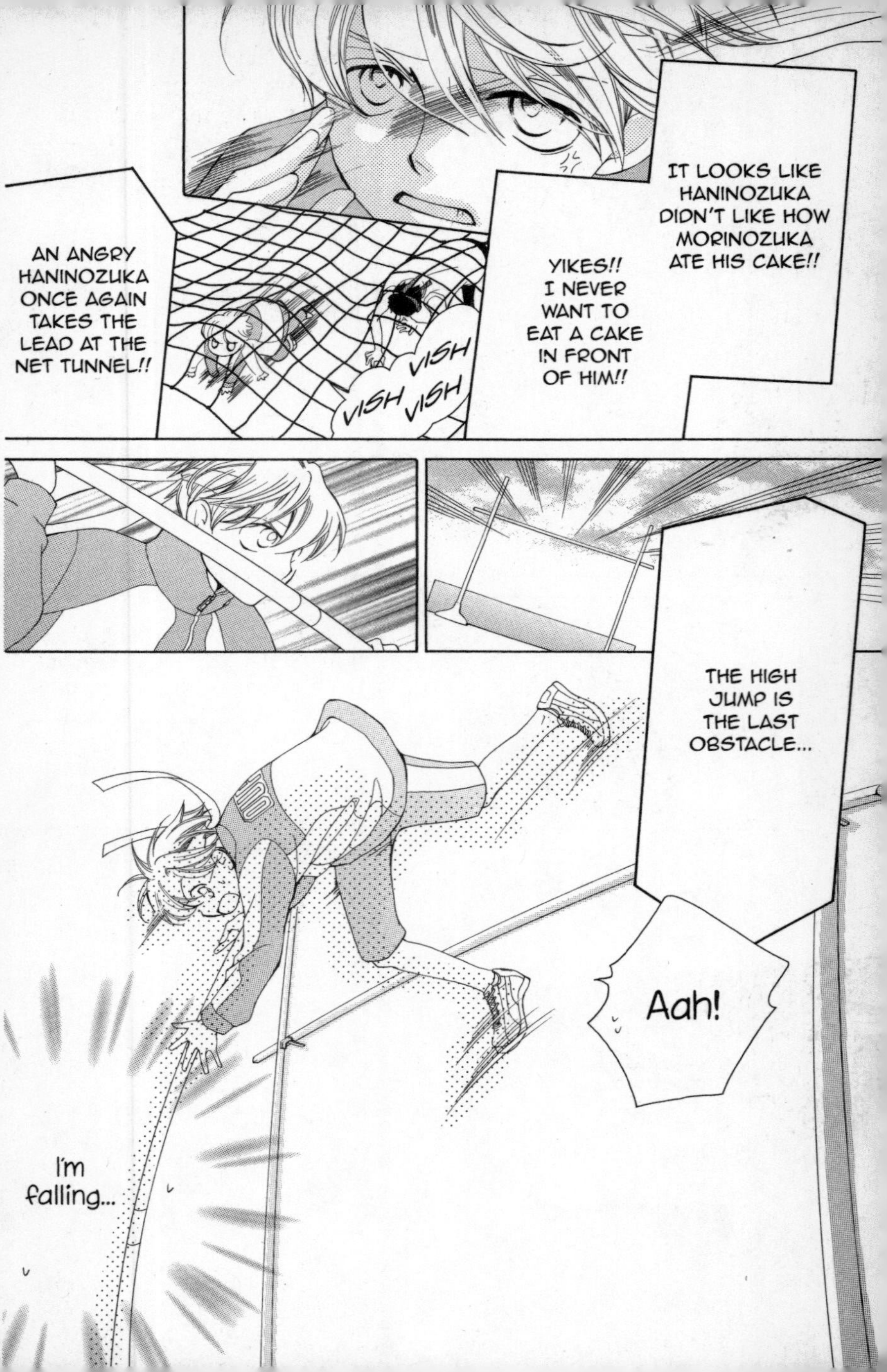

IT LOOKS LIKE HANINOZUKA DIDN'T LIKE HOW MORINOZUKA ATE HIS CAKE!!
YIKES!! I NEVER WANT TO EAT A CAKE IN FRONT OF HIM!!
VISH VISH VISH VISH
AN ANGRY HANINOZUKA ONCE AGAIN TAKES THE LEAD AT THE NET TUNNEL!!
THE HIGH JUMP IS THE LAST OBSTACLE...
Aah!
I'm falling...

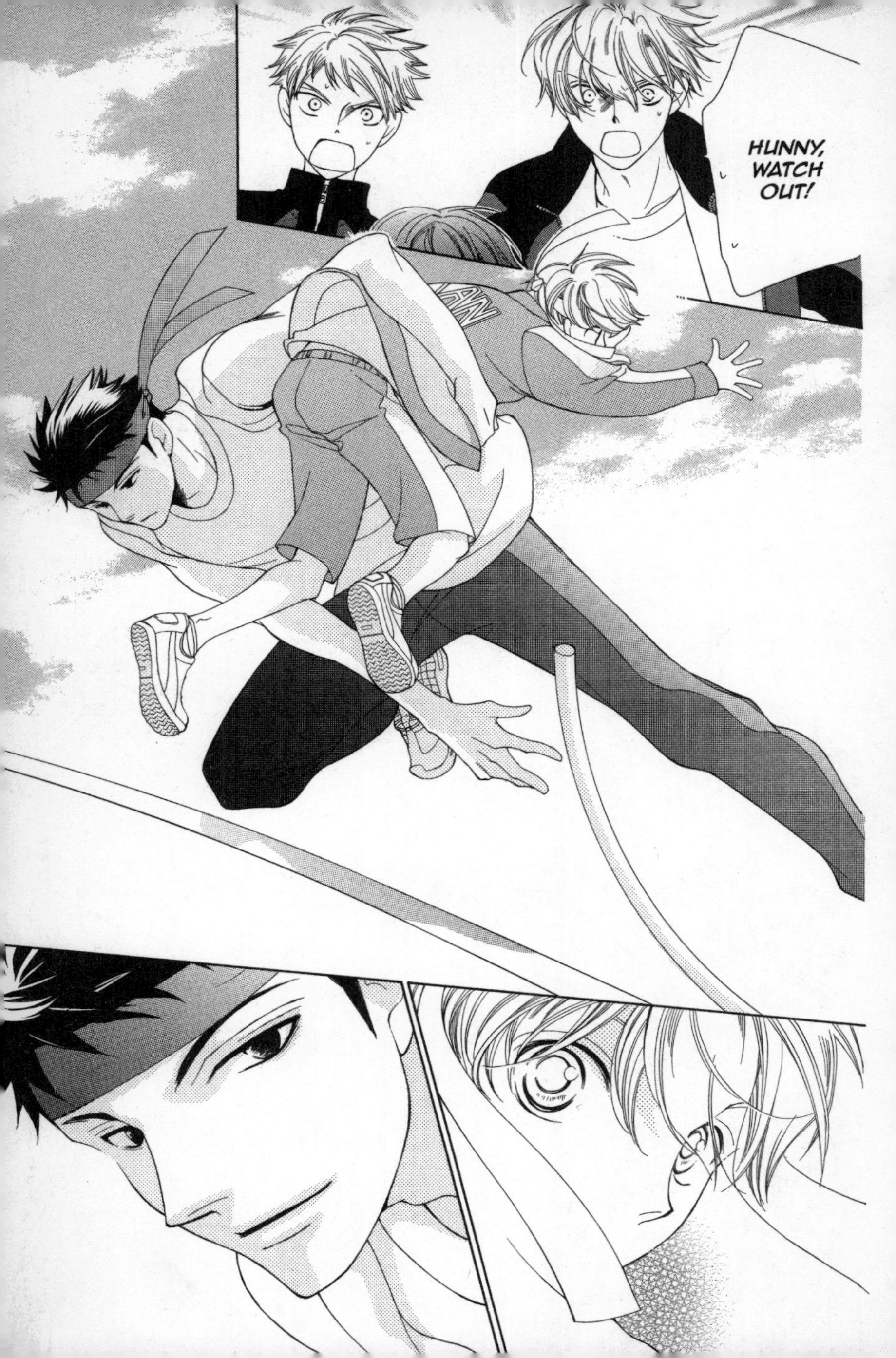
HUNNY, WATCH OUT!

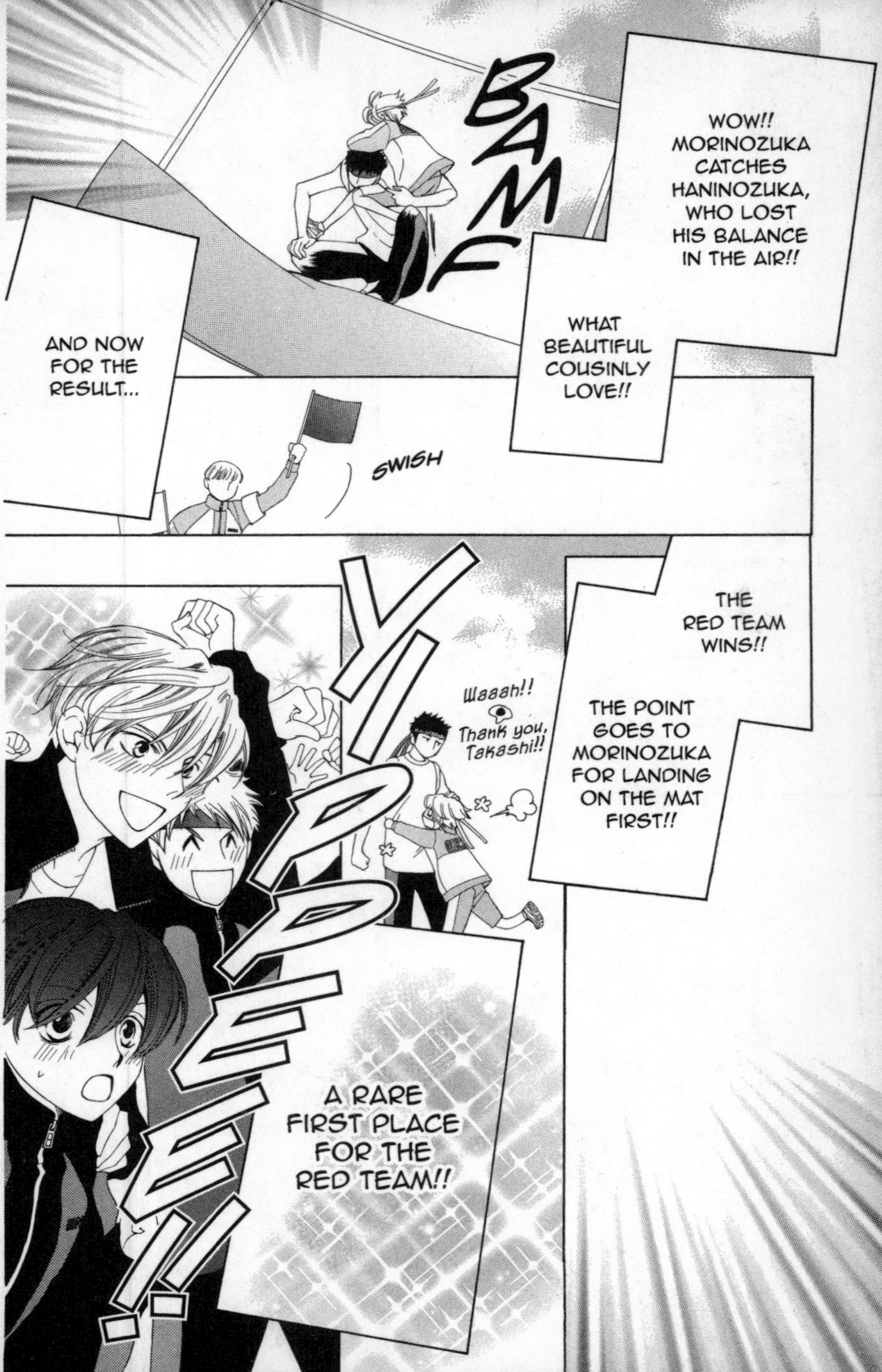
WOW!! MORINOZUKA CATCHES HANINOZUKA, WHO LOST HIS BALANCE IN THE AIR!!
BAMF
WHAT BEAUTIFUL COUSINLY LOVE!!
AND NOW FOR THE RESULT...
SWISH
THE RED TEAM WINS!!
THE POINT GOES TO MORINOZUKA FOR LANDING ON THE MAT FIRST!!
Waaah!!
Thank you, Takashi!!
YIPPEE!!
A RARE FIRST PLACE FOR THE RED TEAM!!

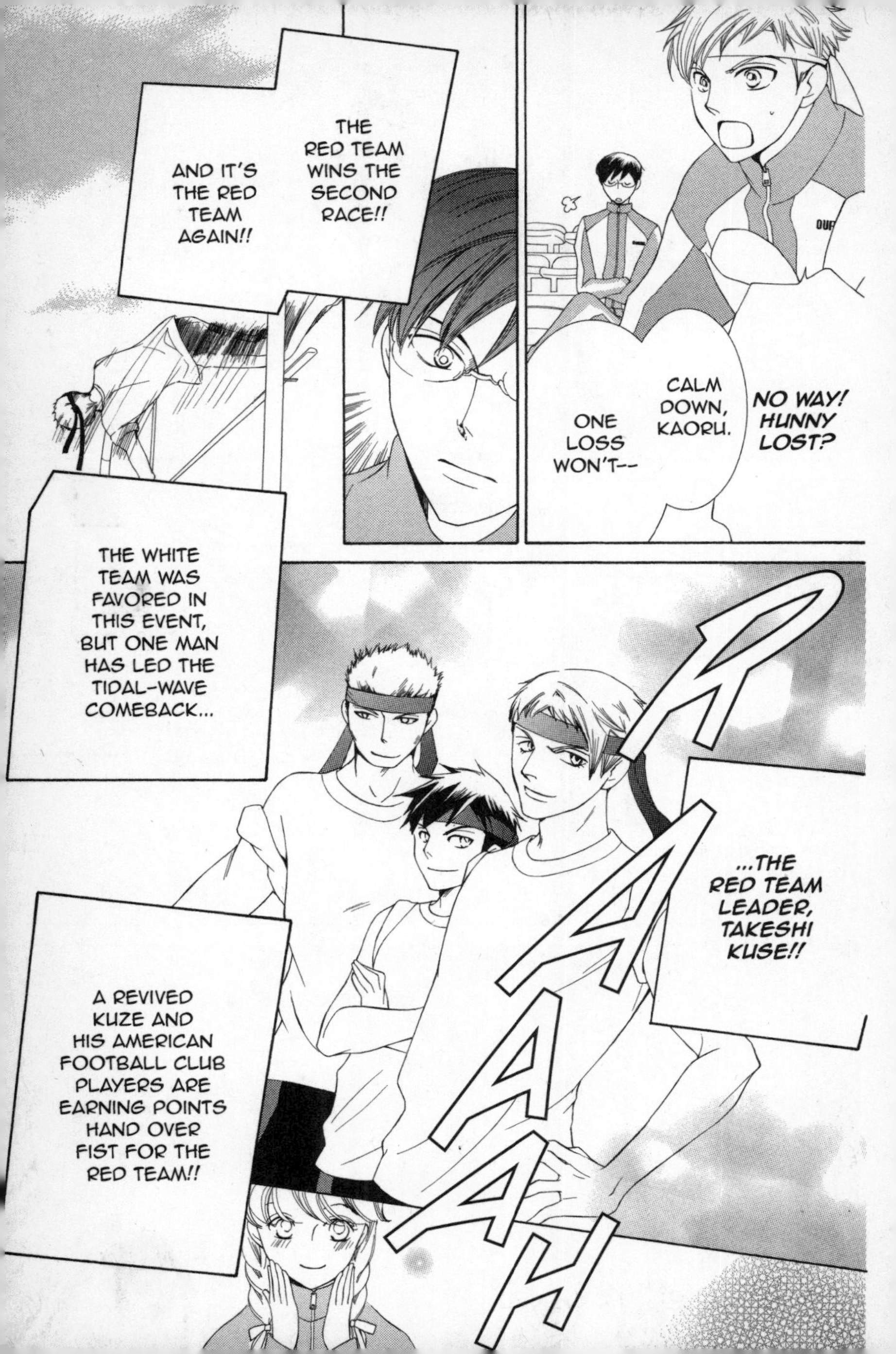
NO WAY! HUNNY LOST?
CALM DOWN, KAORU.
ONE LOSS WON'T--
THE RED TEAM WINS THE SECOND RACE!!
AND IT'S THE RED TEAM AGAIN!!
THE WHITE TEAM WAS FAVORED IN THIS EVENT, BUT ONE MAN HAS LED THE TIDAL-WAVE COMEBACK...
...THE RED TEAM LEADER, TAKESHI KUSE!!
KAAAH
A REVIVED KUZE AND HIS AMERICAN FOOTBALL CLUB PLAYERS ARE EARNING POINTS HAND OVER FIST FOR THE RED TEAM!!

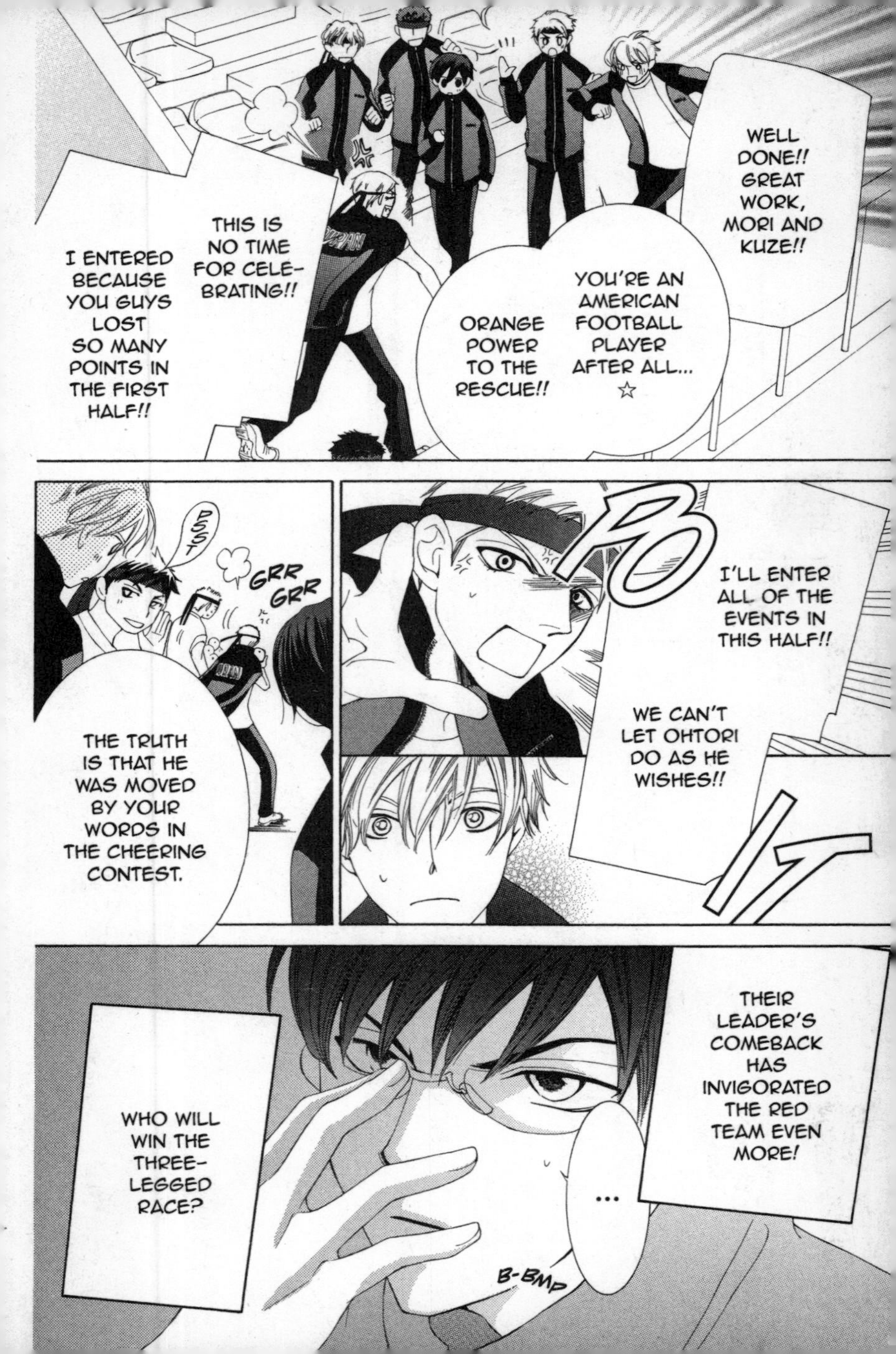
WELL DONE!! GREAT WORK, MORI AND KUZE!!
YOU'RE AN AMERICAN FOOTBALL PLAYER AFTER ALL... ☆
ORANGE POWER TO THE RESCUE!!
THIS IS NO TIME FOR CELE-BRATING!!
I ENTERED BECAUSE YOU GUYS LOST SO MANY POINTS IN THE FIRST HALF!!
I'LL ENTER ALL OF THE EVENTS IN THIS HALF!!
WE CAN'T LET OHTORI DO AS HE WISHES!!
PSST
GRR GRR
THE TRUTH IS THAT HE WAS MOVED BY YOUR WORDS IN THE CHEERING CONTEST.
THEIR LEADER'S COMEBACK HAS INVIGORATED THE RED TEAM EVEN MORE!
...
WHO WILL WIN THE THREE-LEGGED RACE?
B-BMP

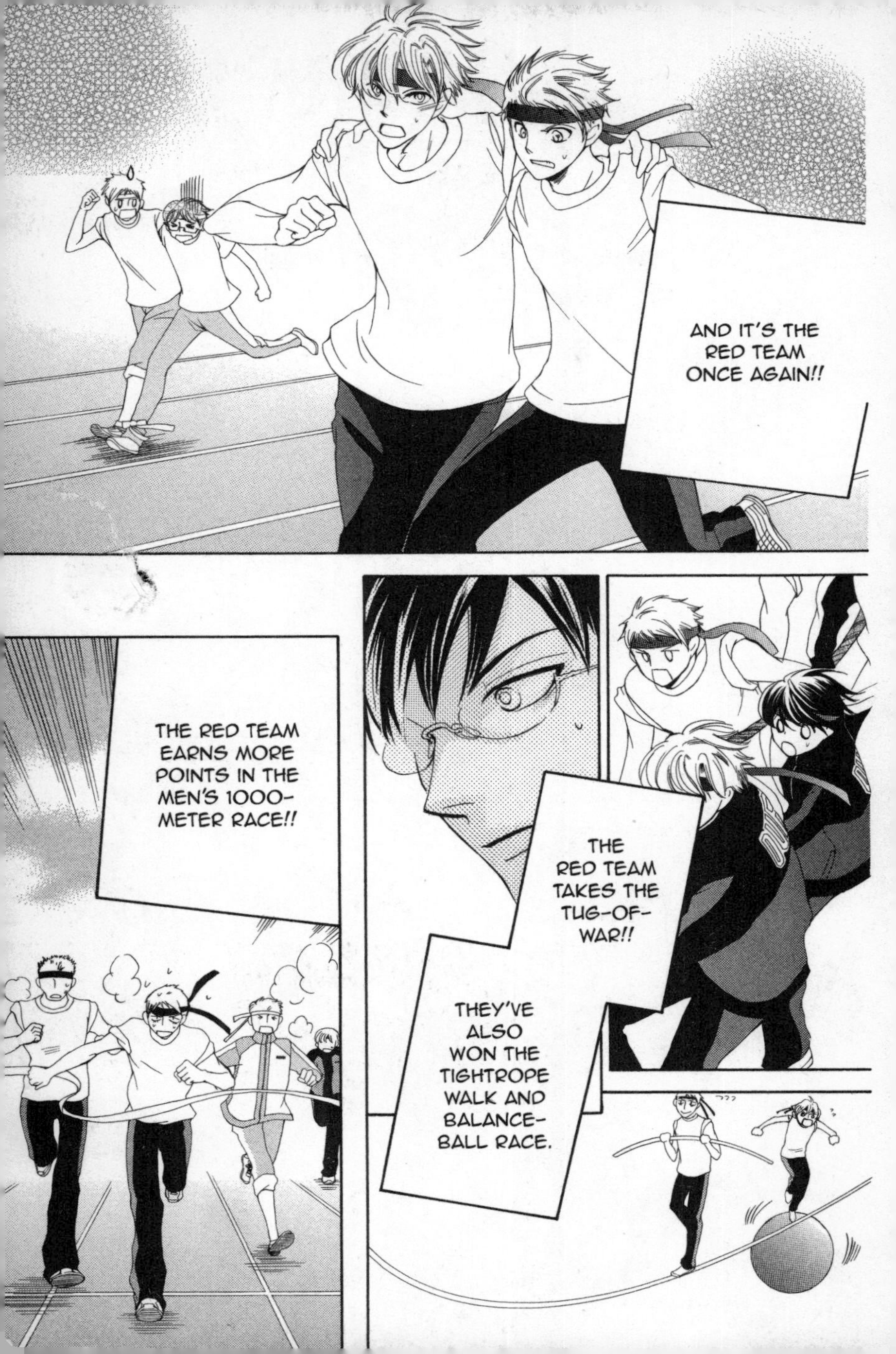
AND IT'S THE RED TEAM ONCE AGAIN!!
THE RED TEAM TAKES THE TUG-OF-WAR!!
THEY'VE ALSO WON THE TIGHTROPE WALK AND BALANCE-BALL RACE.
THE RED TEAM EARNS MORE POINTS IN THE MEN'S 1000-METER RACE!!

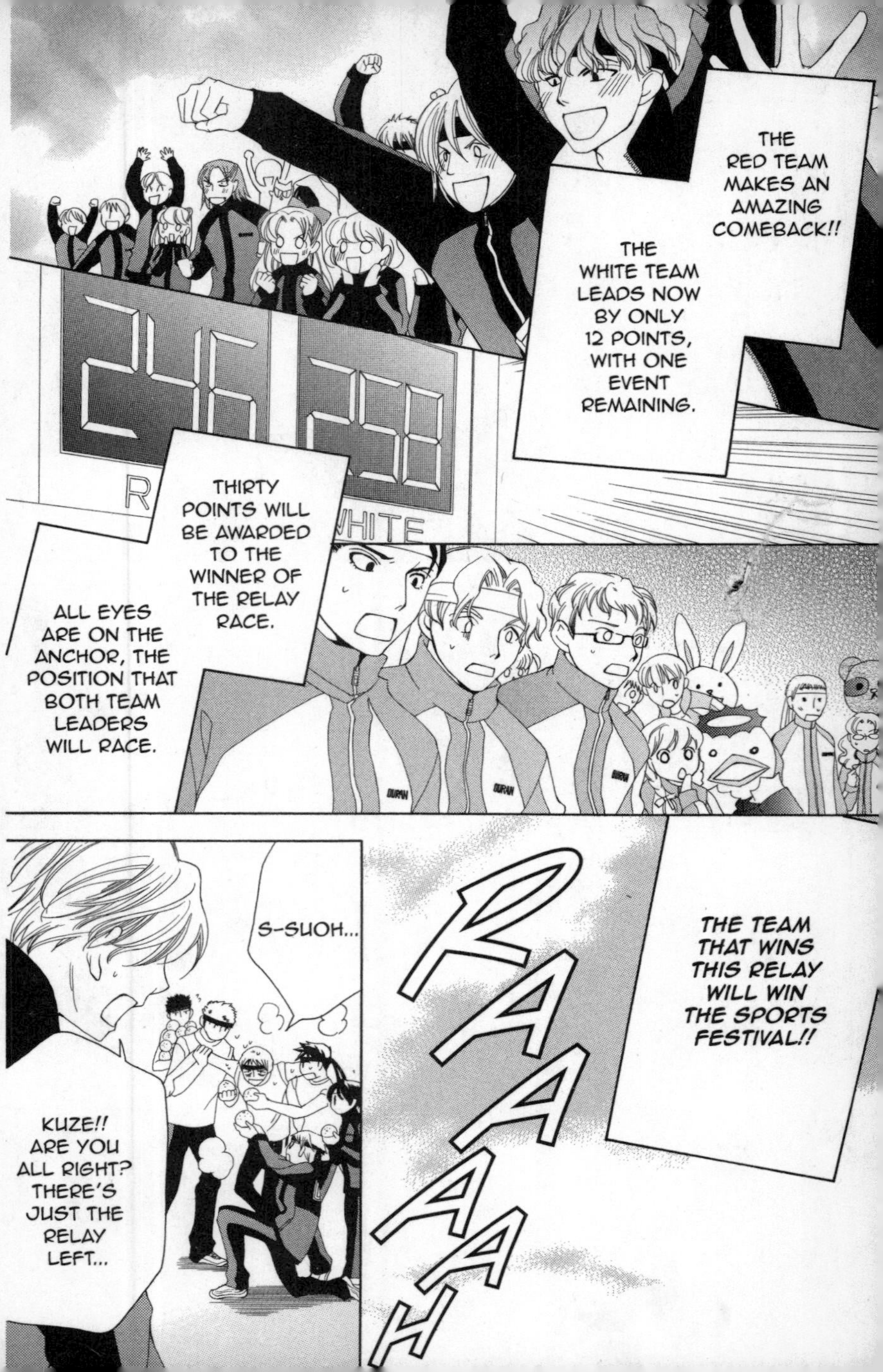
THE RED TEAM MAKES AN AMAZING COMEBACK!!
THE WHITE TEAM LEADS NOW BY ONLY 12 POINTS, WITH ONE EVENT REMAINING.
246
258
THIRTY POINTS WILL BE AWARDED TO THE WINNER OF THE RELAY RACE.
ALL EYES ARE ON THE ANCHOR, THE POSITION THAT BOTH TEAM LEADERS WILL RACE.
THE TEAM THAT WINS THIS RELAY WILL WIN THE SPORTS FESTIVAL!!
RAAAAAH
S-SUOH...
KUZE!! ARE YOU ALL RIGHT? THERE'S JUST THE RELAY LEFT...

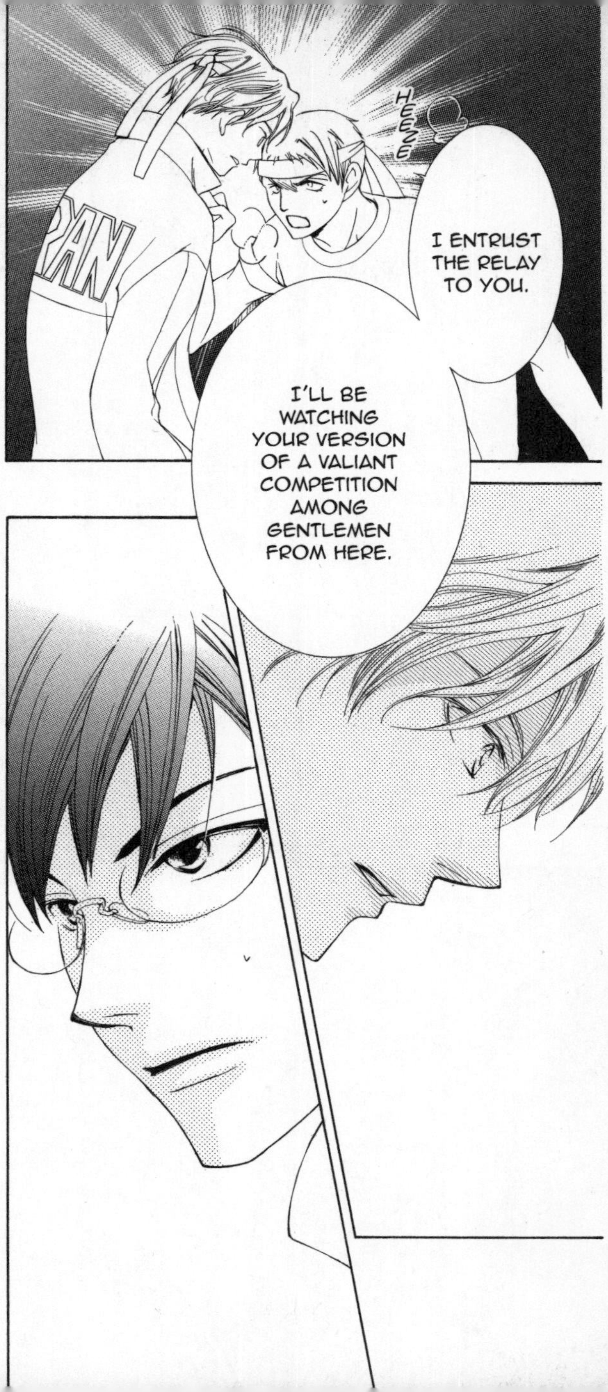
HEEZE
I ENTRUST THE RELAY TO YOU.
I'LL BE WATCHING YOUR VERSION OF A VALIANT COMPETITION AMONG GENTLEMEN FROM HERE.

3

WHEN I HEARD THE POLL RESULTS, MY REACTION WAS "WHAT?! FIRST PLACE IS HARUHI AND SECOND PLACE IS TAMAKI?! DID SOMEBODY PLAY A DIRTY TRICK?" THIS MADE ME THINK, "MAYBE I'M THE ONE WITH DIRTY TRICKS," WHILE MY EDITOR YAMASHII INSISTED, "NO, WE DIDN'T!!"

IN ANY CASE, I WAS THRILLED TO SEE THAT SO MANY PEOPLE VOTED!

WE DISQUALIFIED VOTES FOR THE TWINS AS A UNIT, SO IT'S HARD TO TELL HOW THE RESULTS WOULD HAVE TURNED OUT IF WE HAD ALLOWED THEM. (I APOLOGIZE TO ALL OF YOU WHO VOTED FOR THE TWINS.)

I'VE JUST NOW RECEIVED THE VOTES FROM MY EDITOR, AND I'M LOOKING FORWARD TO READING THEM. I'M EXCITED!!

THANK YOU VERY MUCH!

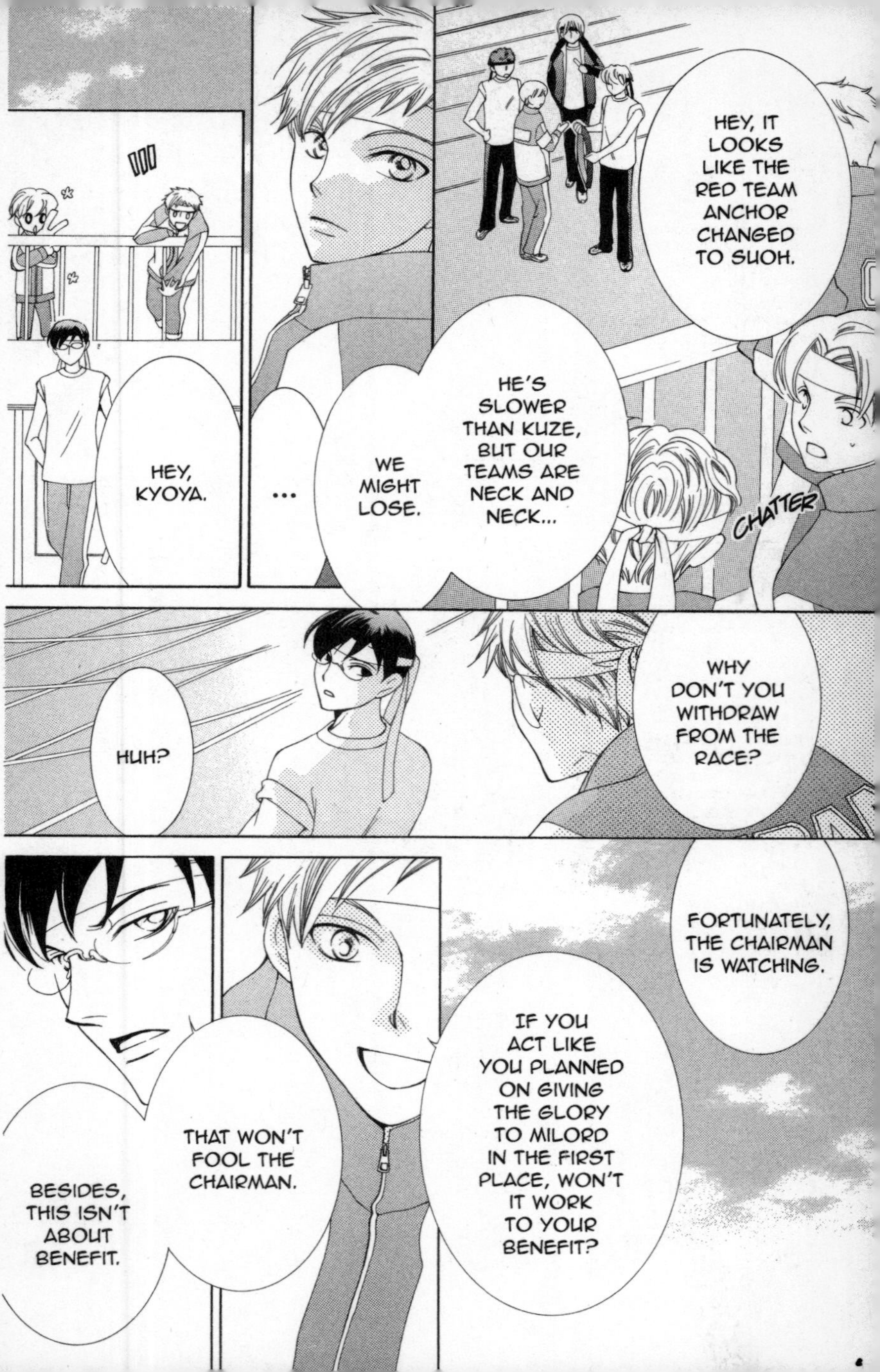
HEY, IT LOOKS LIKE THE RED TEAM ANCHOR CHANGED TO SUOH.
CHATTER
HE'S SLOWER THAN KUZE, BUT OUR TEAMS ARE NECK AND NECK...
WE MIGHT LOSE.
...
HEY, KYOYA.
WHY DON'T YOU WITHDRAW FROM THE RACE?
HUH?
FORTUNATELY, THE CHAIRMAN IS WATCHING.
IF YOU ACT LIKE YOU PLANNED ON GIVING THE GLORY TO MILORD IN THE FIRST PLACE, WON'T IT WORK TO YOUR BENEFIT?
THAT WON'T FOOL THE CHAIRMAN.
BESIDES, THIS ISN'T ABOUT BENEFIT.

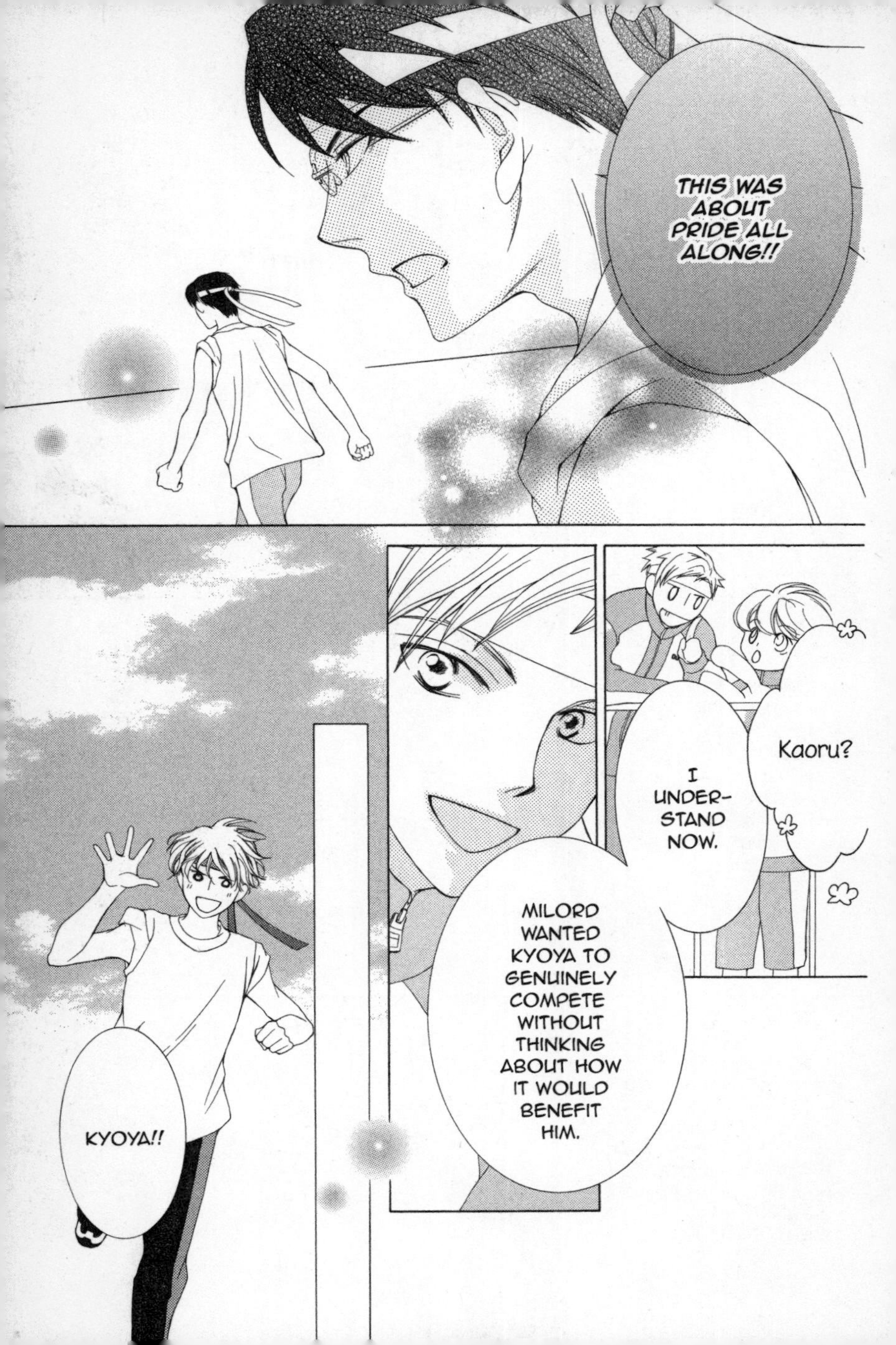
THIS WAS ABOUT PRIDE ALL ALONG!!
Kaoru?
I UNDER-STAND NOW.
MILORD WANTED KYOYA TO GENUINELY COMPETE WITHOUT THINKING ABOUT HOW IT WOULD BENEFIT HIM.
KYOYA!!

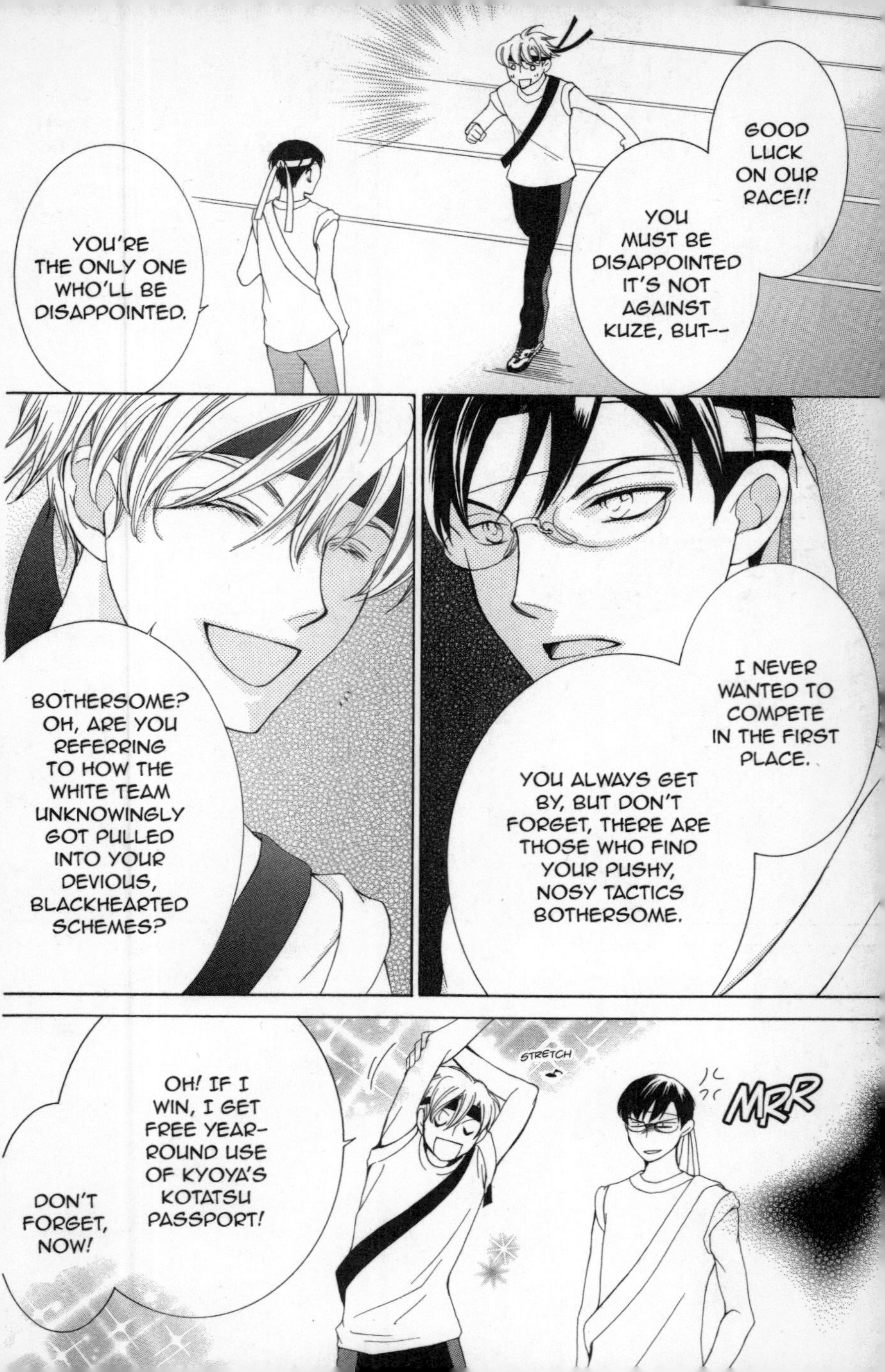
GOOD LUCK ON OUR RACE!!
YOU MUST BE DISAPPOINTED IT'S NOT AGAINST KUZE, BUT--
YOU'RE THE ONLY ONE WHO'LL BE DISAPPOINTED.
I NEVER WANTED TO COMPETE IN THE FIRST PLACE.
YOU ALWAYS GET BY, BUT DON'T FORGET, THERE ARE THOSE WHO FIND YOUR PUSHY, NOSY TACTICS BOTHERSOME.
BOTHERSOME? OH, ARE YOU REFERRING TO HOW THE WHITE TEAM UNKNOWINGLY GOT PULLED INTO YOUR DEVIOUS, BLACKHEARTED SCHEMES?
MRR
STRETCH
OH! IF I WIN, I GET FREE YEAR-ROUND USE OF KYOYA'S KOTATSU PASSPORT!
DON'T FORGET, NOW!

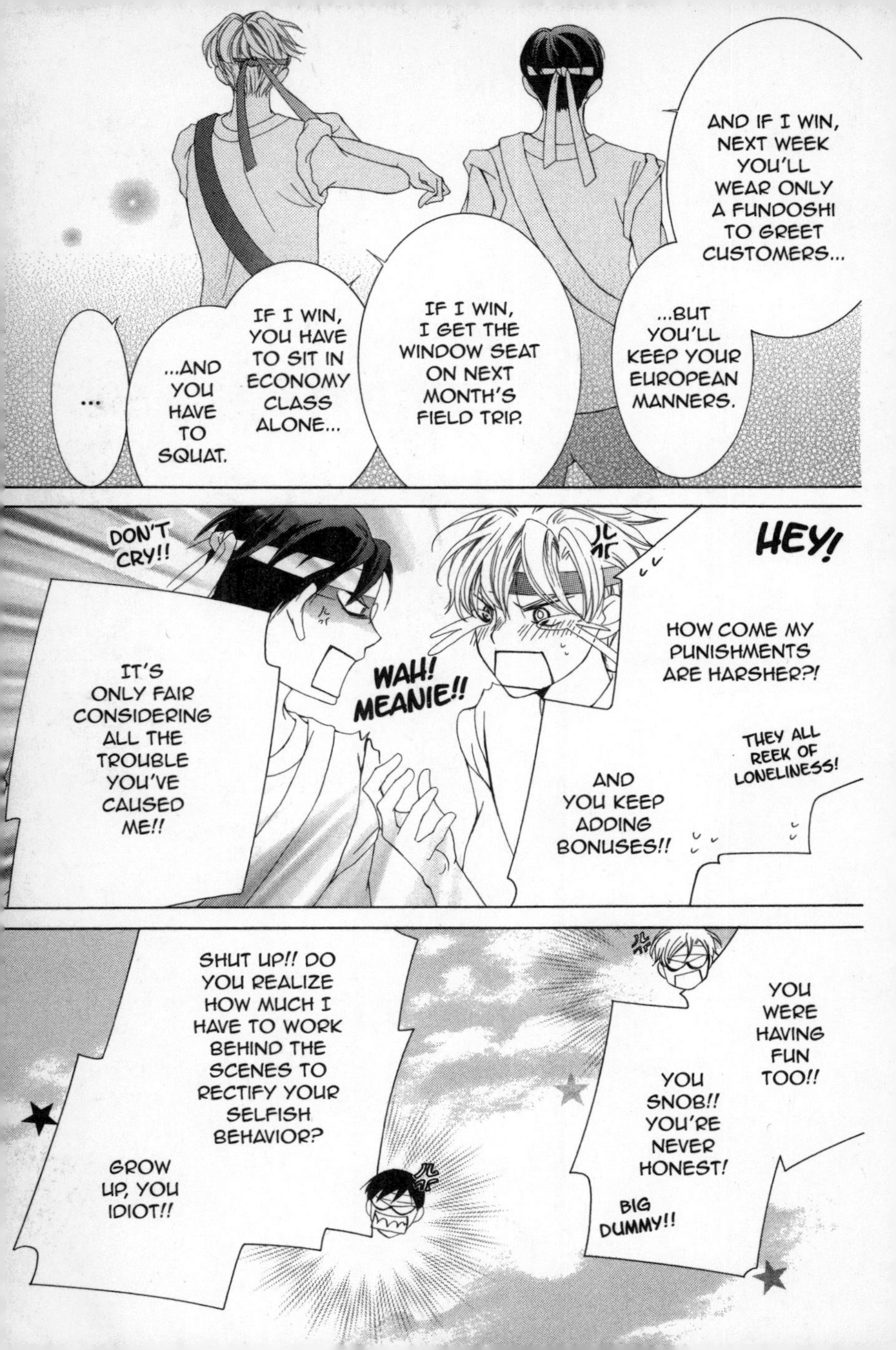
AND IF I WIN, NEXT WEEK YOU'LL WEAR ONLY A FUNDOSHI TO GREET CUSTOMERS...
...BUT YOU'LL KEEP YOUR EUROPEAN MANNERS.
IF I WIN, I GET THE WINDOW SEAT ON NEXT MONTH'S FIELD TRIP.
IF I WIN, YOU HAVE TO SIT IN ECONOMY CLASS ALONE...
...AND YOU HAVE TO SQUAT.
...
HEY!
HOW COME MY PUNISHMENTS ARE HARSHER?!
THEY ALL REEK OF LONELINESS!
AND YOU KEEP ADDING BONUSES!!
WAH! MEANIE!!
DON'T CRY!!
IT'S ONLY FAIR CONSIDERING ALL THE TROUBLE YOU'VE CAUSED ME!!
YOU WERE HAVING FUN TOO!!
YOU SNOB!! YOU'RE NEVER HONEST!
BIG DUMMY!!
SHUT UP!! DO YOU REALIZE HOW MUCH I HAVE TO WORK BEHIND THE SCENES TO RECTIFY YOUR SELFISH BEHAVIOR?
GROW UP, YOU IDIOT!!

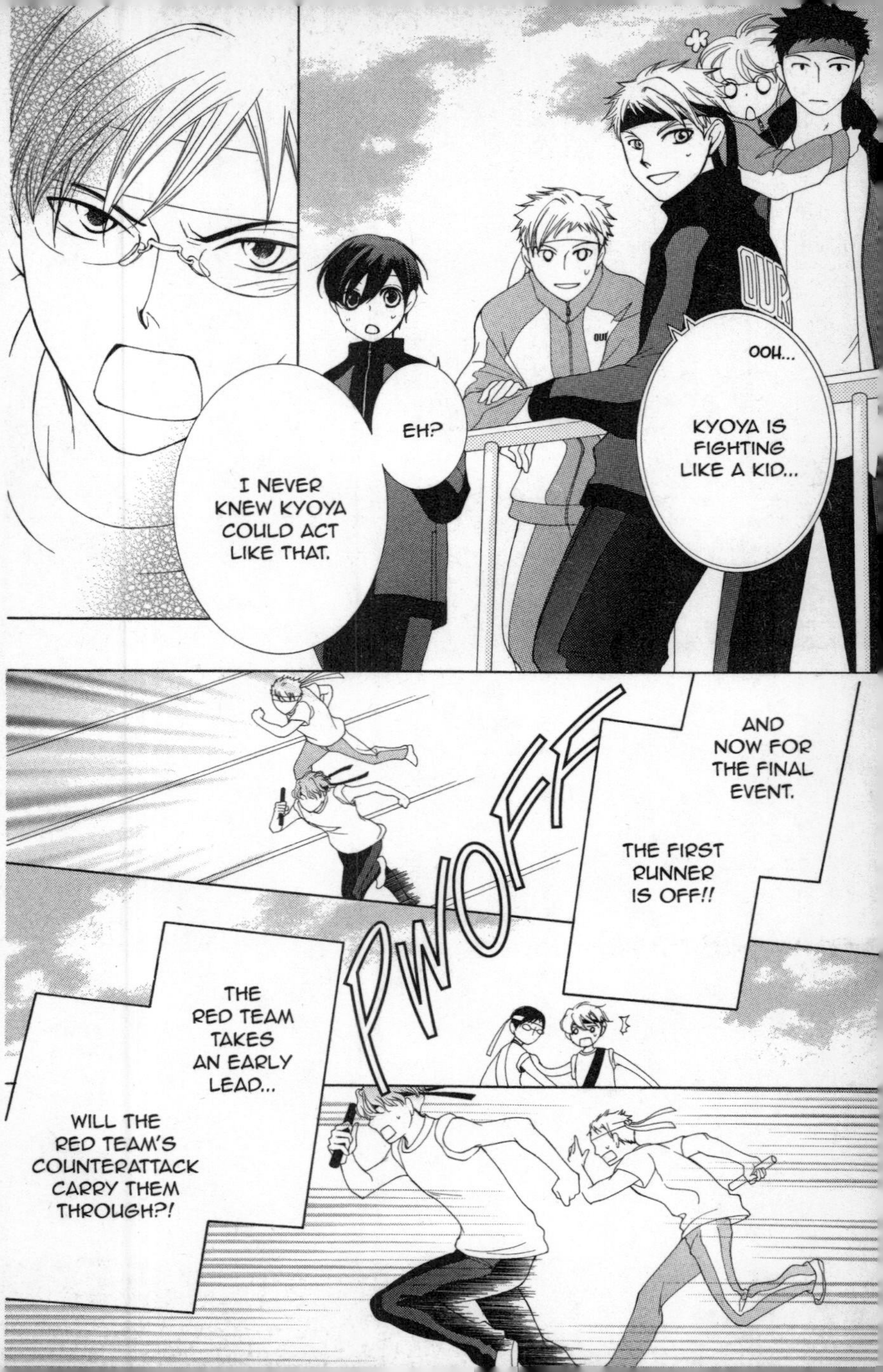
OOH...
KYOYA IS FIGHTING LIKE A KID...
EH?
I NEVER KNEW KYOYA COULD ACT LIKE THAT.
AND NOW FOR THE FINAL EVENT.
THE FIRST RUNNER IS OFF!!
PWOFF
THE RED TEAM TAKES AN EARLY LEAD...
WILL THE RED TEAM'S COUNTERATTACK CARRY THEM THROUGH?!

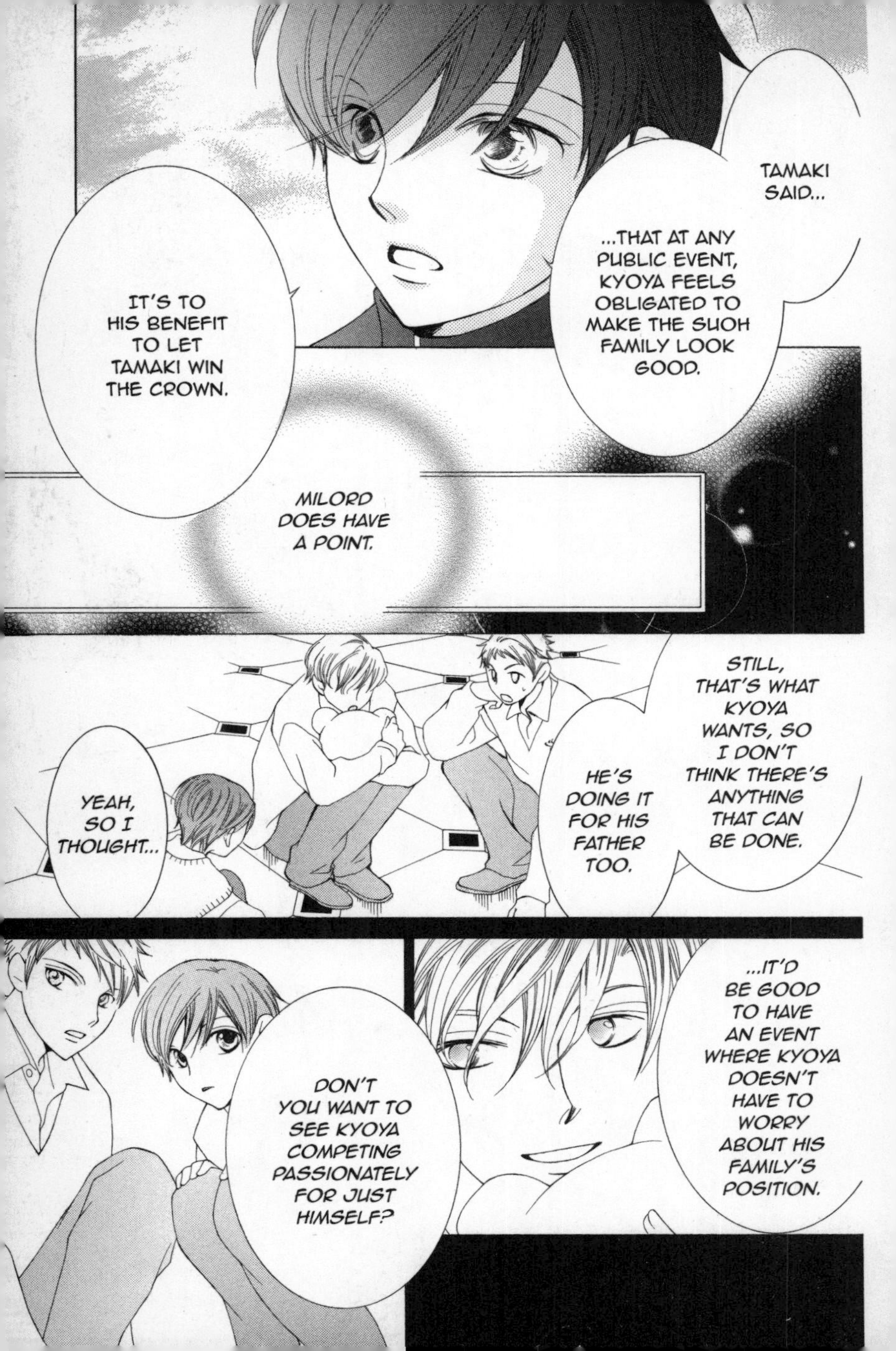
TAMAKI SAID...
...THAT AT ANY PUBLIC EVENT, KYOYA FEELS OBLIGATED TO MAKE THE SUOH FAMILY LOOK GOOD.
IT'S TO HIS BENEFIT TO LET TAMAKI WIN THE CROWN.
MILORD DOES HAVE A POINT.
STILL, THAT'S WHAT KYOYA WANTS, SO I DON'T THINK THERE'S ANYTHING THAT CAN BE DONE.
HE'S DOING IT FOR HIS FATHER TOO.
YEAH, SO I THOUGHT...
...IT'D BE GOOD TO HAVE AN EVENT WHERE KYOYA DOESN'T HAVE TO WORRY ABOUT HIS FAMILY'S POSITION.
DON'T YOU WANT TO SEE KYOYA COMPETING PASSIONATELY FOR JUST HIMSELF?

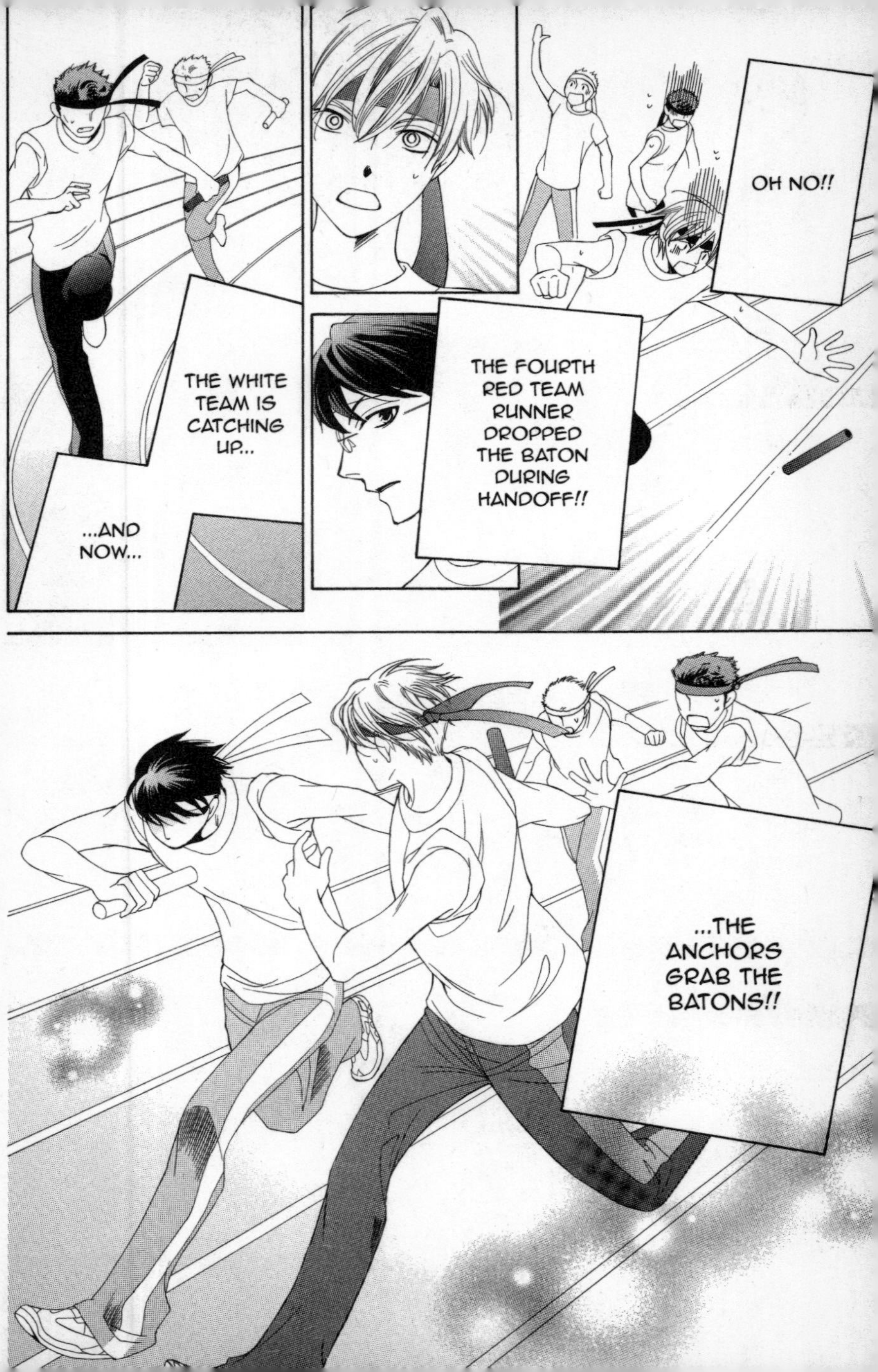
OH NO!!
THE FOURTH RED TEAM RUNNER DROPPED THE BATON DURING HANDOFF!!
THE WHITE TEAM IS CATCHING UP...
...AND NOW...
...THE ANCHORS GRAB THE BATONS!!

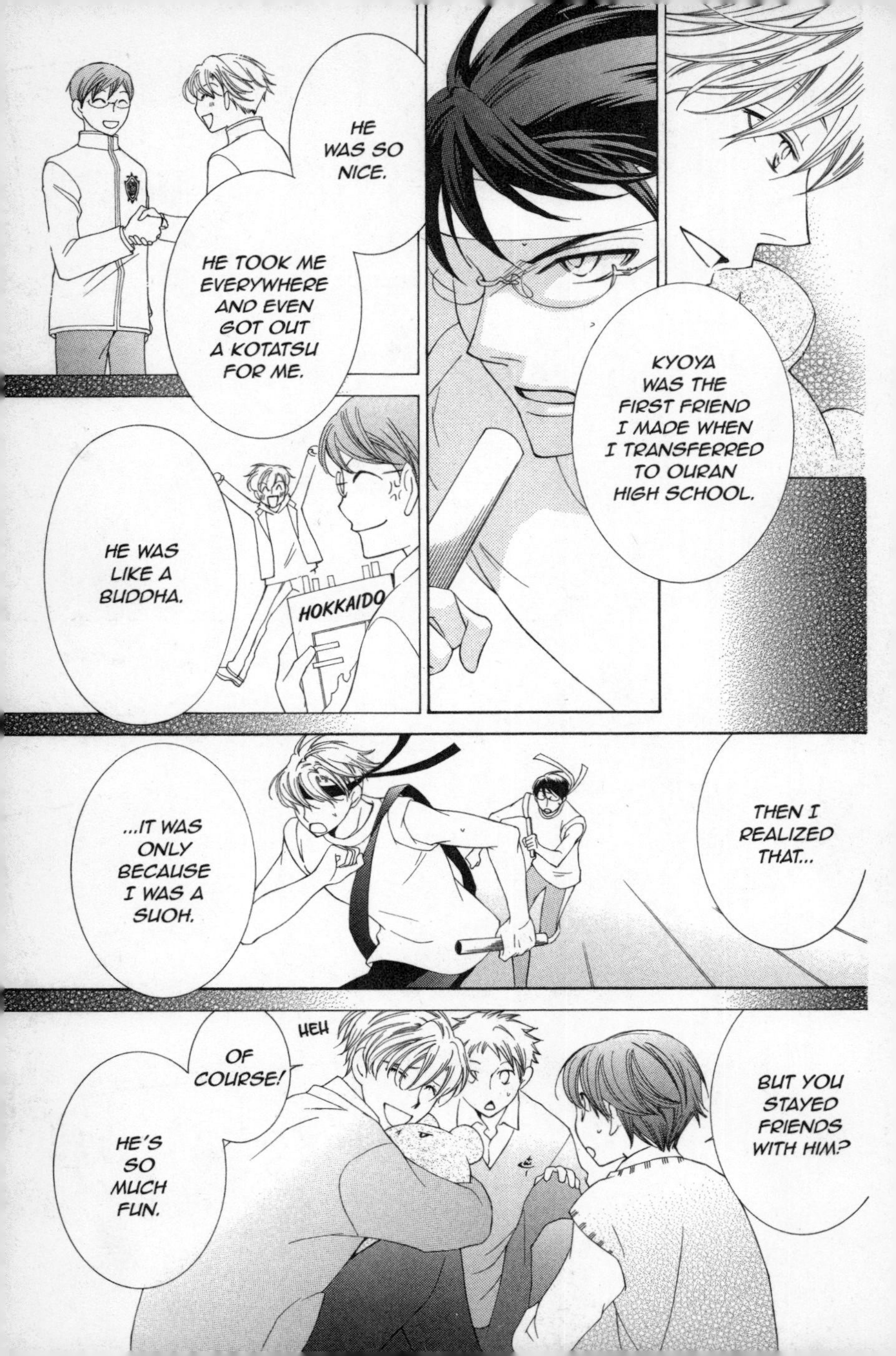
KYOYA WAS THE FIRST FRIEND I MADE WHEN I TRANSFERRED TO OURAN HIGH SCHOOL.
HE WAS SO NICE.
HE TOOK ME EVERYWHERE AND EVEN GOT OUT A KOTATSU FOR ME.
HOKKAIDO
HE WAS LIKE A BUDDHA.
THEN I REALIZED THAT...
...IT WAS ONLY BECAUSE I WAS A SUOH.
BUT YOU STAYED FRIENDS WITH HIM?
HEH
OF COURSE!
HE'S SO MUCH FUN.

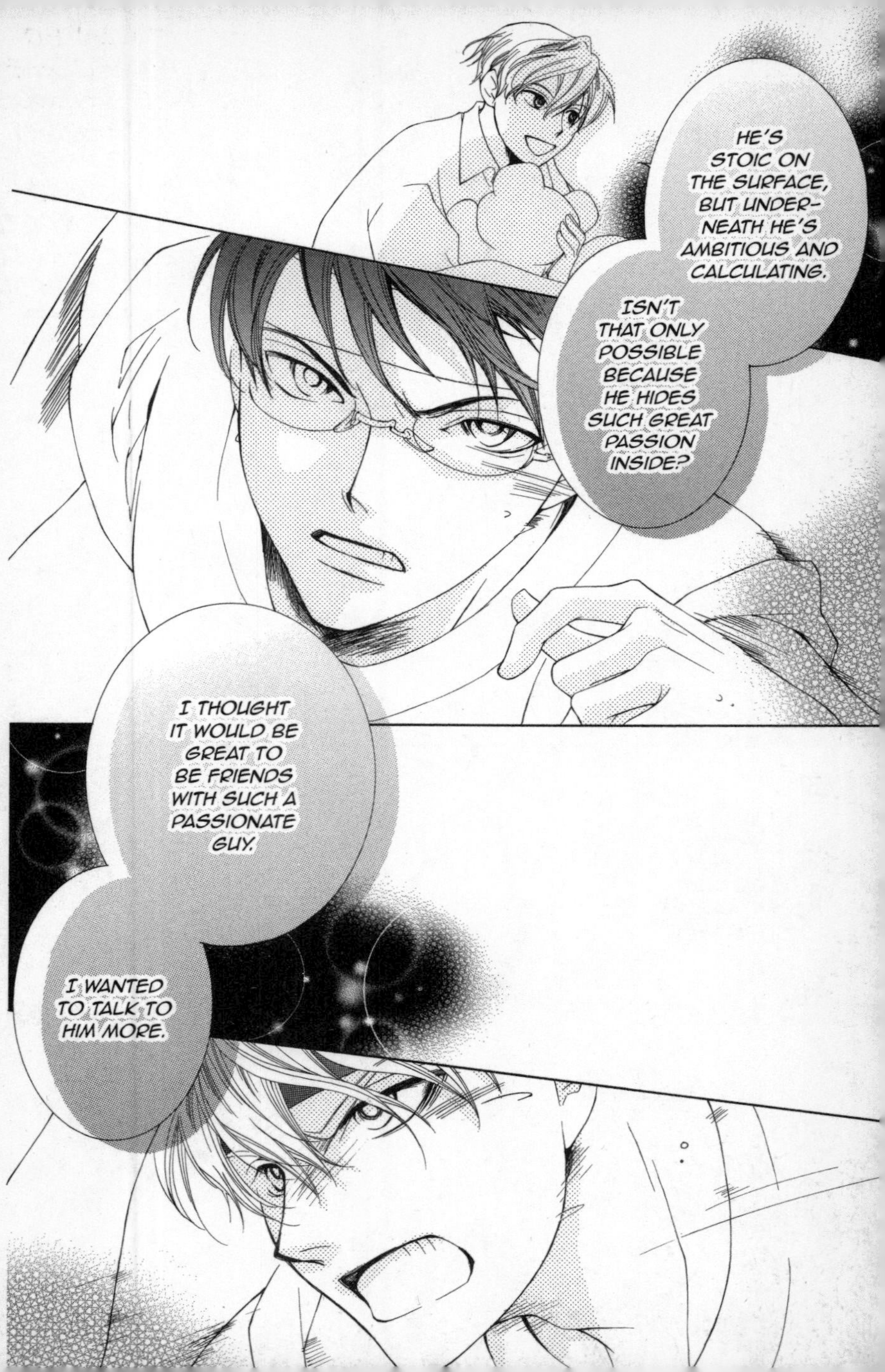
HE'S STOIC ON THE SURFACE, BUT UNDER-NEATH HE'S AMBITIOUS AND CALCULATING.
ISN'T THAT ONLY POSSIBLE BECAUSE HE HIDES SUCH GREAT PASSION INSIDE?
I THOUGHT IT WOULD BE GREAT TO BE FRIENDS WITH SUCH A PASSIONATE GUY.
I WANTED TO TALK TO HIM MORE.

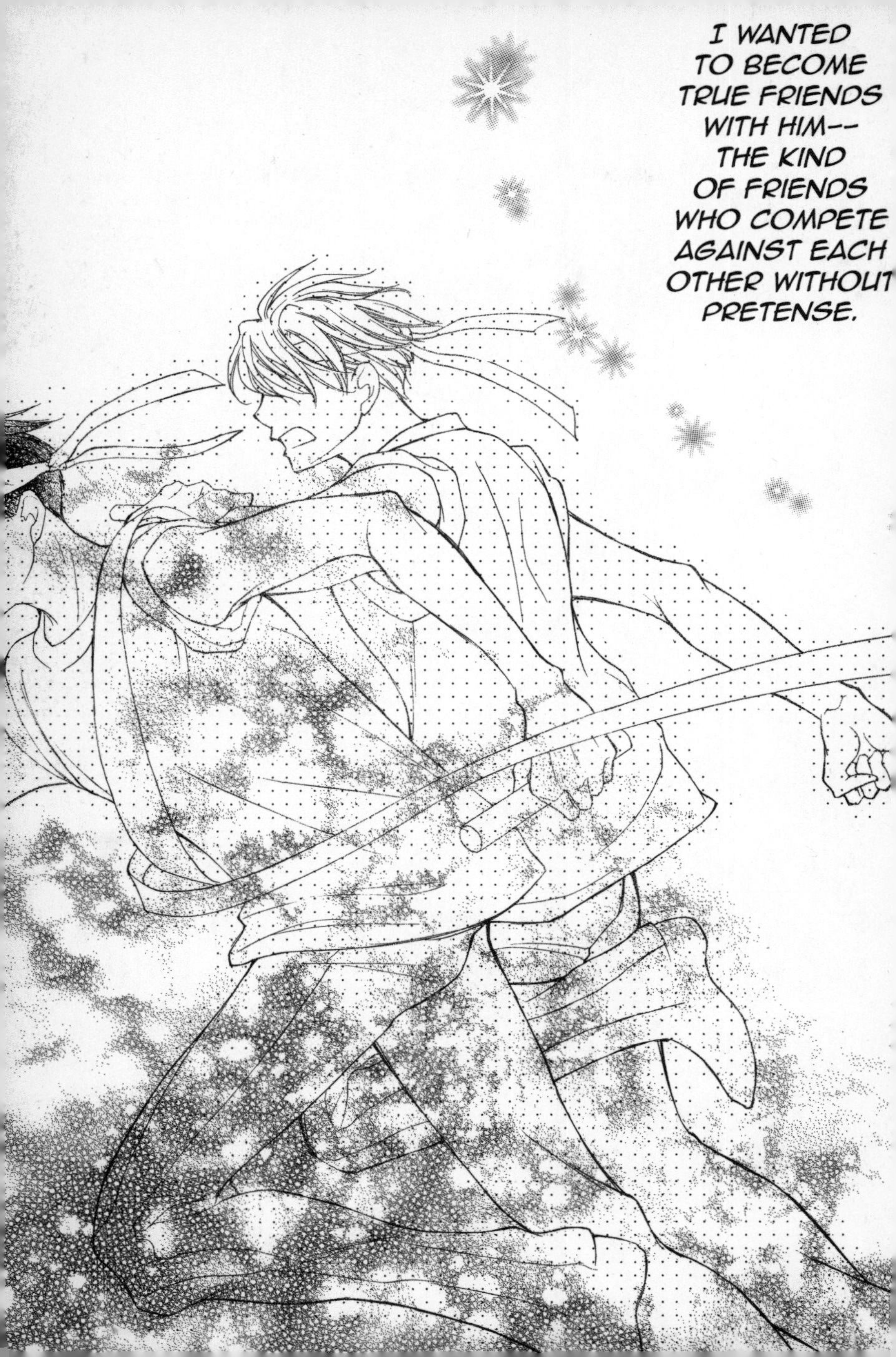
I WANTED TO BECOME TRUE FRIENDS WITH HIM-- THE KIND OF FRIENDS WHO COMPETE AGAINST EACH OTHER WITHOUT PRETENSE.

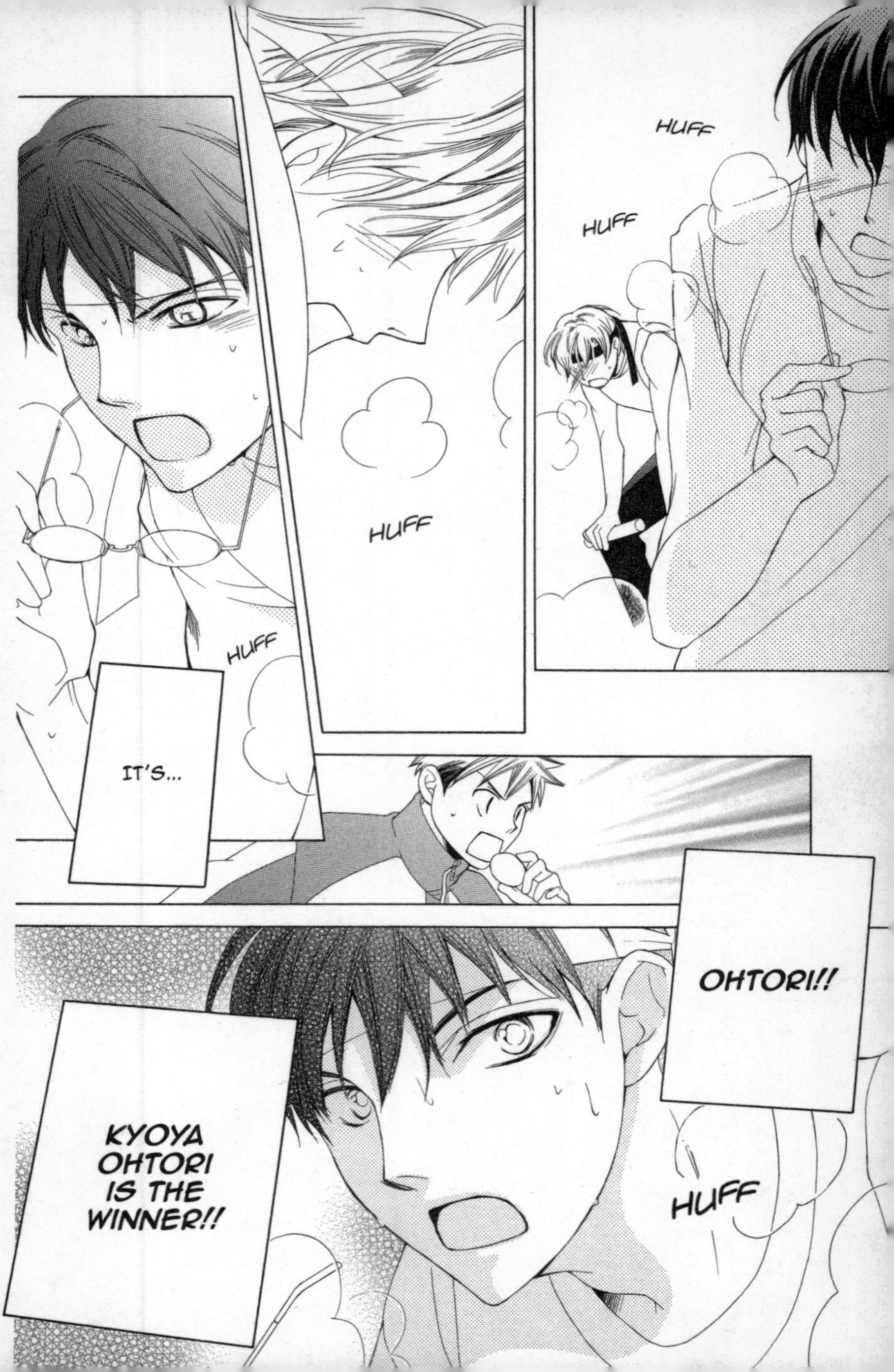
HUFF
HUFF
HUFF
HUFF
IT'S...
OHTORI!!
KYOYA OHTORI IS THE WINNER!!
HUFF

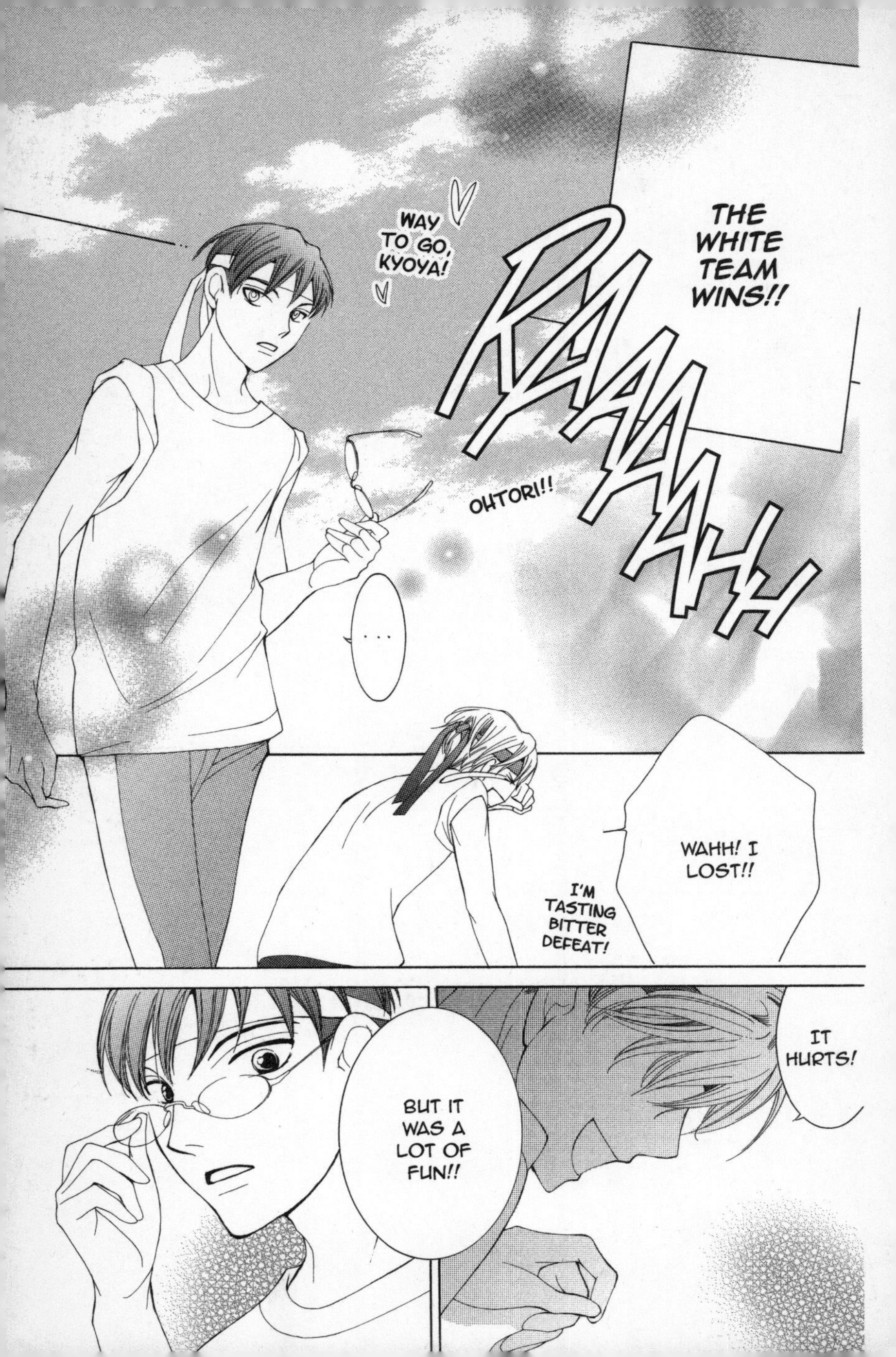
THE WHITE TEAM WINS!!
KAAAAAHH
OHTORI!!
WAY TO GO, KYOYA!
...
WAHH! I LOST!!
I'M TASTING BITTER DEFEAT!
IT HURTS!
BUT IT WAS A LOT OF FUN!!

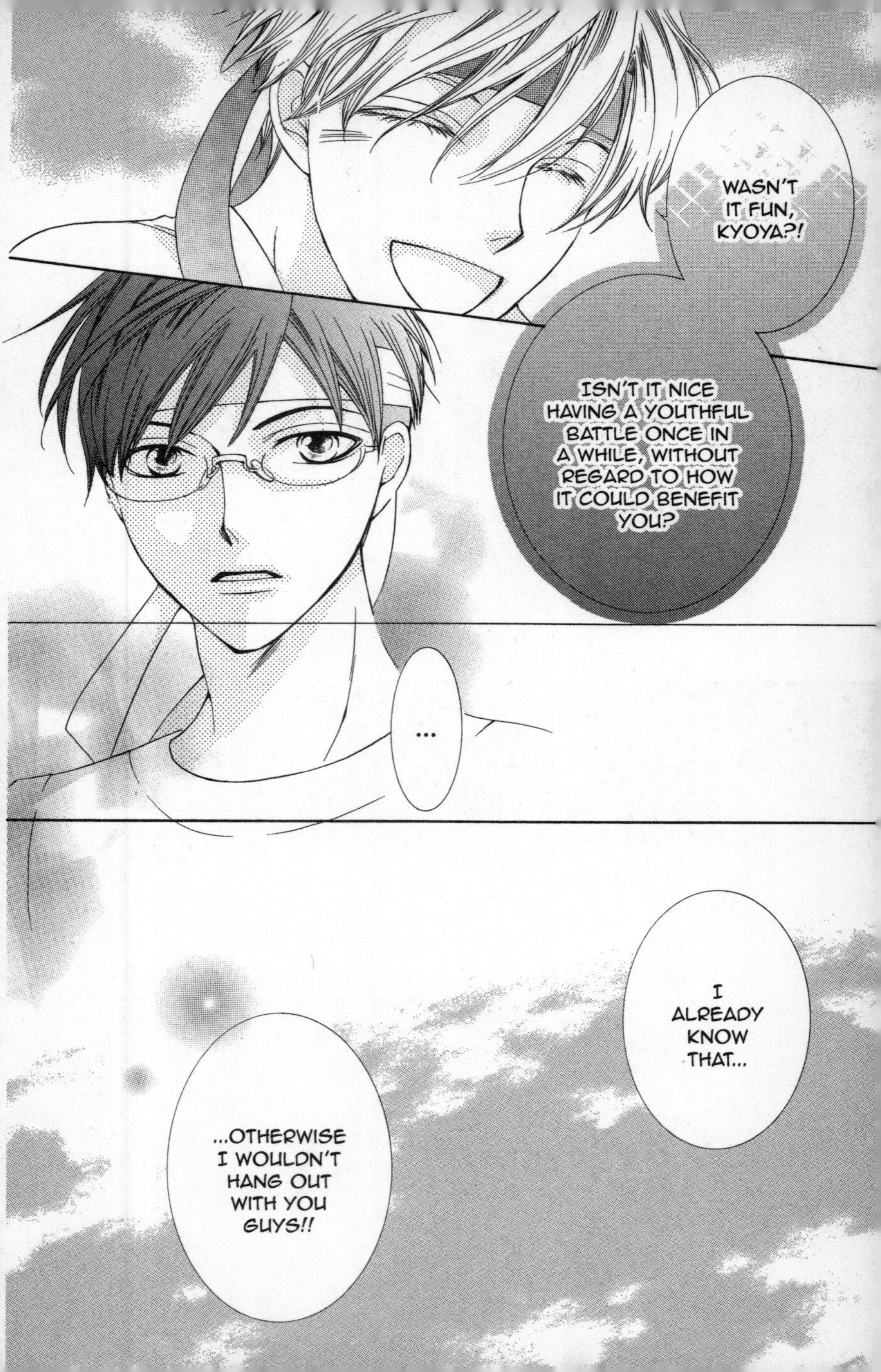
WASN'T IT FUN, KYOYA?!
ISN'T IT NICE HAVING A YOUTHFUL BATTLE ONCE IN A WHILE, WITHOUT REGARD TO HOW IT COULD BENEFIT YOU?
...
I ALREADY KNOW THAT...
...OTHERWISE I WOULDN'T HANG OUT WITH YOU GUYS!!

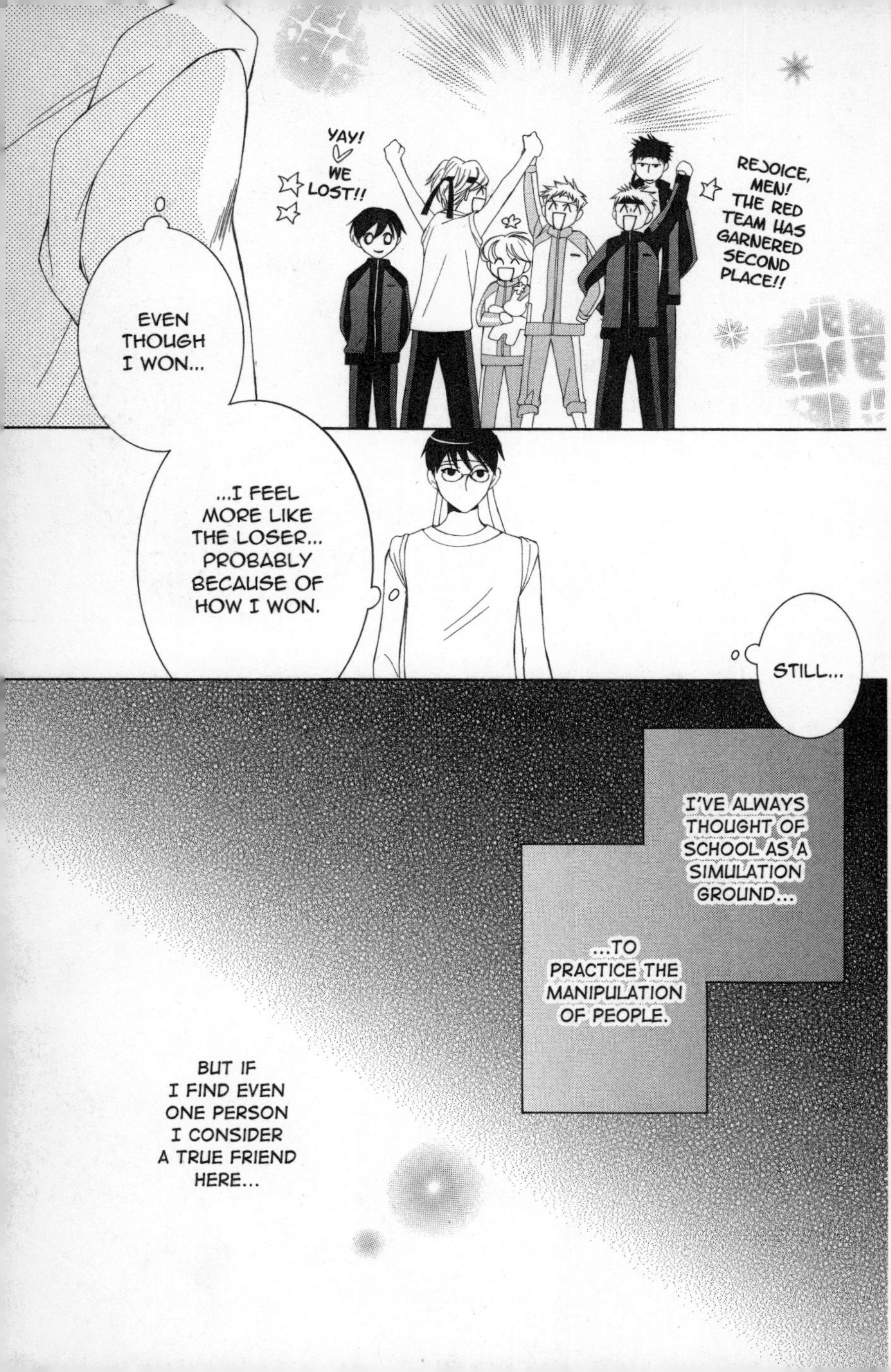
REJOICE, MEN! THE RED TEAM HAS GARNERED SECOND PLACE!!
YAY! WE LOST!!
EVEN THOUGH I WON...
...I FEEL MORE LIKE THE LOSER... PROBABLY BECAUSE OF HOW I WON.
STILL...
I'VE ALWAYS THOUGHT OF SCHOOL AS A SIMULATION GROUND...
...TO PRACTICE THE MANIPULATION OF PEOPLE.
BUT IF I FIND EVEN ONE PERSON I CONSIDER A TRUE FRIEND HERE...

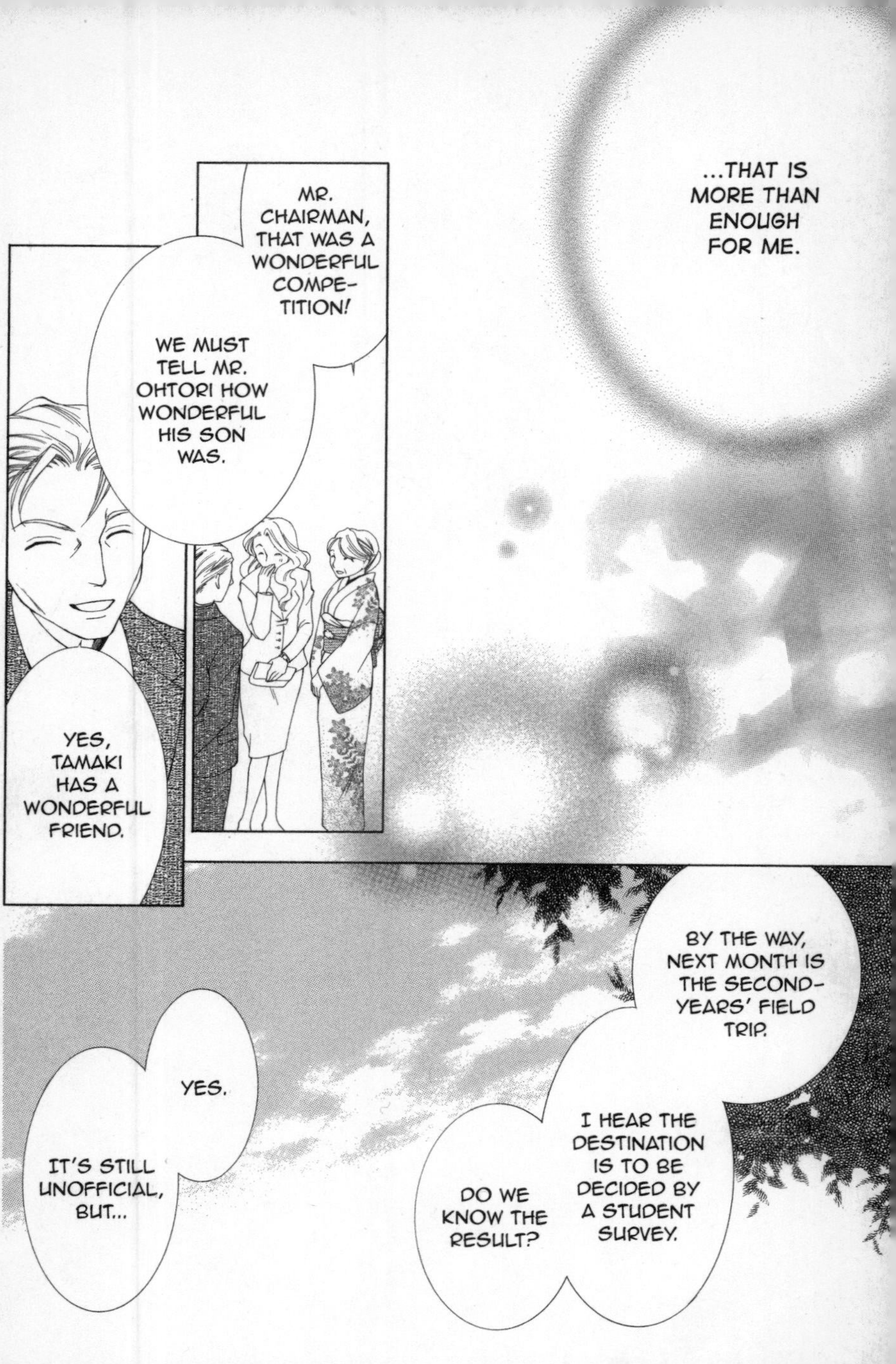
...THAT IS MORE THAN ENOUGH FOR ME.
MR. CHAIRMAN, THAT WAS A WONDERFUL COMPE-TITION!
WE MUST TELL MR. OHTORI HOW WONDERFUL HIS SON WAS.
YES, TAMAKI HAS A WONDERFUL FRIEND.
BY THE WAY, NEXT MONTH IS THE SECOND-YEARS' FIELD TRIP.
I HEAR THE DESTINATION IS TO BE DECIDED BY A STUDENT SURVEY.
DO WE KNOW THE RESULT?
YES.
IT'S STILL UNOFFICIAL, BUT...

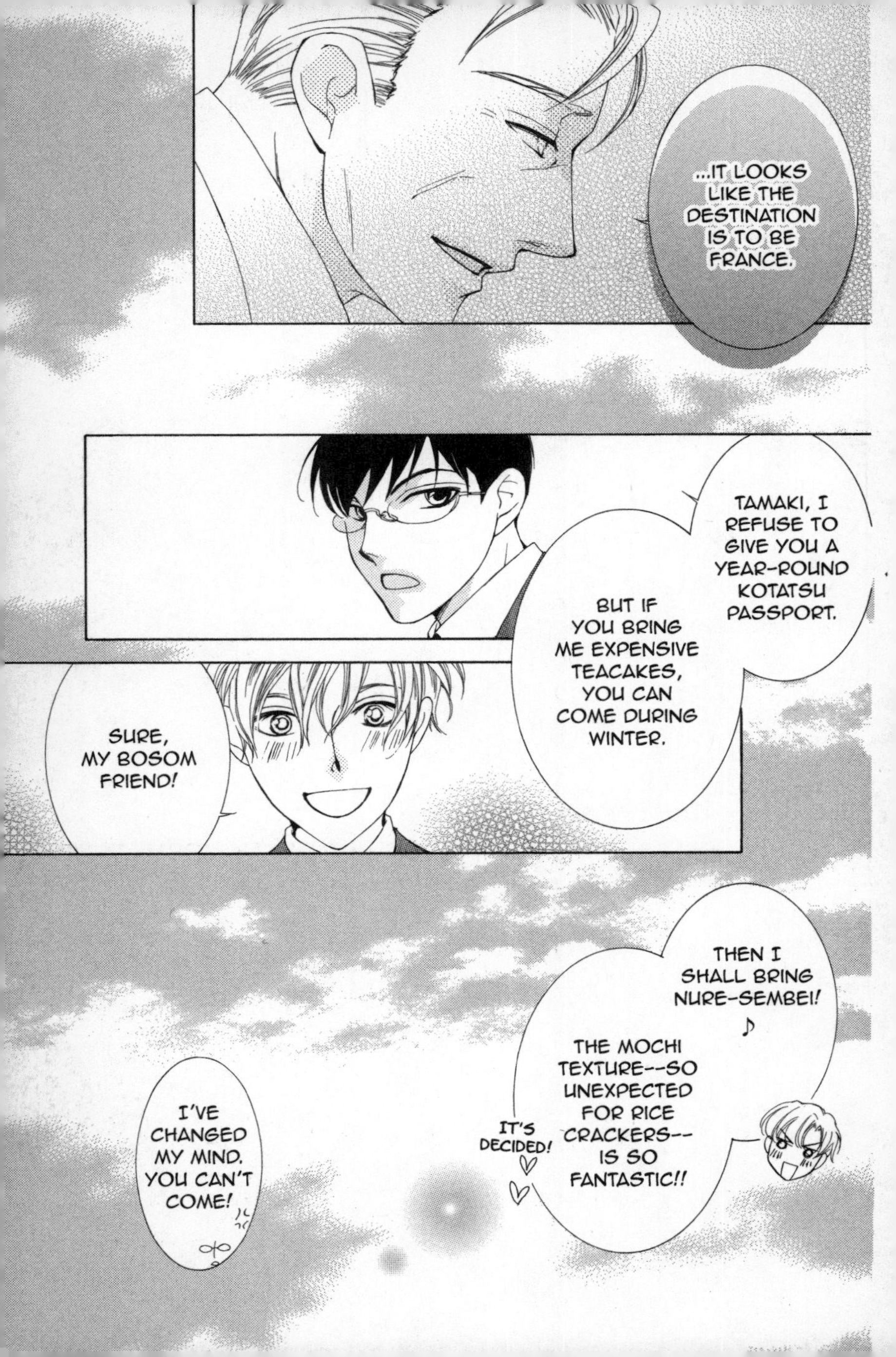
...IT LOOKS LIKE THE DESTINATION IS TO BE FRANCE.
TAMAKI, I REFUSE TO GIVE YOU A YEAR-ROUND KOTATSU PASSPORT.
BUT IF YOU BRING ME EXPENSIVE TEACAKES, YOU CAN COME DURING WINTER.
SURE, MY BOSOM FRIEND!
THEN I SHALL BRING NURE-SEMBEI! ♪
THE MOCHI TEXTURE--SO UNEXPECTED FOR RICE CRACKERS--IS SO FANTASTIC!!
IT'S DECIDED!
I'VE CHANGED MY MIND. YOU CAN'T COME!

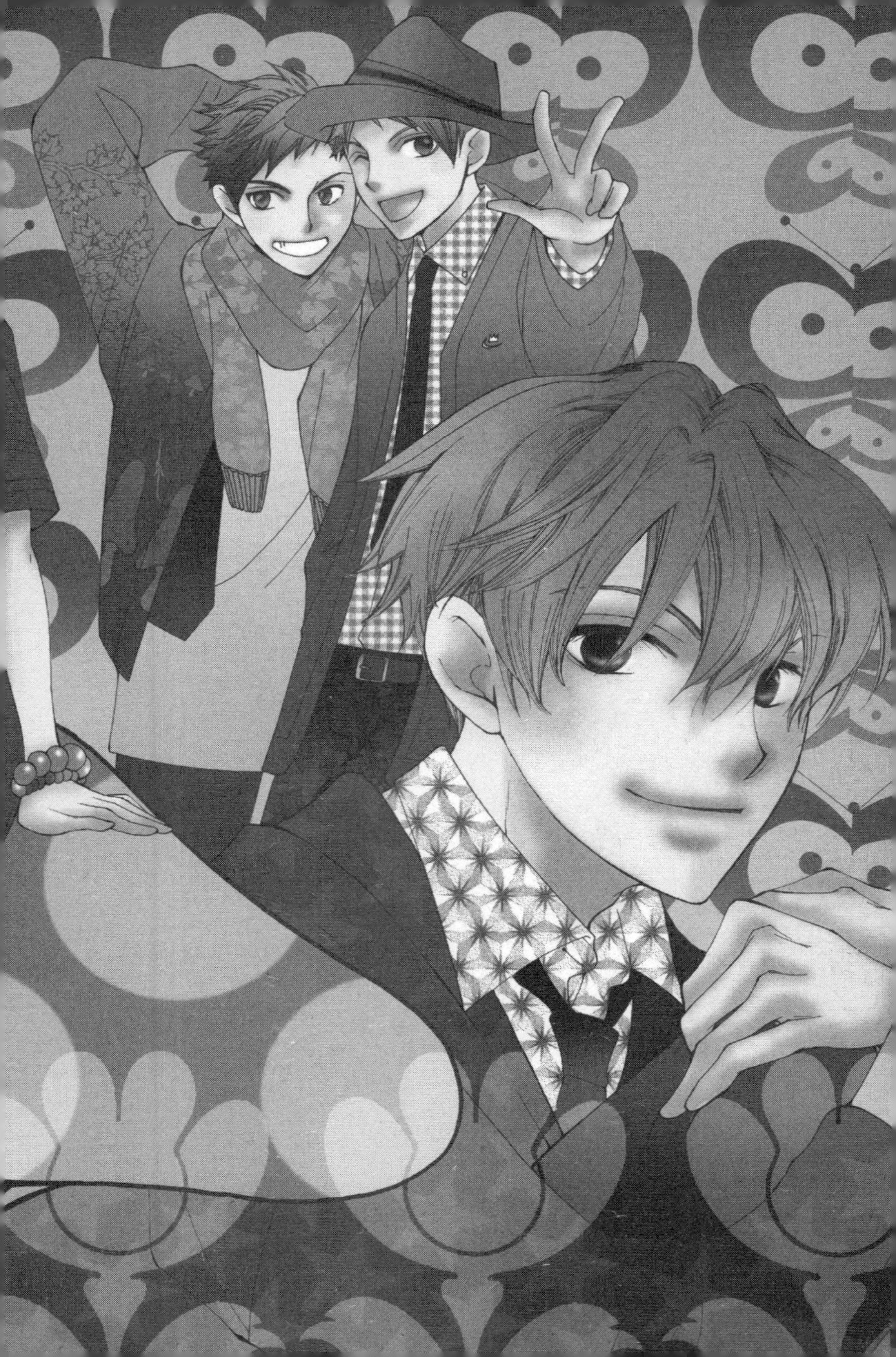

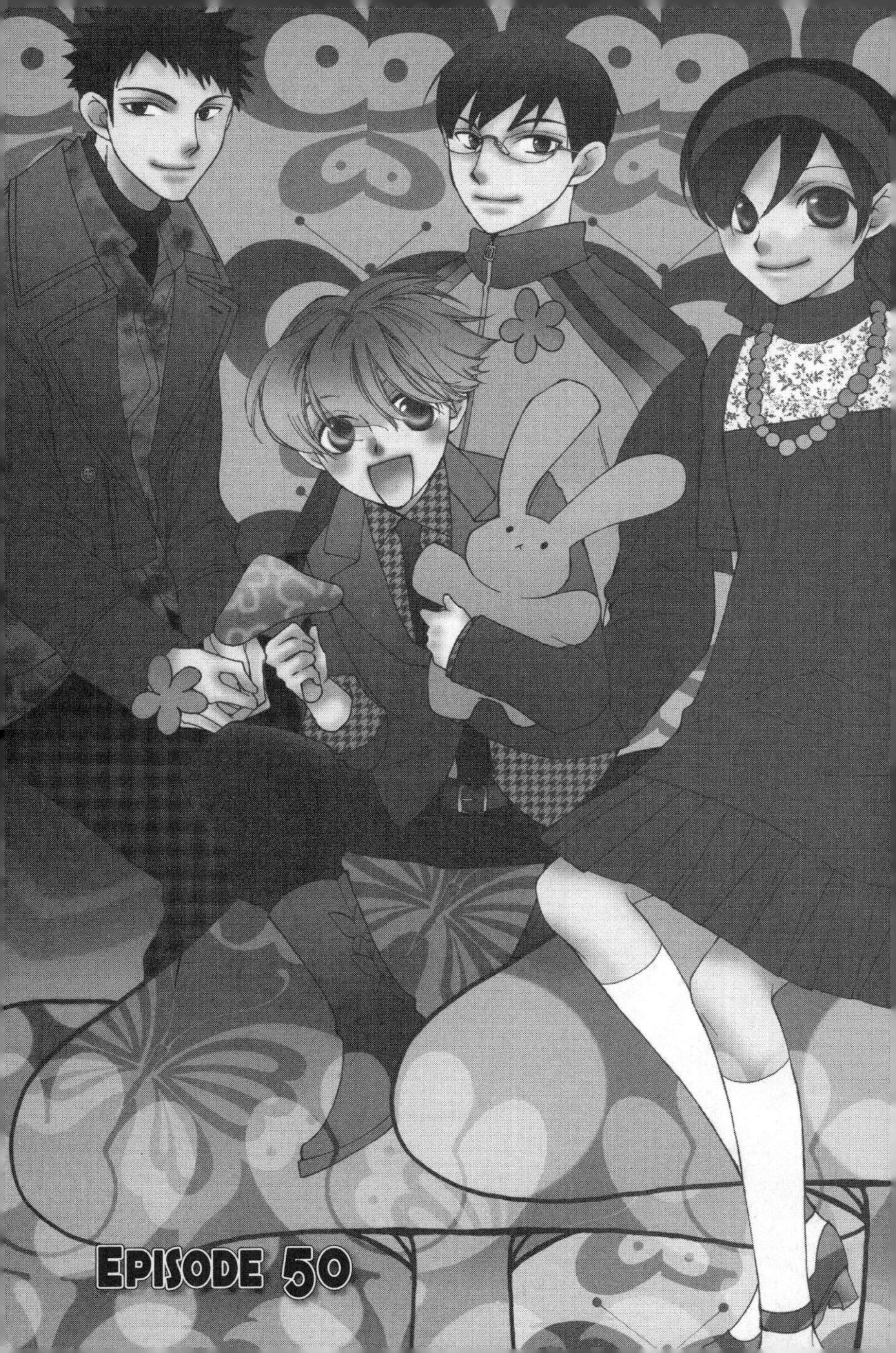
EPISODE 50

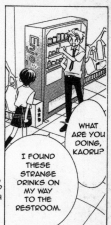

WHAT ARE YOU DOING, KAORU?
I FOUND THESE STRANGE DRINKS ON MY WAY TO THE RESTROOM.

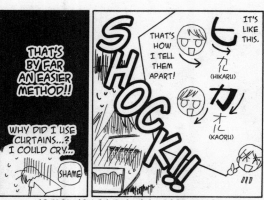

AN APOLOGY.

IN VOLUME 10, EPISODE 42, KAORU WAS SWITCHED WITH HIKARU IN ONE PANEL.

I AM SO SORRY!!

THIS IS PRETTY EMBARRASSING, ESPECIALLY SINCE I FEATURED A PAGE ON HOW TO DISTINGUISH BETWEEN THE TWINS AT THE END OF THE VOLUME. ♥ GYAAH!!

BUT, TO TELL THE TRUTH, I MADE THE SAME MISTAKE OF SWITCHING HIKARU AND KAORU IN EPISODE 51. (I SCREAMED WHEN I SAW *LALA*.) AGAIN...

THANK YOU TO THOSE OF YOU WHO POINTED OUT MY MISTAKE IN VOLUME 10!

PLUS ANOTHER SHOCK...
HOW TO DISTINGUISH BETWEEN THE TWINS FROM VOLUME 10... I'VE BEEN TELLING THEM APART BY USING A DIFFERENT METHOD.
YAMASHII
HUH? WHAT METHOD?
IT'S LIKE THIS.
THAT'S HOW I TELL THEM APART!
ヒカル
(HIKARU)
カオル
(KAORU)
SHOCK!!!
THAT'S BY FAR AN EASIER METHOD!!
WHY DID I USE CURTAINS...? I COULD CRY...
SHAME

SO FROM NOW ON, THIS ↗ IS A GOOD METHOD.

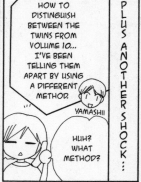

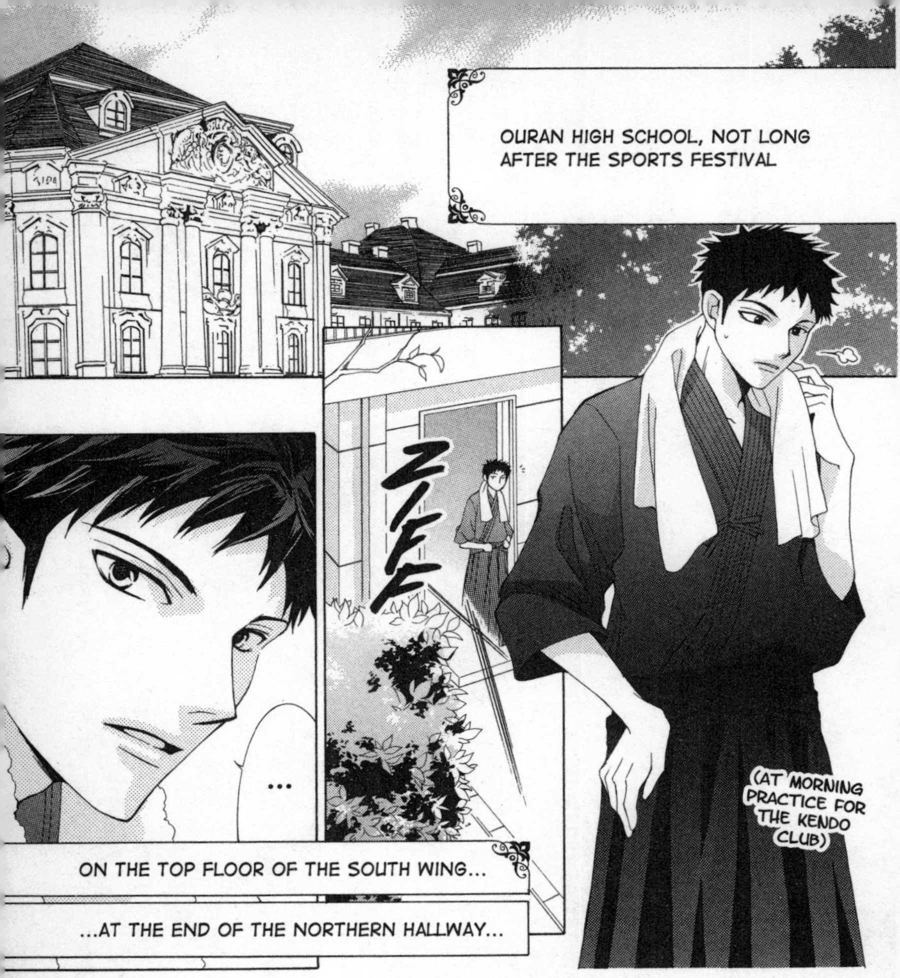
OURAN HIGH SCHOOL, NOT LONG AFTER THE SPORTS FESTIVAL
(AT MORNING PRACTICE FOR THE KENDO CLUB)
ZEE
...
ON THE TOP FLOOR OF THE SOUTH WING...
...AT THE END OF THE NORTHERN HALLWAY...

7D DRIED MANGOES

FELLOW MANGAKA MIDORI SHIINO RECOMMENDED THESE, AND I'M HOOKED.

THEY'RE DELICIOUS!!

PLEASE TRY THEM!

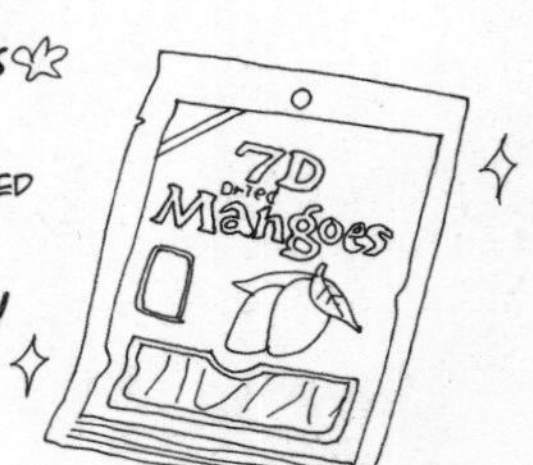
7D
Dried
Mangoes

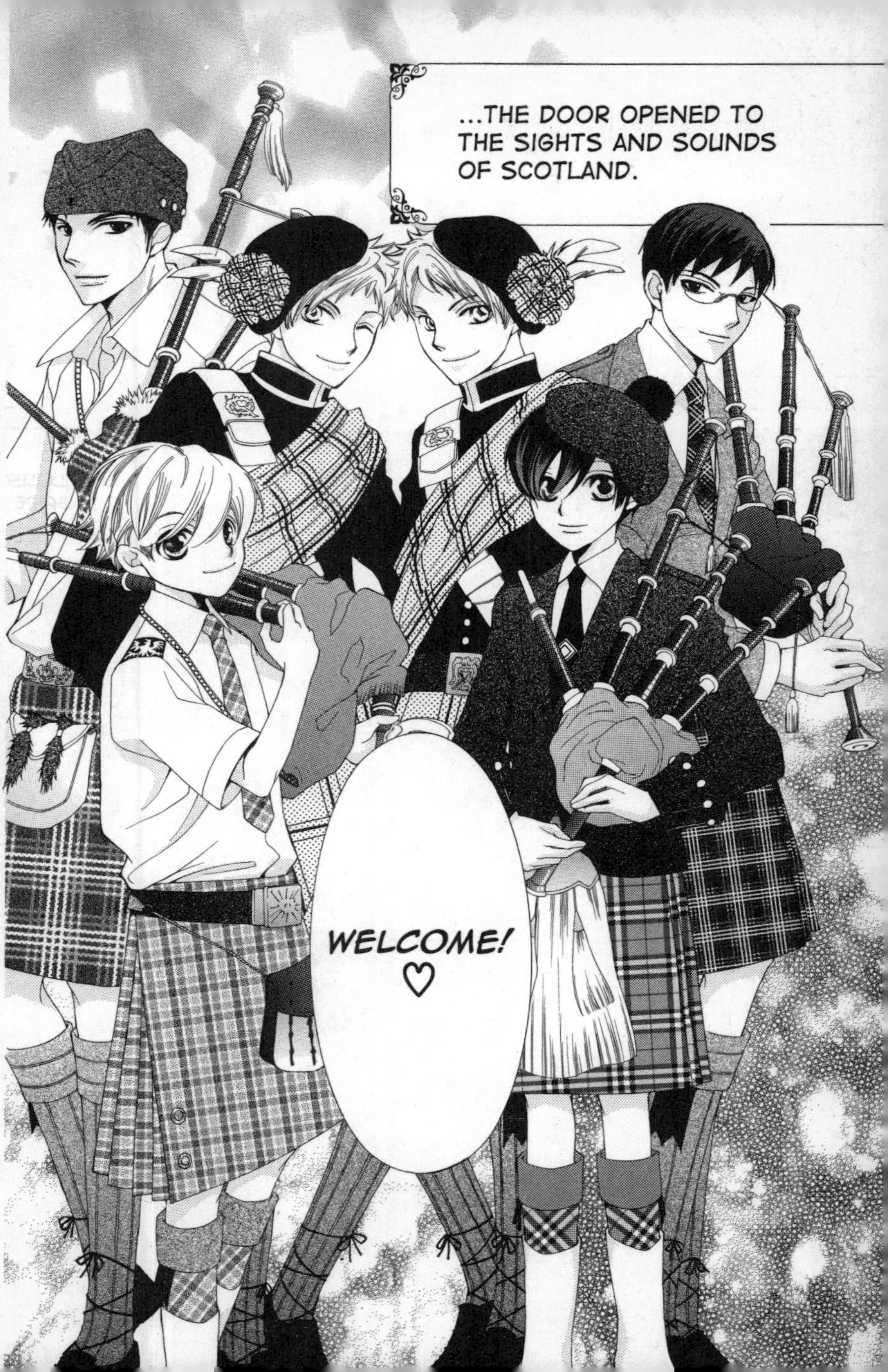
...THE DOOR OPENED TO THE SIGHTS AND SOUNDS OF SCOTLAND.
WELCOME! ♡

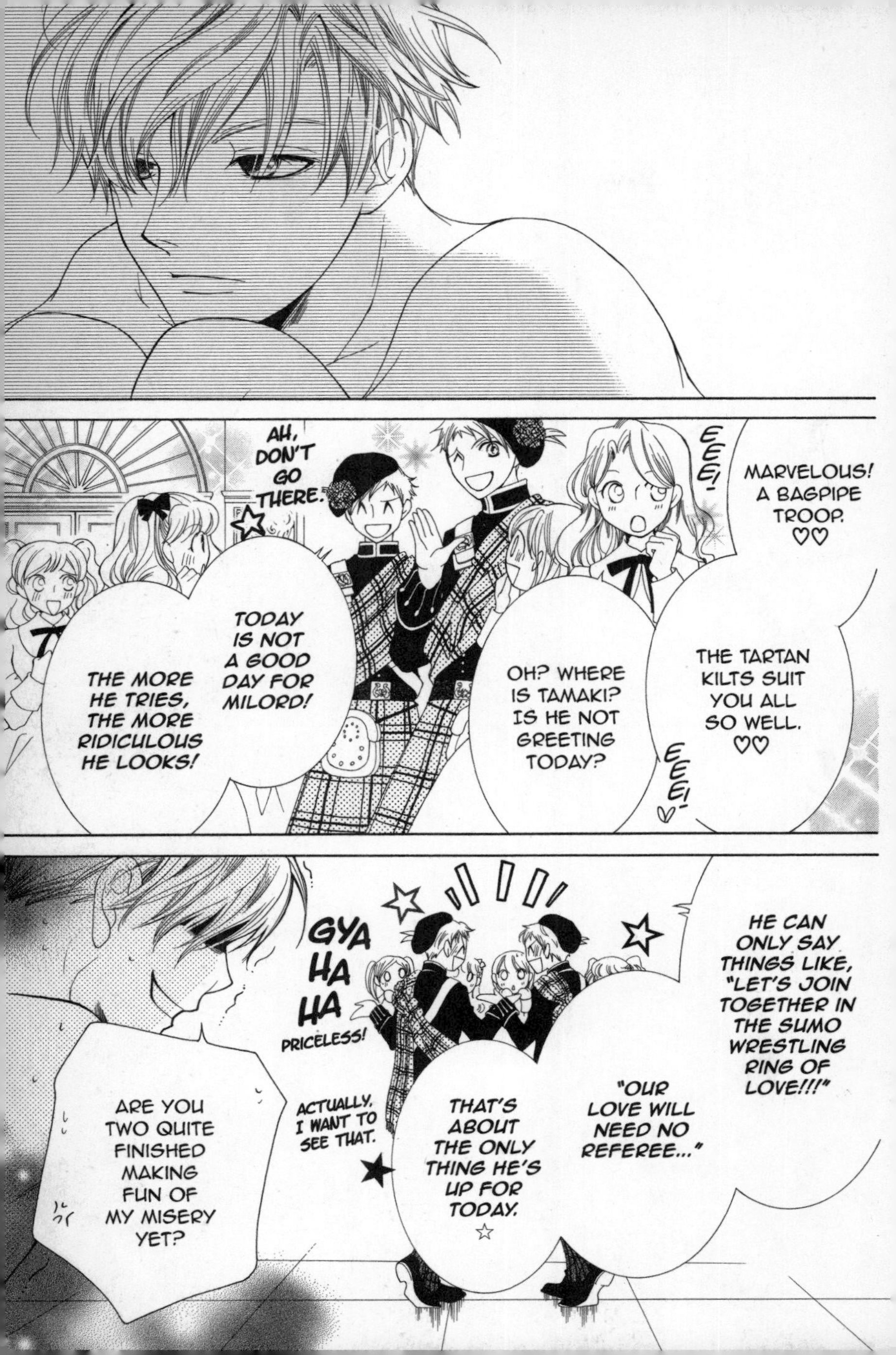
MARVELOUS! A BAGPIPE TROOP. ♡♡
EEE!
THE TARTAN KILTS SUIT YOU ALL SO WELL. ♡♡
EEE!
OH? WHERE IS TAMAKI? IS HE NOT GREETING TODAY?
AH, DON'T GO THERE.
TODAY IS NOT A GOOD DAY FOR MILORD!
THE MORE HE TRIES, THE MORE RIDICULOUS HE LOOKS!
HE CAN ONLY SAY THINGS LIKE, "LET'S JOIN TOGETHER IN THE SUMO WRESTLING RING OF LOVE!!!"
"OUR LOVE WILL NEED NO REFEREE..."
THAT'S ABOUT THE ONLY THING HE'S UP FOR TODAY. ☆
GYA HA HA
PRICELESS!
ACTUALLY, I WANT TO SEE THAT.
ARE YOU TWO QUITE FINISHED MAKING FUN OF MY MISERY YET?

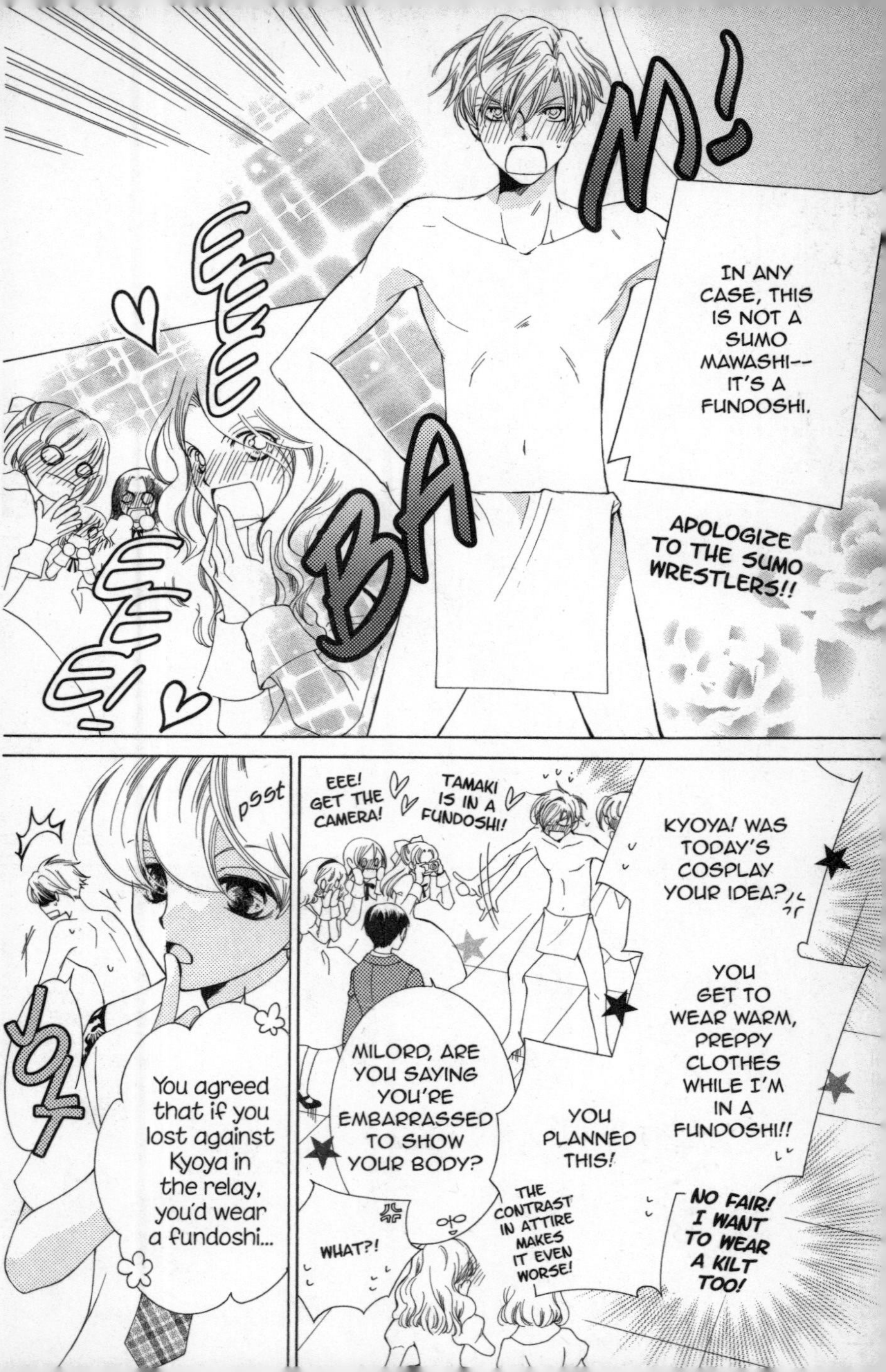
BAM!
IN ANY CASE, THIS IS NOT A SUMO MAWASHI-- IT'S A FUNDOSHI.
APOLOGIZE TO THE SUMO WRESTLERS!!
EEEEEE!
KYOYA! WAS TODAY'S COSPLAY YOUR IDEA?
TAMAKI IS IN A FUNDOSHI!
EEE! GET THE CAMERA!
YOU GET TO WEAR WARM, PREPPY CLOTHES WHILE I'M IN A FUNDOSHI!!
MILORD, ARE YOU SAYING YOU'RE EMBARRASSED TO SHOW YOUR BODY?
YOU PLANNED THIS!
NO FAIR! I WANT TO WEAR A KILT TOO!
THE CONTRAST IN ATTIRE MAKES IT EVEN WORSE!
WHAT?!
psst
JOLT
You agreed that if you lost against Kyoya in the relay, you'd wear a fundoshi...

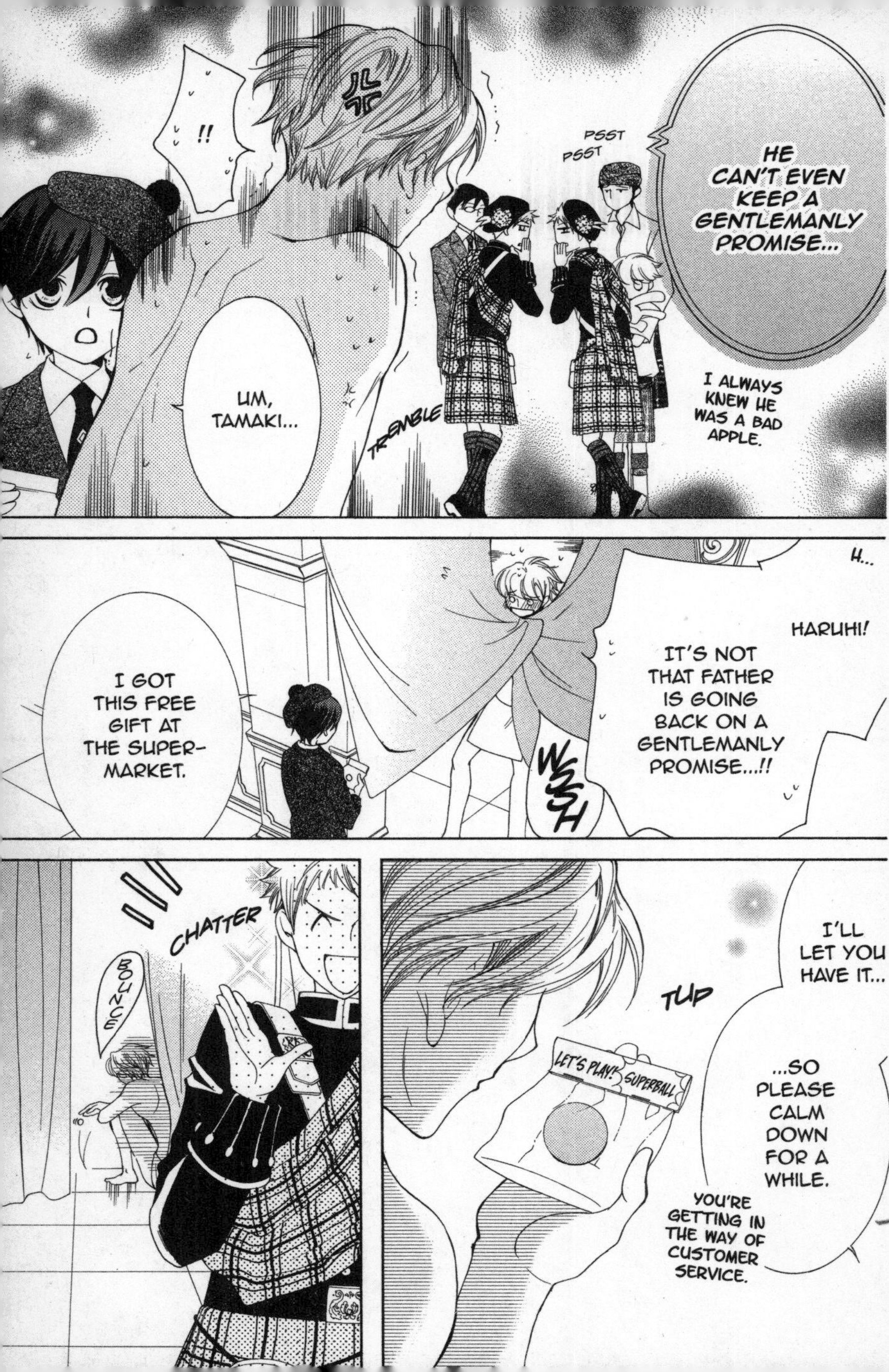
HE CAN'T EVEN KEEP A GENTLEMANLY PROMISE...
PSST
PSST
I ALWAYS KNEW HE WAS A BAD APPLE.
TREMBLE
UM, TAMAKI...
!!
H...
HARUHI!
IT'S NOT THAT FATHER IS GOING BACK ON A GENTLEMANLY PROMISE...!!
WSSH
I GOT THIS FREE GIFT AT THE SUPER-MARKET.
I'LL LET YOU HAVE IT...
...SO PLEASE CALM DOWN FOR A WHILE.
TUP
LET'S PLAY! SUPERBALL
YOU'RE GETTING IN THE WAY OF CUSTOMER SERVICE.
CHATTER
BOUNCE

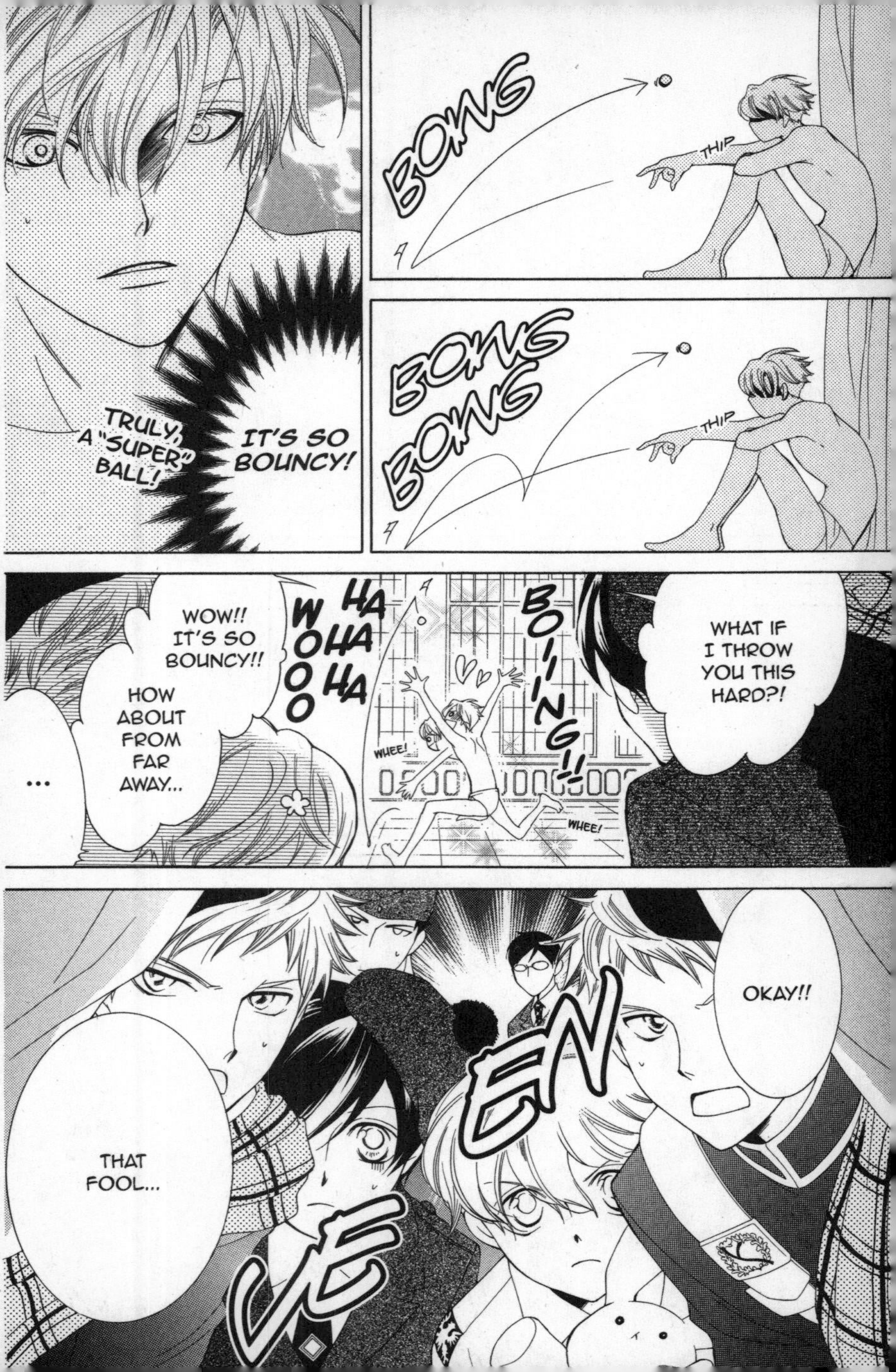

BONG
THIP
BONG BONG
THIP
IT'S SO BOUNCY!
TRULY, A "SUPER" BALL!
WHAT IF I THROW YOU THIS HARD?!
BOIING!!
WHEE!
HA HA HA
WOOOO
WHEE!
WOW!! IT'S SO BOUNCY!!
HOW ABOUT FROM FAR AWAY...
...
OKAY!!
EN
JE
THAT FOOL...

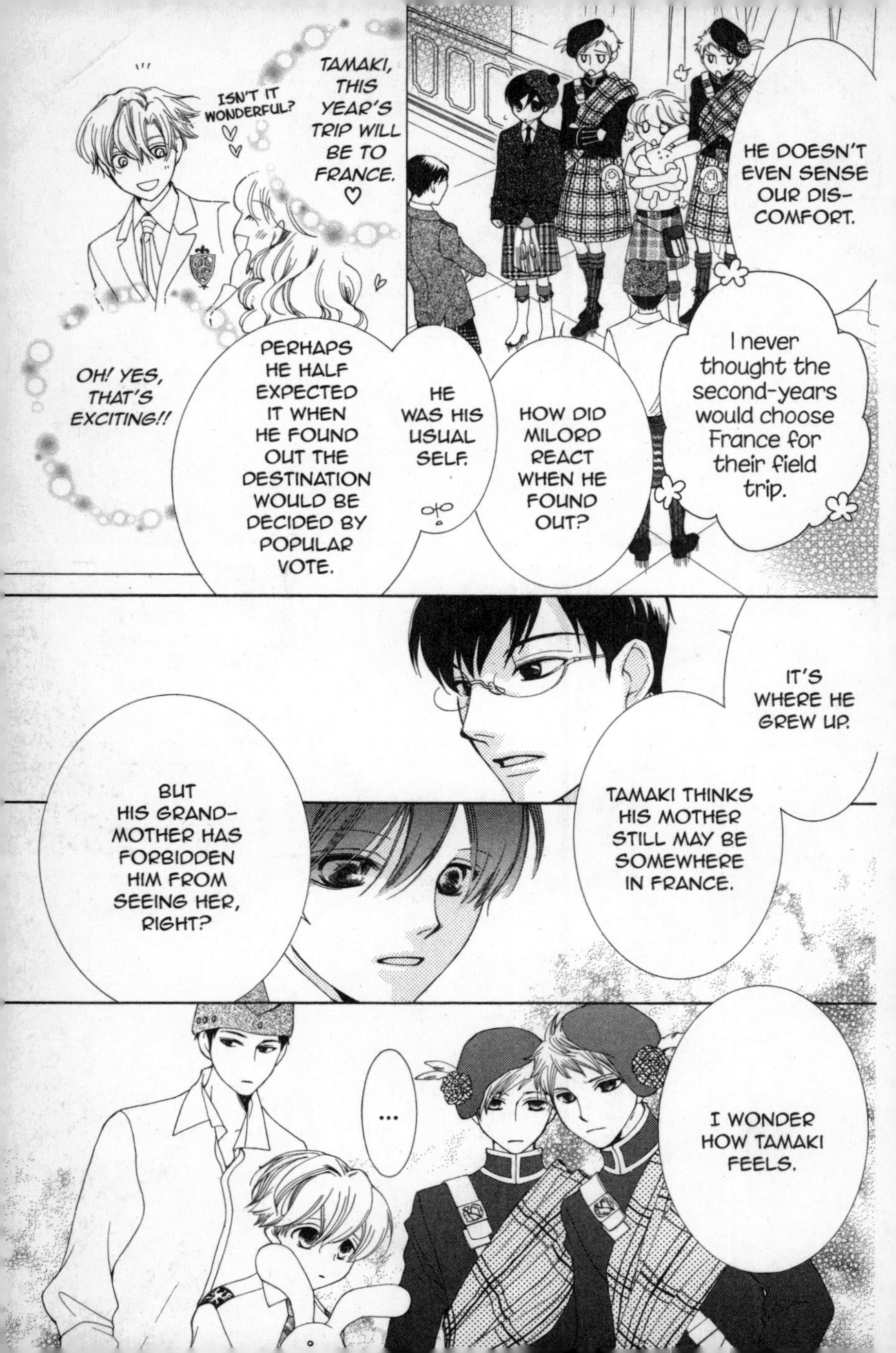
HE DOESN'T EVEN SENSE OUR DIS-COMFORT.
I never thought the second-years would choose France for their field trip.
HOW DID MILORD REACT WHEN HE FOUND OUT?
HE WAS HIS USUAL SELF.
PERHAPS HE HALF EXPECTED IT WHEN HE FOUND OUT THE DESTINATION WOULD BE DECIDED BY POPULAR VOTE.
TAMAKI, THIS YEAR'S TRIP WILL BE TO FRANCE. ♡
ISN'T IT WONDERFUL? ♡
OH! YES, THAT'S EXCITING!!
IT'S WHERE HE GREW UP.
TAMAKI THINKS HIS MOTHER STILL MAY BE SOMEWHERE IN FRANCE.
BUT HIS GRAND-MOTHER HAS FORBIDDEN HIM FROM SEEING HER, RIGHT?
I WONDER HOW TAMAKI FEELS.
...

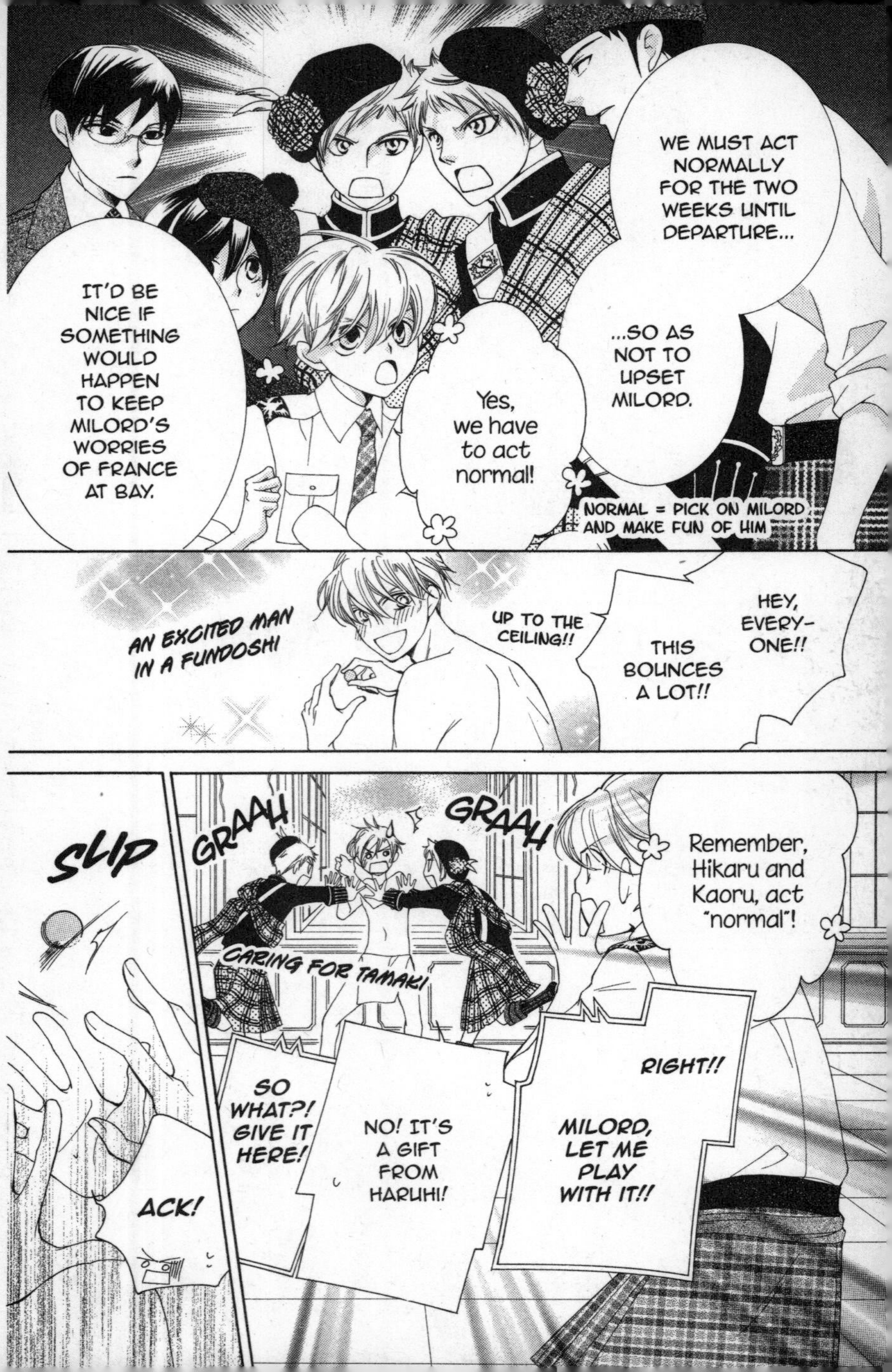
WE MUST ACT NORMALLY FOR THE TWO WEEKS UNTIL DEPARTURE...
...SO AS NOT TO UPSET MILORD.
Yes, we have to act normal!
IT'D BE NICE IF SOMETHING WOULD HAPPEN TO KEEP MILORD'S WORRIES OF FRANCE AT BAY.
NORMAL = PICK ON MILORD AND MAKE FUN OF HIM
HEY, EVERYONE!!
THIS BOUNCES A LOT!!
UP TO THE CEILING!!
AN EXCITED MAN IN A FUNDOSHI
Remember, Hikaru and Kaoru, act "normal"!
GRAAH
GRAAH
RIGHT!!
MILORD, LET ME PLAY WITH IT!!
NO! IT'S A GIFT FROM HARUHI!
SO WHAT?! GIVE IT HERE!
CARING FOR TAMAKI
SLIP
ACK!

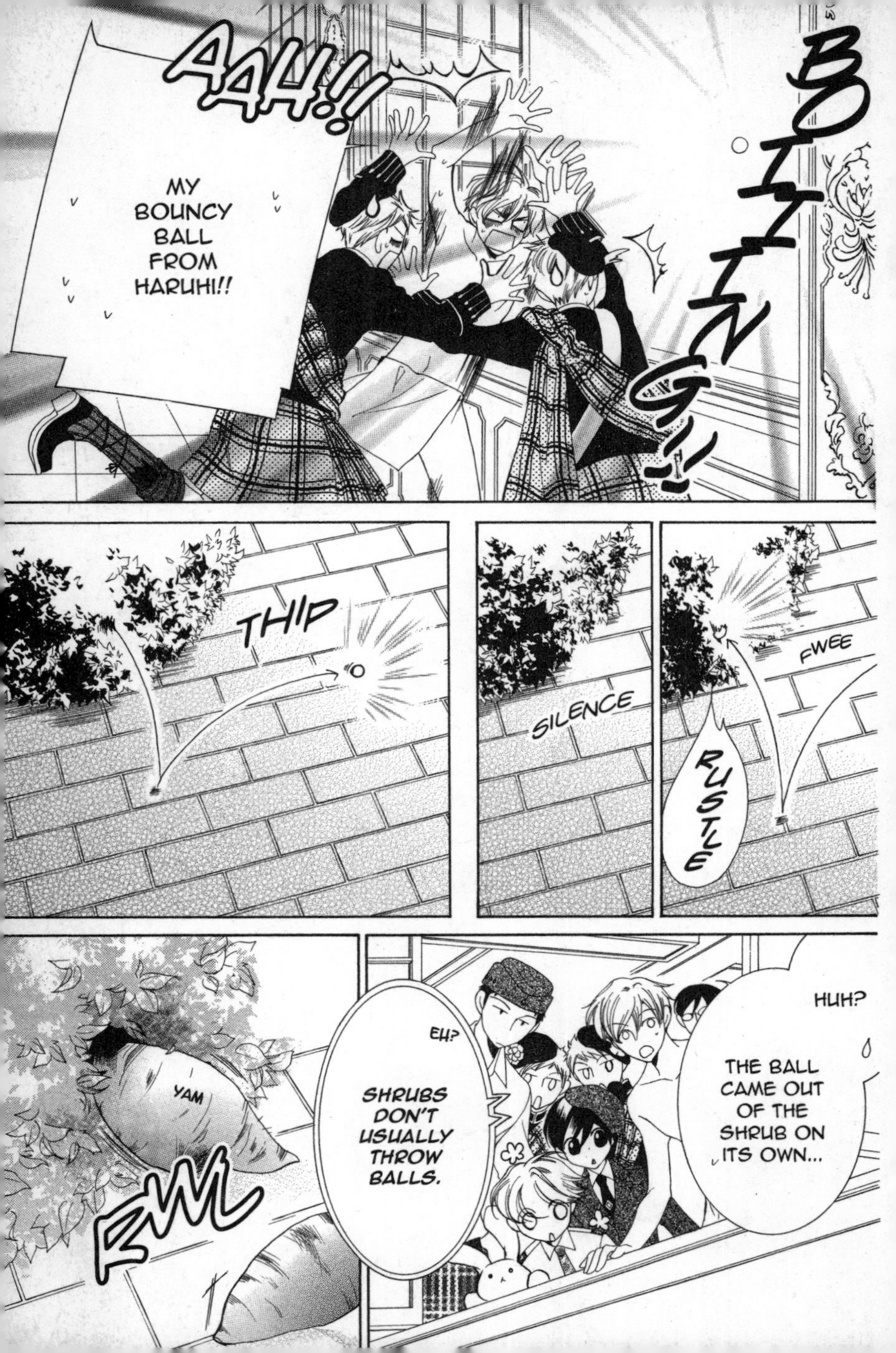
BOIING!!
AAH!!!
MY BOUNCY BALL FROM HARUHI!!
FWEE
RUSTLE
SILENCE
THIP
HUH?
THE BALL CAME OUT OF THE SHRUB ON ITS OWN...
EH?
SHRUBS DON'T USUALLY THROW BALLS.
YAM
RWL

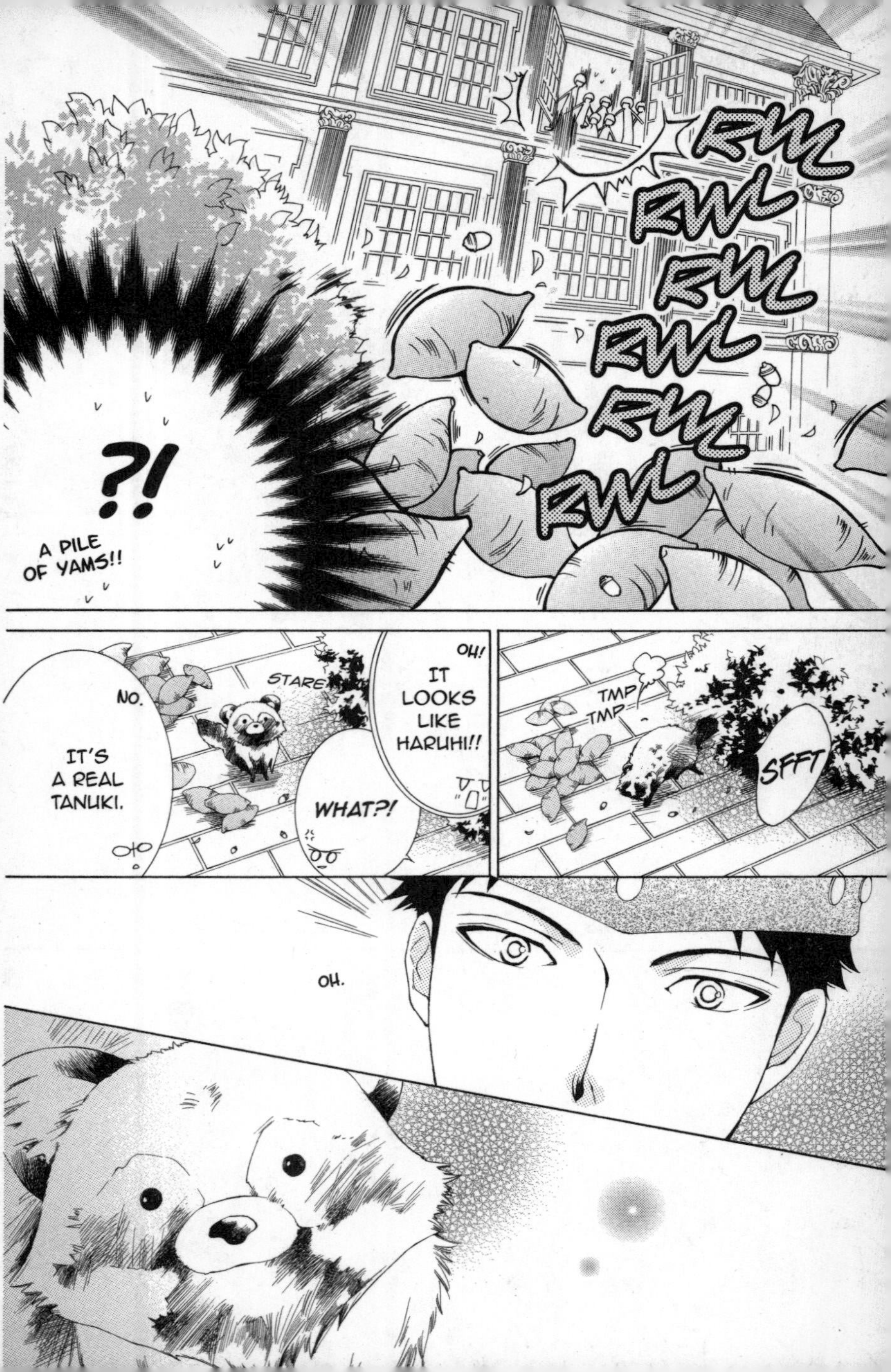

RWL RWL RWL RWL RWL RWL
?!
A PILE OF YAMS!!
TMP TMP
SFFT
OH! IT LOOKS LIKE HARUHI!!
STARE
WHAT?!
NO.
IT'S A REAL TANUKI.
OH.

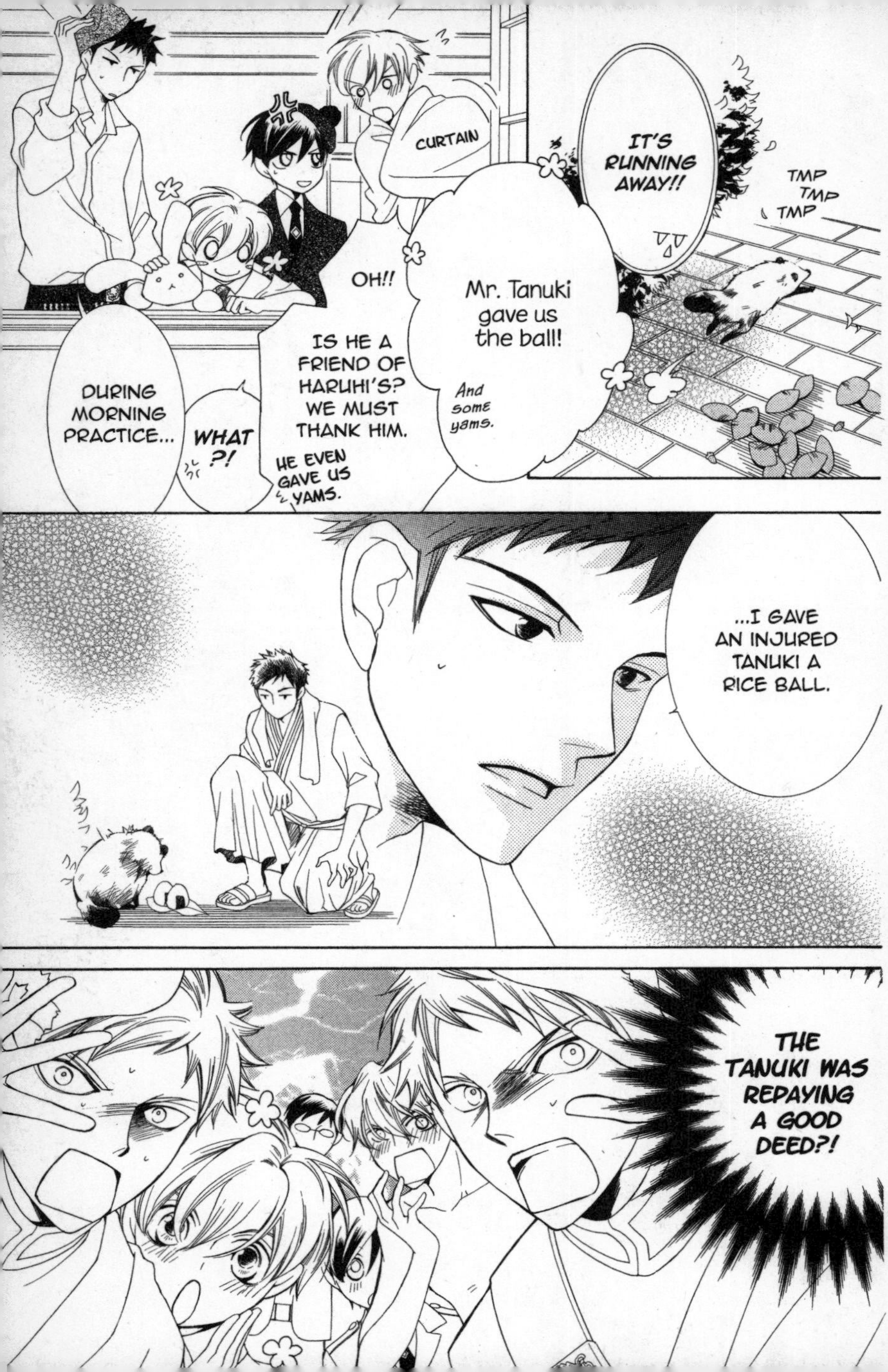
IT'S RUNNING AWAY!!
TMP TMP TMP
CURTAIN
Mr. Tanuki gave us the ball!
And some yams.
OH!!
IS HE A FRIEND OF HARUHI'S? WE MUST THANK HIM.
HE EVEN GAVE US YAMS.
WHAT ?!
DURING MORNING PRACTICE...
...I GAVE AN INJURED TANUKI A RICE BALL.
THE TANUKI WAS REPAYING A GOOD DEED?!

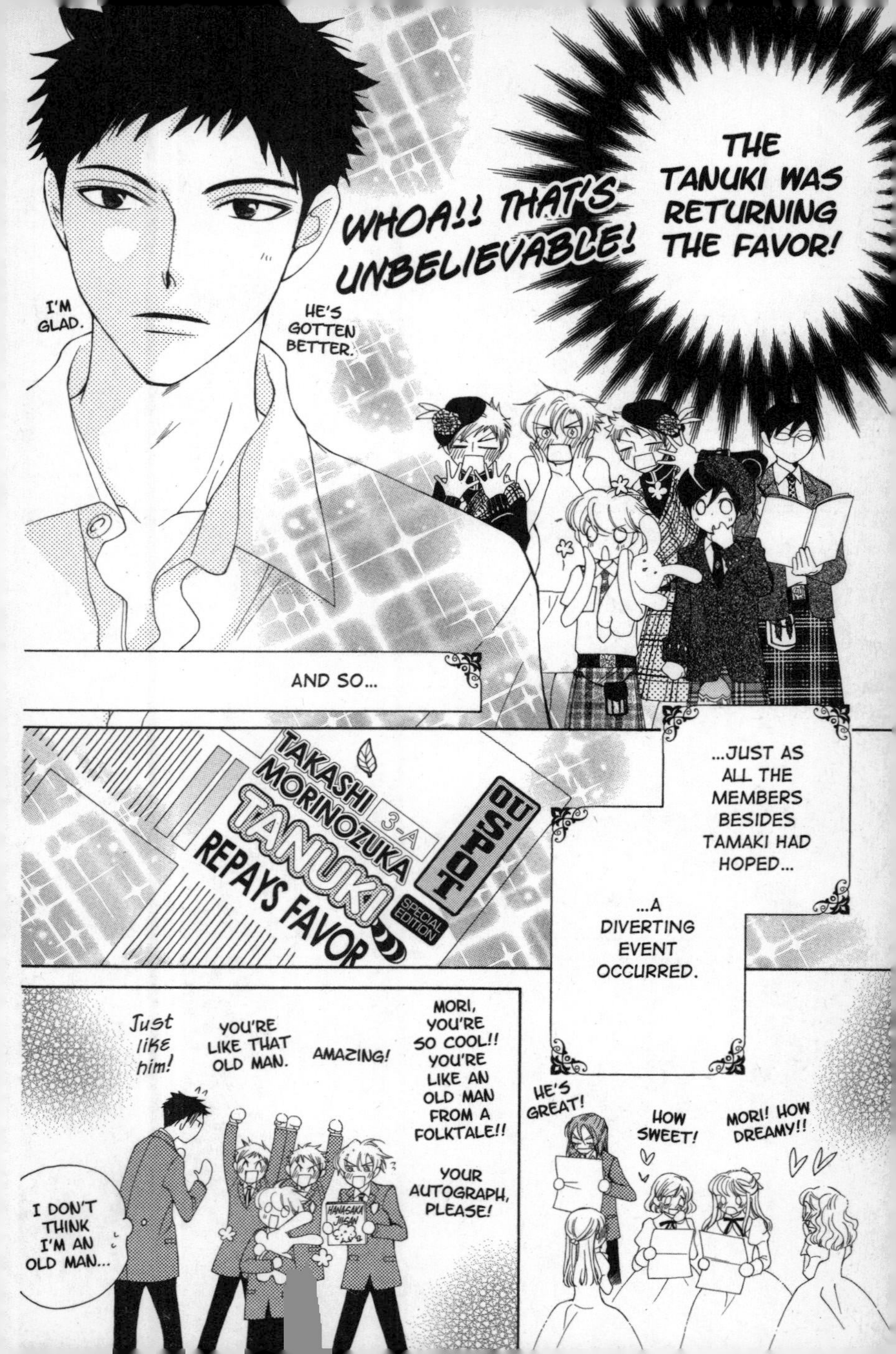
THE TANUKI WAS RETURNING THE FAVOR!
WHOA!! THAT'S UNBELIEVABLE!
HE'S GOTTEN BETTER.
I'M GLAD.
AND SO...
...JUST AS ALL THE MEMBERS BESIDES TAMAKI HAD HOPED...
...A DIVERTING EVENT OCCURRED.
OU SPOT
SPECIAL EDITION
TAKASHI MORINOZUKA 3-A
TANUKI REPAYS FAVOR
MORI! HOW DREAMY!!
HOW SWEET!
HE'S GREAT!
MORI, YOU'RE SO COOL!! YOU'RE LIKE AN OLD MAN FROM A FOLKTALE!!
YOUR AUTOGRAPH, PLEASE!
AMAZING!
YOU'RE LIKE THAT OLD MAN.
Just like him!
HANASAKA JIISAN
I DON'T THINK I'M AN OLD MAN...

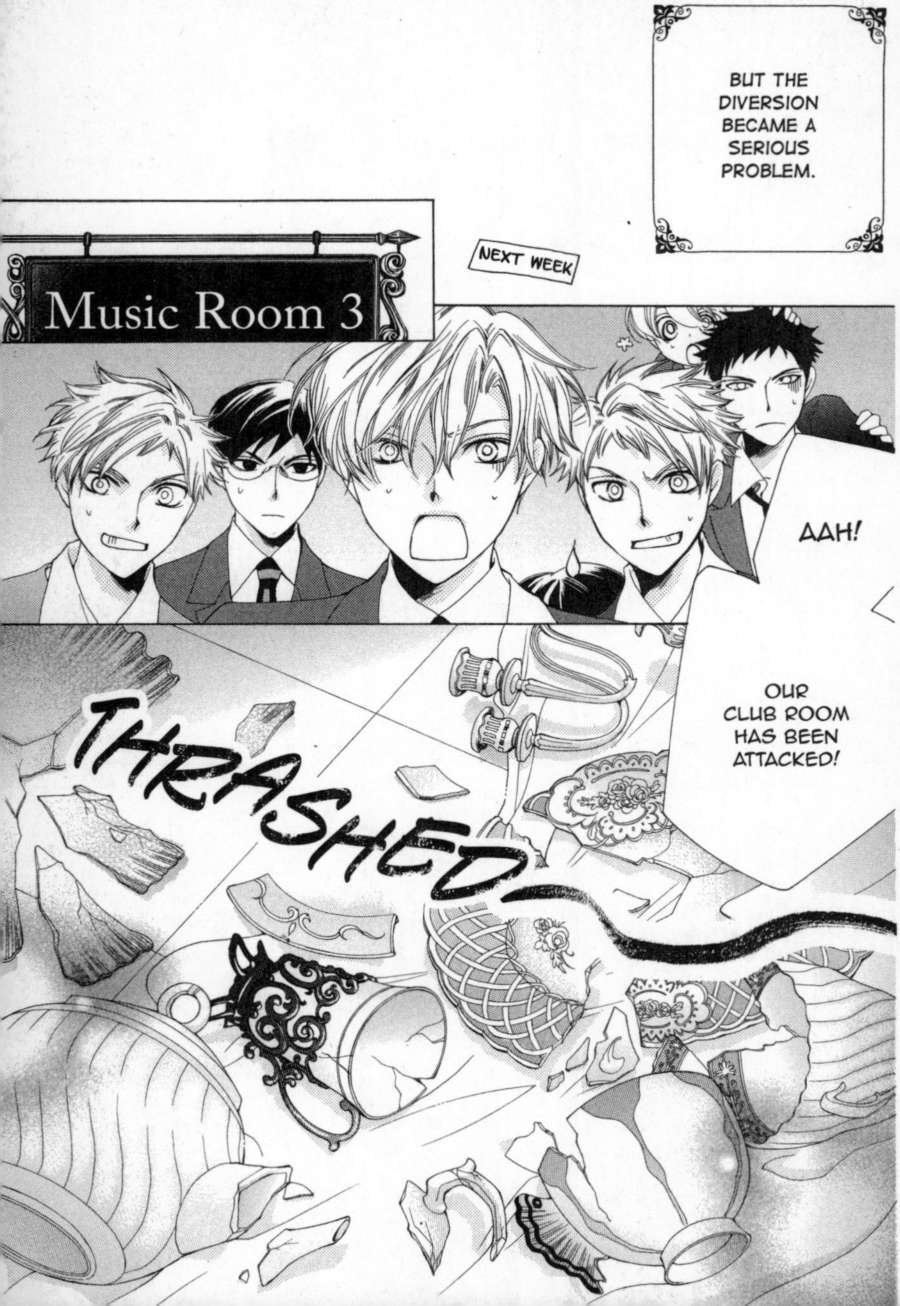
BUT THE DIVERSION BECAME A SERIOUS PROBLEM.
NEXT WEEK
Music Room 3
AAH!
OUR CLUB ROOM HAS BEEN ATTACKED!
THRASHED

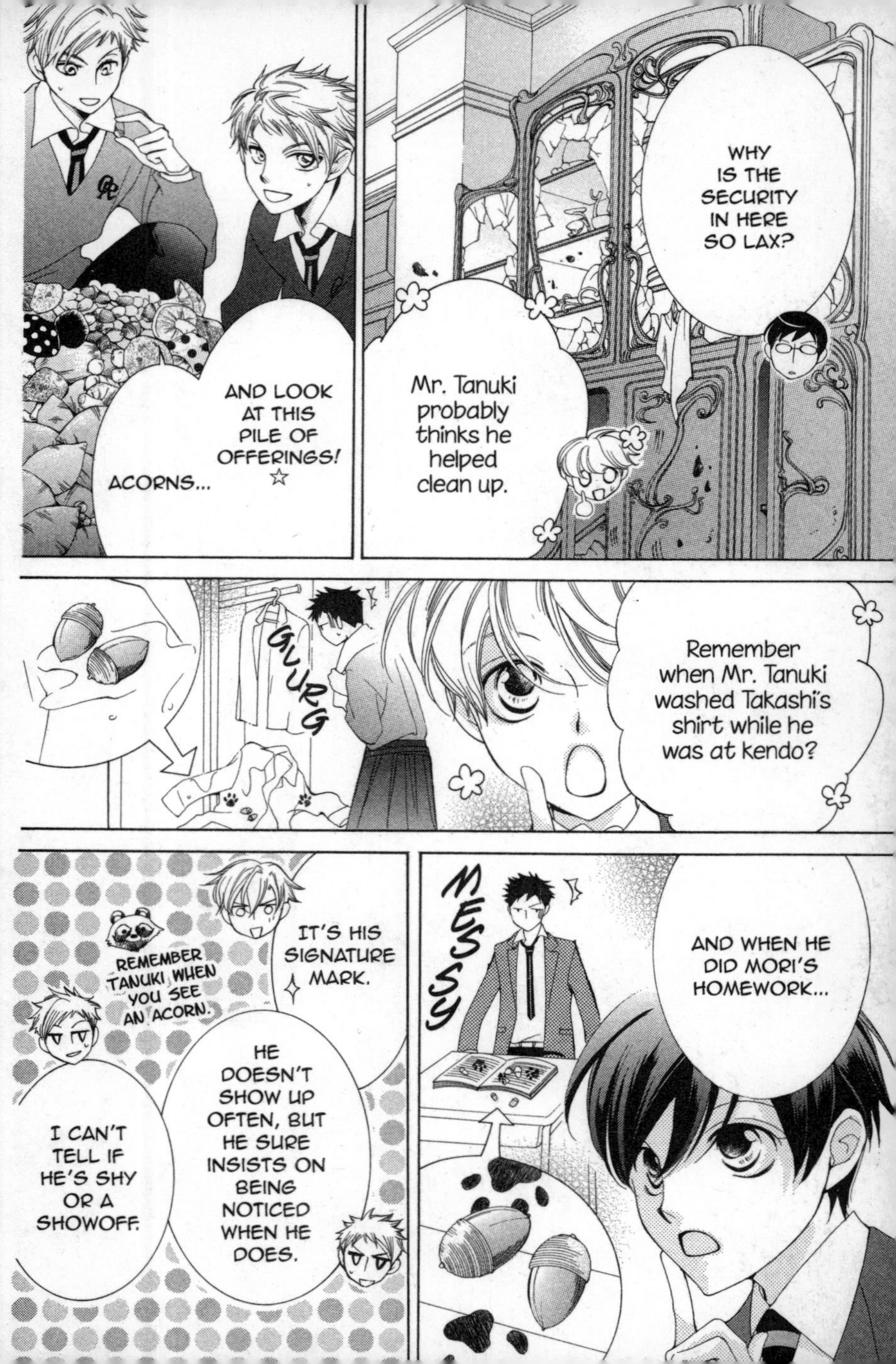
WHY IS THE SECURITY IN HERE SO LAX?
Mr. Tanuki probably thinks he helped clean up.
AND LOOK AT THIS PILE OF OFFERINGS! ☆
ACORNS...
Remember when Mr. Tanuki washed Takashi's shirt while he was at kendo?
GUURG
AND WHEN HE DID MORI'S HOMEWORK...
MESSY
IT'S HIS SIGNATURE MARK.
REMEMBER TANUKI WHEN YOU SEE AN ACORN.
HE DOESN'T SHOW UP OFTEN, BUT HE SURE INSISTS ON BEING NOTICED WHEN HE DOES.
I CAN'T TELL IF HE'S SHY OR A SHOWOFF.

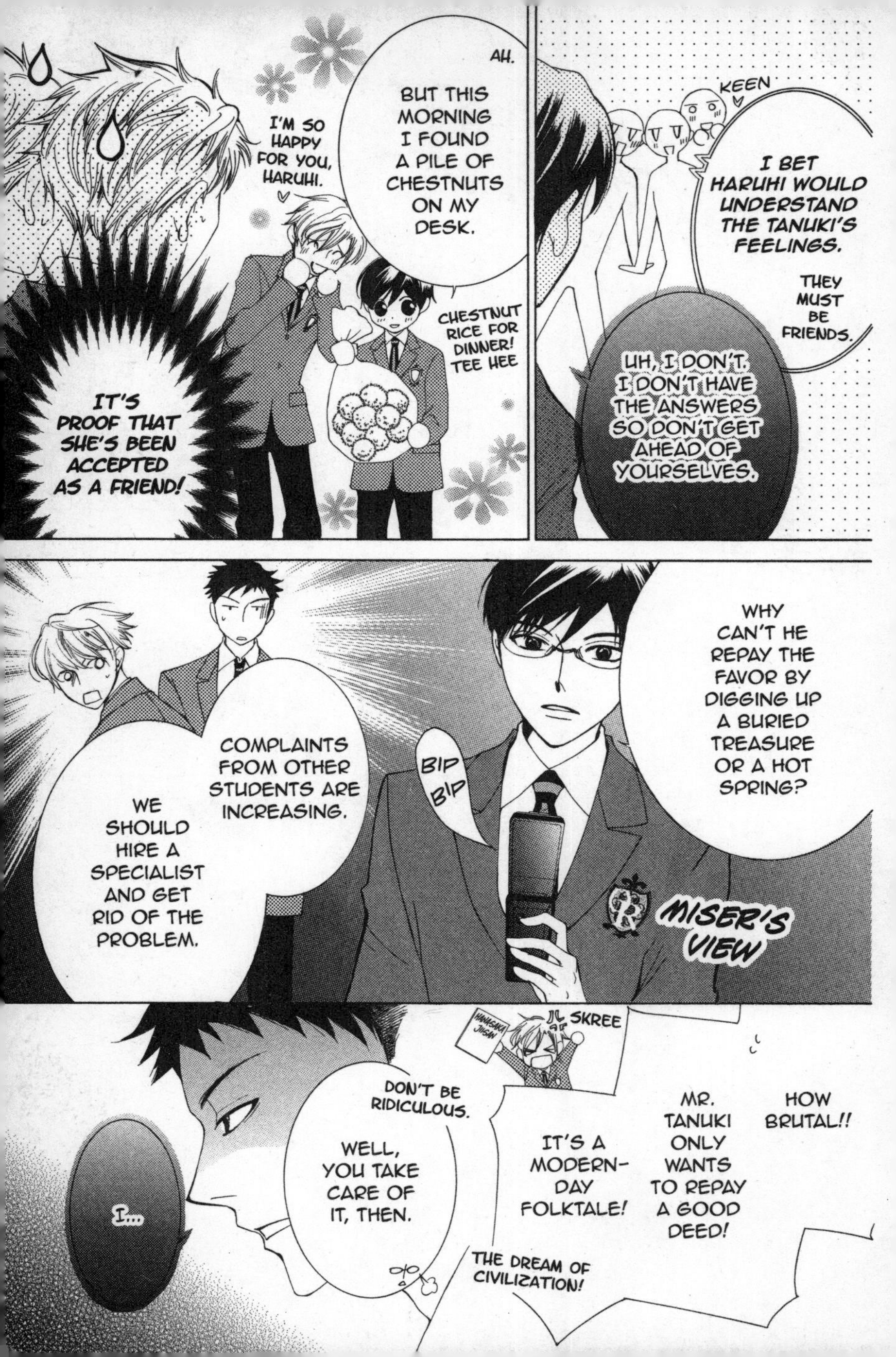
KEEN
I BET HARUHI WOULD UNDERSTAND THE TANUKI'S FEELINGS.
THEY MUST BE FRIENDS.
UH, I DON'T. I DON'T HAVE THE ANSWERS SO DON'T GET AHEAD OF YOURSELVES.
AH.
BUT THIS MORNING I FOUND A PILE OF CHESTNUTS ON MY DESK.
I'M SO HAPPY FOR YOU, HARUHI.
CHESTNUT RICE FOR DINNER! TEE HEE
IT'S PROOF THAT SHE'S BEEN ACCEPTED AS A FRIEND!
WHY CAN'T HE REPAY THE FAVOR BY DIGGING UP A BURIED TREASURE OR A HOT SPRING?
BIP BIP
MISER'S VIEW
COMPLAINTS FROM OTHER STUDENTS ARE INCREASING.
WE SHOULD HIRE A SPECIALIST AND GET RID OF THE PROBLEM.
SKREE
HOW BRUTAL!!
MR. TANUKI ONLY WANTS TO REPAY A GOOD DEED!
IT'S A MODERN-DAY FOLKTALE!
THE DREAM OF CIVILIZATION!
DON'T BE RIDICULOUS.
WELL, YOU TAKE CARE OF IT, THEN.
I...

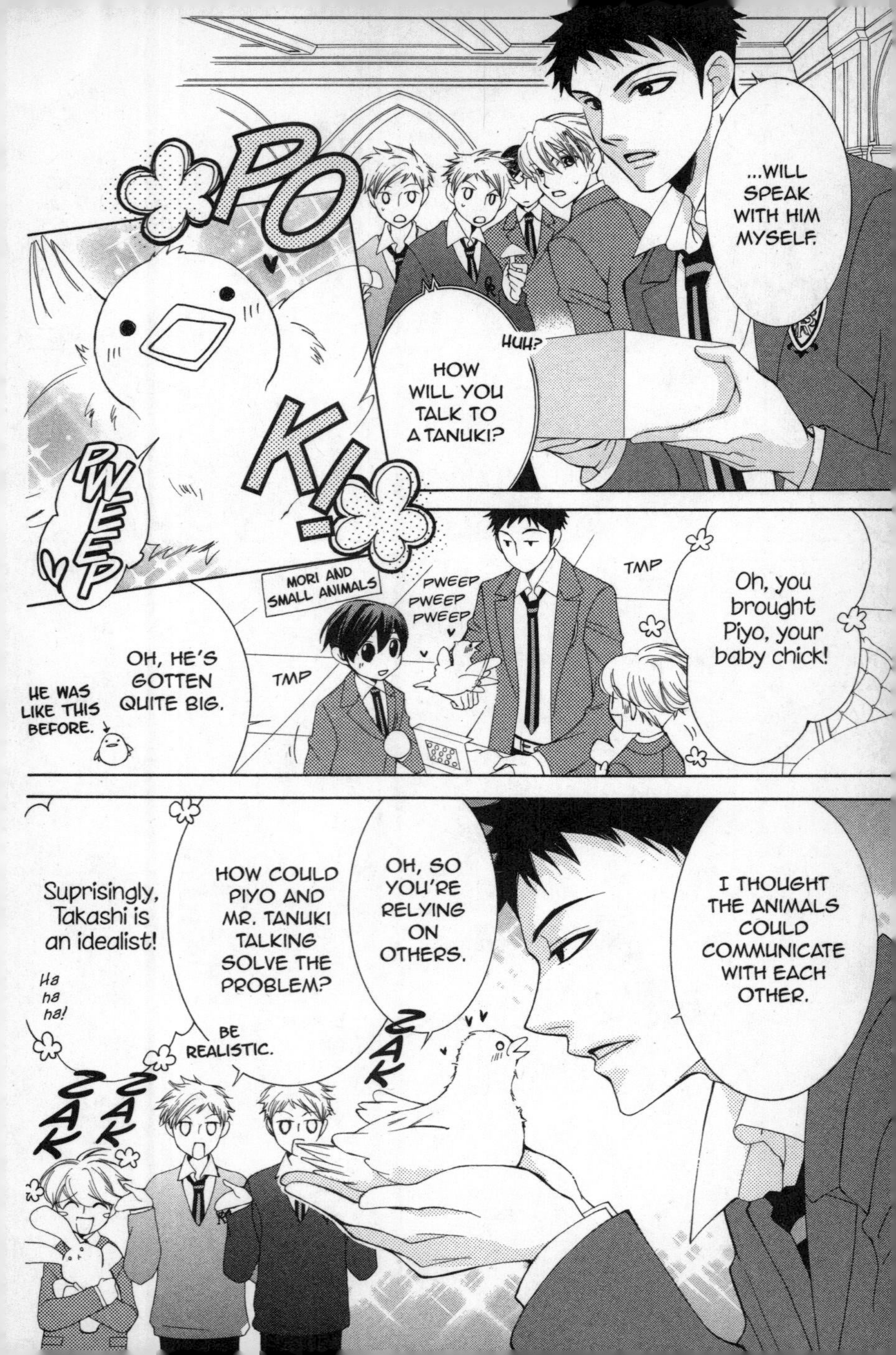
...WILL SPEAK WITH HIM MYSELF.
HUH?
HOW WILL YOU TALK TO A TANUKI?
POKI!
PWEEP
Oh, you brought Piyo, your baby chick!
TMP
PWEEP PWEEP PWEEP
TMP
MORI AND SMALL ANIMALS
OH, HE'S GOTTEN QUITE BIG.
HE WAS LIKE THIS BEFORE.
I THOUGHT THE ANIMALS COULD COMMUNICATE WITH EACH OTHER.
OH, SO YOU'RE RELYING ON OTHERS.
ZAK
HOW COULD PIYO AND MR. TANUKI TALKING SOLVE THE PROBLEM?
BE REALISTIC.
Suprisingly, Takashi is an idealist!
Ha ha ha!
ZAK
ZAK

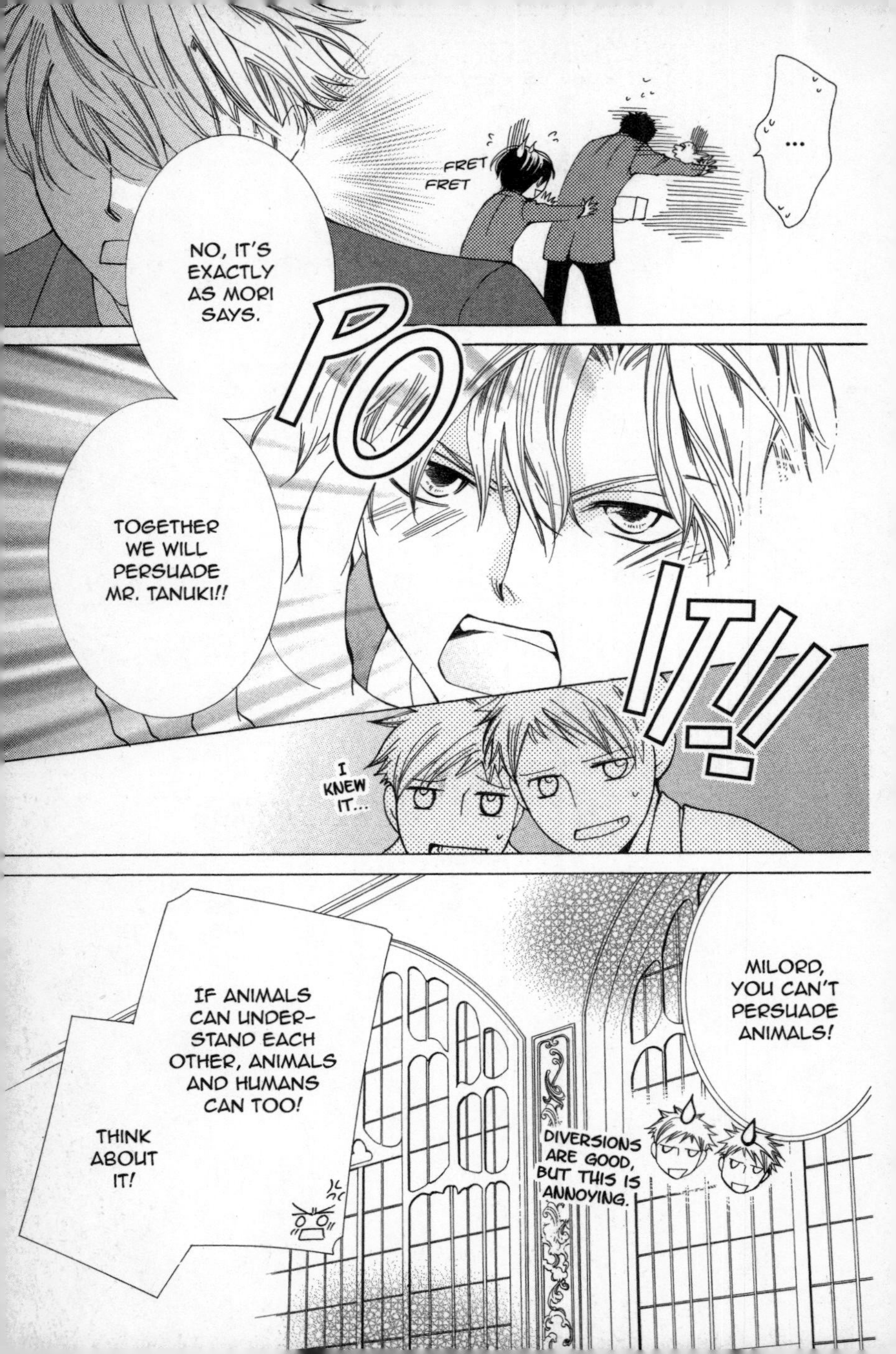
...
FRET FRET
NO, IT'S EXACTLY AS MORI SAYS.
TOGETHER WE WILL PERSUADE MR. TANUKI!!
POIT!!
I KNEW IT...
MILORD, YOU CAN'T PERSUADE ANIMALS!
DIVERSIONS ARE GOOD, BUT THIS IS ANNOYING.
IF ANIMALS CAN UNDER-STAND EACH OTHER, ANIMALS AND HUMANS CAN TOO!
THINK ABOUT IT!

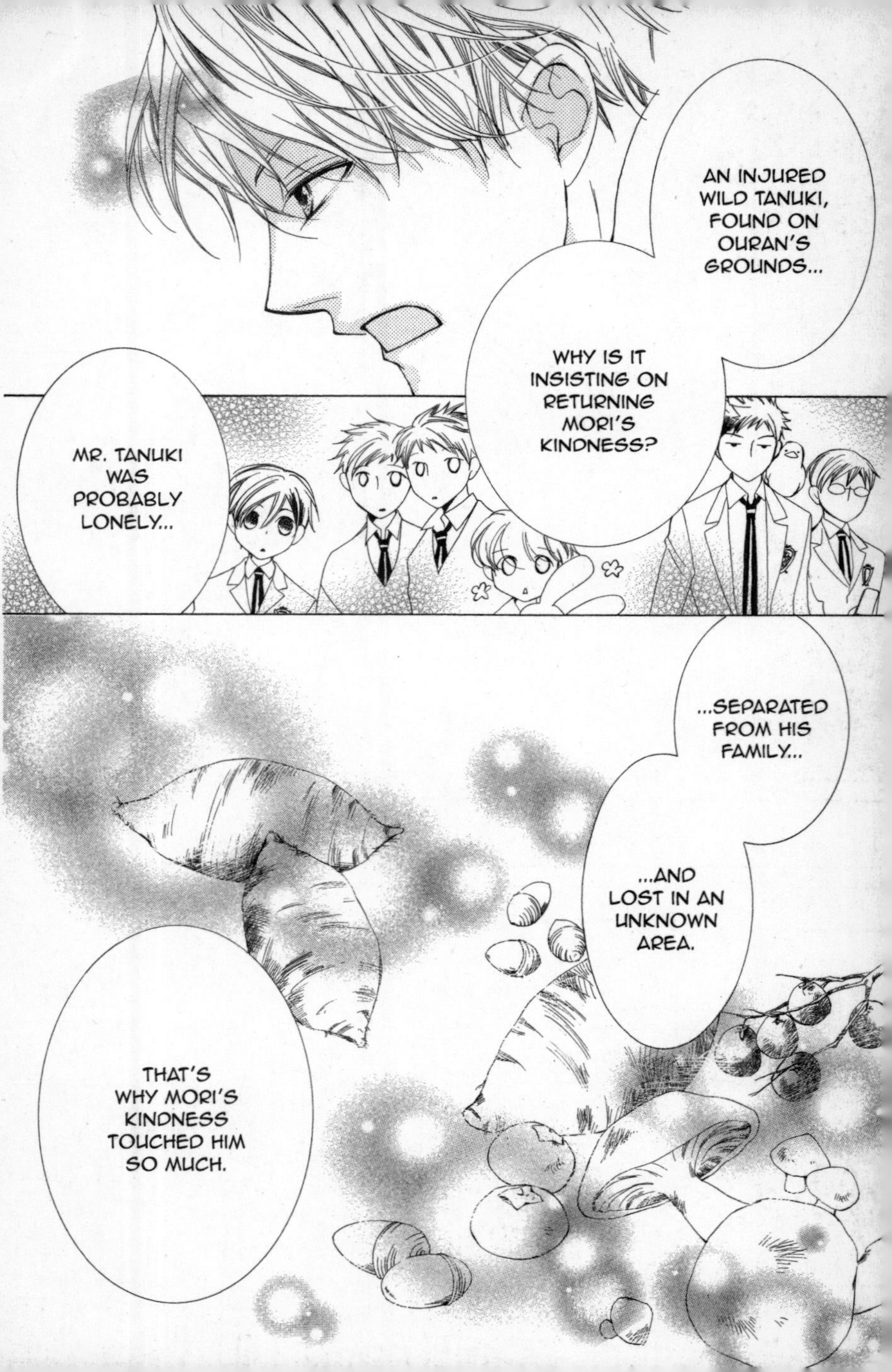
AN INJURED WILD TANUKI, FOUND ON OURAN'S GROUNDS...
WHY IS IT INSISTING ON RETURNING MORI'S KINDNESS?
MR. TANUKI WAS PROBABLY LONELY...
...SEPARATED FROM HIS FAMILY...
...AND LOST IN AN UNKNOWN AREA.
THAT'S WHY MORI'S KINDNESS TOUCHED HIM SO MUCH.

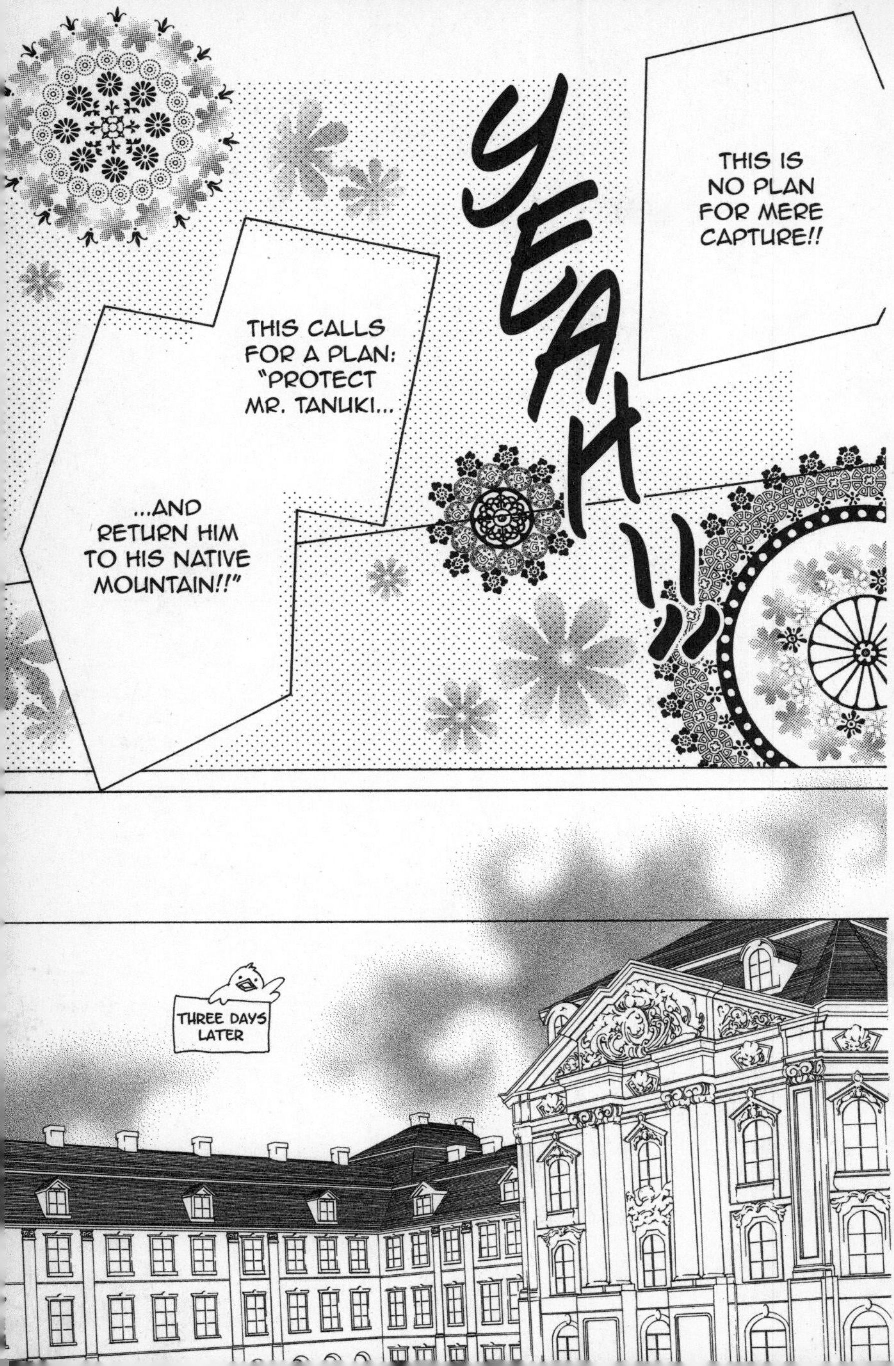
THIS IS NO PLAN FOR MERE CAPTURE!!
YEAH!!!
THIS CALLS FOR A PLAN: "PROTECT MR. TANUKI...
...AND RETURN HIM TO HIS NATIVE MOUNTAIN!!"
THREE DAYS LATER

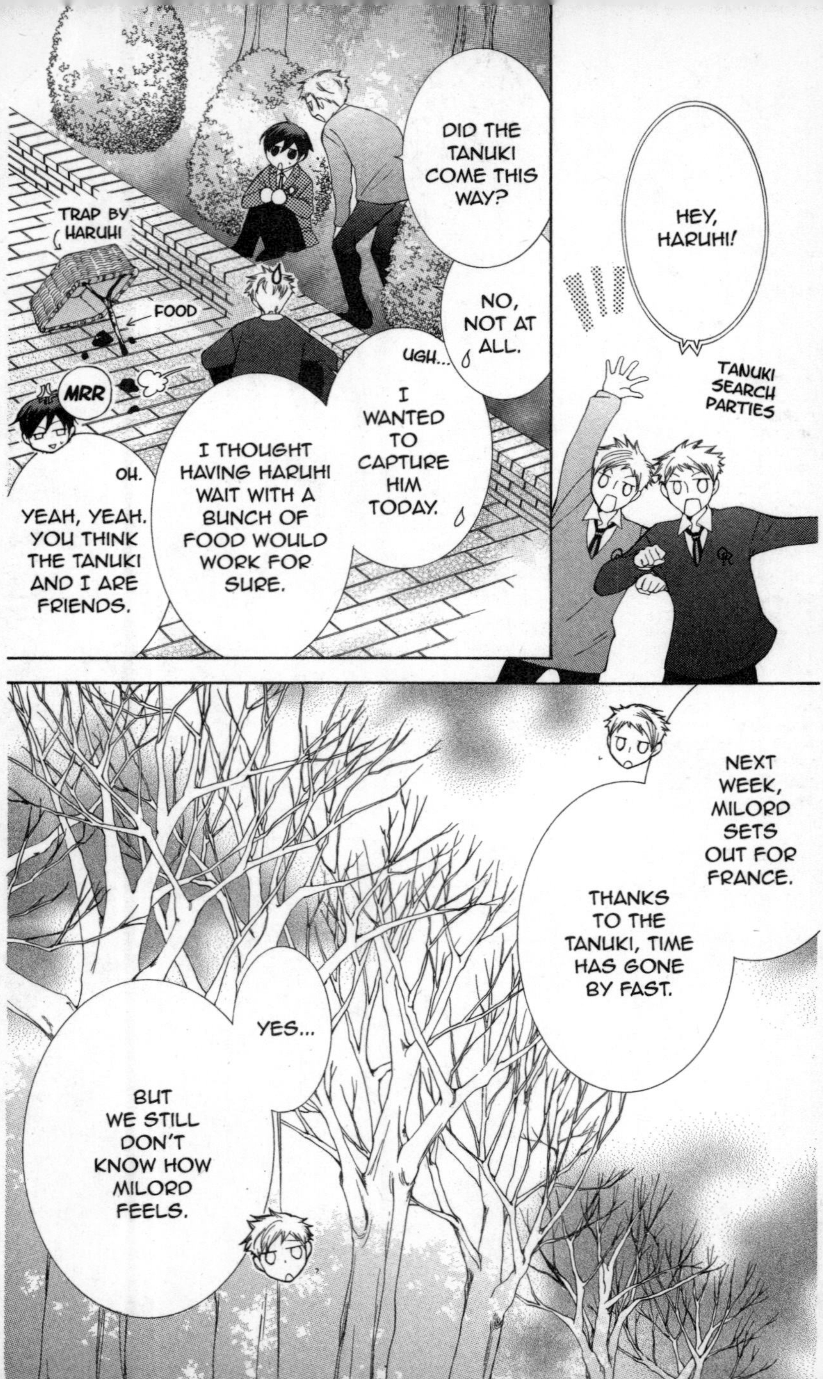
HEY, HARUHI!
TANUKI SEARCH PARTIES
DID THE TANUKI COME THIS WAY?
NO, NOT AT ALL.
TRAP BY HARUHI
FOOD
UGH...
I WANTED TO CAPTURE HIM TODAY.
I THOUGHT HAVING HARUHI WAIT WITH A BUNCH OF FOOD WOULD WORK FOR SURE.
MRR
OH.
YEAH, YEAH. YOU THINK THE TANUKI AND I ARE FRIENDS.
NEXT WEEK, MILORD SETS OUT FOR FRANCE.
THANKS TO THE TANUKI, TIME HAS GONE BY FAST.
YES...
BUT WE STILL DON'T KNOW HOW MILORD FEELS.

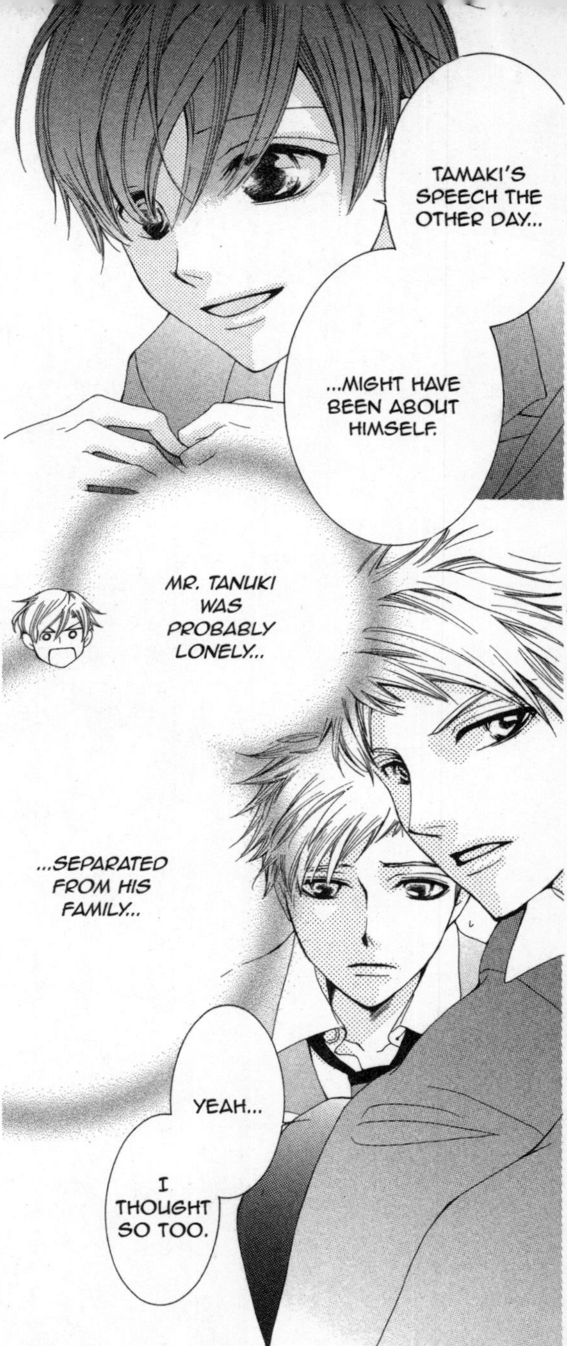
TAMAKI'S SPEECH THE OTHER DAY...
...MIGHT HAVE BEEN ABOUT HIMSELF.
MR. TANUKI WAS PROBABLY LONELY...
...SEPARATED FROM HIS FAMILY...
YEAH...
I THOUGHT SO TOO.

4

BETWEEN EPISODES 50 AND 51, I TOOK A RESEARCH TRIP TO **FRANCE** WITH YUI FROM MY STAFF!

I HAD ORIGINALLY PLANNED TO GO LAST FALL, BUT I WAS WORRIED ABOUT MY HEALTH AND PUT IT OFF. (THINKING A DOMESTIC TRIP WOULD BE BETTER, I WENT TO OKINAWA AND HUIS TEN BOSCH.)

← I GUESS I WAS PLENTY HEALTHY...

AFTER THAT, I RECEIVED SO MUCH WORK I THOUGHT I WOULDN'T HAVE TIME TO TAKE A TRIP, BUT I MADE IT WORK SOMEHOW.

WELL, IT WAS SUCH A WHIRLWIND TRIP THAT I GOT QUITE TIRED, BUT FRANCE WAS SO MUCH FUN! NICE IS THE BEST!! PARIS IS THE BEST TOO!!

FLOATING DOWN THE SEINE IN A BOAT FELT SO WONDERFUL!!

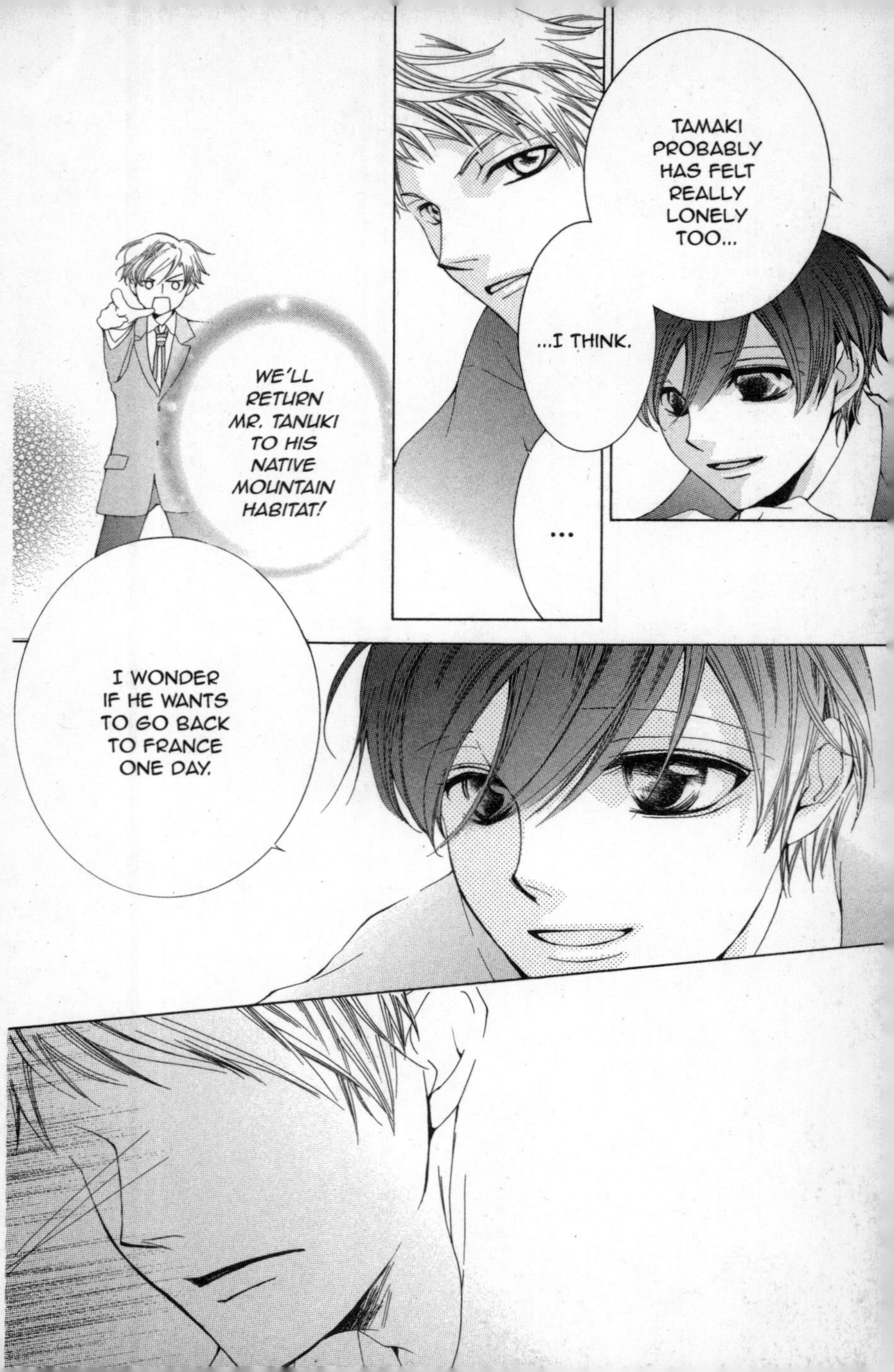
TAMAKI PROBABLY HAS FELT REALLY LONELY TOO...
...I THINK.
...
WE'LL RETURN MR. TANUKI TO HIS NATIVE MOUNTAIN HABITAT!
I WONDER IF HE WANTS TO GO BACK TO FRANCE ONE DAY.

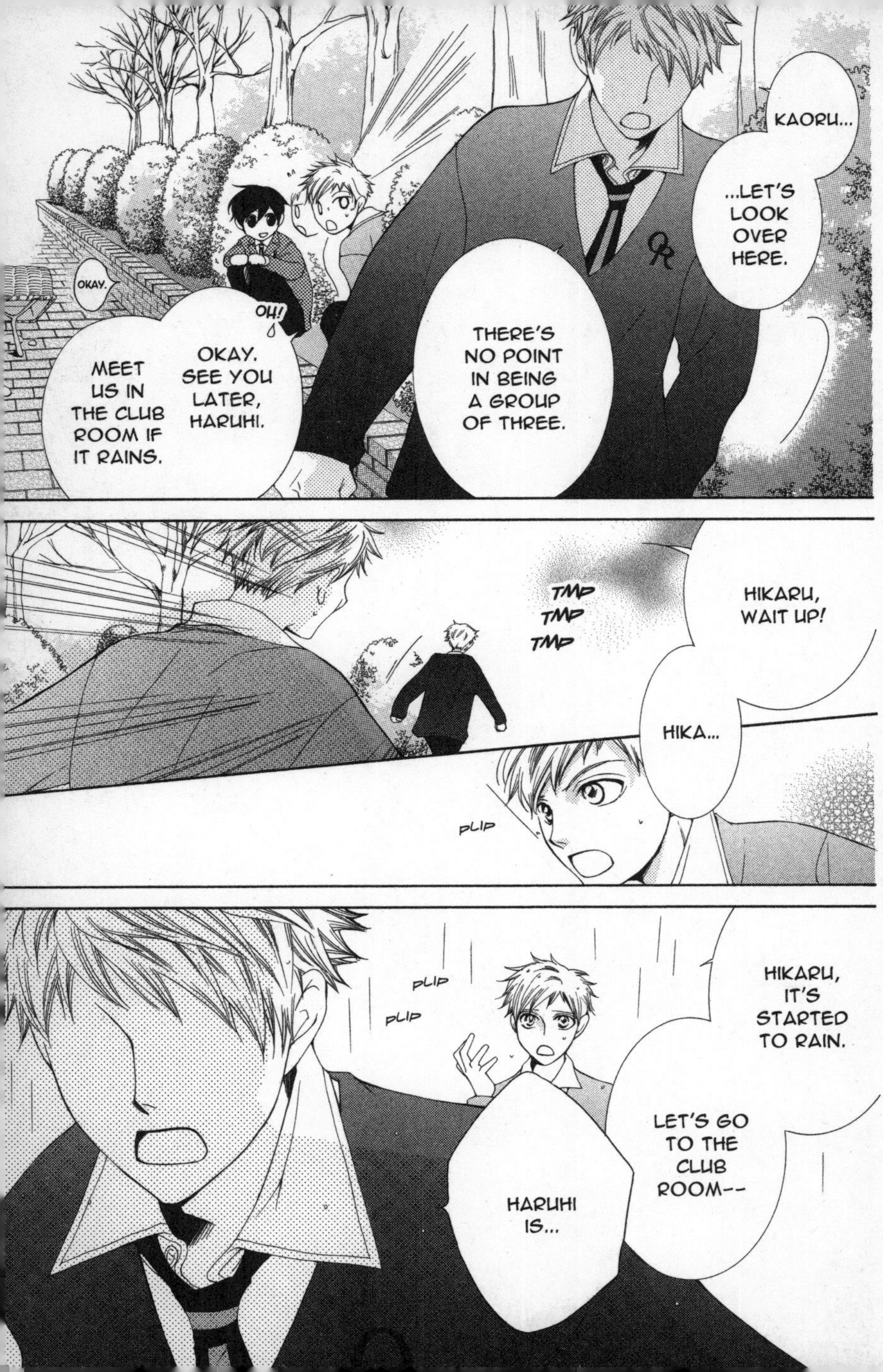
KAORU...
...LET'S LOOK OVER HERE.
THERE'S NO POINT IN BEING A GROUP OF THREE.
OKAY. SEE YOU LATER, HARUHI.
OH!
MEET US IN THE CLUB ROOM IF IT RAINS.
OKAY.
HIKARU, WAIT UP!
TMP TMP TMP
HIKA...
PLIP
HIKARU, IT'S STARTED TO RAIN.
LET'S GO TO THE CLUB ROOM--
HARUHI IS...
PLIP
PLIP

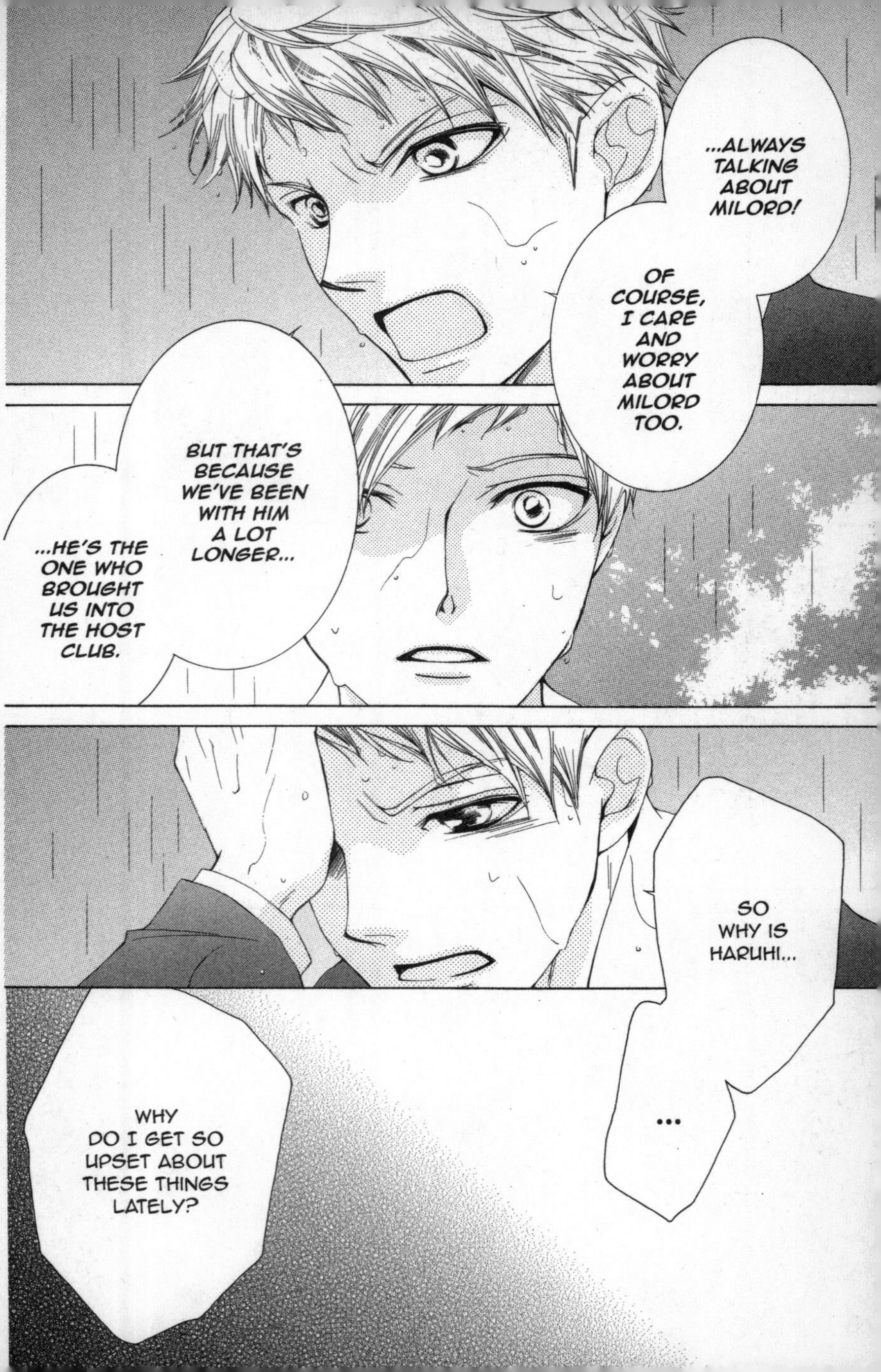
...ALWAYS TALKING ABOUT MILORD!
OF COURSE, I CARE AND WORRY ABOUT MILORD TOO.
BUT THAT'S BECAUSE WE'VE BEEN WITH HIM A LOT LONGER...
...HE'S THE ONE WHO BROUGHT US INTO THE HOST CLUB.
SO WHY IS HARUHI...
...
WHY DO I GET SO UPSET ABOUT THESE THINGS LATELY?

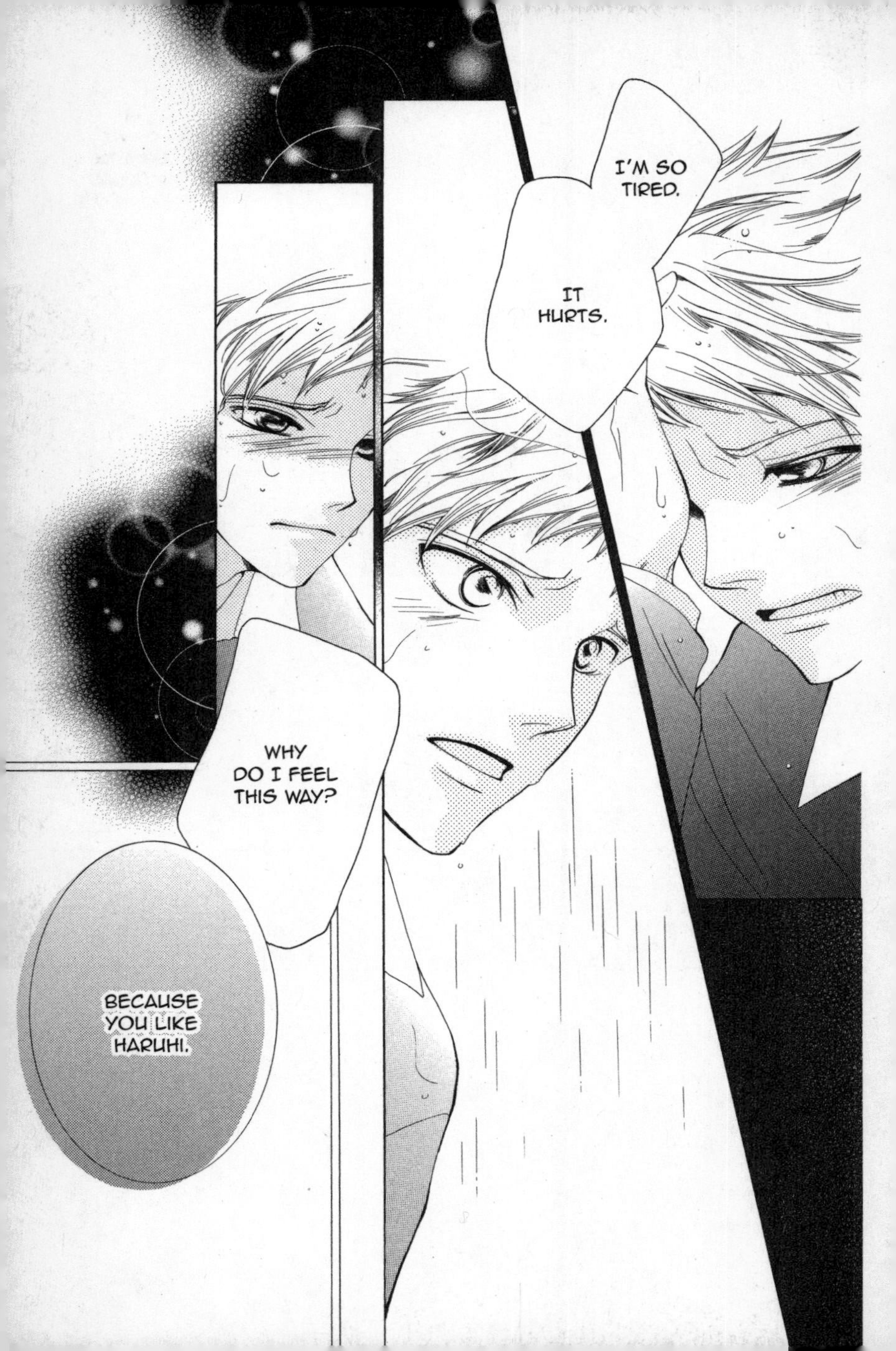
I'M SO TIRED.
IT HURTS.
WHY DO I FEEL THIS WAY?
BECAUSE YOU LIKE HARUHI.

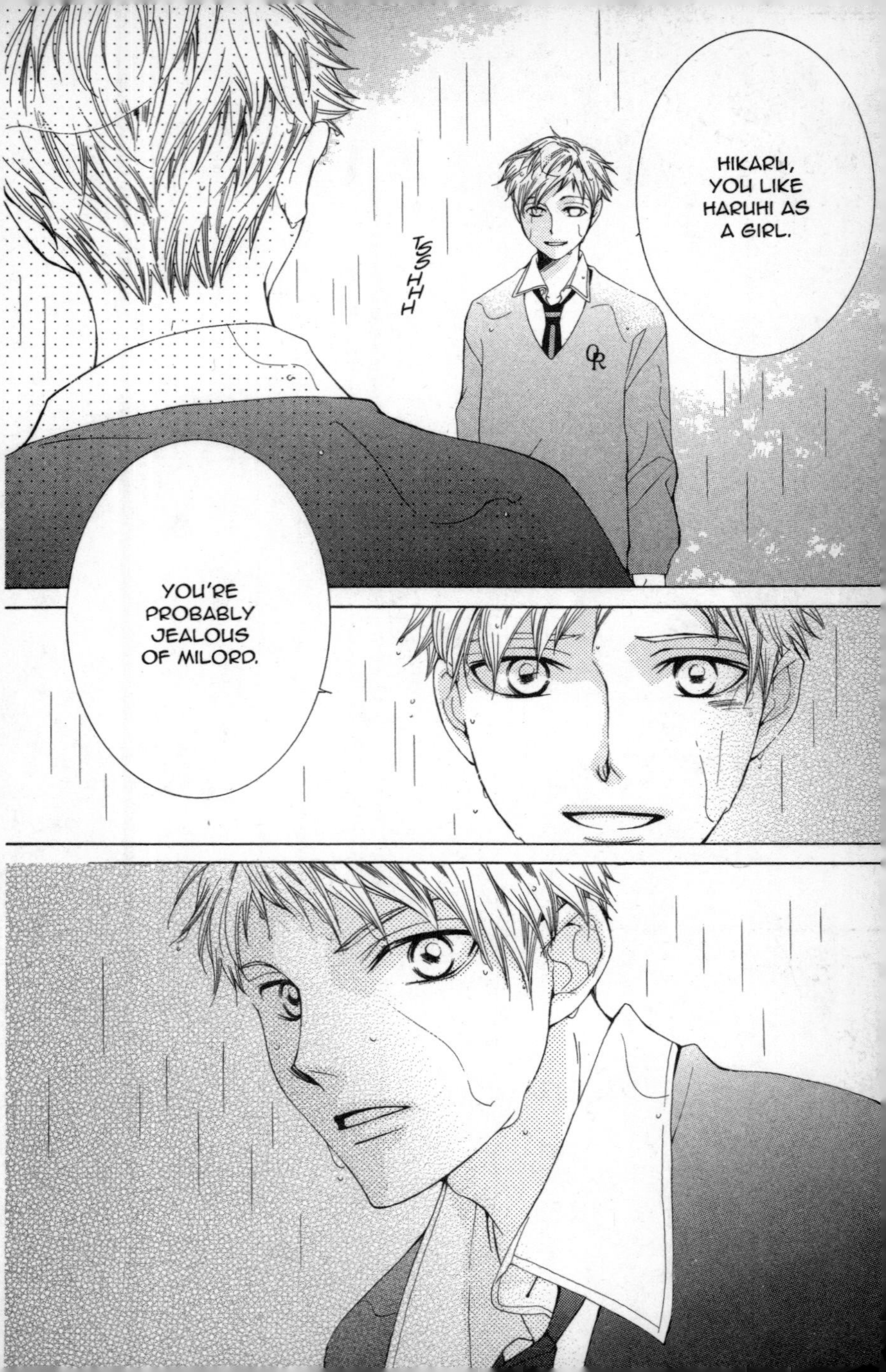
HIKARU, YOU LIKE HARUHI AS A GIRL.
TSSHHH
YOU'RE PROBABLY JEALOUS OF MILORD.

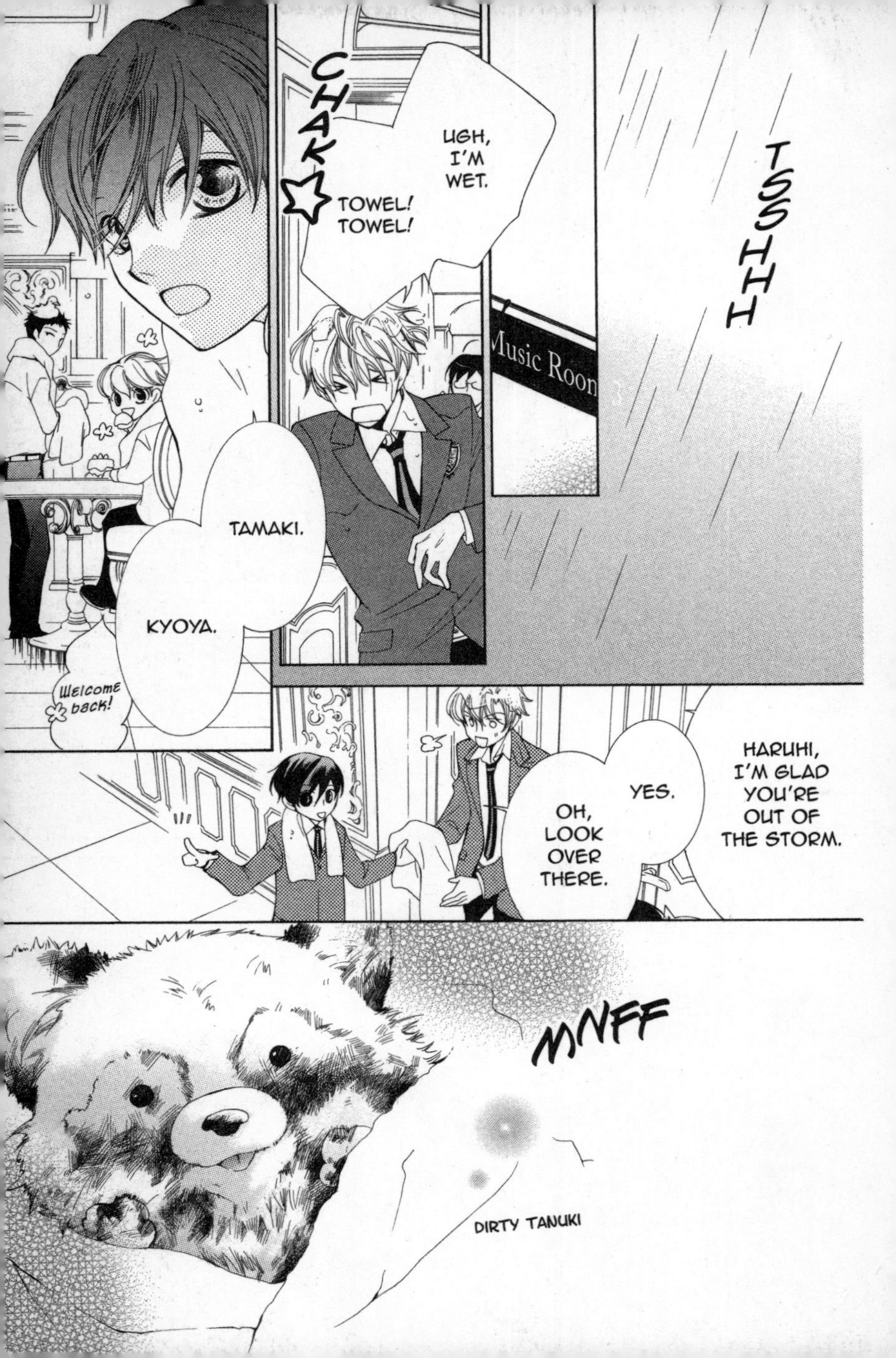
TSSHHH
CHAK
UGH, I'M WET.
TOWEL! TOWEL!
TAMAKI.
KYOYA.
Welcome back!
HARUHI, I'M GLAD YOU'RE OUT OF THE STORM.
YES.
OH, LOOK OVER THERE.
MNFF
DIRTY TANUKI

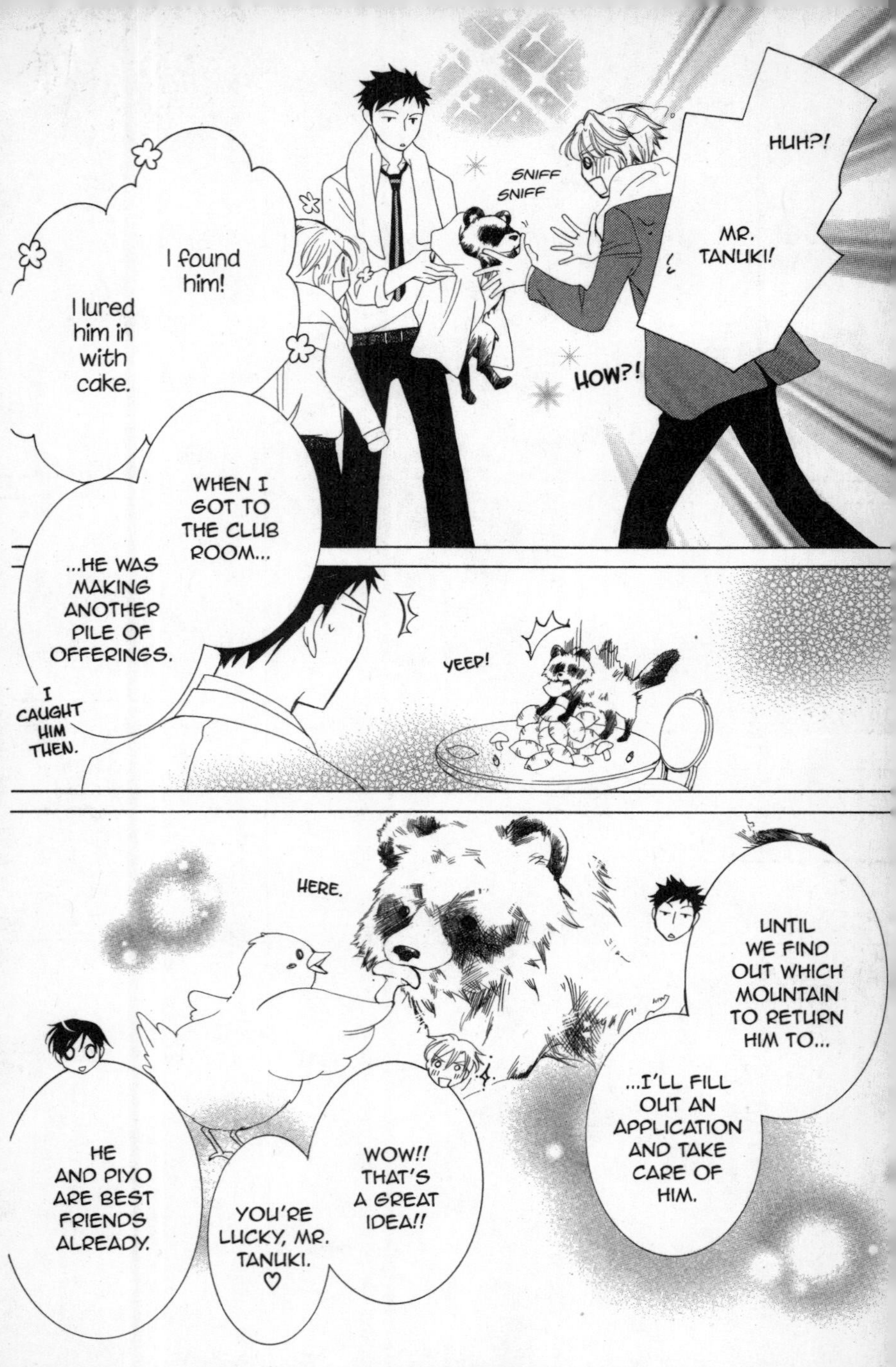
HUH?!
MR. TANUKI!
SNIFF SNIFF
HOW?!
I found him!
I lured him in with cake.
WHEN I GOT TO THE CLUB ROOM...
...HE WAS MAKING ANOTHER PILE OF OFFERINGS.
YEEP!
I CAUGHT HIM THEN.
UNTIL WE FIND OUT WHICH MOUNTAIN TO RETURN HIM TO...
...I'LL FILL OUT AN APPLICATION AND TAKE CARE OF HIM.
HERE.
WOW!! THAT'S A GREAT IDEA!!
YOU'RE LUCKY, MR. TANUKI. ♡
HE AND PIYO ARE BEST FRIENDS ALREADY.

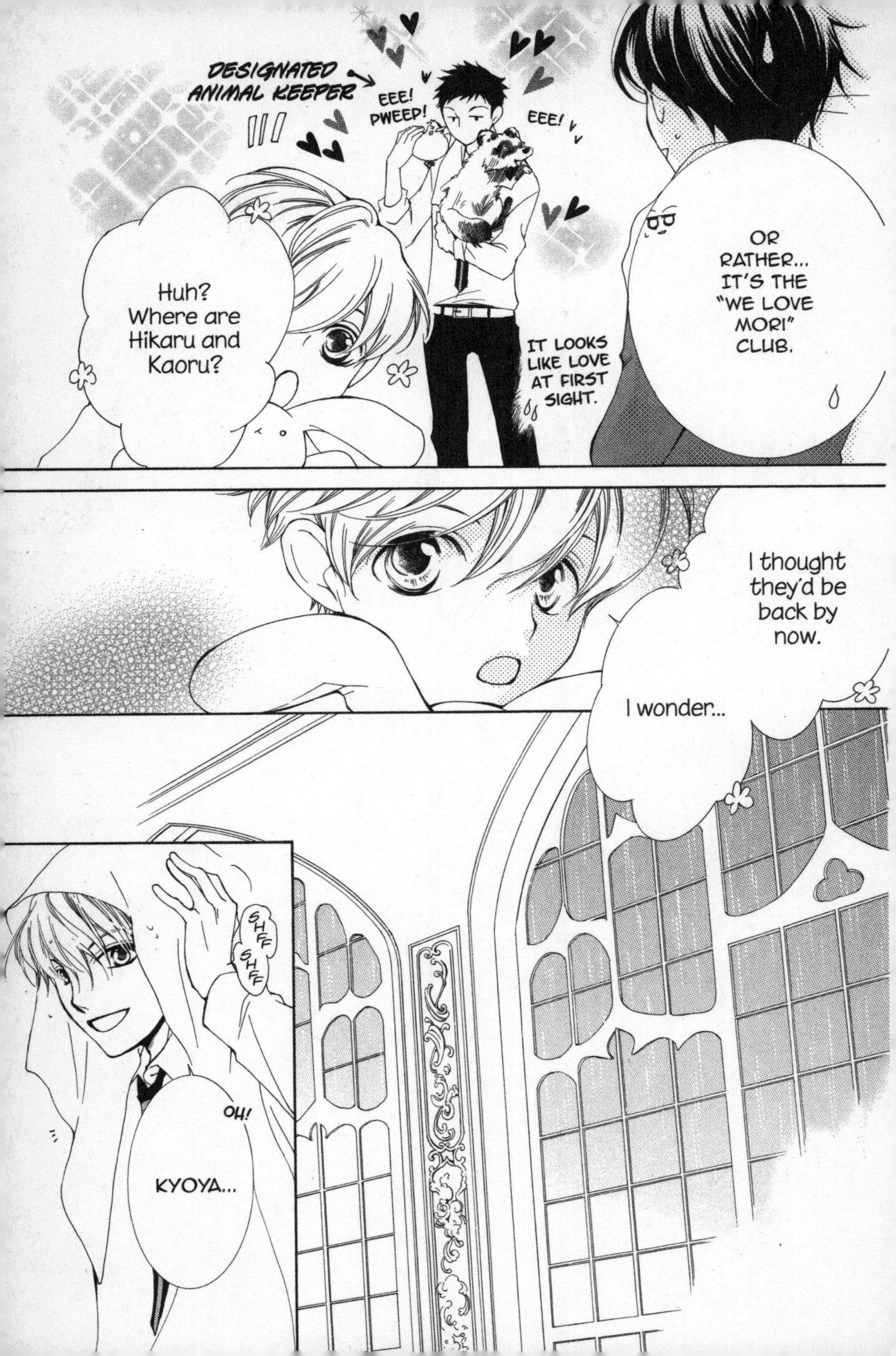
OR RATHER... IT'S THE "WE LOVE MORI" CLUB.
IT LOOKS LIKE LOVE AT FIRST SIGHT.
EEE!
EEE! PWEEP!
DESIGNATED ANIMAL KEEPER
Huh? Where are Hikaru and Kaoru?
I thought they'd be back by now.
I wonder...
SHFF SHFF
OH!
KYOYA...

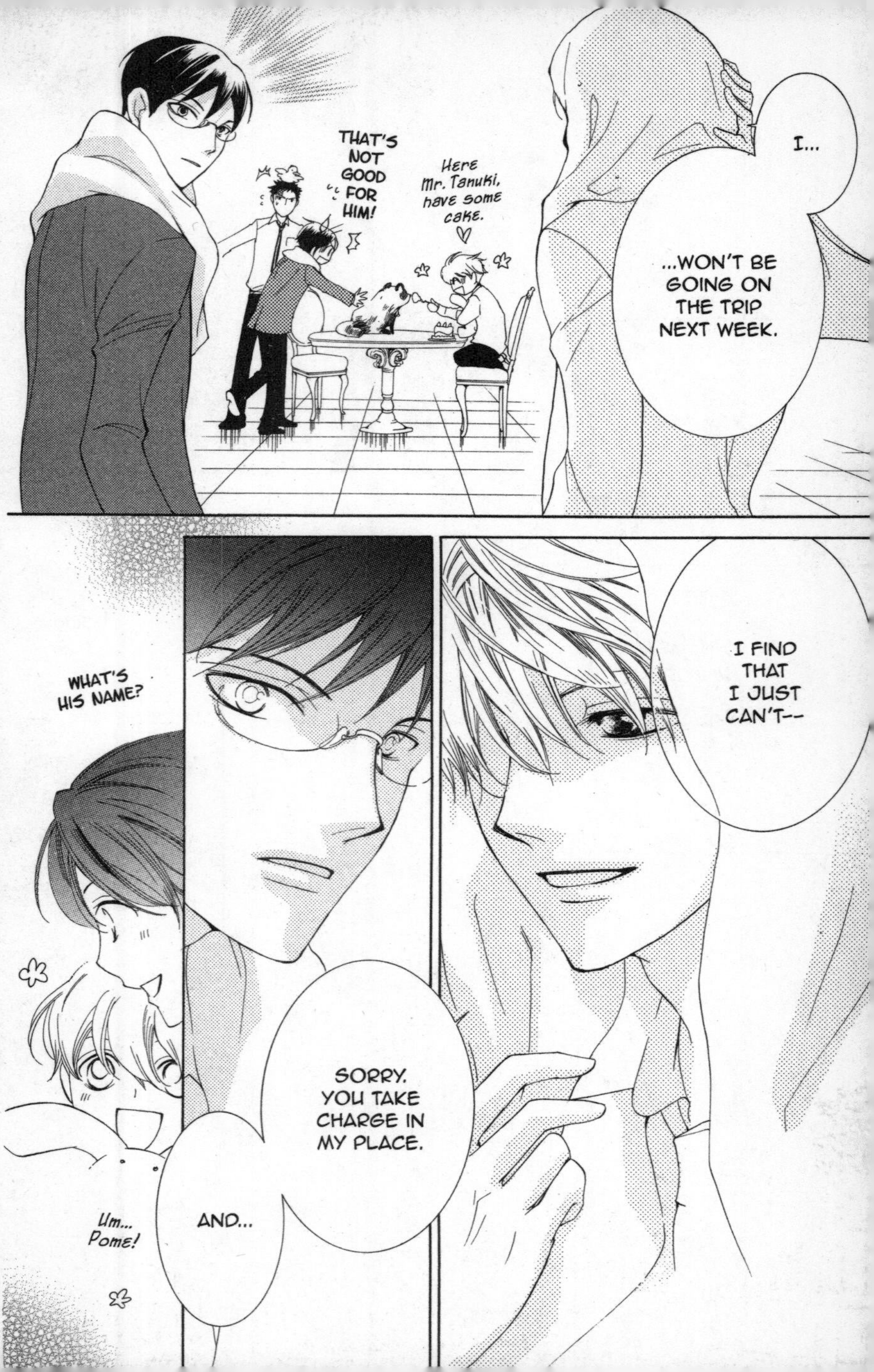
I...
...WON'T BE GOING ON THE TRIP NEXT WEEK.
Here Mr. Tanuki, have some cake.
THAT'S NOT GOOD FOR HIM!
I FIND THAT I JUST CAN'T--
SORRY. YOU TAKE CHARGE IN MY PLACE.
AND...
WHAT'S HIS NAME?
Um... Pome!

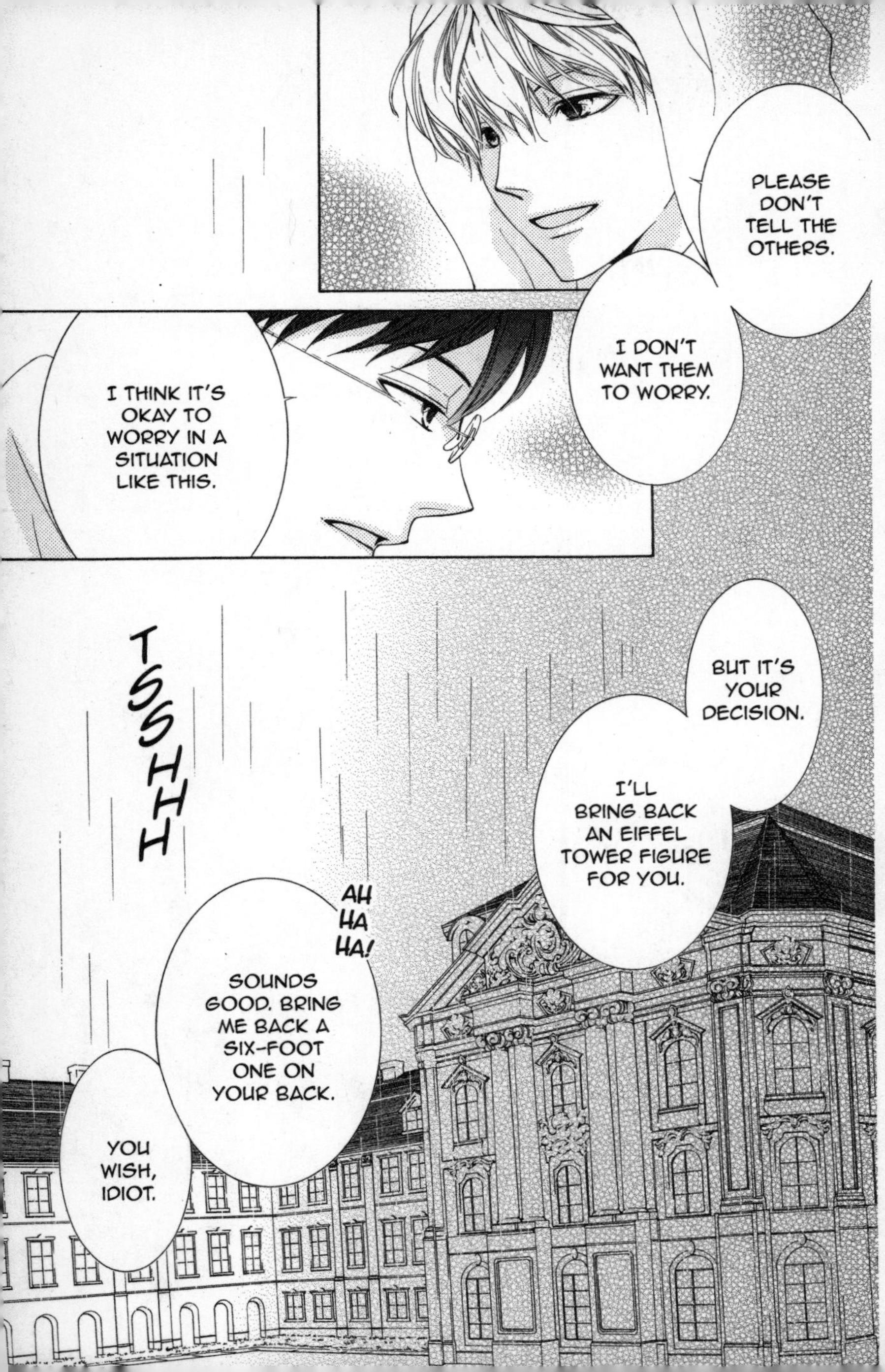
PLEASE DON'T TELL THE OTHERS.
I DON'T WANT THEM TO WORRY.
I THINK IT'S OKAY TO WORRY IN A SITUATION LIKE THIS.
BUT IT'S YOUR DECISION.
TSSHHH
I'LL BRING BACK AN EIFFEL TOWER FIGURE FOR YOU.
AH HA HA!
SOUNDS GOOD. BRING ME BACK A SIX-FOOT ONE ON YOUR BACK.
YOU WISH, IDIOT.

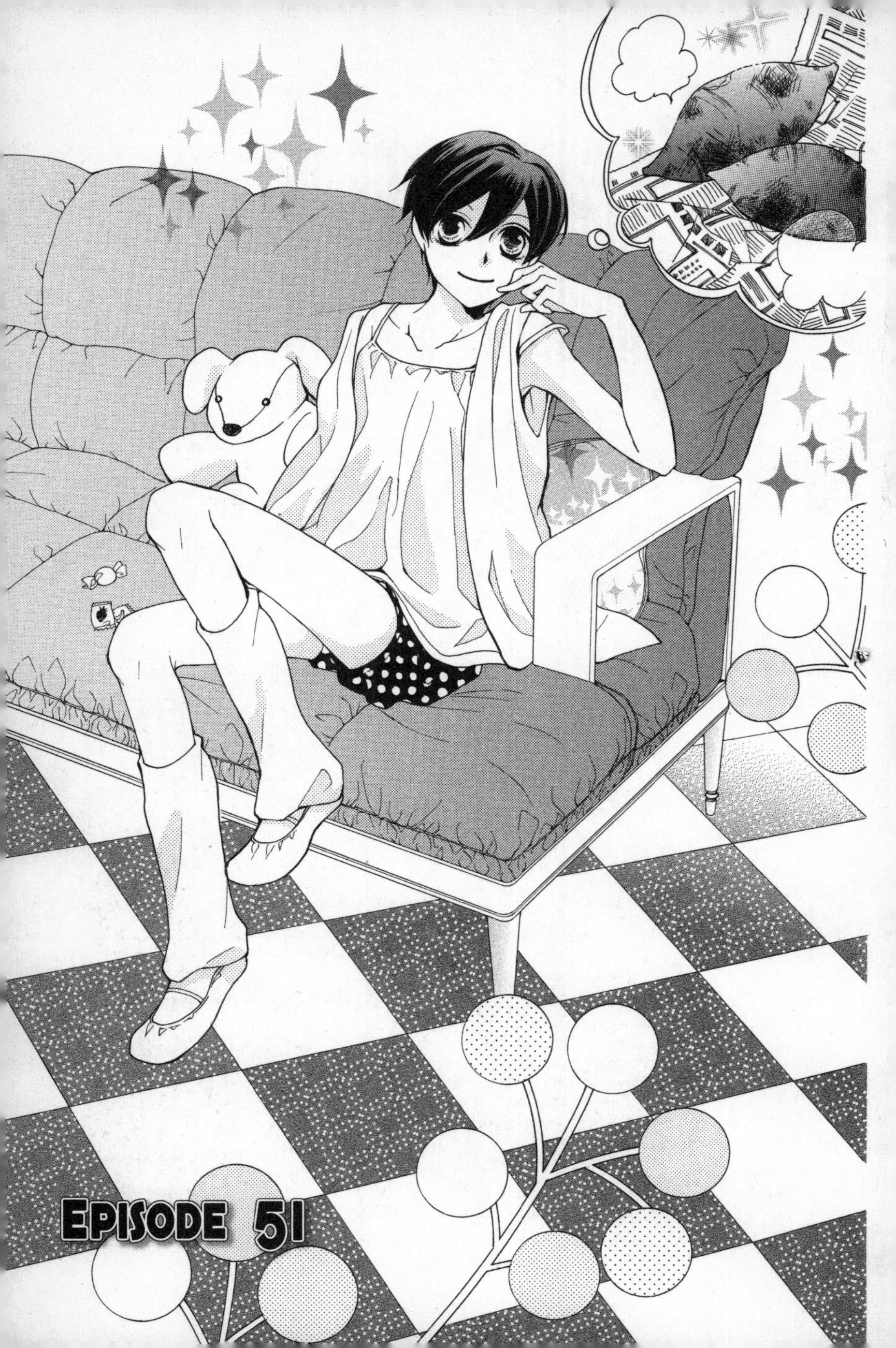
EPISODE 51

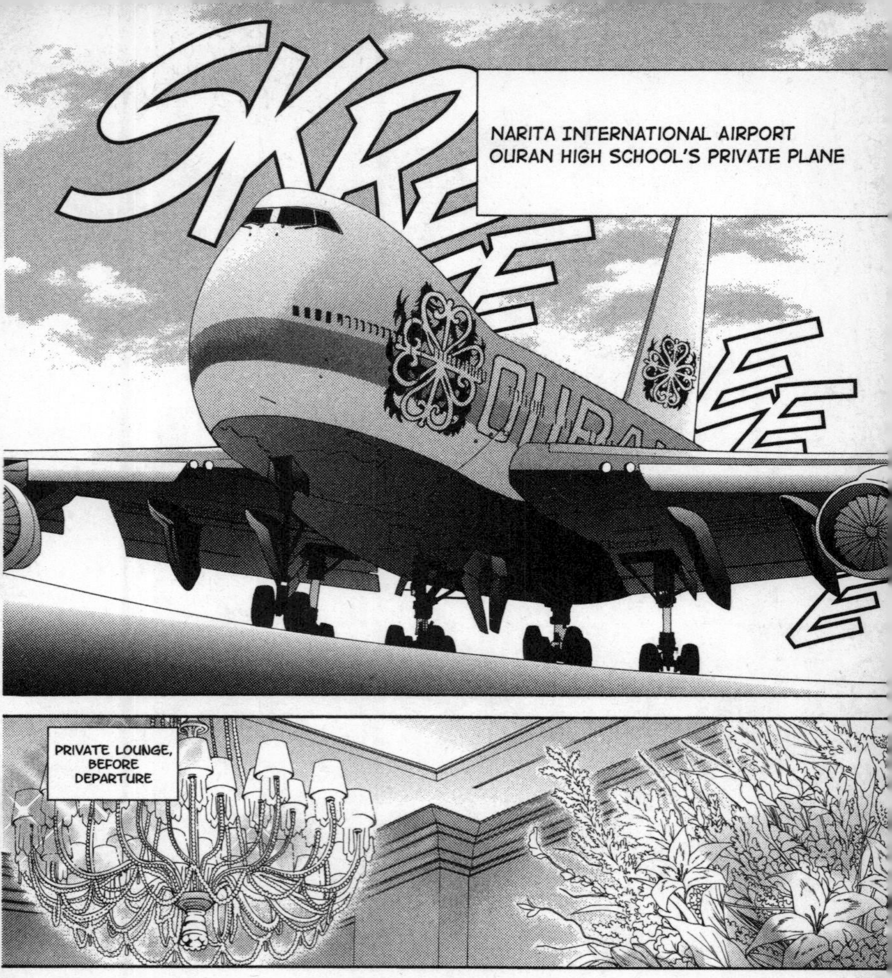
NARITA INTERNATIONAL AIRPORT
OURAN HIGH SCHOOL'S PRIVATE PLANE
SKREEEEE
PRIVATE LOUNGE, BEFORE DEPARTURE

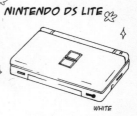

NINTENDO DS LITE

I FINALLY BOUGHT A NINTENDO DS LITE! I HAVEN'T PLAYED MUCH. I PLANNED TO DO SOME BRAIN EXERCISES, BUT I'VE GOTTEN INTO *SUPER MARIO* INSTEAD. IT'S FUN DOING THE MARIO MINI-GAME WHILE TAKING A BREAK FROM CREATING STORYBOARDS.

I'M THINKING PLAYING *ANIMAL CROSSING* NEXT.

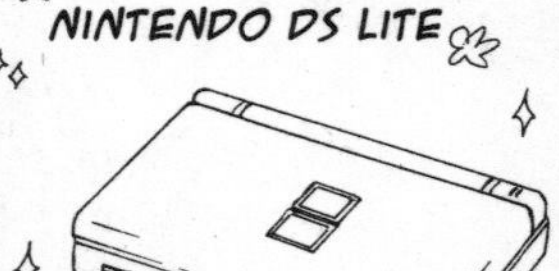
WHITE

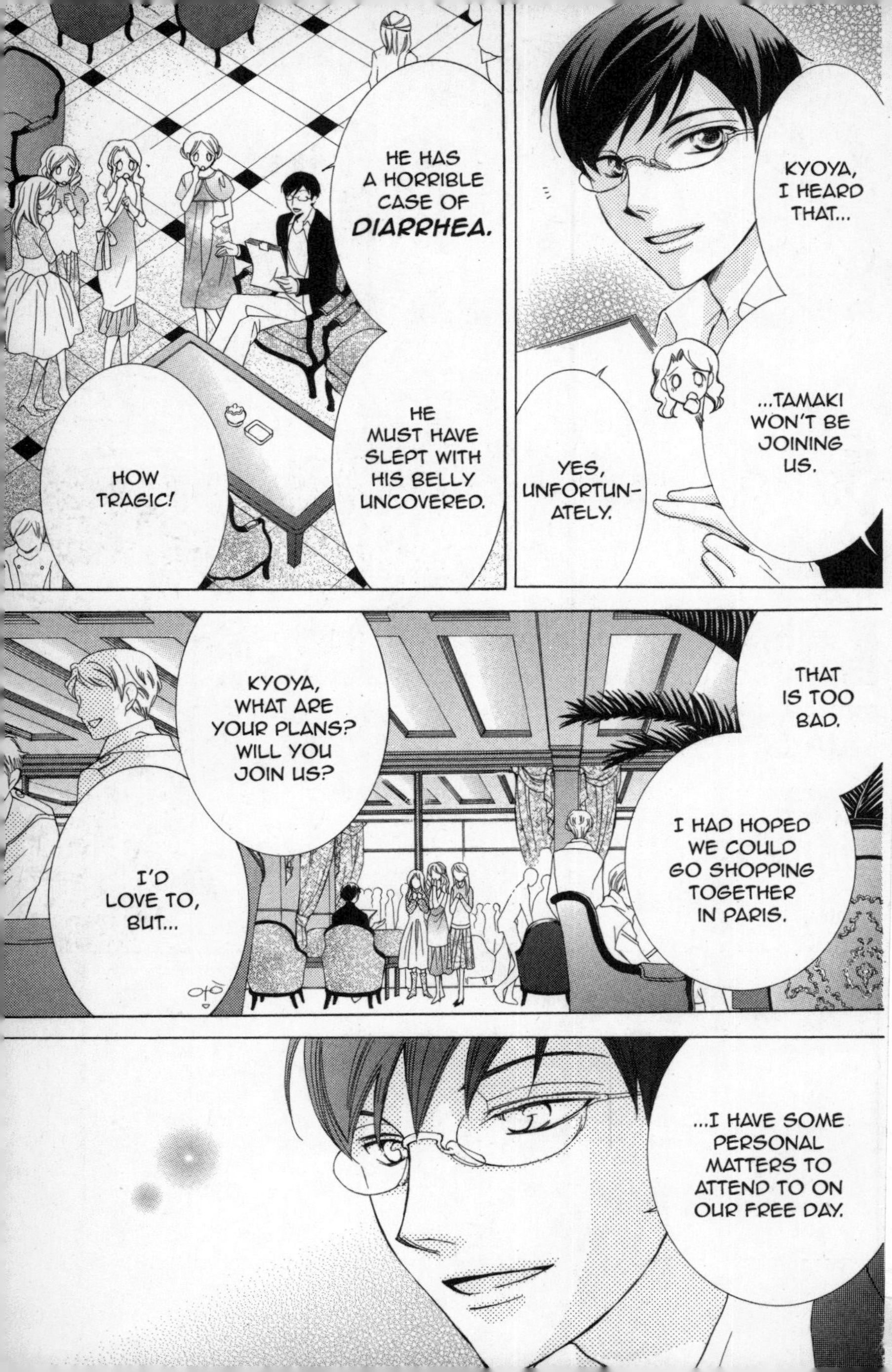
KYOYA, I HEARD THAT...
...TAMAKI WON'T BE JOINING US.
YES, UNFORTUNATELY.
HE HAS A HORRIBLE CASE OF **DIARRHEA.**
HE MUST HAVE SLEPT WITH HIS BELLY UNCOVERED.
HOW TRAGIC!
THAT IS TOO BAD.
I HAD HOPED WE COULD GO SHOPPING TOGETHER IN PARIS.
KYOYA, WHAT ARE YOUR PLANS? WILL YOU JOIN US?
I'D LOVE TO, BUT...
...I HAVE SOME PERSONAL MATTERS TO ATTEND TO ON OUR FREE DAY.

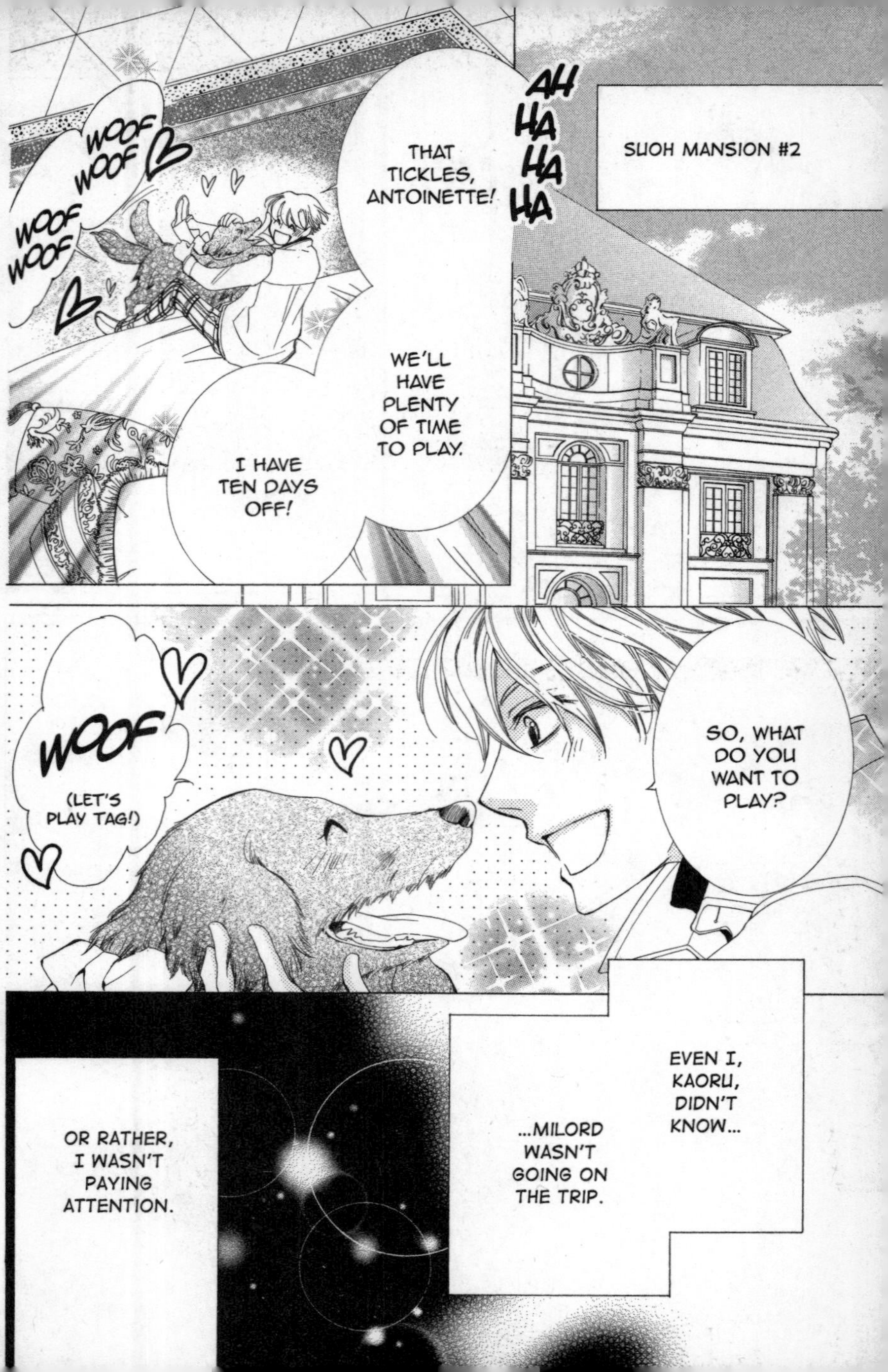

SUOH MANSION #2
AH HA HA HA
THAT TICKLES, ANTOINETTE!
WE'LL HAVE PLENTY OF TIME TO PLAY.
I HAVE TEN DAYS OFF!
WOOF WOOF
WOOF WOOF
SO, WHAT DO YOU WANT TO PLAY?
WOOF
(LET'S PLAY TAG!)
EVEN I, KAORU, DIDN'T KNOW...
...MILORD WASN'T GOING ON THE TRIP.
OR RATHER, I WASN'T PAYING ATTENTION.

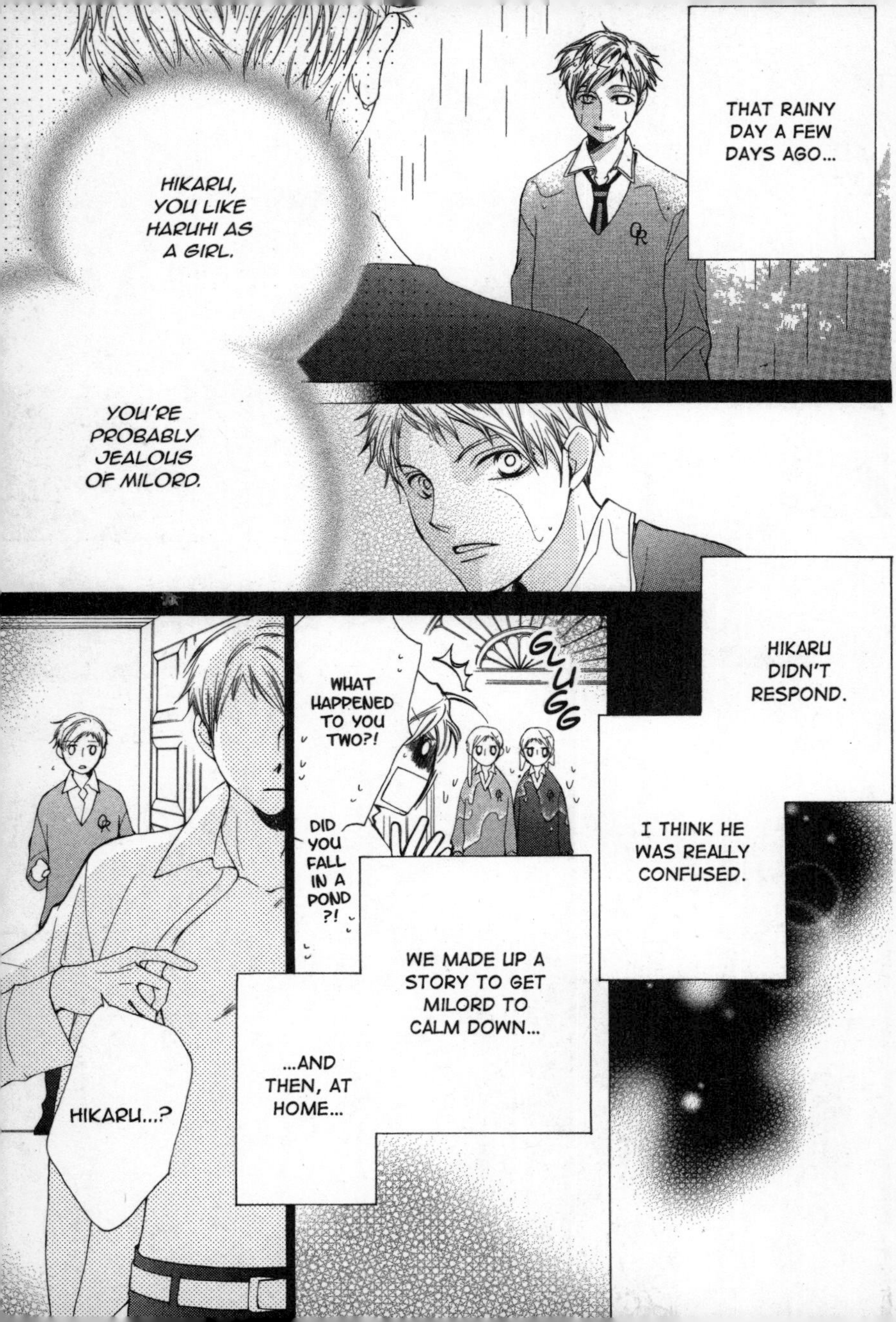
THAT RAINY DAY A FEW DAYS AGO...
HIKARU, YOU LIKE HARUHI AS A GIRL.
YOU'RE PROBABLY JEALOUS OF MILORD.
HIKARU DIDN'T RESPOND.
I THINK HE WAS REALLY CONFUSED.
GLUGG
WHAT HAPPENED TO YOU TWO?!
DID YOU FALL IN A POND?!
WE MADE UP A STORY TO GET MILORD TO CALM DOWN...
...AND THEN, AT HOME...
HIKARU...?

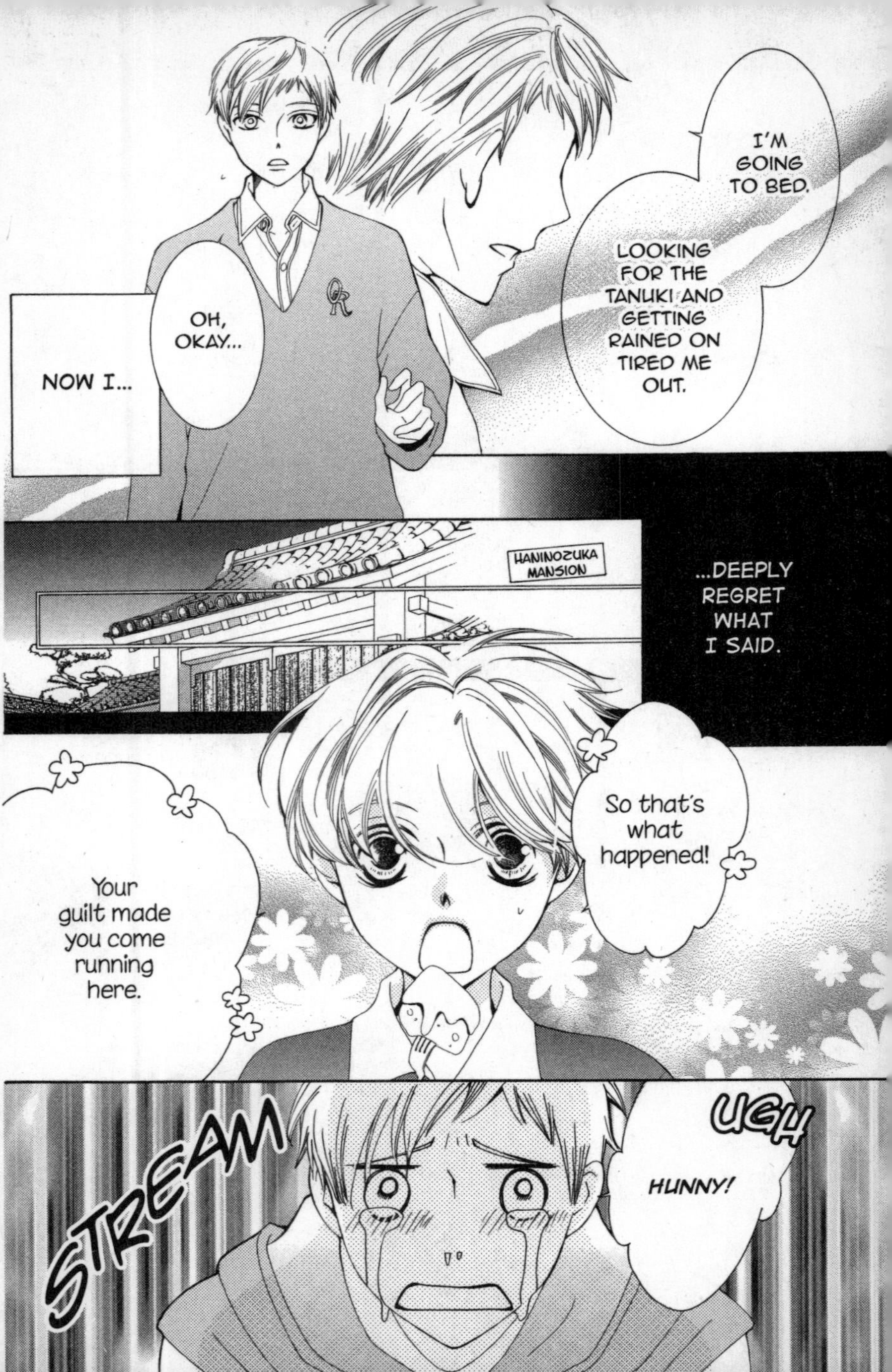
I'M GOING TO BED.
LOOKING FOR THE TANUKI AND GETTING RAINED ON TIRED ME OUT.
OH, OKAY...
NOW I...
...DEEPLY REGRET WHAT I SAID.
HANINOZUKA MANSION
So that's what happened!
Your guilt made you come running here.
UGH
HUNNY!
STREAM

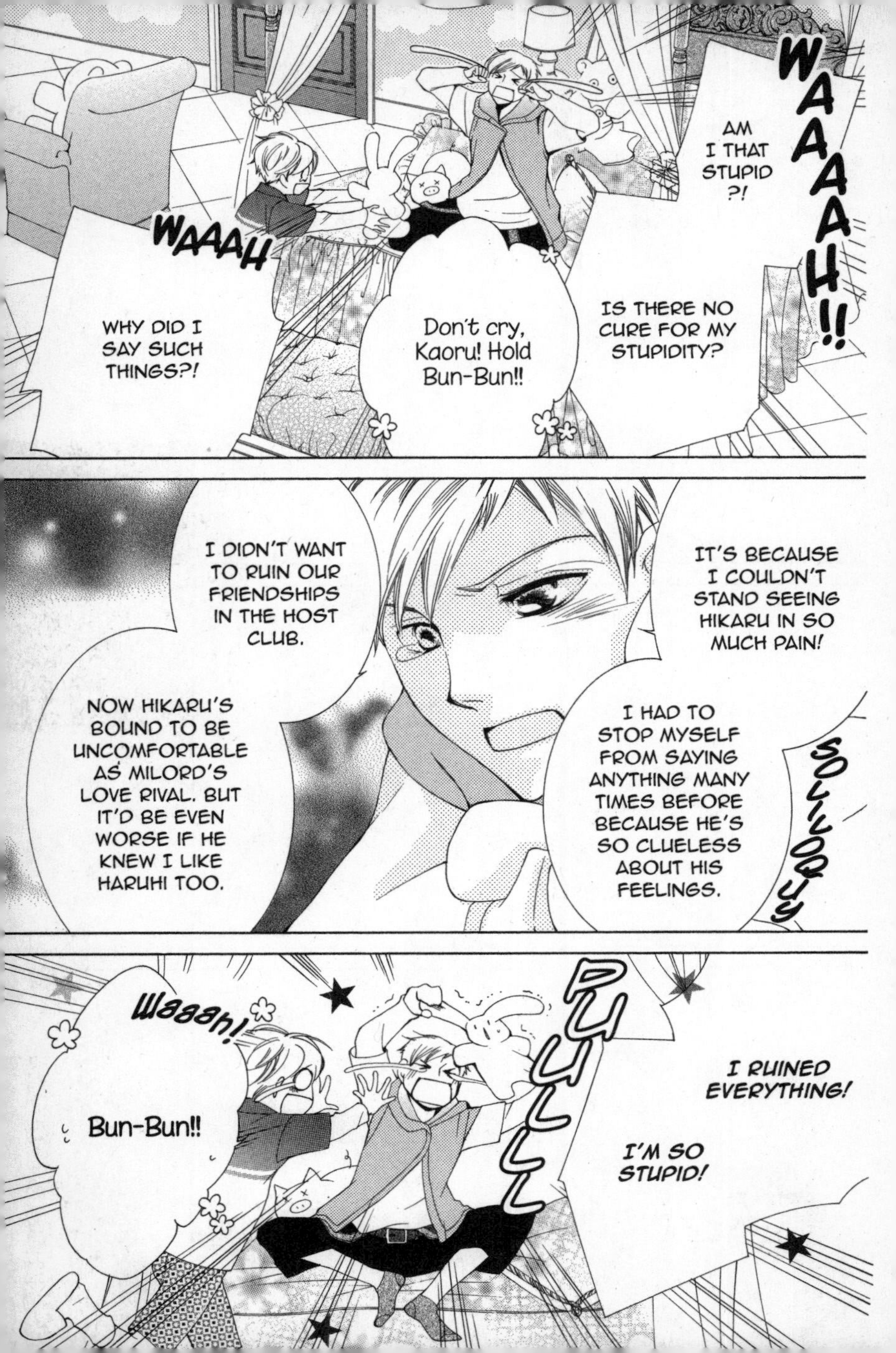
WAAAAAH!!
AM I THAT STUPID?!
IS THERE NO CURE FOR MY STUPIDITY?
Don't cry, Kaoru! Hold Bun-Bun!!
WAAAH
WHY DID I SAY SUCH THINGS?!
SOLILOQUY
IT'S BECAUSE I COULDN'T STAND SEEING HIKARU IN SO MUCH PAIN!
I HAD TO STOP MYSELF FROM SAYING ANYTHING MANY TIMES BEFORE BECAUSE HE'S SO CLUELESS ABOUT HIS FEELINGS.
I DIDN'T WANT TO RUIN OUR FRIENDSHIPS IN THE HOST CLUB.
NOW HIKARU'S BOUND TO BE UNCOMFORTABLE AS MILORD'S LOVE RIVAL. BUT IT'D BE EVEN WORSE IF HE KNEW I LIKE HARUHI TOO.
I RUINED EVERYTHING!
I'M SO STUPID!
PULLLL
Waaah!
Bun-Bun!!

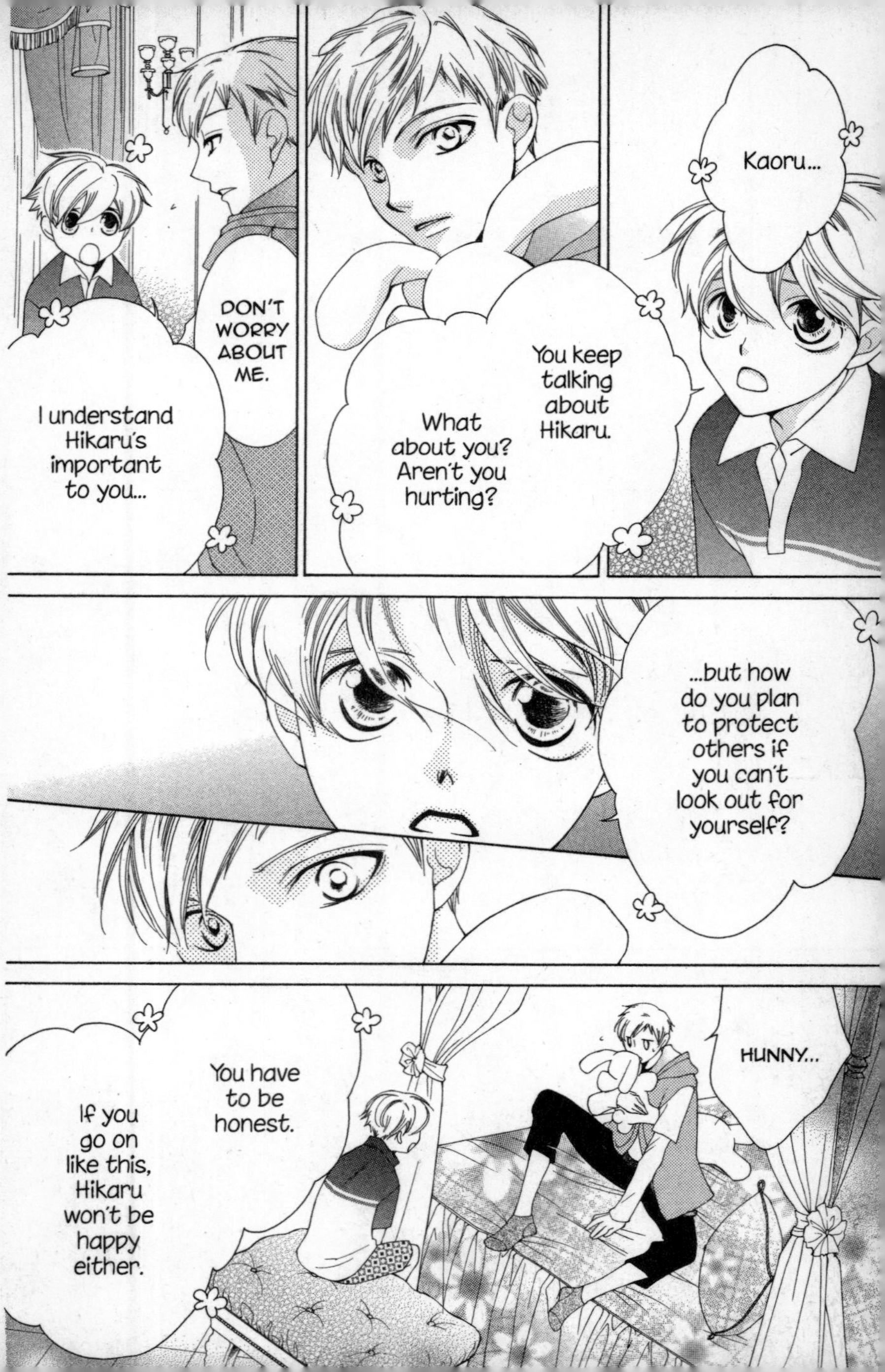
Kaoru...
You keep talking about Hikaru.
What about you? Aren't you hurting?
DON'T WORRY ABOUT ME.
I understand Hikaru's important to you...
...but how do you plan to protect others if you can't look out for yourself?
HUNNY...
You have to be honest.
If you go on like this, Hikaru won't be happy either.

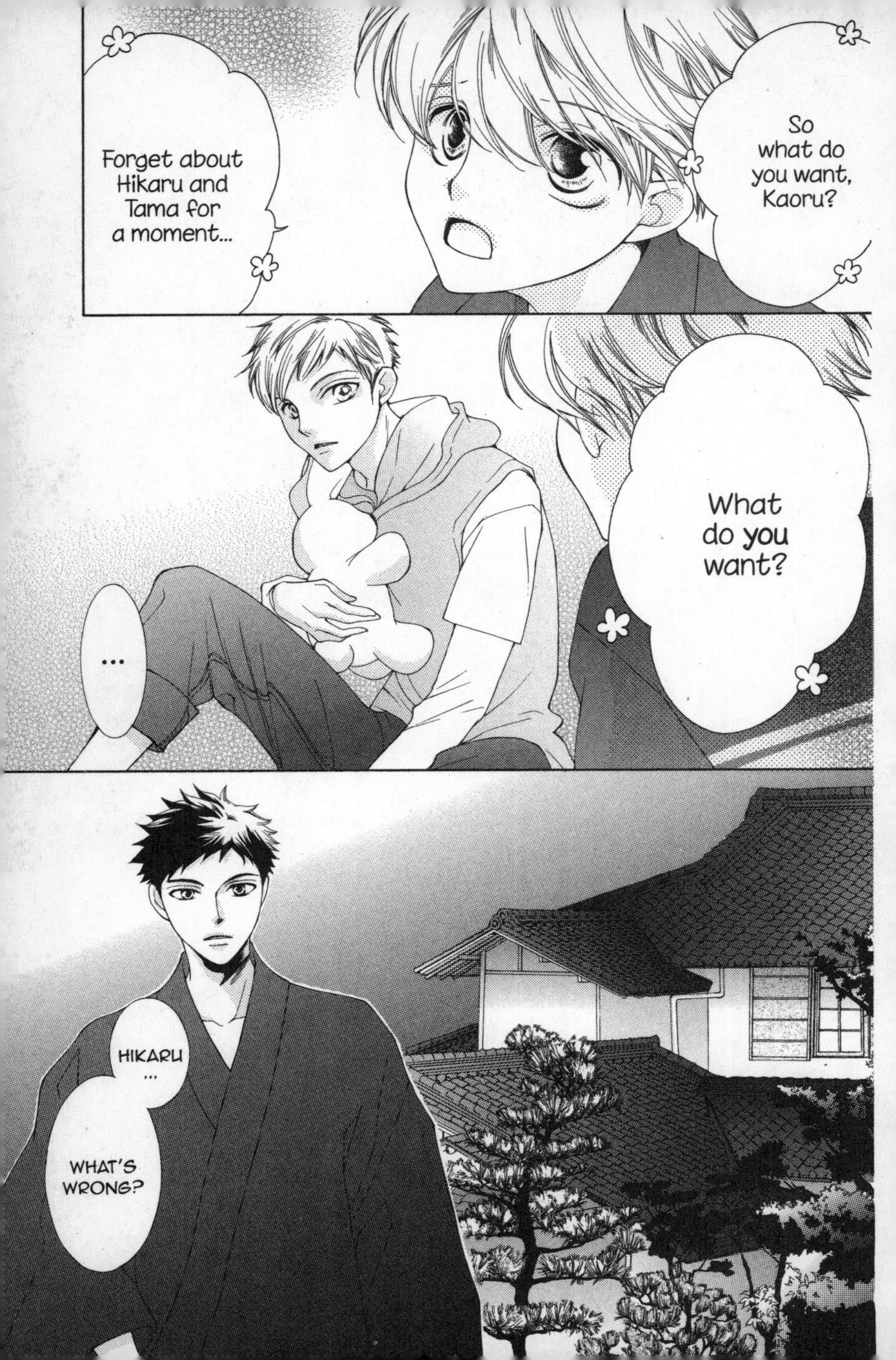
So what do you want, Kaoru?
Forget about Hikaru and Tama for a moment...
What do you want?
...
Hikaru ...
What's wrong?

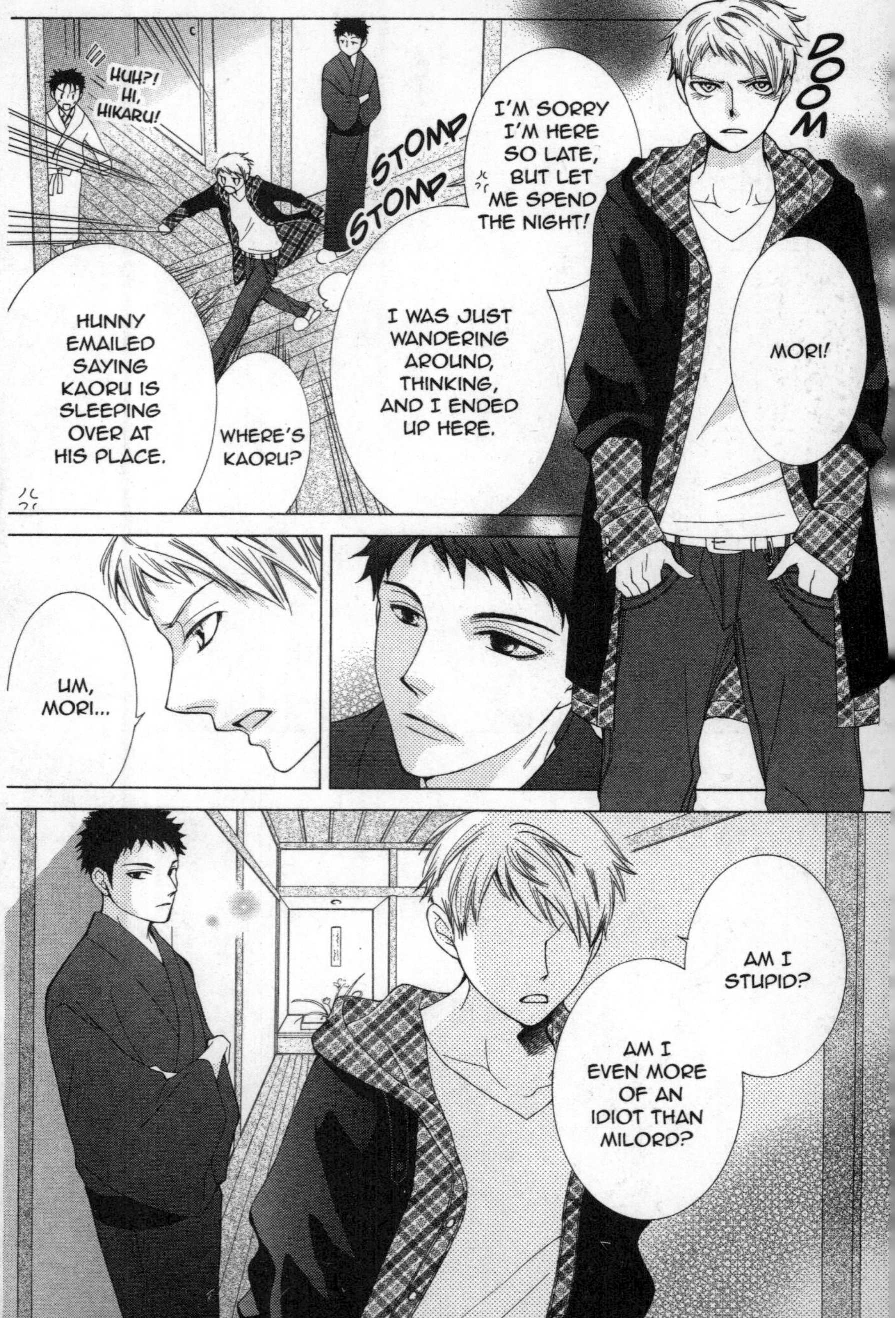
DOOM
MORI!
I'M SORRY I'M HERE SO LATE, BUT LET ME SPEND THE NIGHT!
STOMP STOMP
HUH?! HI, HIKARU!
I WAS JUST WANDERING AROUND, THINKING, AND I ENDED UP HERE.
WHERE'S KAORU?
HUNNY EMAILED SAYING KAORU IS SLEEPING OVER AT HIS PLACE.
UM, MORI...
AM I STUPID?
AM I EVEN MORE OF AN IDIOT THAN MILORD?

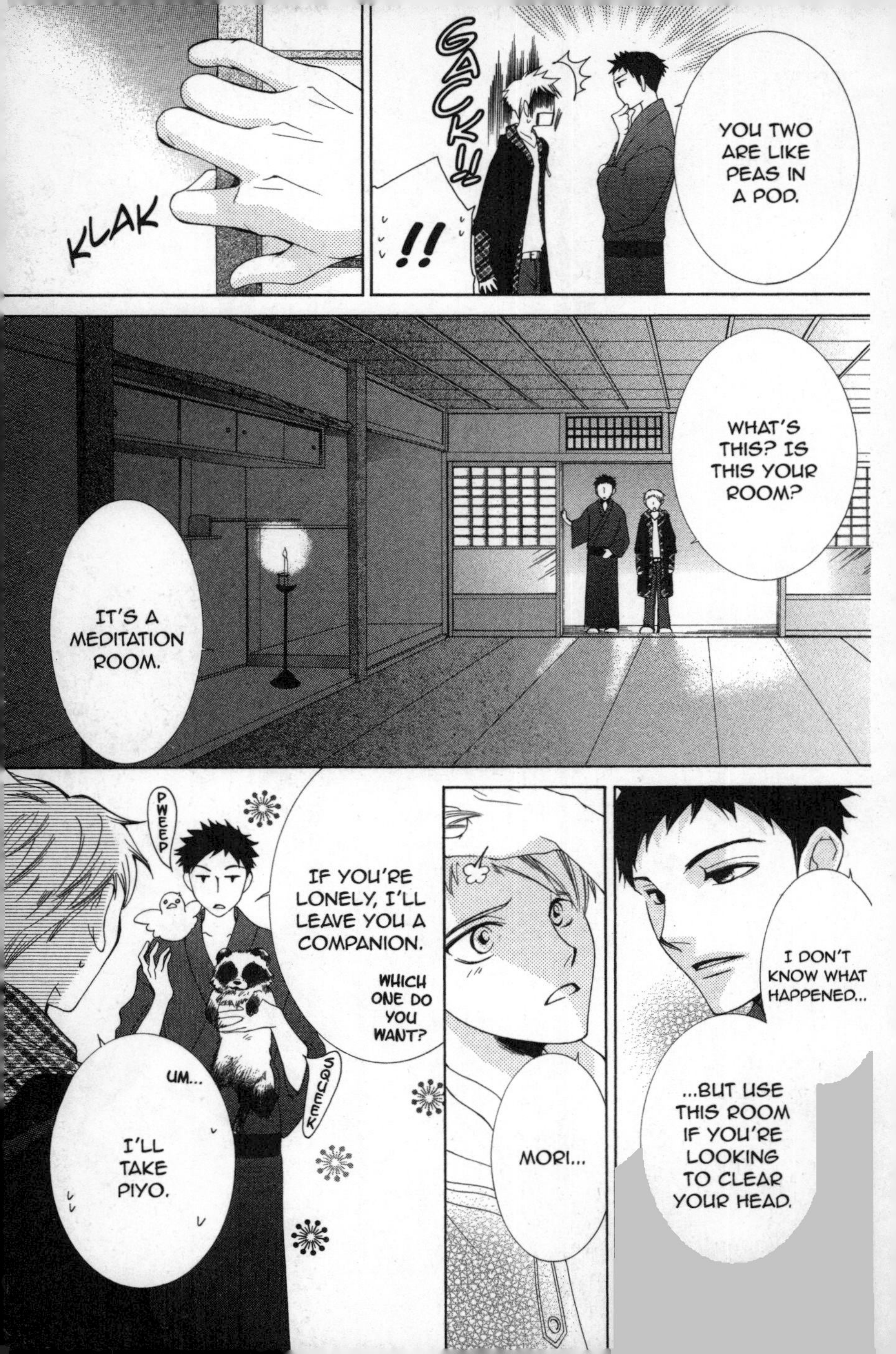
YOU TWO ARE LIKE PEAS IN A POD.
GACK!!
!!
KLAK
WHAT'S THIS? IS THIS YOUR ROOM?
IT'S A MEDITATION ROOM.
I DON'T KNOW WHAT HAPPENED...
...BUT USE THIS ROOM IF YOU'RE LOOKING TO CLEAR YOUR HEAD.
MORI...
IF YOU'RE LONELY, I'LL LEAVE YOU A COMPANION.
WHICH ONE DO YOU WANT?
PWEEP
SQUEEK
UM...
I'LL TAKE PIYO.

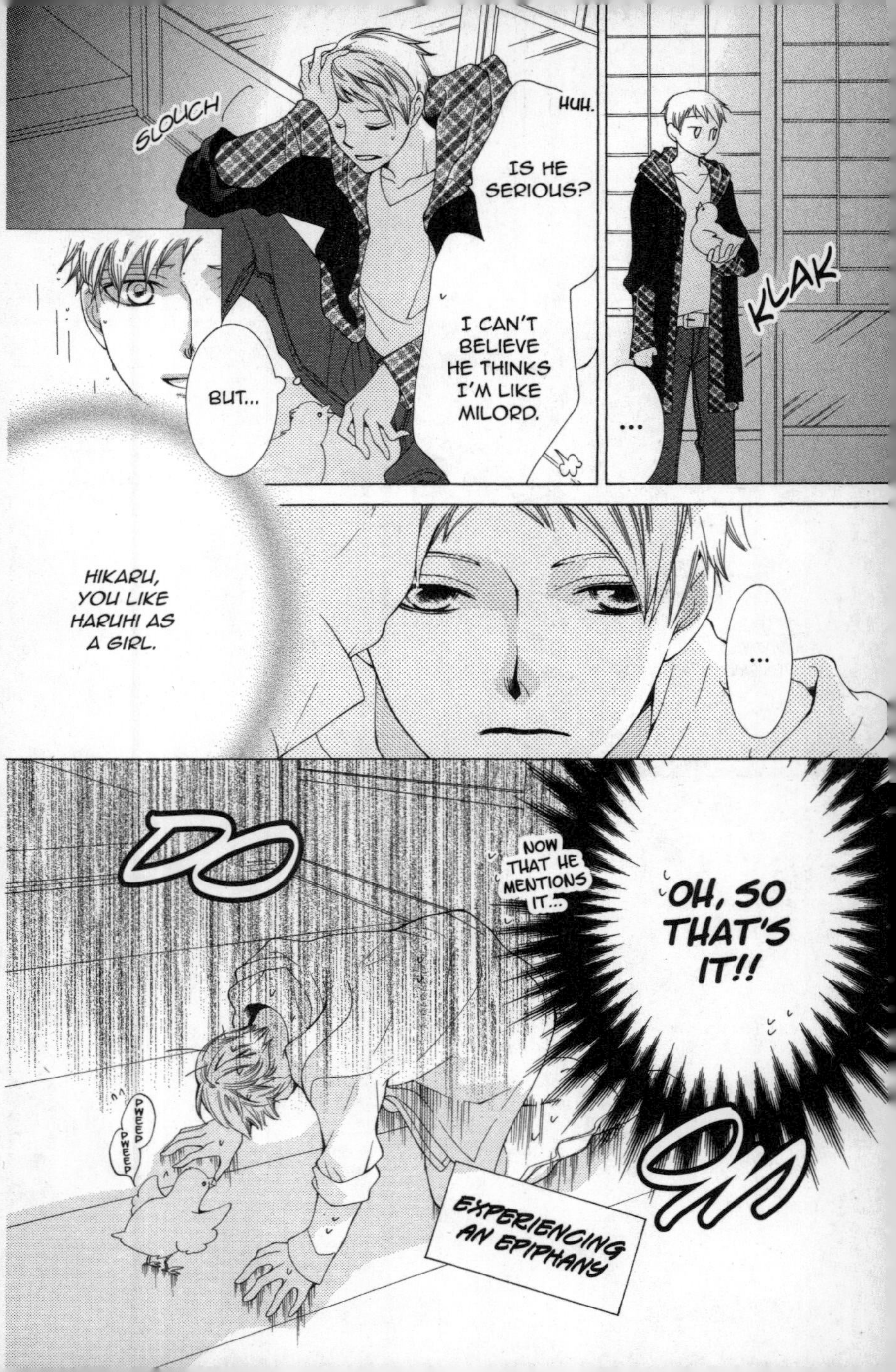
KLAK
...
HUH.
IS HE SERIOUS?
I CAN'T BELIEVE HE THINKS I'M LIKE MILORD.
SLOUCH
BUT...
...
HIKARU, YOU LIKE HARUHI AS A GIRL.
OH, SO THAT'S IT!!
NOW THAT HE MENTIONS IT...
DO
ON
EXPERIENCING AN EPIPHANY
PWEED PWEED

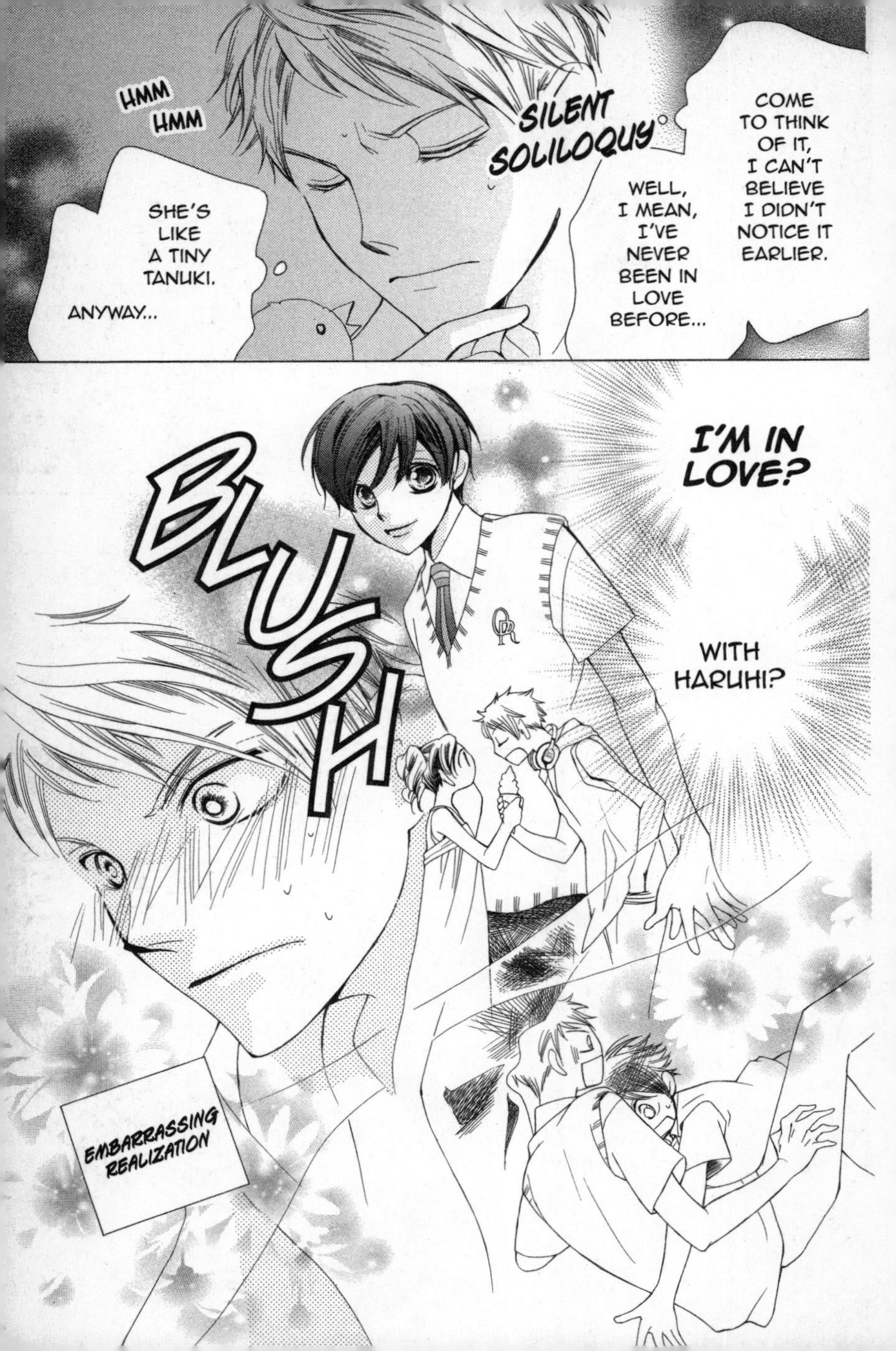
COME TO THINK OF IT, I CAN'T BELIEVE I DIDN'T NOTICE IT EARLIER.
SILENT SOLILOQUY
WELL, I MEAN, I'VE NEVER BEEN IN LOVE BEFORE...
HMM HMM
SHE'S LIKE A TINY TANUKI.
ANYWAY...
I'M IN LOVE?
WITH HARUHI?
BLUSH
EMBARRASSING REALIZATION

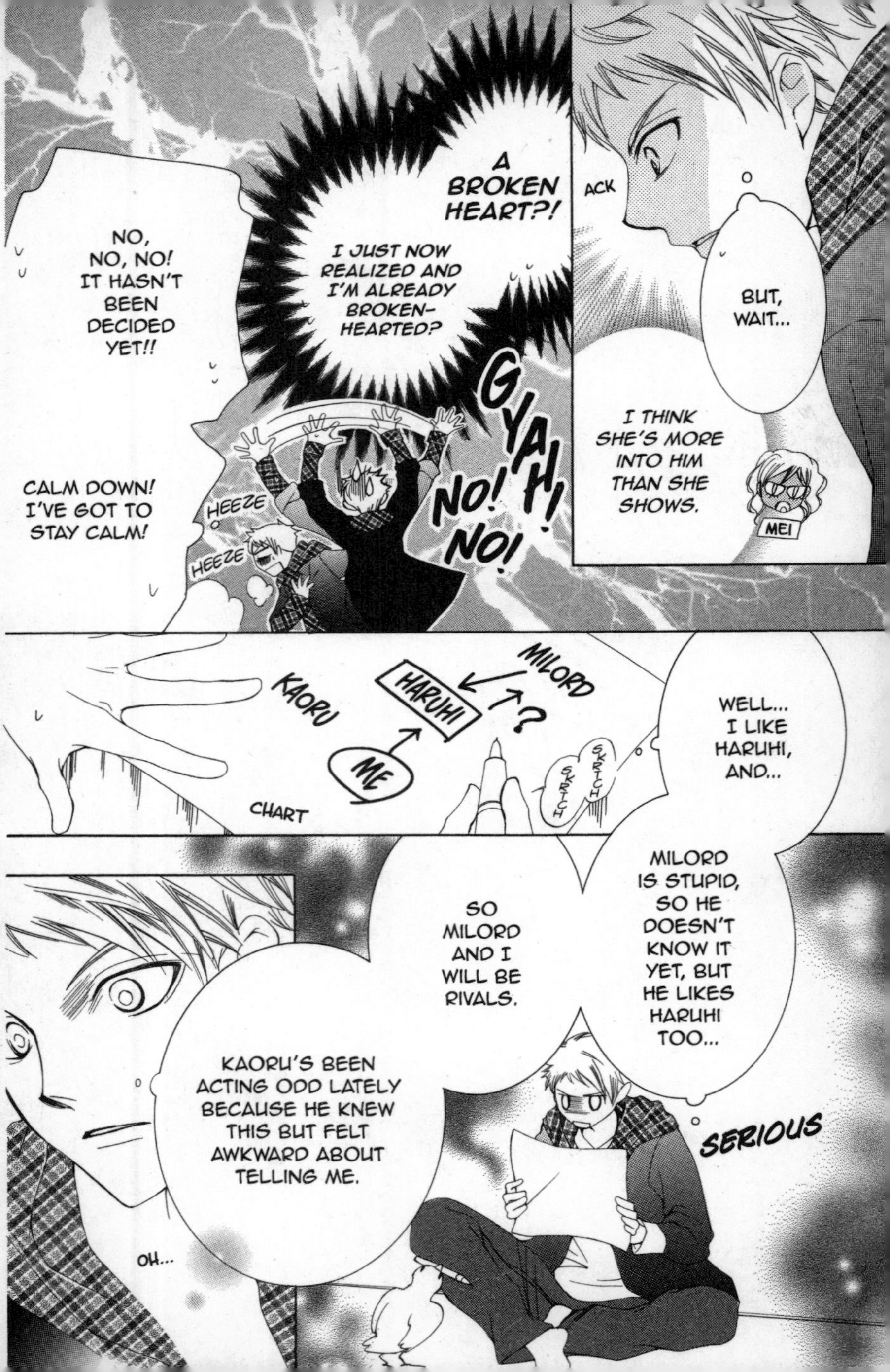
ACK
BUT, WAIT...
I THINK SHE'S MORE INTO HIM THAN SHE SHOWS.
MEI
A BROKEN HEART?!
I JUST NOW REALIZED AND I'M ALREADY BROKEN-HEARTED?
NO, NO, NO! IT HASN'T BEEN DECIDED YET!!
GYAH!!
NO! NO!
HEEZE
HEEZE
CALM DOWN! I'VE GOT TO STAY CALM!
WELL... I LIKE HARUHI, AND...
SKRITCH
SKRITCH
MILORD
HARUHI
?
KAORU
ME
CHART
MILORD IS STUPID, SO HE DOESN'T KNOW IT YET, BUT HE LIKES HARUHI TOO...
SO MILORD AND I WILL BE RIVALS.
SERIOUS
KAORU'S BEEN ACTING ODD LATELY BECAUSE HE KNEW THIS BUT FELT AWKWARD ABOUT TELLING ME.
OH...

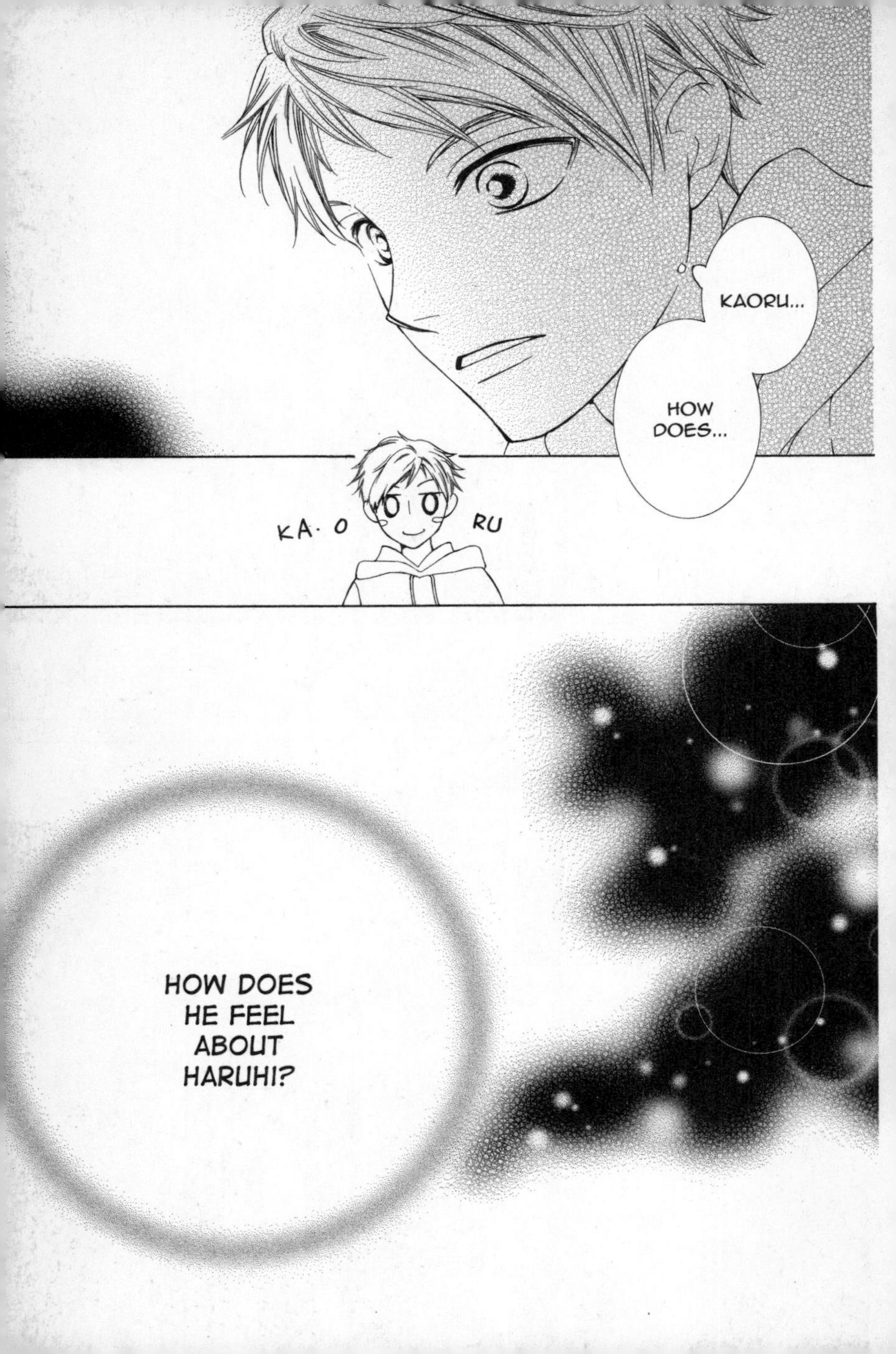
KAORU...
HOW DOES...
KA· O RU
HOW DOES HE FEEL ABOUT HARUHI?

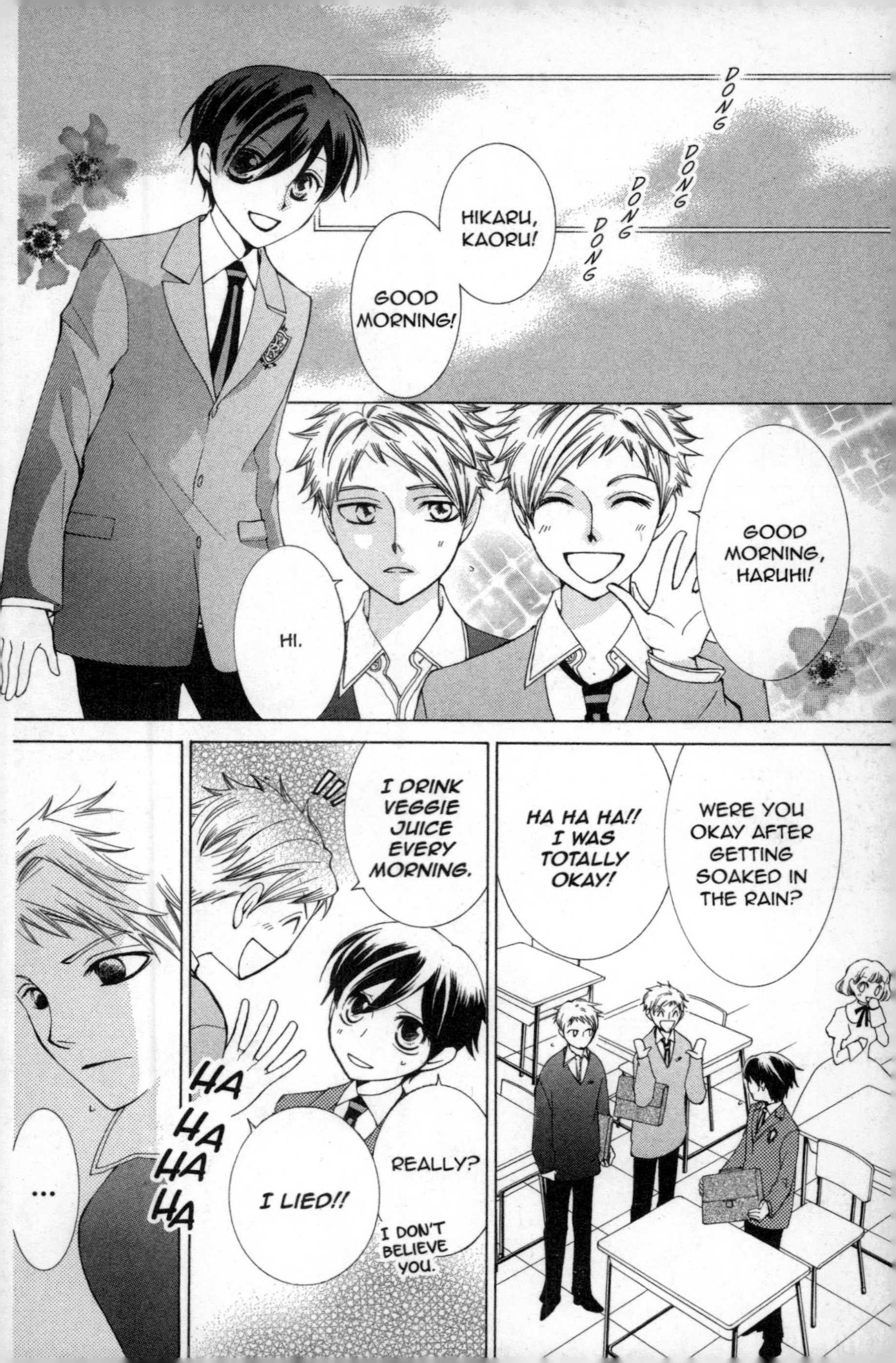
DONG DONG DONG DONG
HIKARU, KAORU!
GOOD MORNING!
GOOD MORNING, HARUHI!
HI.
WERE YOU OKAY AFTER GETTING SOAKED IN THE RAIN?
HA HA HA!! I WAS TOTALLY OKAY!
I DRINK VEGGIE JUICE EVERY MORNING.
REALLY?
I DON'T BELIEVE YOU.
I LIED!!
HA HA HA HA
...

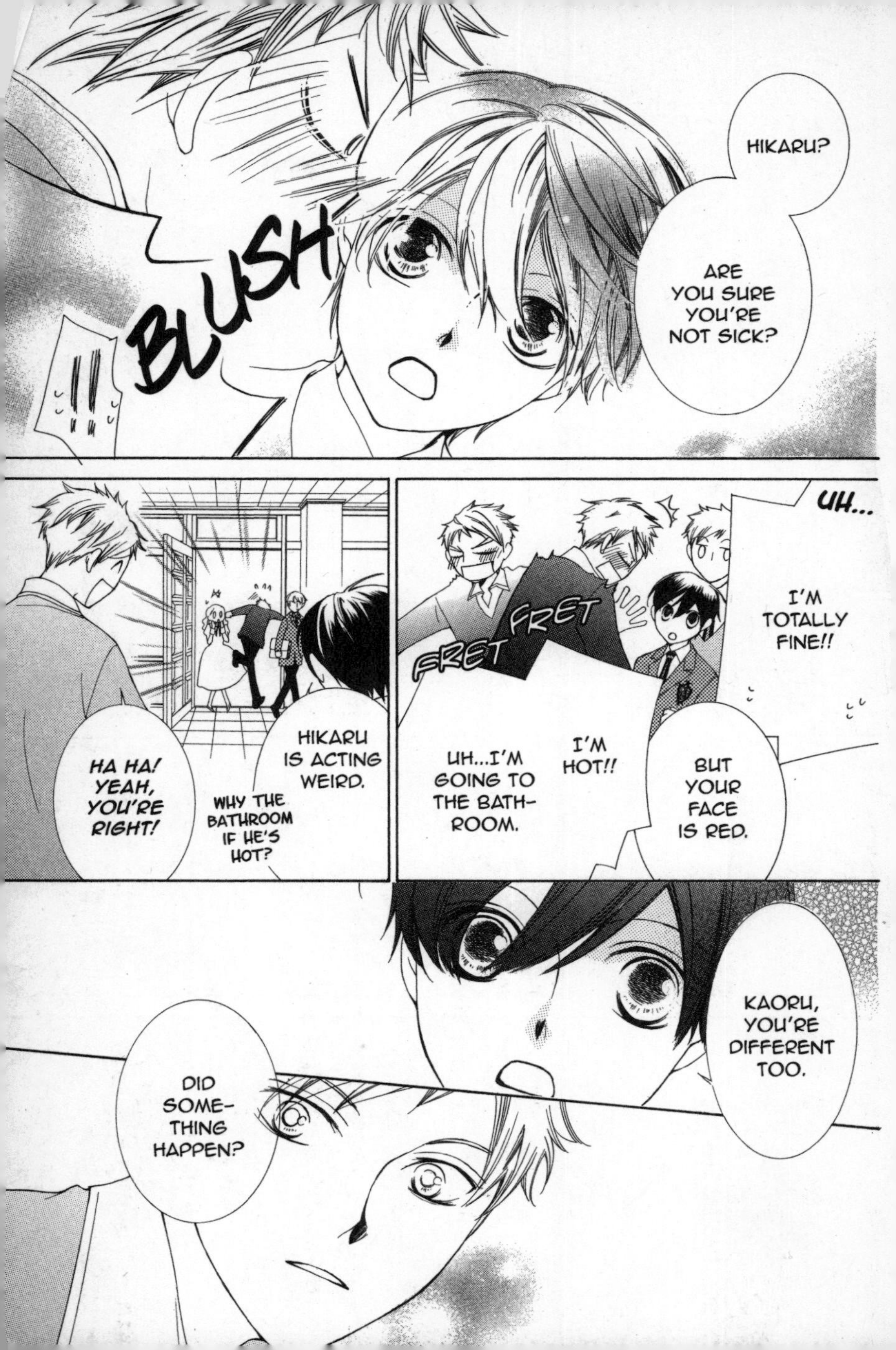
HIKARU?
ARE YOU SURE YOU'RE NOT SICK?
BLUSH
!!
UH...
I'M TOTALLY FINE!!
BUT YOUR FACE IS RED.
I'M HOT!!
UH...I'M GOING TO THE BATH-ROOM.
FRET FRET
HIKARU IS ACTING WEIRD.
WHY THE BATHROOM IF HE'S HOT?
HA HA! YEAH, YOU'RE RIGHT!
KAORU, YOU'RE DIFFERENT TOO.
DID SOME-THING HAPPEN?

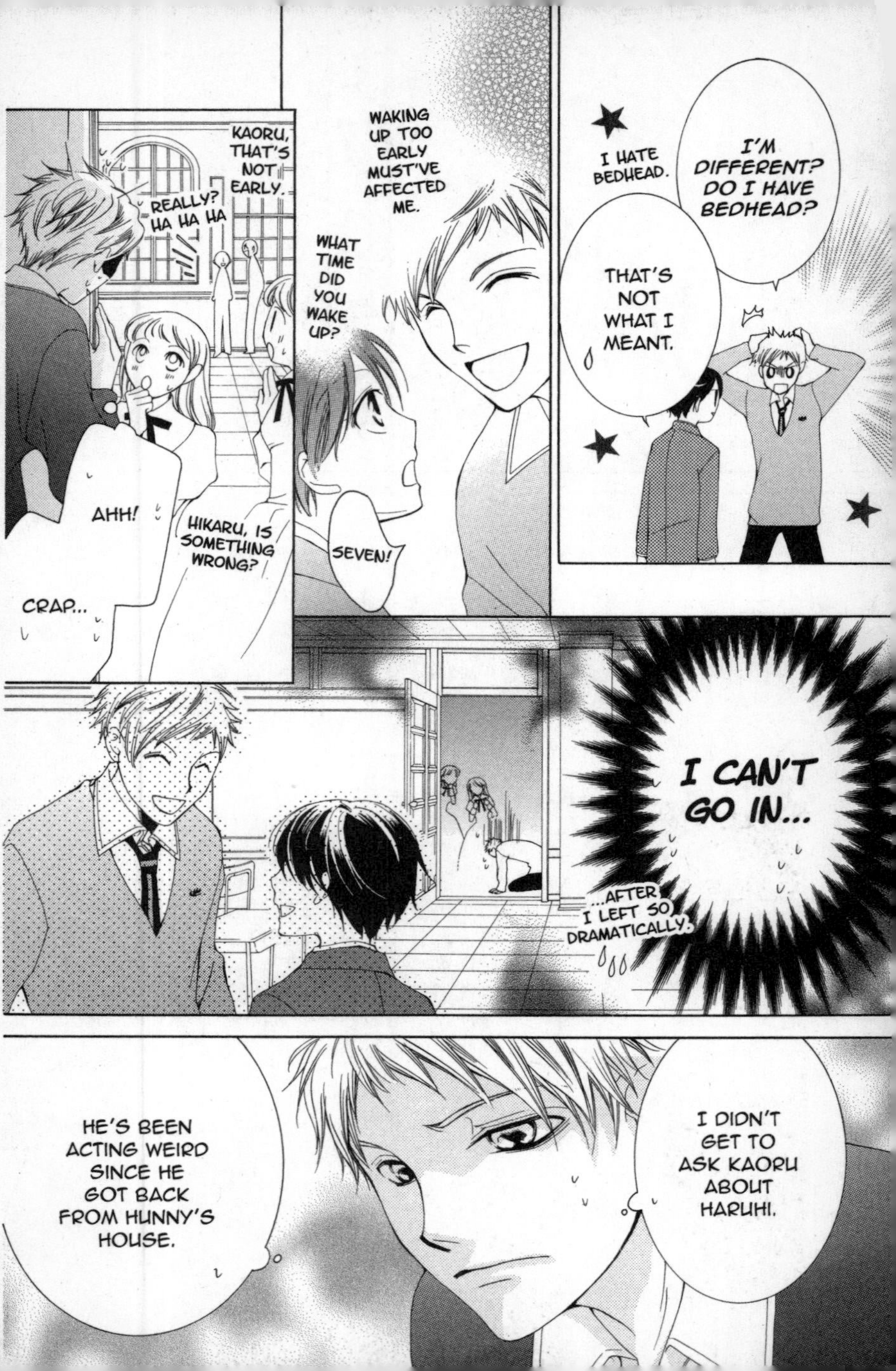
I'M DIFFERENT? DO I HAVE BEDHEAD?
THAT'S NOT WHAT I MEANT.
I HATE BEDHEAD.
WAKING UP TOO EARLY MUST'VE AFFECTED ME.
WHAT TIME DID YOU WAKE UP?
SEVEN!
KAORU, THAT'S NOT EARLY.
REALLY? HA HA HA
HIKARU, IS SOMETHING WRONG?
AHH!
CRAP...
I CAN'T GO IN...
...AFTER I LEFT SO DRAMATICALLY.
I DIDN'T GET TO ASK KAORU ABOUT HARUHI.
HE'S BEEN ACTING WEIRD SINCE HE GOT BACK FROM HUNNY'S HOUSE.

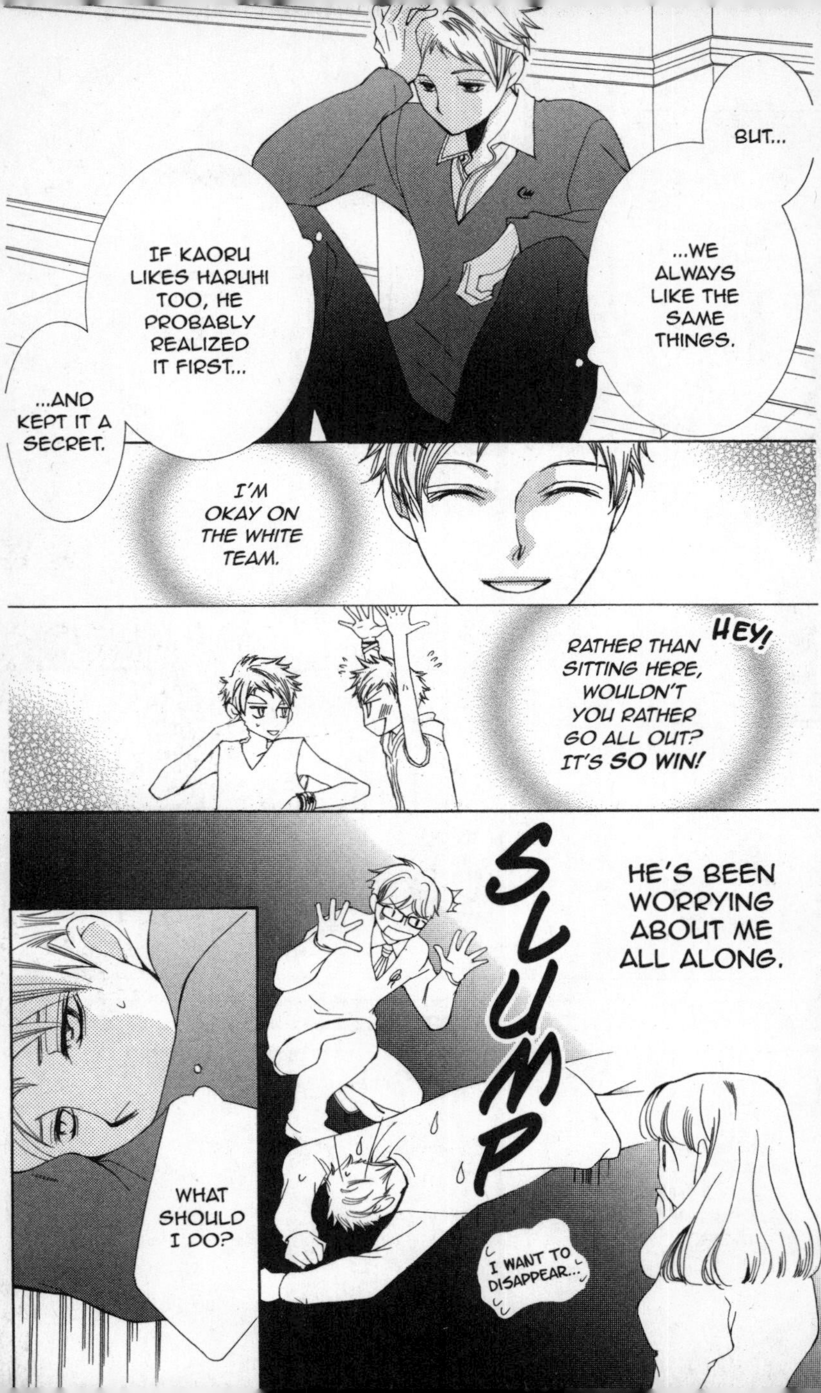
BUT...
...WE ALWAYS LIKE THE SAME THINGS.
IF KAORU LIKES HARUHI TOO, HE PROBABLY REALIZED IT FIRST...
...AND KEPT IT A SECRET.
I'M OKAY ON THE WHITE TEAM.
HEY!
RATHER THAN SITTING HERE, WOULDN'T YOU RATHER GO ALL OUT? IT'S SO WIN!
HE'S BEEN WORRYING ABOUT ME ALL ALONG.
SLUMP
I WANT TO DISAPPEAR...
WHAT SHOULD I DO?

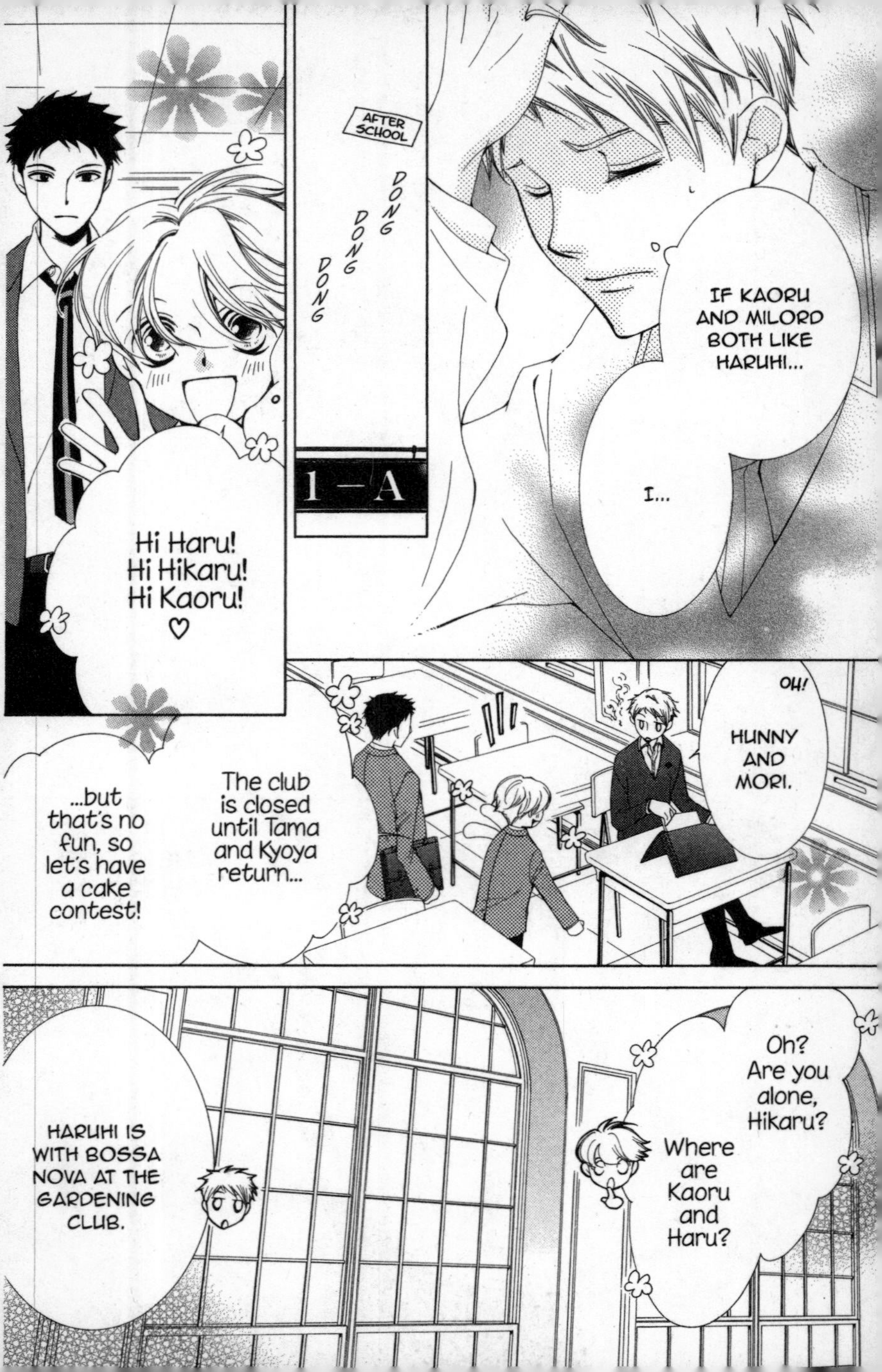
IF KAORU AND MILORD BOTH LIKE HARUHI...
I...
AFTER SCHOOL
DONG DONG DONG
1-A
Hi Haru! Hi Hikaru! Hi Kaoru! ♡
OH!
HUNNY AND MORI.
The club is closed until Tama and Kyoya return...
...but that's no fun, so let's have a cake contest!
Oh? Are you alone, Hikaru?
Where are Kaoru and Haru?
HARUHI IS WITH BOSSA NOVA AT THE GARDENING CLUB.

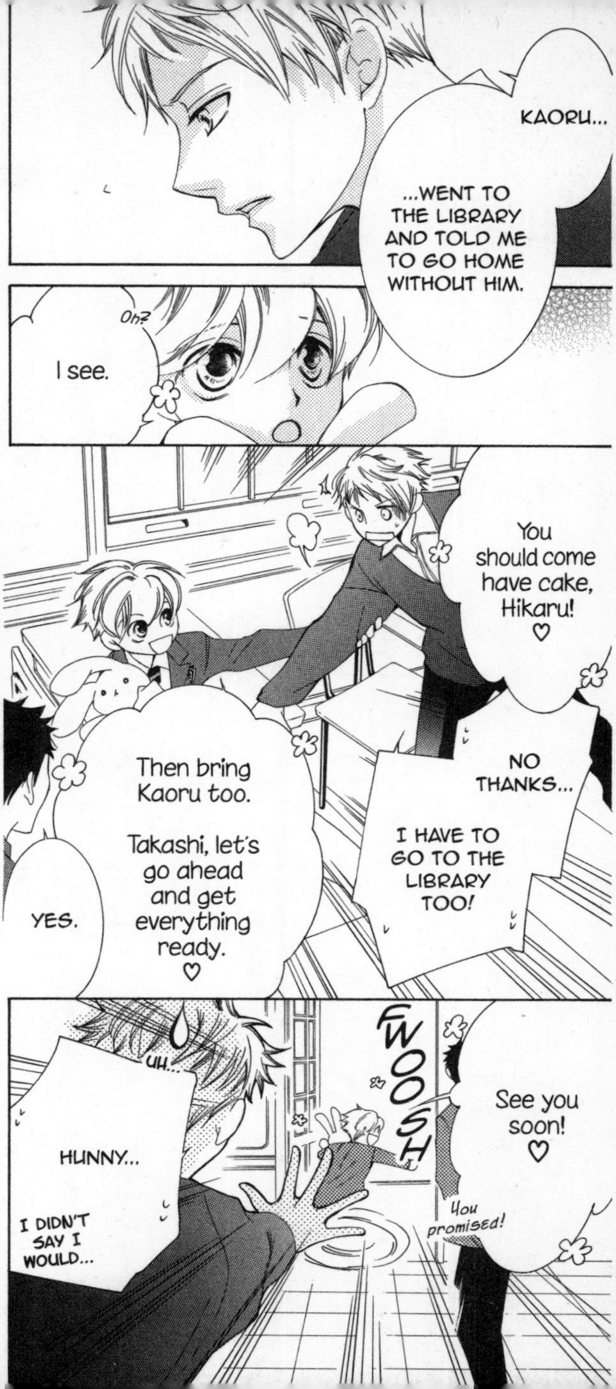
KAORU...
...WENT TO THE LIBRARY AND TOLD ME TO GO HOME WITHOUT HIM.
Oh?
I see.
You should come have cake, Hikaru! ♡
NO THANKS...
I HAVE TO GO TO THE LIBRARY TOO!
Then bring Kaoru too.
Takashi, let's go ahead and get everything ready. ♡
YES.
FWOOSH
See you soon! ♡
You promised!
UH...
HUNNY...
I DIDN'T SAY I WOULD...

5

✿I WAS SUPPOSED TO WRITE A LOG OF MY TRIP TO FRANCE FOR THE END OF THIS VOLUME, BUT WHEN I DREW UP THE STORYBOARD IT DIDN'T FIT IN THREE PAGES SO I CHANGED MY MIND.

MAYBE I'LL WRITE IT FOR THE NEXT VOLUME. I'LL DO IT IF I CAN.

✿I APOLOGIZE FOR LEAVING VOLUME 11 AT A BAD SPOT... *HOST CLUB'S* SELLING POINT IS HOW EVERYBODY GETS ALONG, BUT IT'S GETTING A LITTLE SERIOUS NOW. PLEASE BE PATIENT WITH ME! THE OTHER DAY I WENT TO THE DRAMA CD VOICE RECORDING SESSION AND THOUGHT, "IT'S BEST WHEN ALL THE CHARACTERS ARE HAVING FUN." (OR RATHER, I WAS LAUGHING HYSTERICALLY.)

SO, WITH THIS IN MIND, I'M LOOKING FORWARD TO SEEING ALL OF YOU AGAIN IN VOLUME 12. ♡♡
THANK YOU. ♡♡

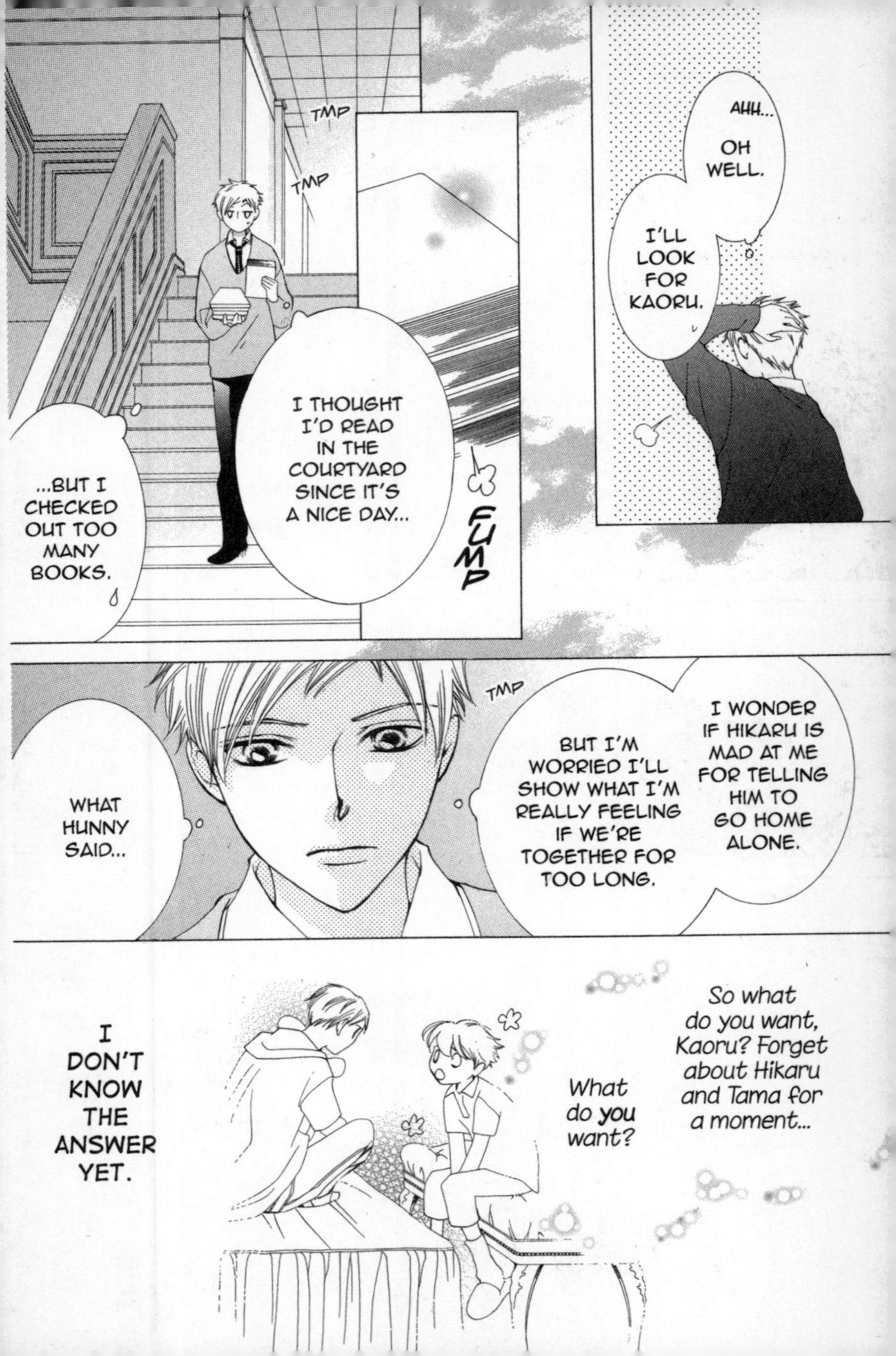
AHH... OH WELL.
I'LL LOOK FOR KAORU.
FUMP
TMP
TMP
I THOUGHT I'D READ IN THE COURTYARD SINCE IT'S A NICE DAY...
...BUT I CHECKED OUT TOO MANY BOOKS.
TMP
I WONDER IF HIKARU IS MAD AT ME FOR TELLING HIM TO GO HOME ALONE.
BUT I'M WORRIED I'LL SHOW WHAT I'M REALLY FEELING IF WE'RE TOGETHER FOR TOO LONG.
WHAT HUNNY SAID...
So what do you want, Kaoru? Forget about Hikaru and Tama for a moment...
What do **you** want?
I DON'T KNOW THE ANSWER YET.

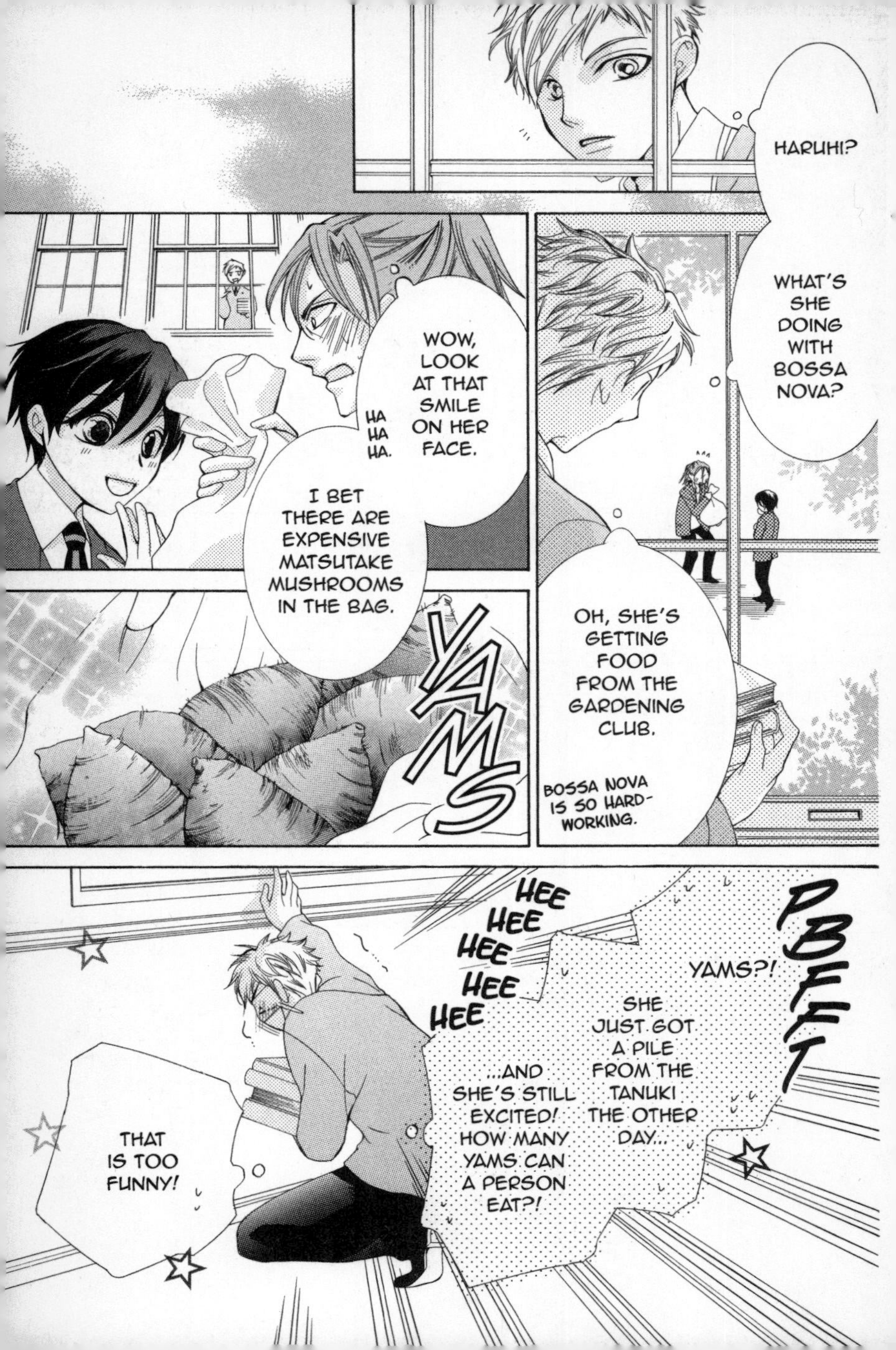
HARUHI?
WHAT'S SHE DOING WITH BOSSA NOVA?
OH, SHE'S GETTING FOOD FROM THE GARDENING CLUB.
BOSSA NOVA IS SO HARD-WORKING.
WOW, LOOK AT THAT SMILE ON HER FACE.
HA HA HA.
I BET THERE ARE EXPENSIVE MATSUTAKE MUSHROOMS IN THE BAG.
YAMS
PBFFT
YAMS?!
SHE JUST GOT A PILE FROM THE TANUKI THE OTHER DAY...
...AND SHE'S STILL EXCITED! HOW MANY YAMS CAN A PERSON EAT?!
HEE HEE HEE HEE HEE
THAT IS TOO FUNNY!

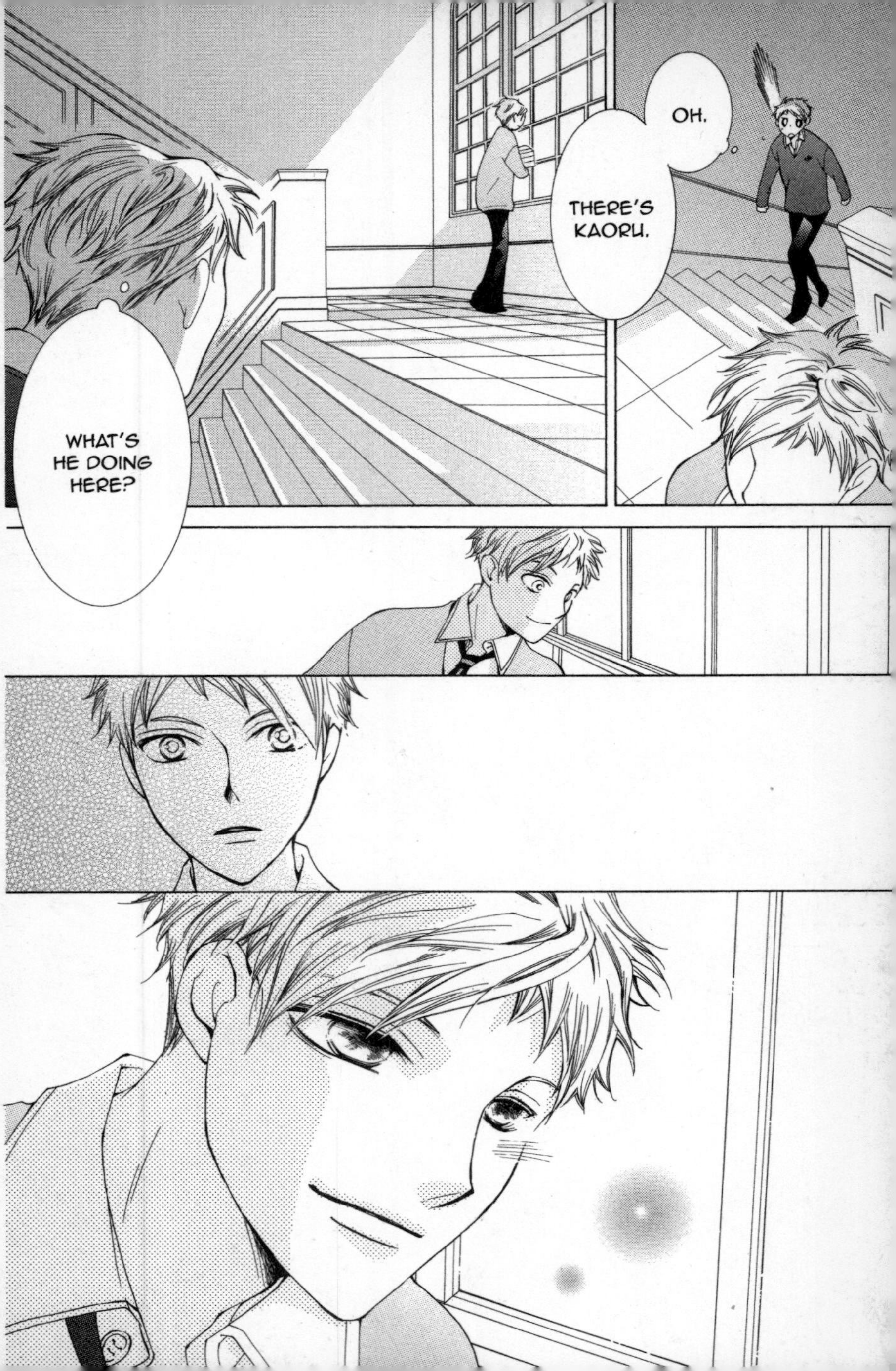
OH.
THERE'S KAORU.
WHAT'S HE DOING HERE?

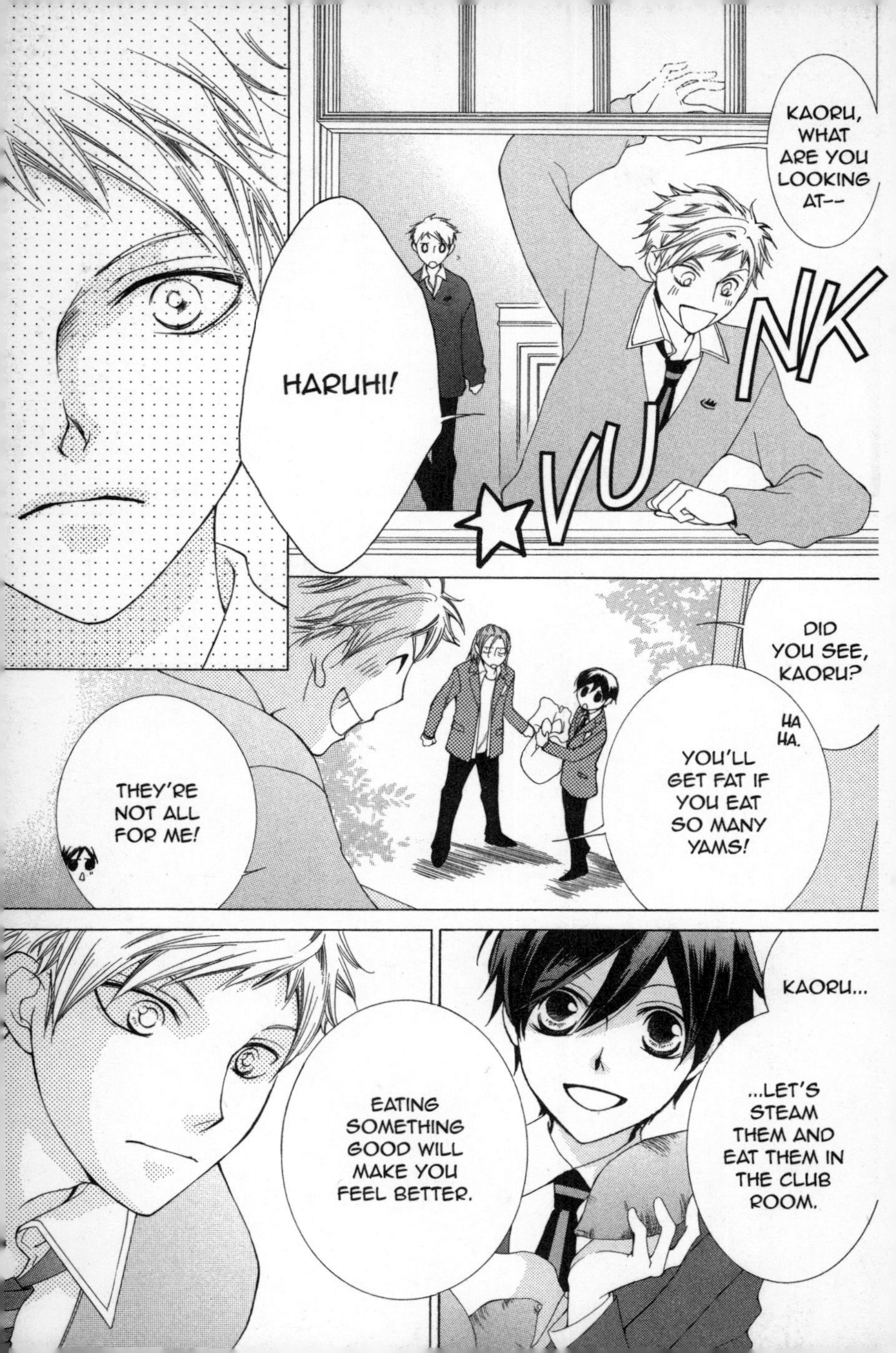
KAORU, WHAT ARE YOU LOOKING AT--
VUNK
HARUHI!
DID YOU SEE, KAORU?
HA HA.
YOU'LL GET FAT IF YOU EAT SO MANY YAMS!
THEY'RE NOT ALL FOR ME!
KAORU...
...LET'S STEAM THEM AND EAT THEM IN THE CLUB ROOM.
EATING SOMETHING GOOD WILL MAKE YOU FEEL BETTER.

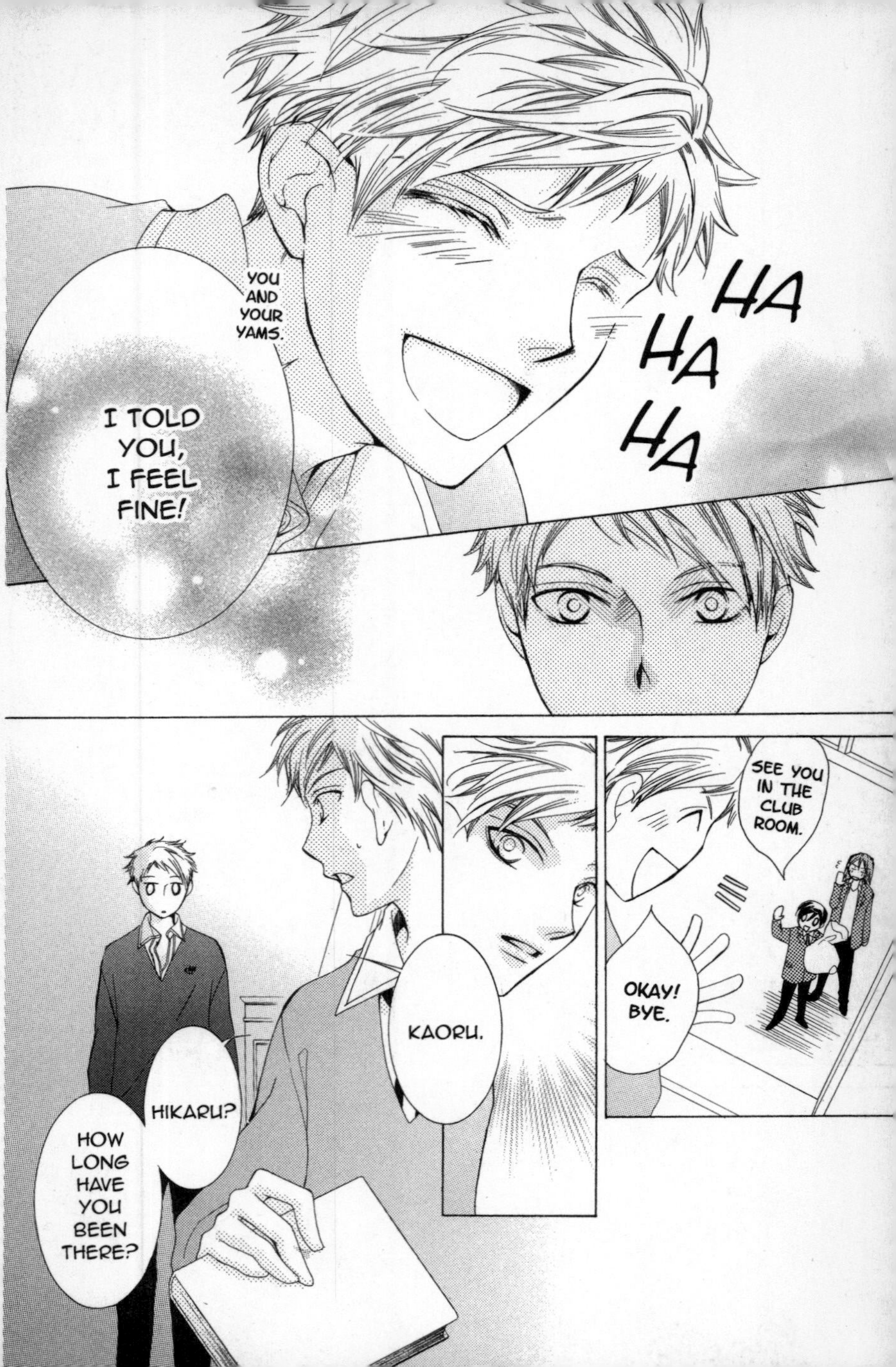
HA HA HA
YOU AND YOUR YAMS.
I TOLD YOU, I FEEL FINE!
SEE YOU IN THE CLUB ROOM.
OKAY! BYE.
KAORU.
HIKARU?
HOW LONG HAVE YOU BEEN THERE?

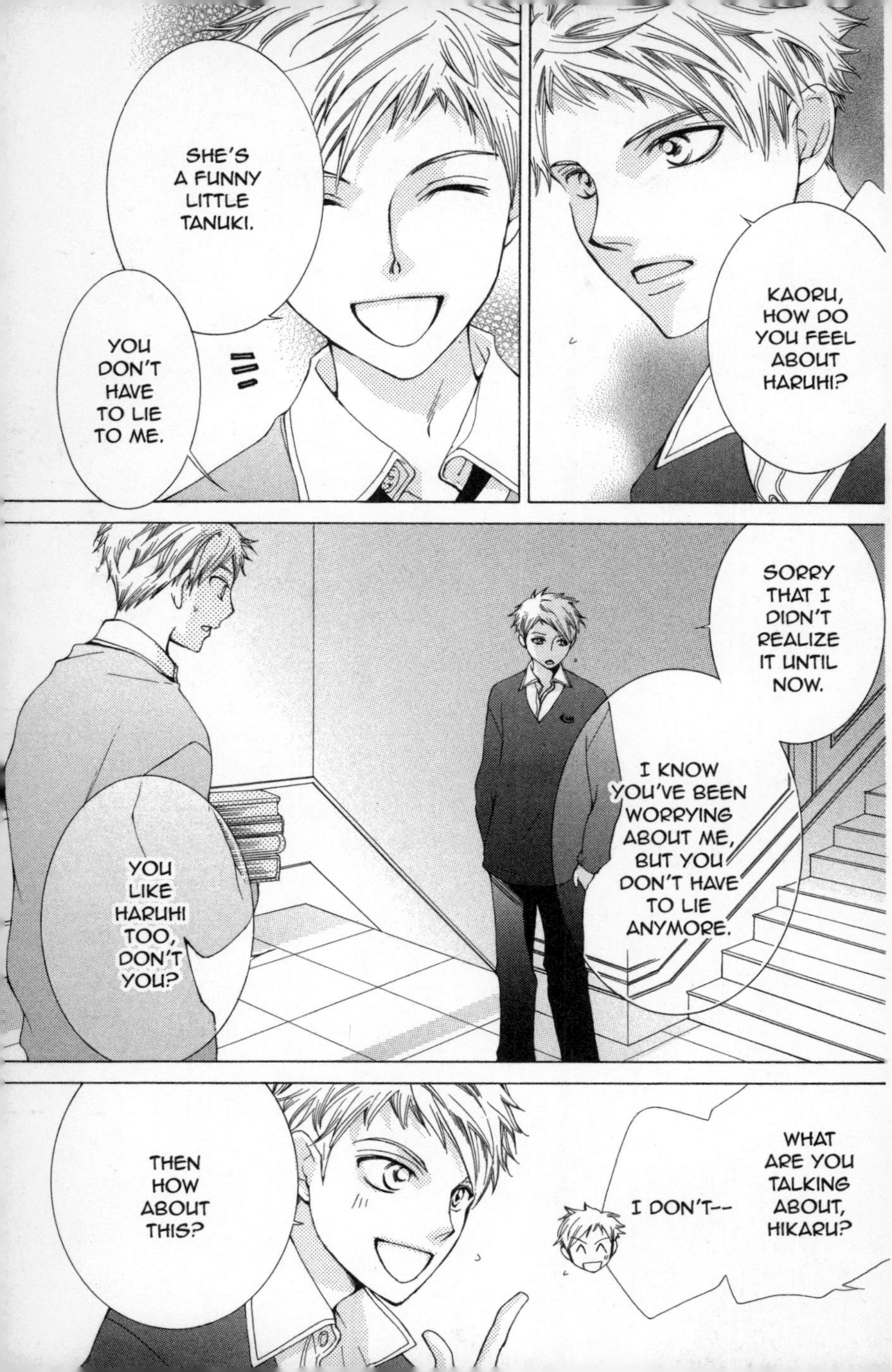
KAORU, HOW DO YOU FEEL ABOUT HARUHI?
SHE'S A FUNNY LITTLE TANUKI.
YOU DON'T HAVE TO LIE TO ME.
SORRY THAT I DIDN'T REALIZE IT UNTIL NOW.
I KNOW YOU'VE BEEN WORRYING ABOUT ME, BUT YOU DON'T HAVE TO LIE ANYMORE.
YOU LIKE HARUHI TOO, DON'T YOU?
WHAT ARE YOU TALKING ABOUT, HIKARU?
I DON'T--
THEN HOW ABOUT THIS?

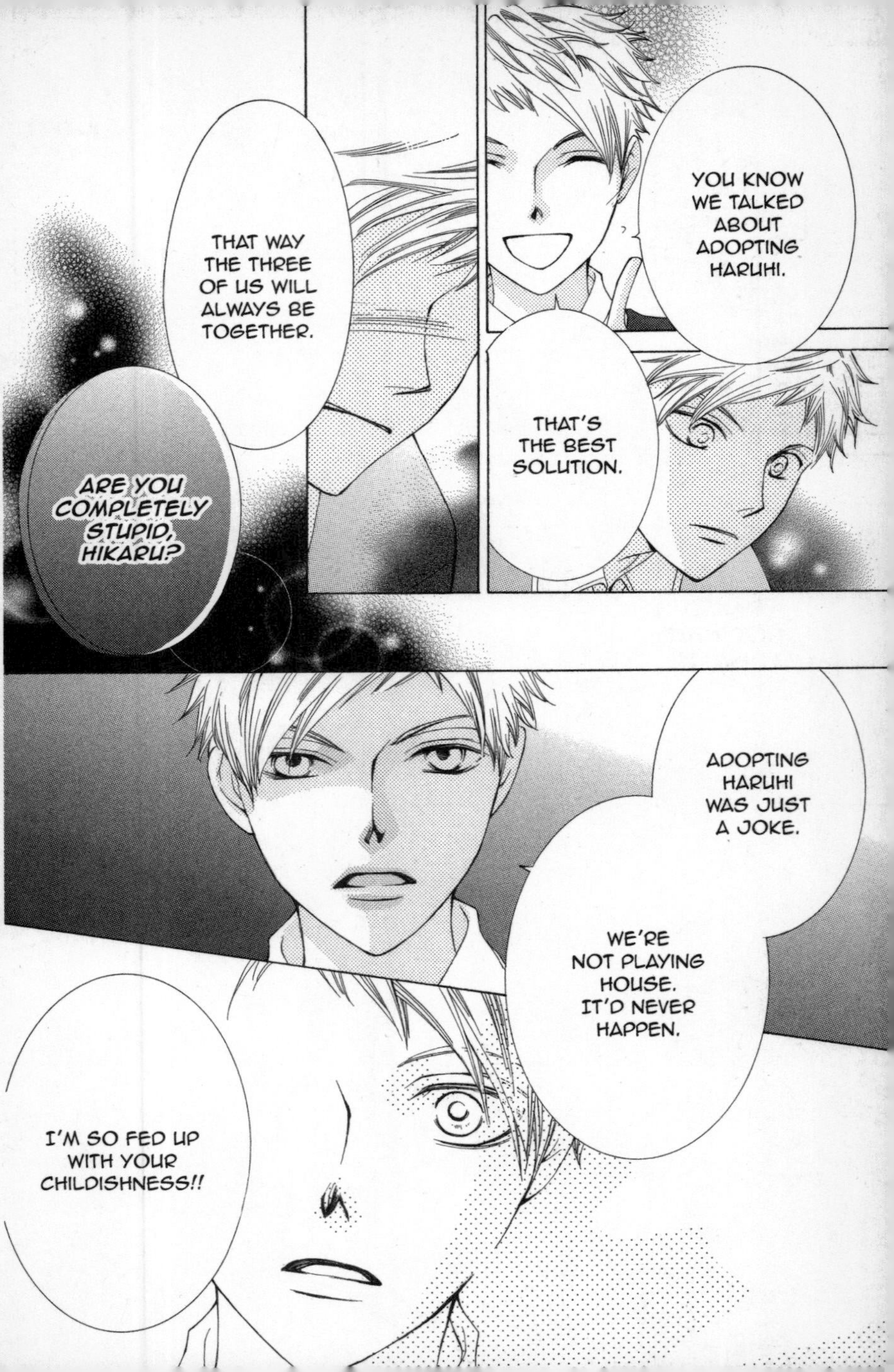
YOU KNOW WE TALKED ABOUT ADOPTING HARUHI.
THAT'S THE BEST SOLUTION.
THAT WAY THE THREE OF US WILL ALWAYS BE TOGETHER.
ARE YOU COMPLETELY STUPID, HIKARU?
ADOPTING HARUHI WAS JUST A JOKE.
WE'RE NOT PLAYING HOUSE. IT'D NEVER HAPPEN.
I'M SO FED UP WITH YOUR CHILDISHNESS!!

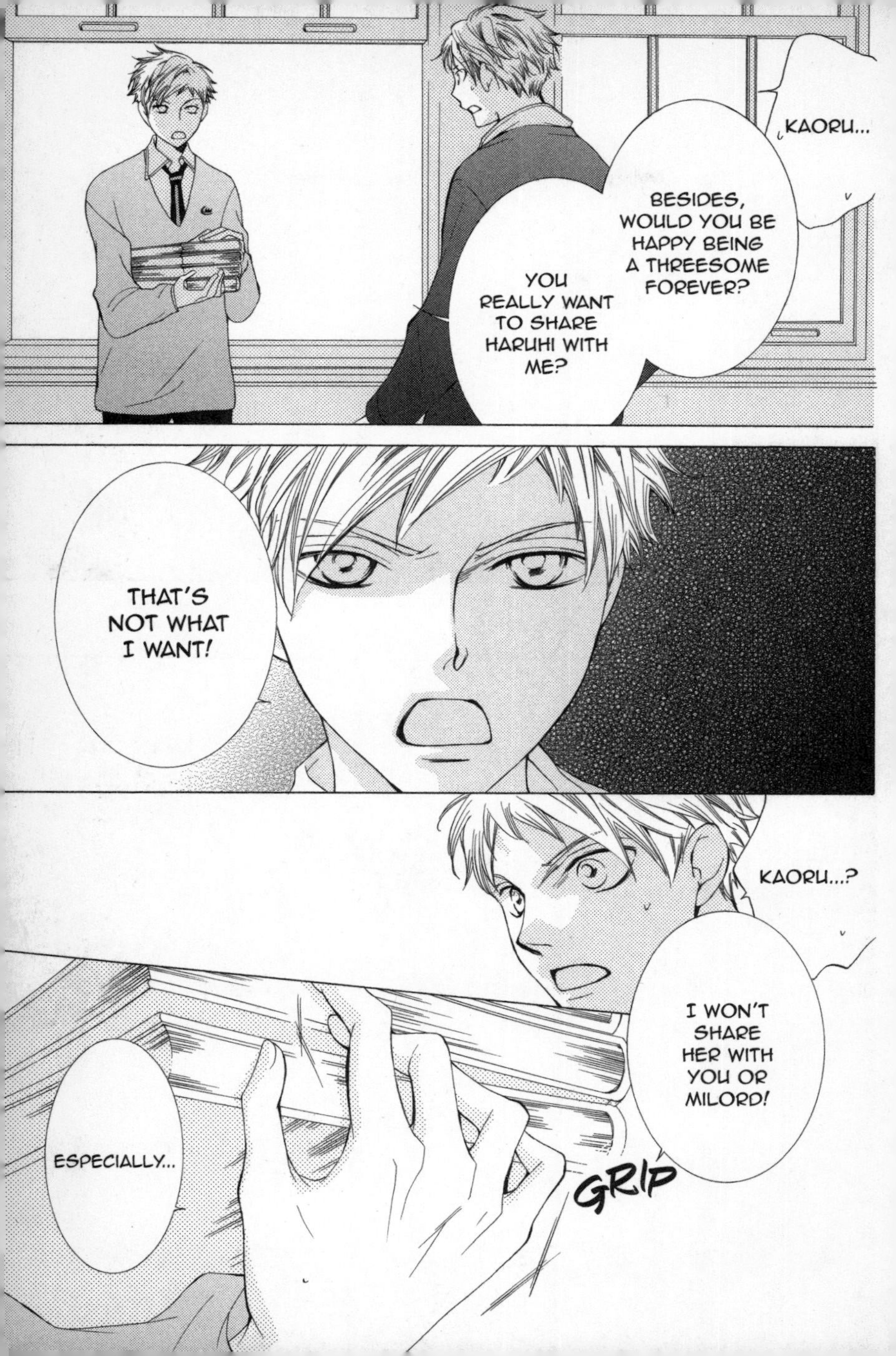
KAORU...
YOU REALLY WANT TO SHARE HARUHI WITH ME?
BESIDES, WOULD YOU BE HAPPY BEING A THREESOME FOREVER?
THAT'S NOT WHAT I WANT!
KAORU...?
I WON'T SHARE HER WITH YOU OR MILORD!
GRIP
ESPECIALLY...

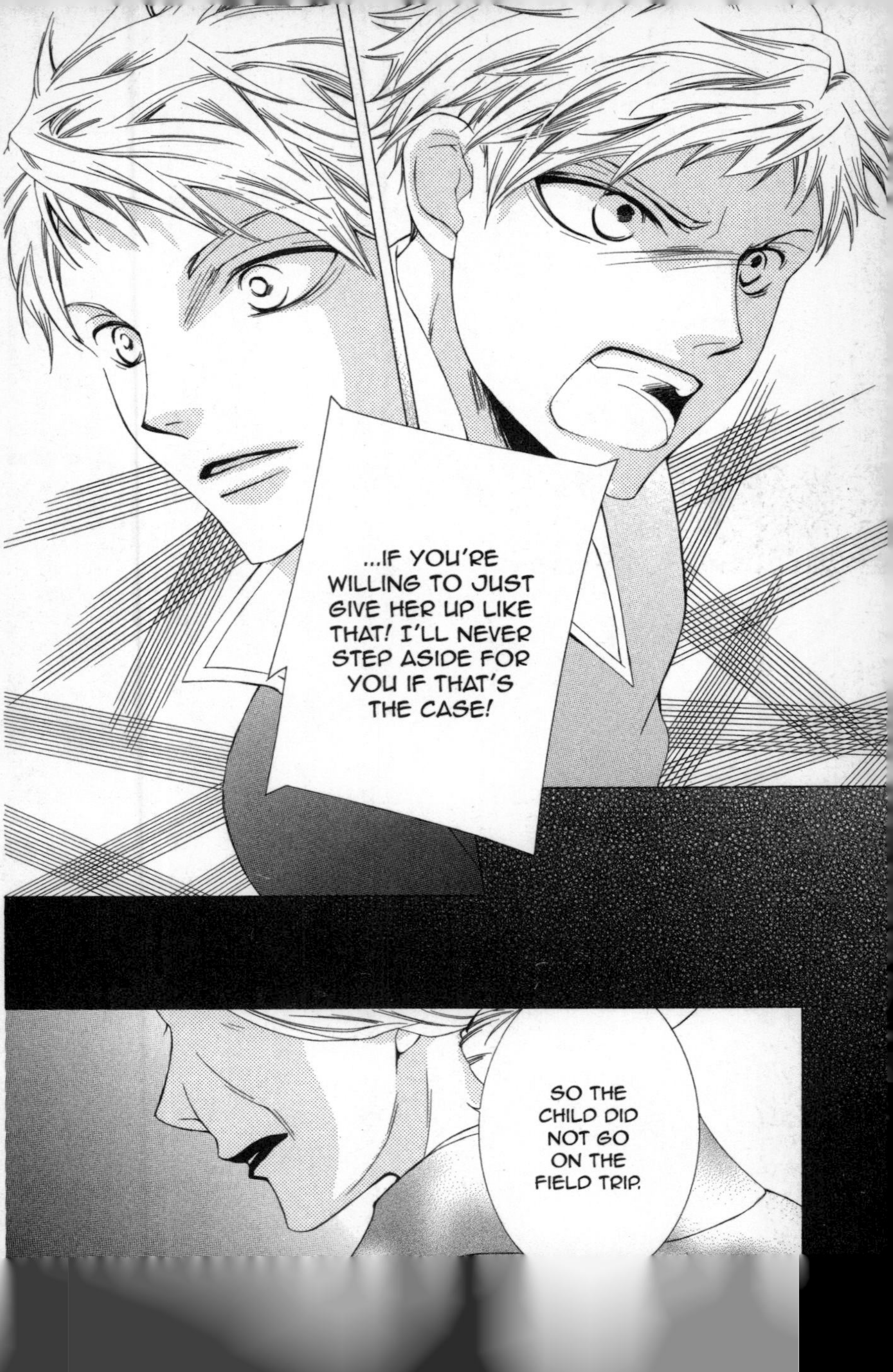
...IF YOU'RE WILLING TO JUST GIVE HER UP LIKE THAT! I'LL NEVER STEP ASIDE FOR YOU IF THAT'S THE CASE!
SO THE CHILD DID NOT GO ON THE FIELD TRIP.

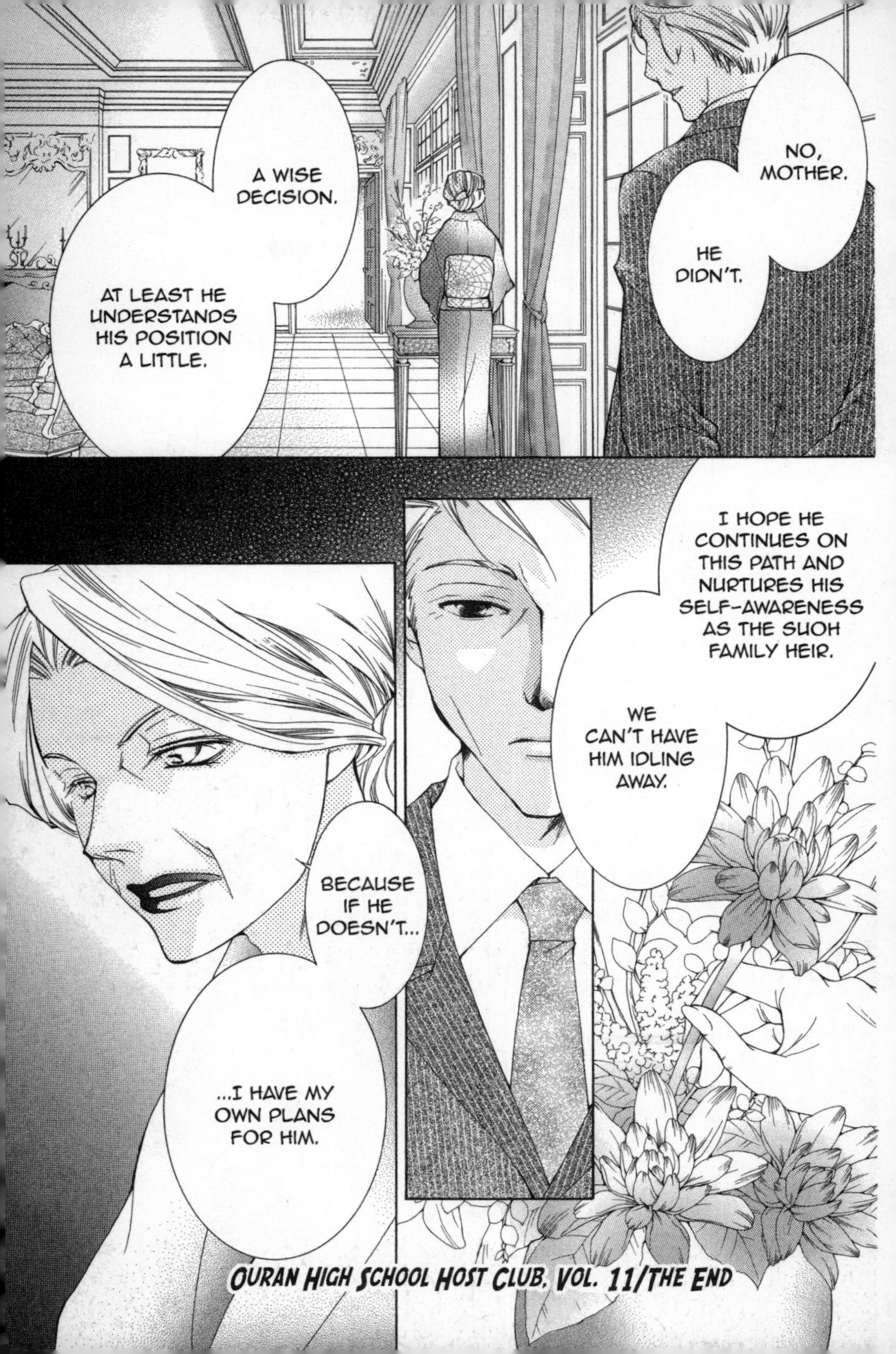
NO, MOTHER.
HE DIDN'T.
A WISE DECISION.
AT LEAST HE UNDERSTANDS HIS POSITION A LITTLE.
I HOPE HE CONTINUES ON THIS PATH AND NURTURES HIS SELF-AWARENESS AS THE SUOH FAMILY HEIR.
WE CAN'T HAVE HIM IDLING AWAY.
BECAUSE IF HE DOESN'T...
...I HAVE MY OWN PLANS FOR HIM.
OURAN HIGH SCHOOL HOST CLUB, VOL. 11/THE END

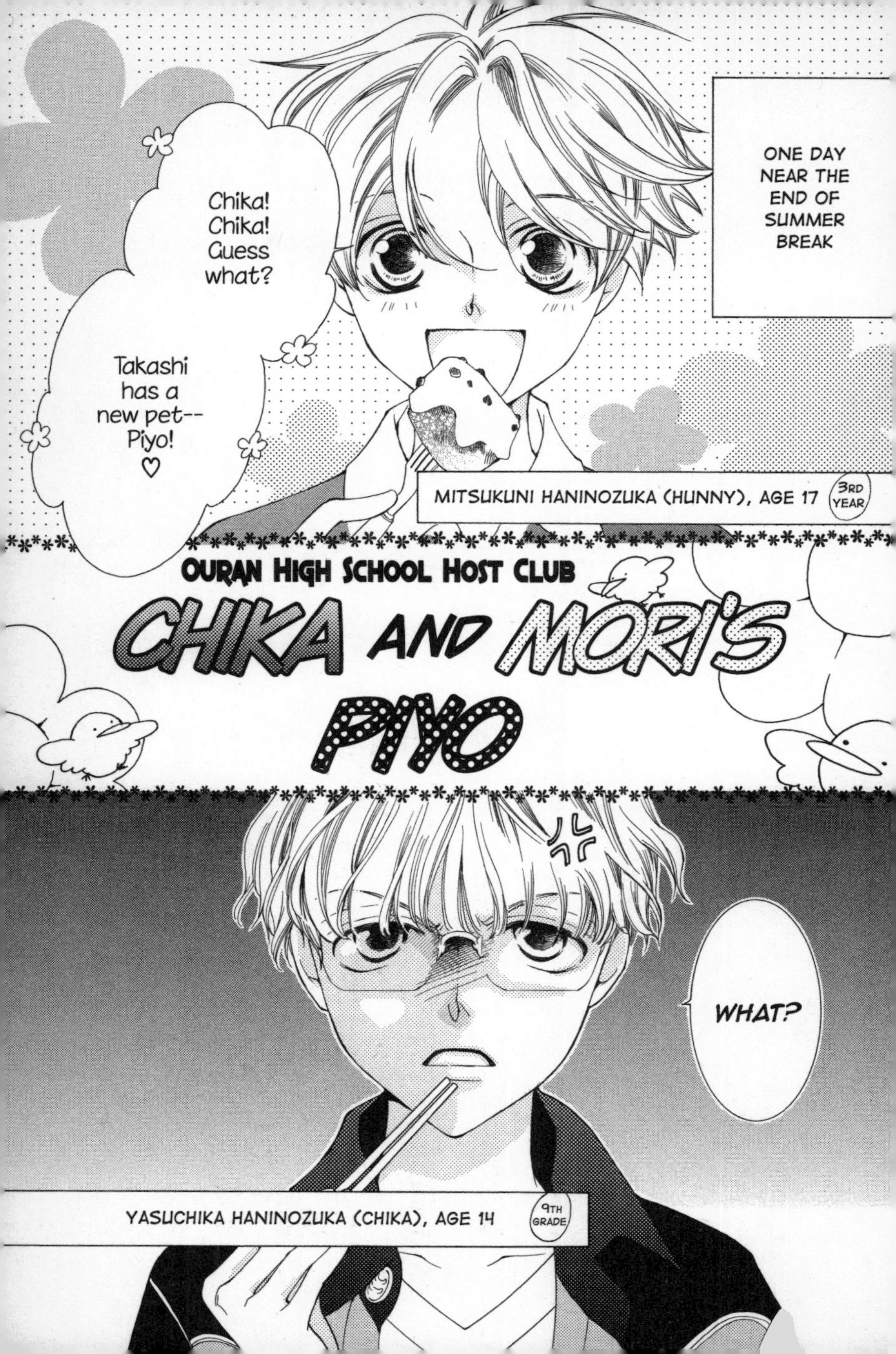
ONE DAY NEAR THE END OF SUMMER BREAK
Chika! Chika! Guess what?
Takashi has a new pet-- Piyo! ♡
MITSUKUNI HANINOZUKA (HUNNY), AGE 17 3RD YEAR
OURAN HIGH SCHOOL HOST CLUB
CHIKA AND MORI'S PIYO
WHAT?
YASUCHIKA HANINOZUKA (CHIKA), AGE 14 9TH GRADE

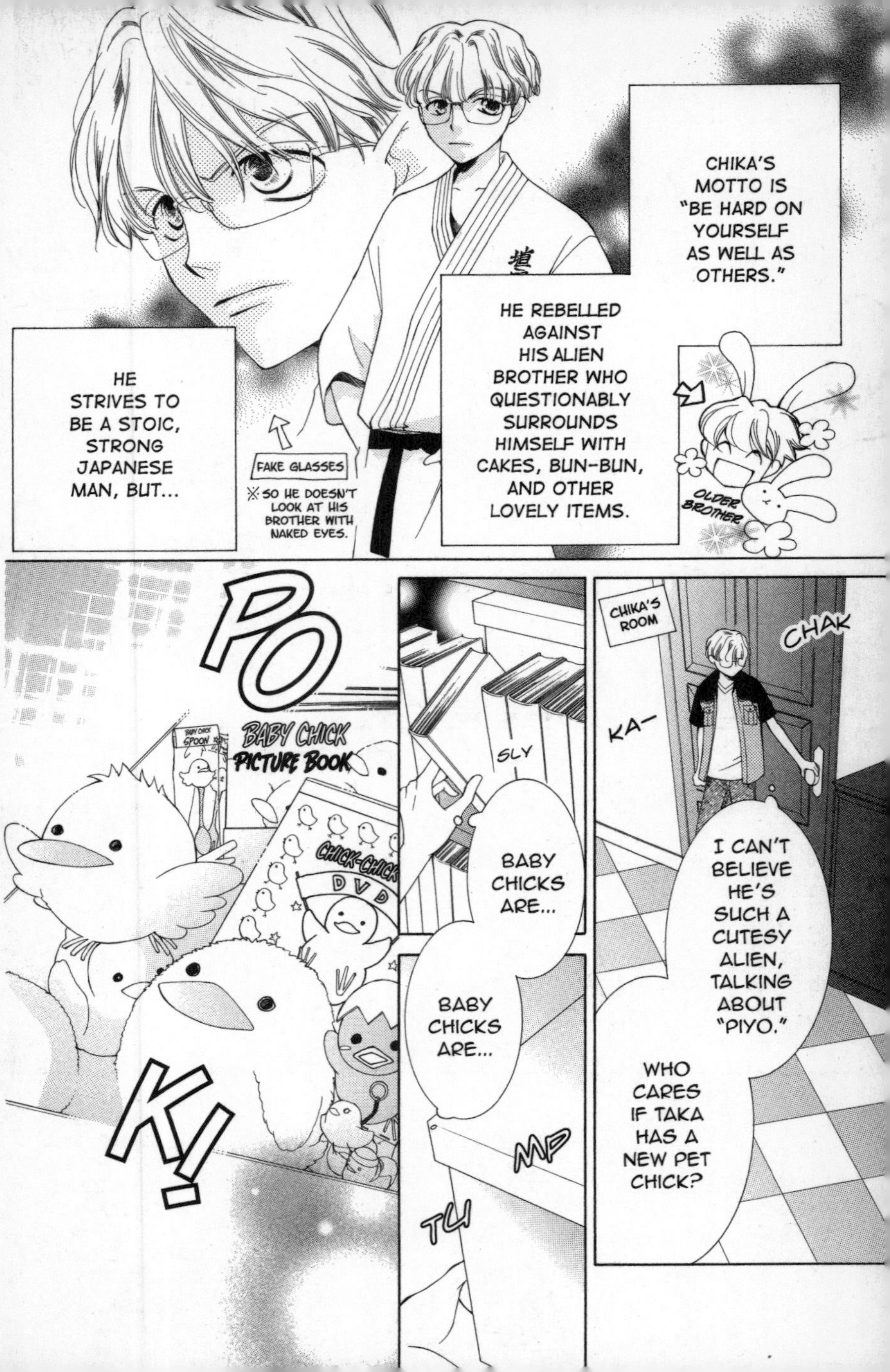

CHIKA'S MOTTO IS "BE HARD ON YOURSELF AS WELL AS OTHERS."
HE REBELLED AGAINST HIS ALIEN BROTHER WHO QUESTIONABLY SURROUNDS HIMSELF WITH CAKES, BUN-BUN, AND OTHER LOVELY ITEMS.
OLDER BROTHER
FAKE GLASSES
※SO HE DOESN'T LOOK AT HIS BROTHER WITH NAKED EYES.
HE STRIVES TO BE A STOIC, STRONG JAPANESE MAN, BUT...
CHIKA'S ROOM
CHAK
KA-
I CAN'T BELIEVE HE'S SUCH A CUTESY ALIEN, TALKING ABOUT "PIYO."
WHO CARES IF TAKA HAS A NEW PET CHICK?
SLY
BABY CHICKS ARE...
BABY CHICKS ARE...
MP
TU
PO
BABY CHICK PICTURE BOOK
BABY CHICK SPOON
CHICK-CHICK DVD
K!

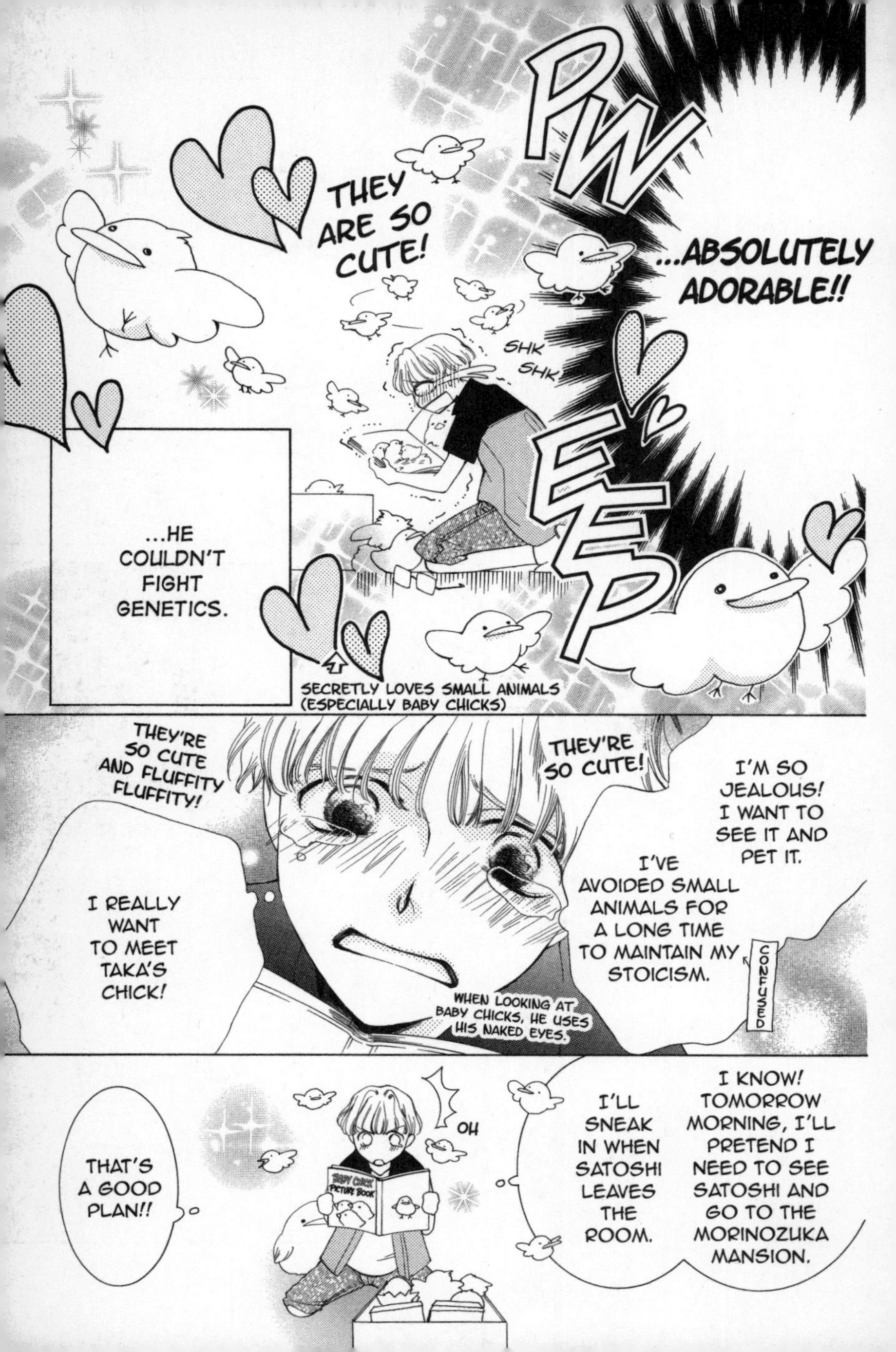
PWEEP
...ABSOLUTELY ADORABLE!!
THEY ARE SO CUTE!
SHK SHK
...HE COULDN'T FIGHT GENETICS.
SECRETLY LOVES SMALL ANIMALS (ESPECIALLY BABY CHICKS)
I'M SO JEALOUS! I WANT TO SEE IT AND PET IT.
CONFUSED
I'VE AVOIDED SMALL ANIMALS FOR A LONG TIME TO MAINTAIN MY STOICISM.
THEY'RE SO CUTE!
THEY'RE SO CUTE AND FLUFFITY FLUFFITY!
WHEN LOOKING AT BABY CHICKS, HE USES HIS NAKED EYES.
I REALLY WANT TO MEET TAKA'S CHICK!
I KNOW! TOMORROW MORNING, I'LL PRETEND I NEED TO SEE SATOSHI AND GO TO THE MORINOZUKA MANSION.
I'LL SNEAK IN WHEN SATOSHI LEAVES THE ROOM.
OH
BABY CHICK PICTURE BOOK
THAT'S A GOOD PLAN!!

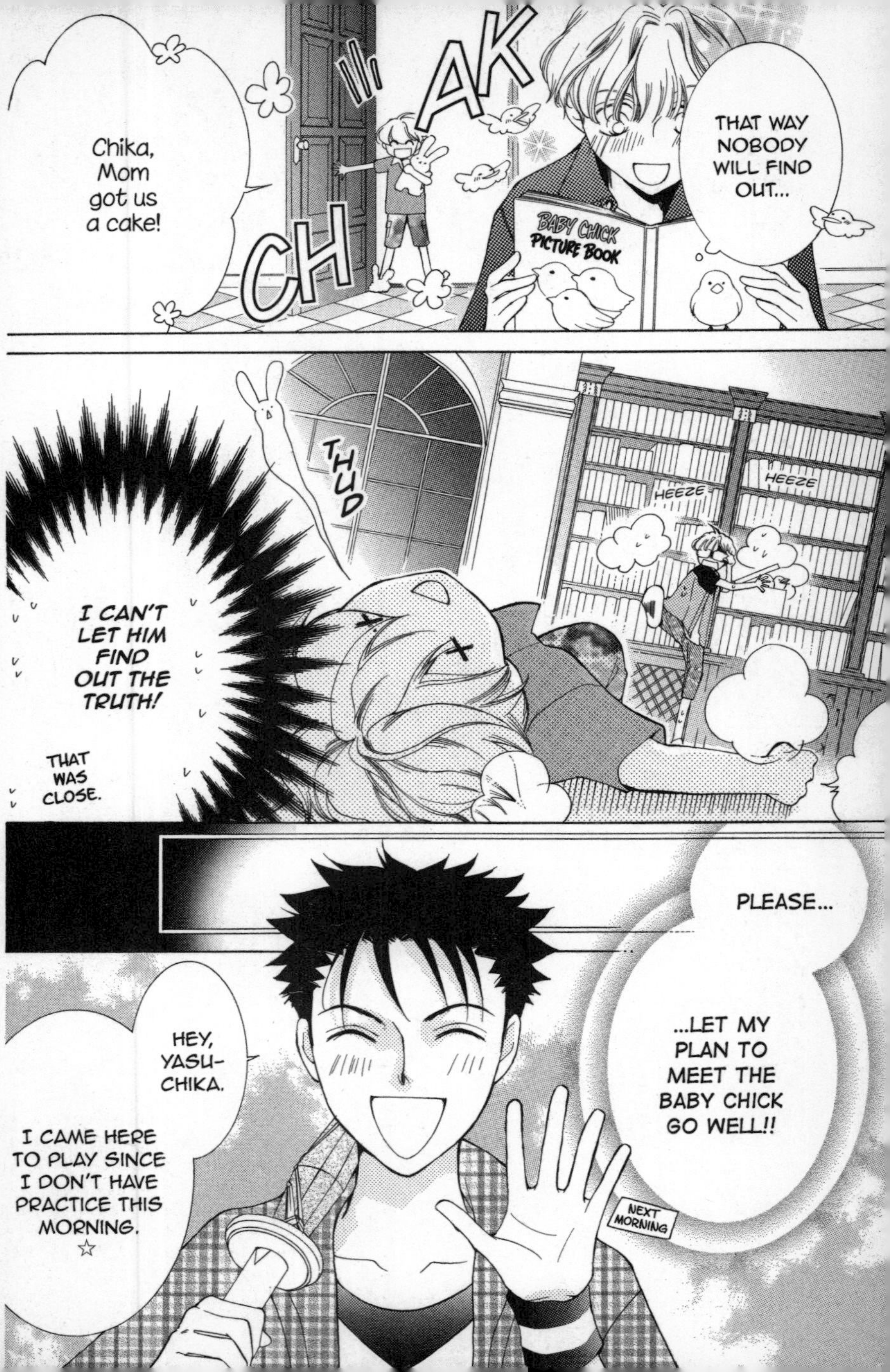
THAT WAY NOBODY WILL FIND OUT...
BABY CHICK PICTURE BOOK
CHAK
Chika, Mom got us a cake!
HEEZE
HEEZE
THUD
I CAN'T LET HIM FIND OUT THE TRUTH!
THAT WAS CLOSE.
PLEASE...
...LET MY PLAN TO MEET THE BABY CHICK GO WELL!!
NEXT MORNING
HEY, YASU-CHIKA.
I CAME HERE TO PLAY SINCE I DON'T HAVE PRACTICE THIS MORNING. ☆

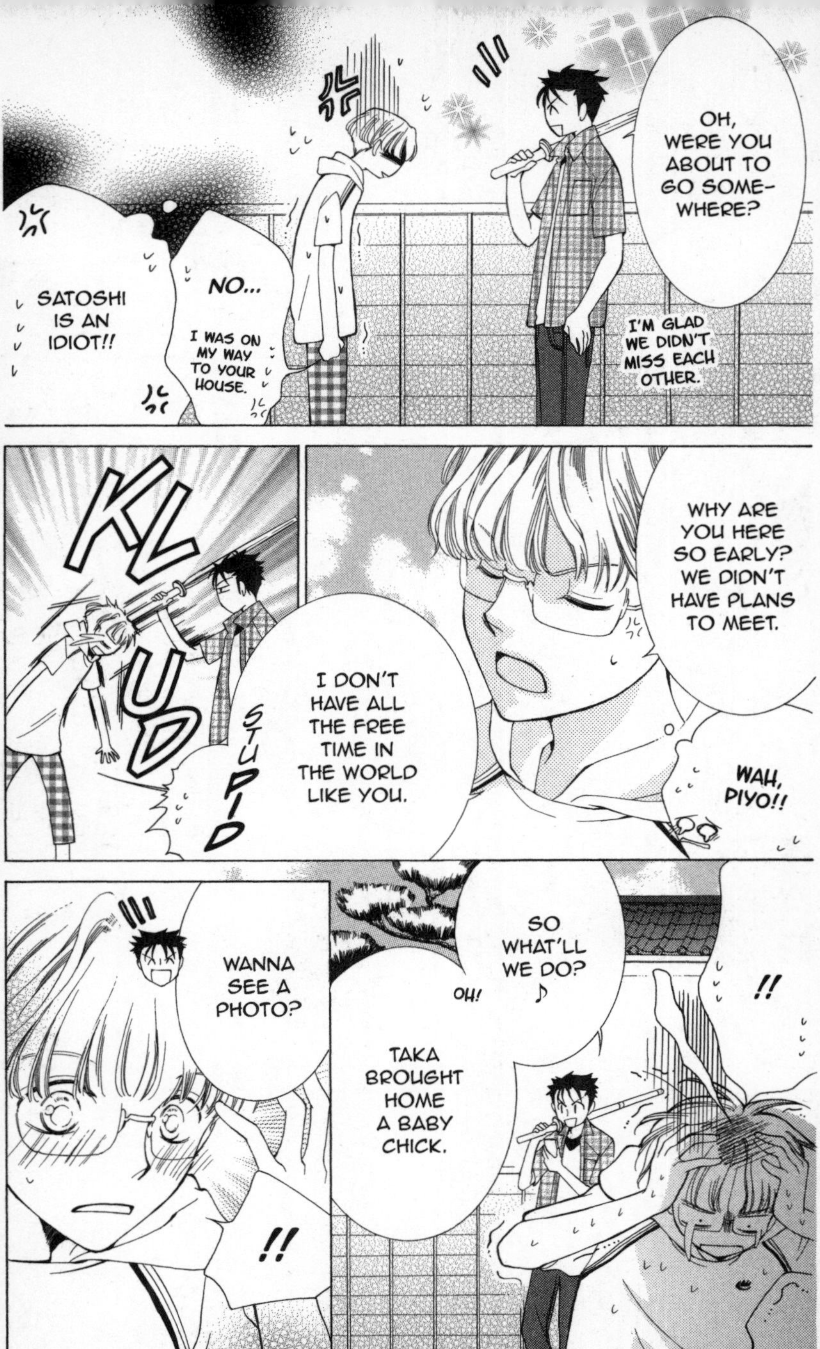
OH, WERE YOU ABOUT TO GO SOME-WHERE?
I'M GLAD WE DIDN'T MISS EACH OTHER.
NO...
I WAS ON MY WAY TO YOUR HOUSE.
SATOSHI IS AN IDIOT!!
WHY ARE YOU HERE SO EARLY? WE DIDN'T HAVE PLANS TO MEET.
WAH, PIYO!!
I DON'T HAVE ALL THE FREE TIME IN THE WORLD LIKE YOU.
KLUD
STUPID
!!
SO WHAT'LL WE DO? ♪
OH!
TAKA BROUGHT HOME A BABY CHICK.
WANNA SEE A PHOTO?
!!

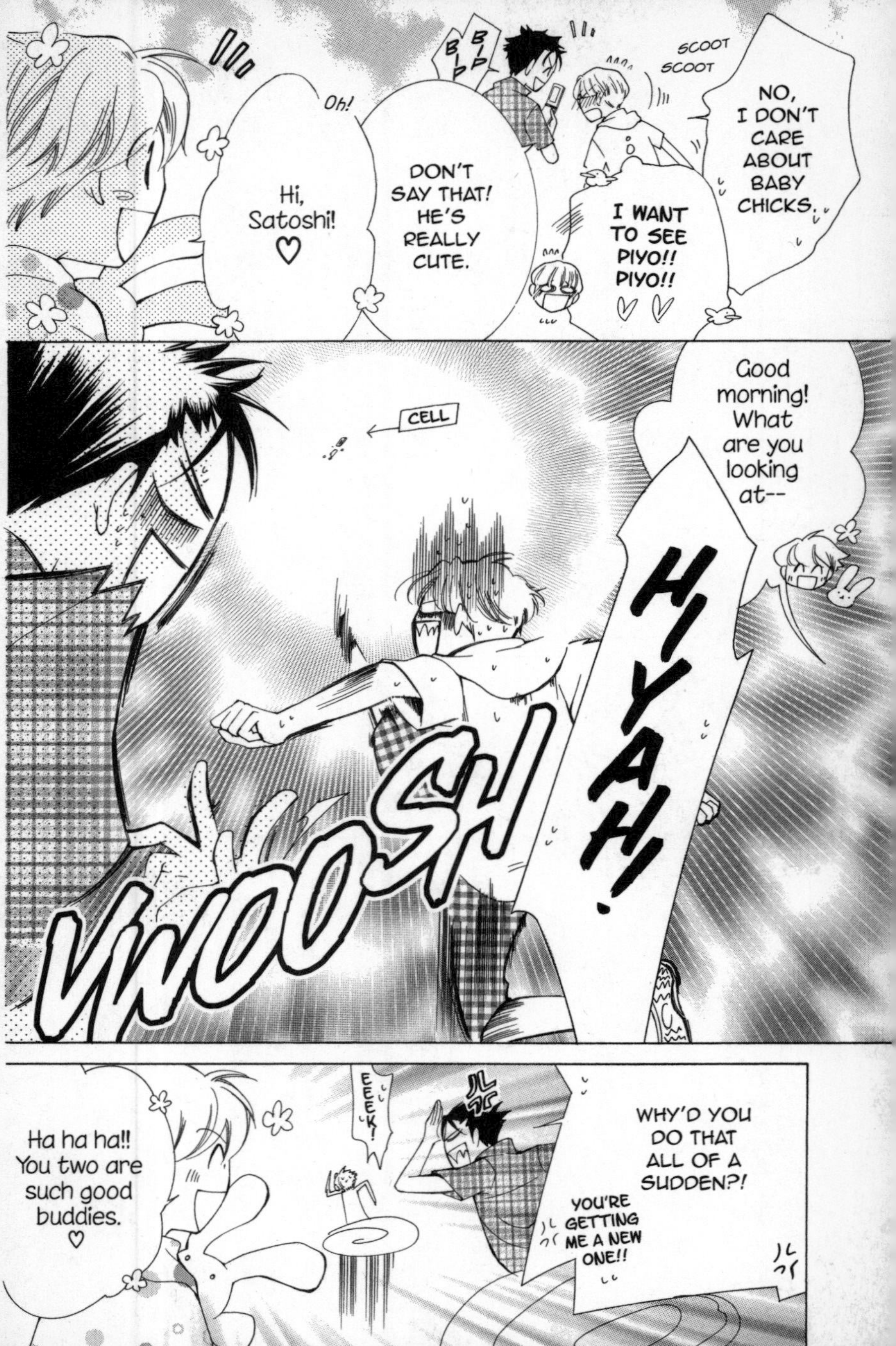
SCOOT SCOOT
NO, I DON'T CARE ABOUT BABY CHICKS.
I WANT TO SEE PIYO!! PIYO!! ♡ ♡
BIP BIP
DON'T SAY THAT! HE'S REALLY CUTE.
Oh!
Hi, Satoshi! ♡
Good morning! What are you looking at--
HIYAH!
CELL
VWOOSH
WHY'D YOU DO THAT ALL OF A SUDDEN?!
YOU'RE GETTING ME A NEW ONE!!
EEEK!
Ha ha ha!! You two are such good buddies. ♡

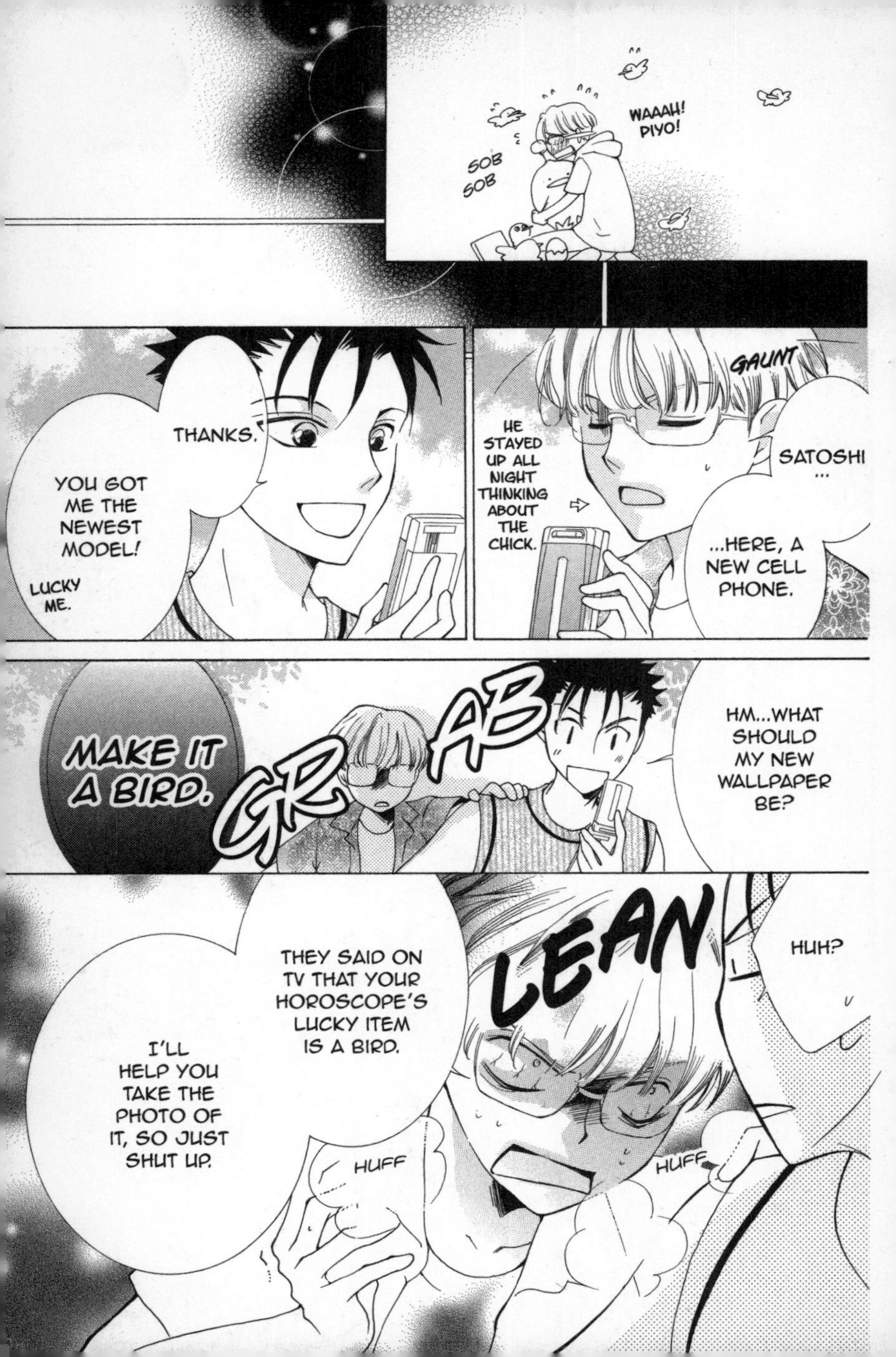
WAAAH! PIYO!
SOB SOB
GAUNT
SATOSHI ...
...HERE, A NEW CELL PHONE.
HE STAYED UP ALL NIGHT THINKING ABOUT THE CHICK.
THANKS.
YOU GOT ME THE NEWEST MODEL!
LUCKY ME.
HM...WHAT SHOULD MY NEW WALLPAPER BE?
GRAB
MAKE IT A BIRD.
HUH?
LEAN
THEY SAID ON TV THAT YOUR HOROSCOPE'S LUCKY ITEM IS A BIRD.
I'LL HELP YOU TAKE THE PHOTO OF IT, SO JUST SHUT UP.
HUFF
HUFF

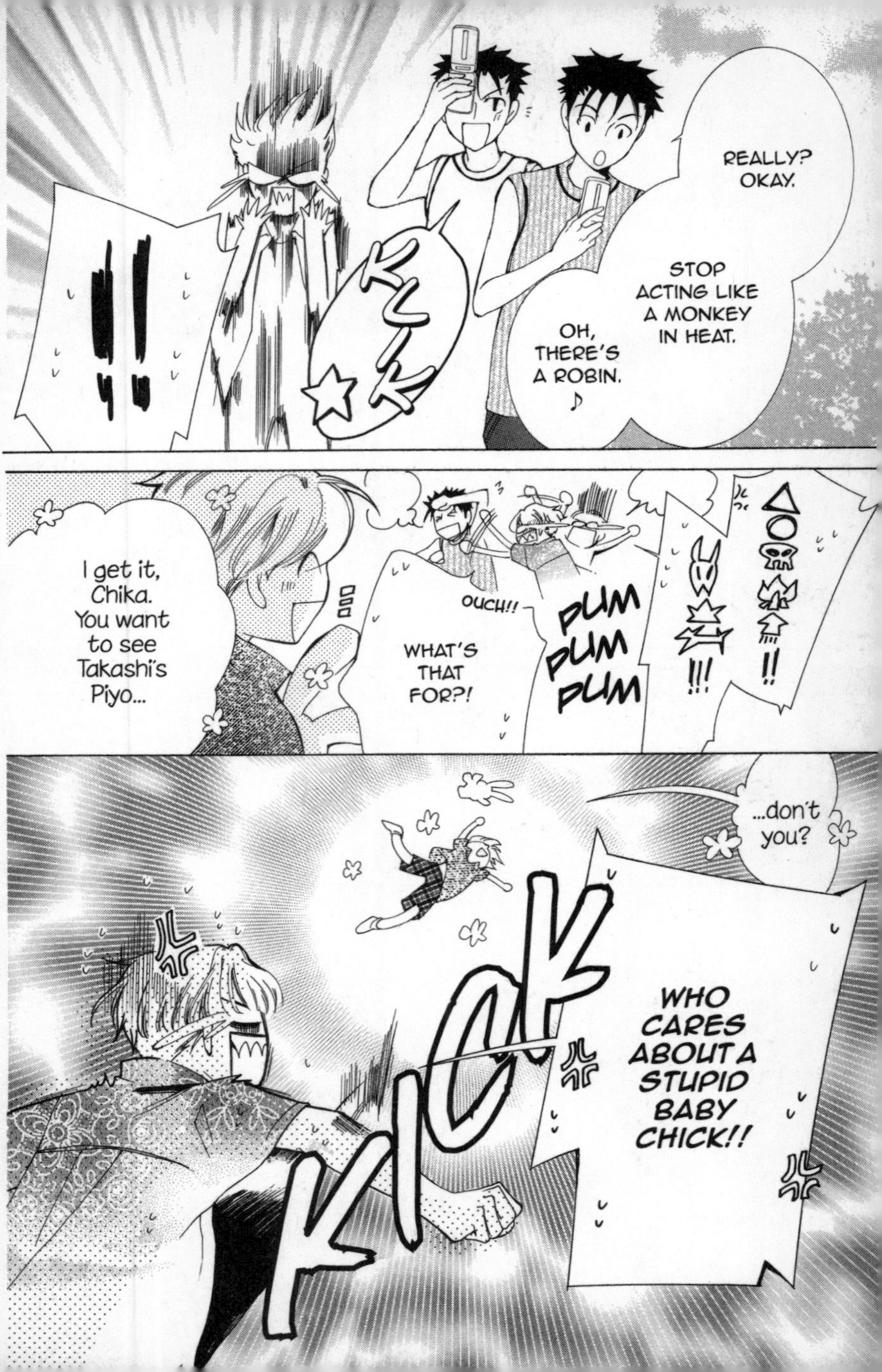
REALLY? OKAY.
STOP ACTING LIKE A MONKEY IN HEAT.
OH, THERE'S A ROBIN. ♪
KLIK
!!
!!
!!!
PUM PUM PUM
OUCH!!
WHAT'S THAT FOR?!
I get it, Chika. You want to see Takashi's Piyo...
...don't you?
WHO CARES ABOUT A STUPID BABY CHICK!!
KICK

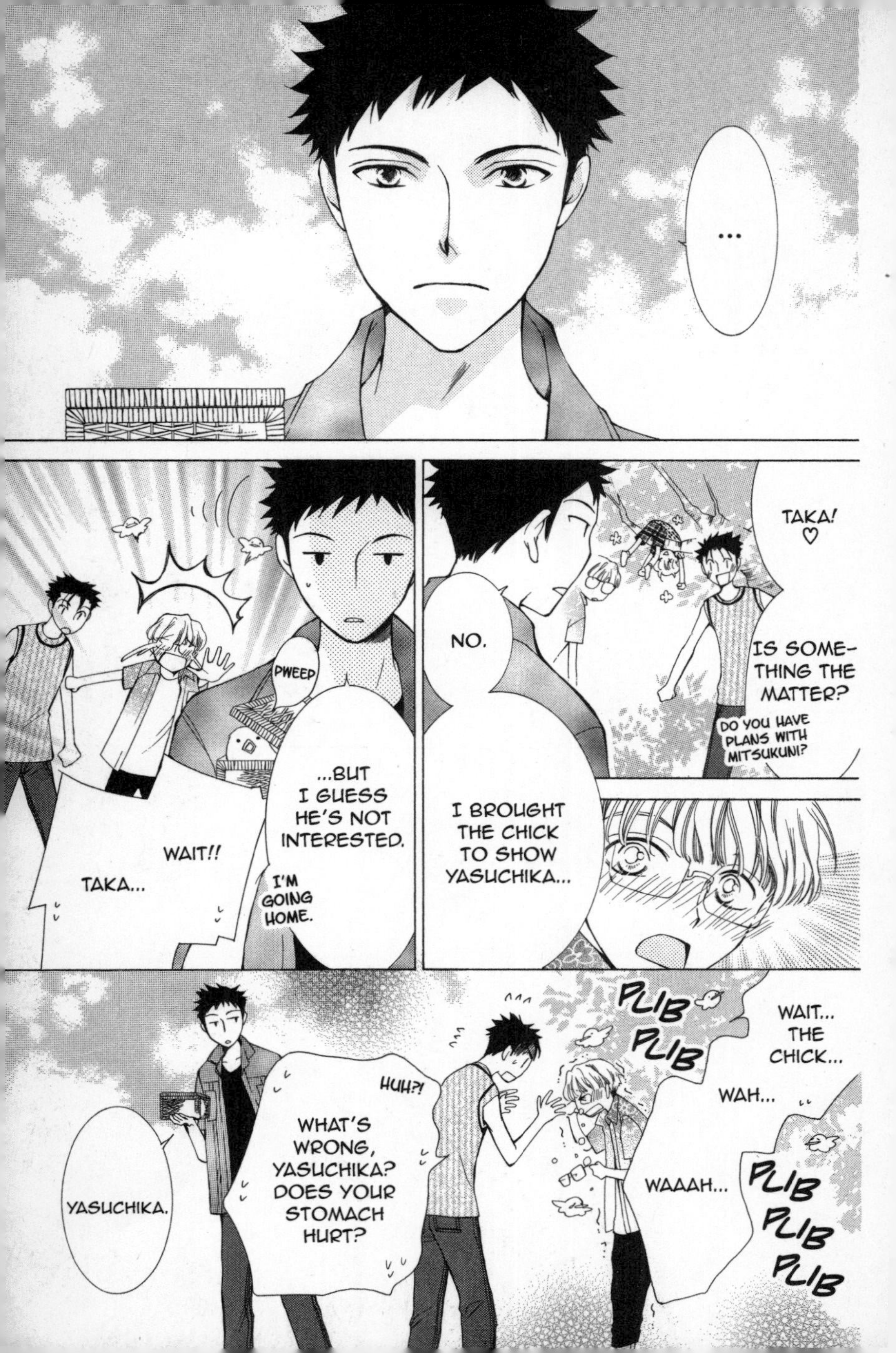
...
TAKA! ♡
IS SOMETHING THE MATTER?
DO YOU HAVE PLANS WITH MITSUKUNI?
NO.
I BROUGHT THE CHICK TO SHOW YASUCHIKA...
...BUT I GUESS HE'S NOT INTERESTED.
I'M GOING HOME.
PWEEP
WAIT!!
TAKA...
WAIT... THE CHICK...
PLIB PLIB
WAH...
WAAAH...
PLIB PLIB PLIB
HUH?!
WHAT'S WRONG, YASUCHIKA? DOES YOUR STOMACH HURT?
YASUCHIKA.

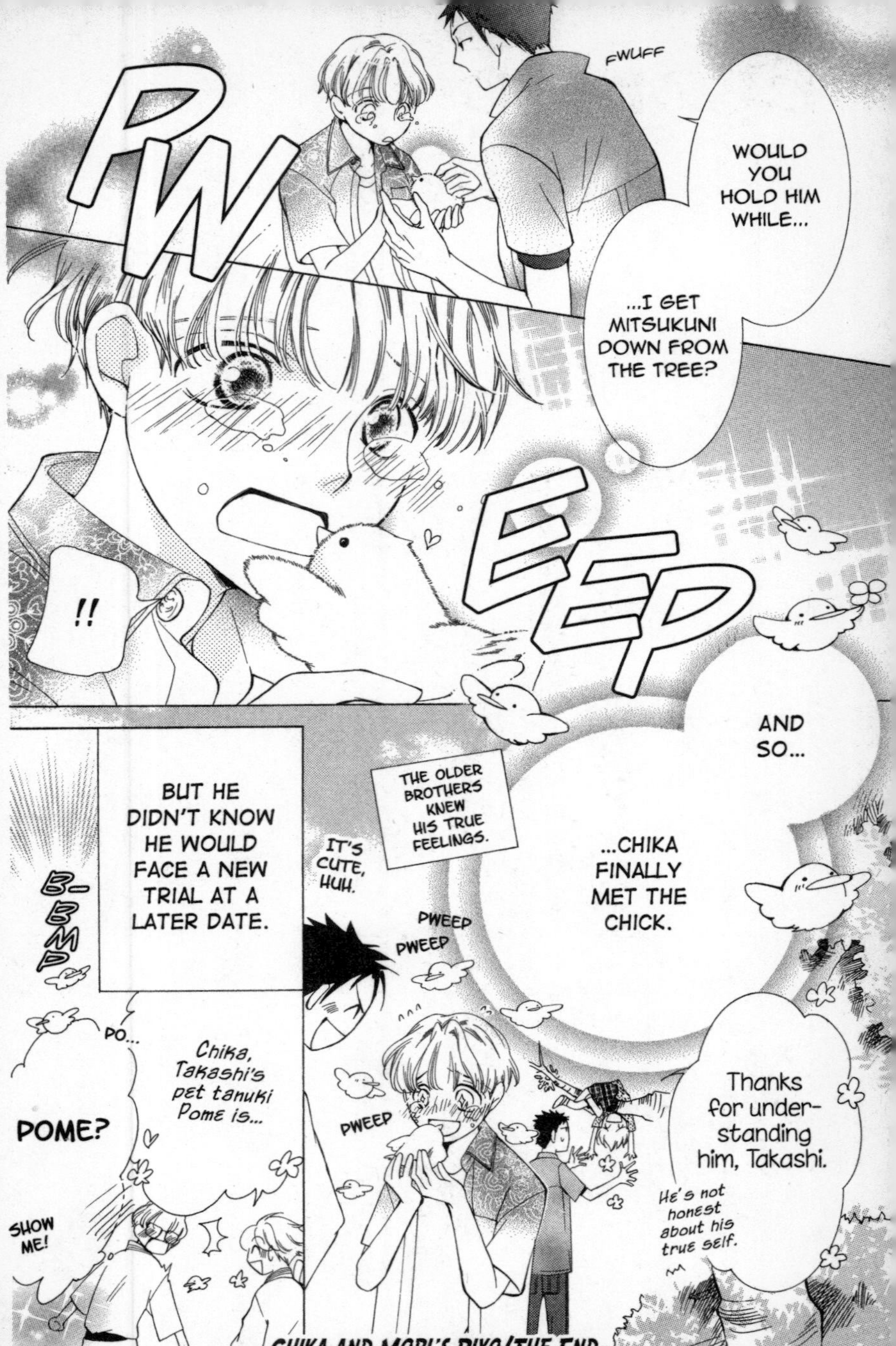
FWUFF
WOULD YOU HOLD HIM WHILE...
...I GET MITSUKUNI DOWN FROM THE TREE?
PW
EEP
!!
AND SO...
...CHIKA FINALLY MET THE CHICK.
THE OLDER BROTHERS KNEW HIS TRUE FEELINGS.
IT'S CUTE, HUH.
PWEEP
PWEEP
Thanks for under-standing him, Takashi.
He's not honest about his true self.
PWEEP
BUT HE DIDN'T KNOW HE WOULD FACE A NEW TRIAL AT A LATER DATE.
B-BMP
Chika, Takashi's pet tanuki Pome is...
PO...
POME?
SHOW ME!

CHIKA AND MORI'S PIYO/THE END

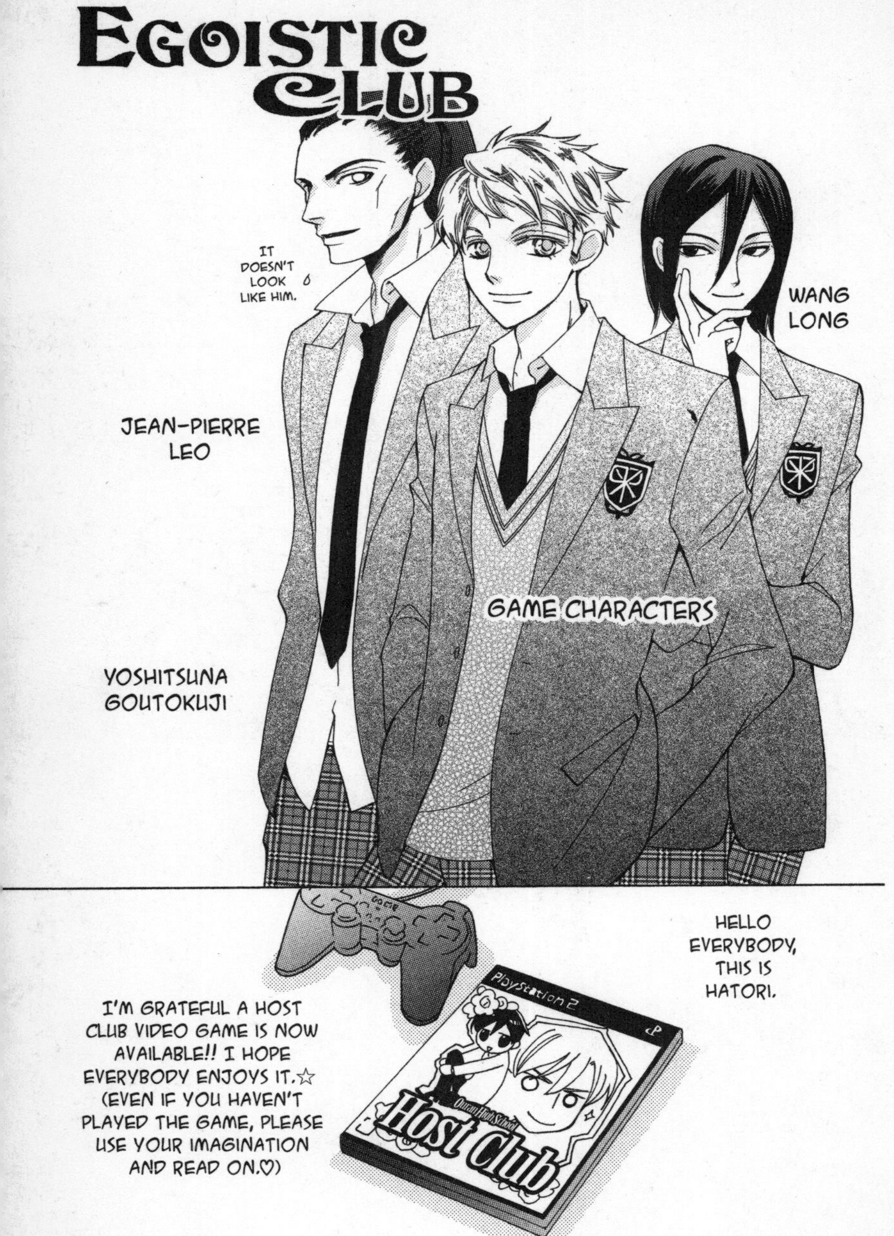
EGOISTIC CLUB
WANG LONG
IT DOESN'T LOOK LIKE HIM.
JEAN-PIERRE LEO
GAME CHARACTERS
YOSHITSUNA GOUTOKUJI
HELLO EVERYBODY, THIS IS HATORI.
I'M GRATEFUL A HOST CLUB VIDEO GAME IS NOW AVAILABLE!! I HOPE EVERYBODY ENJOYS IT.☆ (EVEN IF YOU HAVEN'T PLAYED THE GAME, PLEASE USE YOUR IMAGINATION AND READ ON.♡)
PlayStation 2
Ouran High School
Host Club

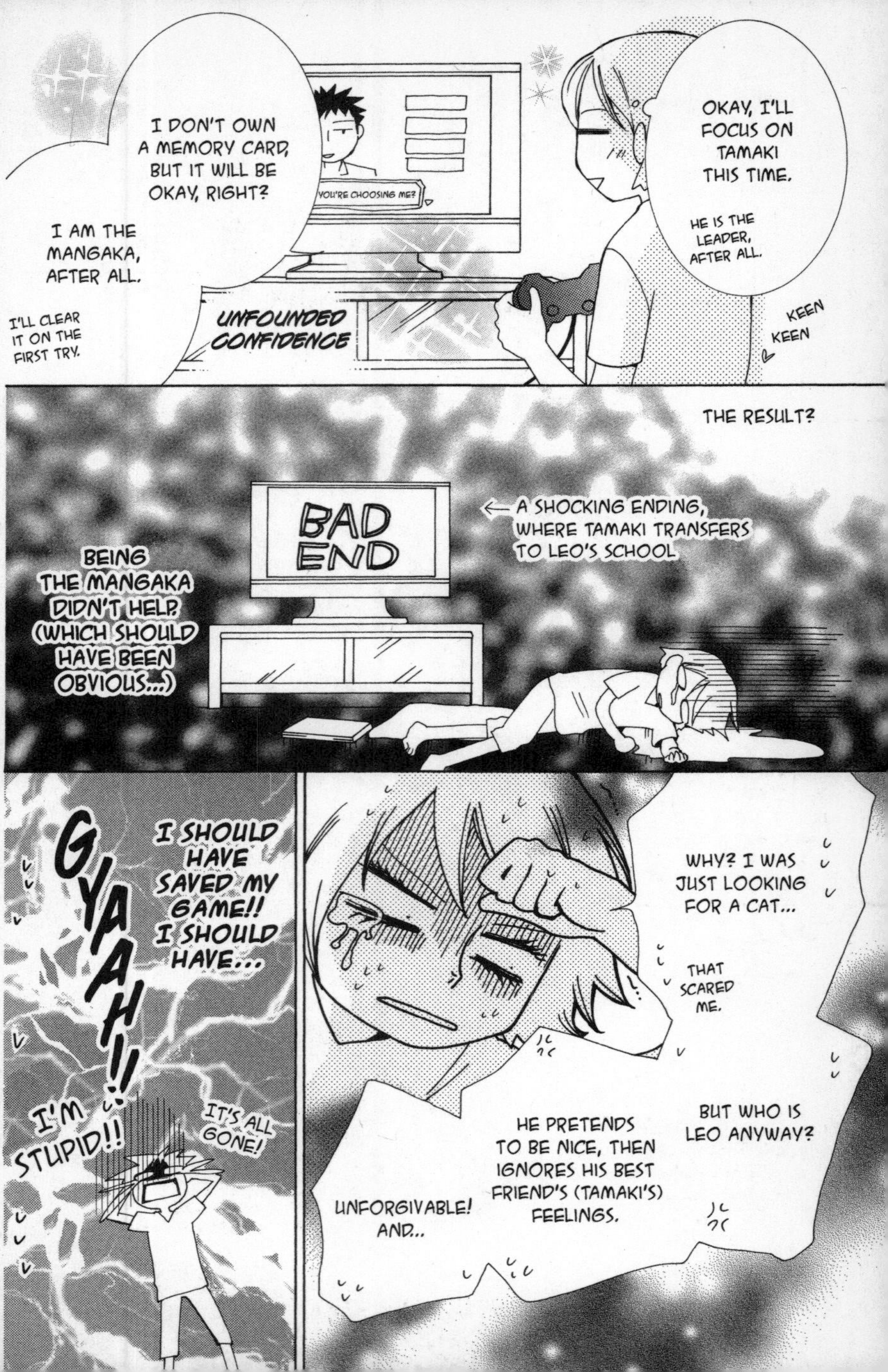
OKAY, I'LL FOCUS ON TAMAKI THIS TIME.
HE IS THE LEADER, AFTER ALL.
KEEN KEEN
YOU'RE CHOOSING ME?
I DON'T OWN A MEMORY CARD, BUT IT WILL BE OKAY, RIGHT?
I AM THE MANGAKA, AFTER ALL.
I'LL CLEAR IT ON THE FIRST TRY.
UNFOUNDED CONFIDENCE
THE RESULT?
← A SHOCKING ENDING, WHERE TAMAKI TRANSFERS TO LEO'S SCHOOL
BAD END
BEING THE MANGAKA DIDN'T HELP. (WHICH SHOULD HAVE BEEN OBVIOUS...)
WHY? I WAS JUST LOOKING FOR A CAT...
THAT SCARED ME.
BUT WHO IS LEO ANYWAY?
HE PRETENDS TO BE NICE, THEN IGNORES HIS BEST FRIEND'S (TAMAKI'S) FEELINGS.
UNFORGIVABLE! AND...
I SHOULD HAVE SAVED MY GAME!! I SHOULD HAVE...
GYAAH!!
IT'S ALL GONE!
I'M STUPID!!

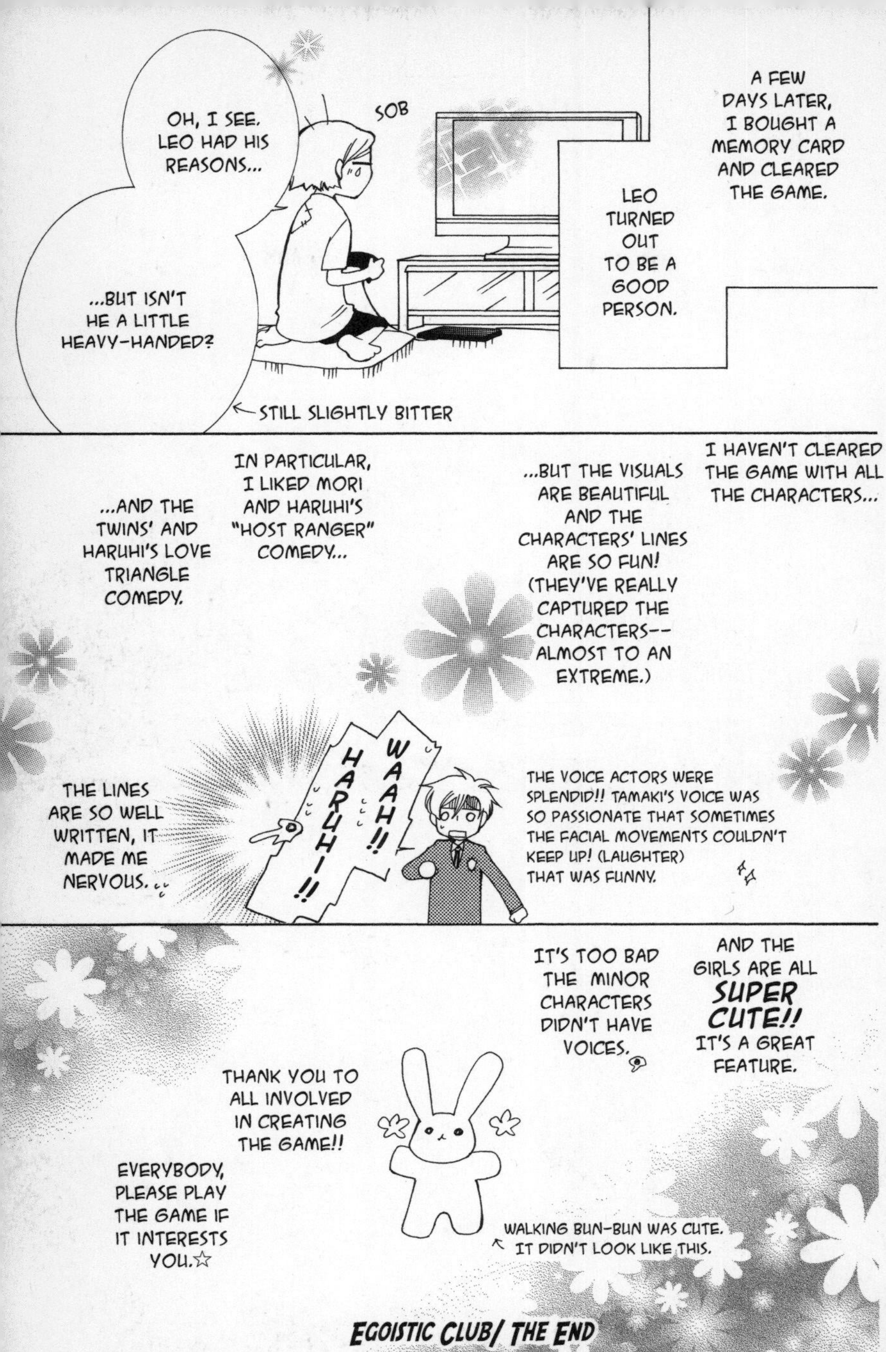
A FEW DAYS LATER, I BOUGHT A MEMORY CARD AND CLEARED THE GAME.
LEO TURNED OUT TO BE A GOOD PERSON.
OH, I SEE. LEO HAD HIS REASONS...
SOB
...BUT ISN'T HE A LITTLE HEAVY-HANDED?
STILL SLIGHTLY BITTER
I HAVEN'T CLEARED THE GAME WITH ALL THE CHARACTERS...
...BUT THE VISUALS ARE BEAUTIFUL AND THE CHARACTERS' LINES ARE SO FUN! (THEY'VE REALLY CAPTURED THE CHARACTERS--ALMOST TO AN EXTREME.)
IN PARTICULAR, I LIKED MORI AND HARUHI'S "HOST RANGER" COMEDY...
...AND THE TWINS' AND HARUHI'S LOVE TRIANGLE COMEDY.
THE VOICE ACTORS WERE SPLENDID!! TAMAKI'S VOICE WAS SO PASSIONATE THAT SOMETIMES THE FACIAL MOVEMENTS COULDN'T KEEP UP! (LAUGHTER) THAT WAS FUNNY.
WAAH!!
HARUHI!!
THE LINES ARE SO WELL WRITTEN, IT MADE ME NERVOUS.
AND THE GIRLS ARE ALL SUPER CUTE!! IT'S A GREAT FEATURE.
IT'S TOO BAD THE MINOR CHARACTERS DIDN'T HAVE VOICES.
THANK YOU TO ALL INVOLVED IN CREATING THE GAME!!
EVERYBODY, PLEASE PLAY THE GAME IF IT INTERESTS YOU.☆
WALKING BUN-BUN WAS CUTE. IT DIDN'T LOOK LIKE THIS.
EGOISTIC CLUB/ THE END

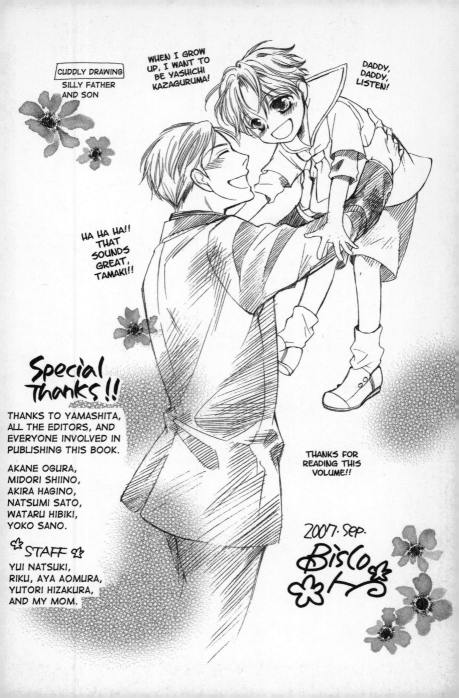

CUDDLY DRAWING

SILLY FATHER AND SON

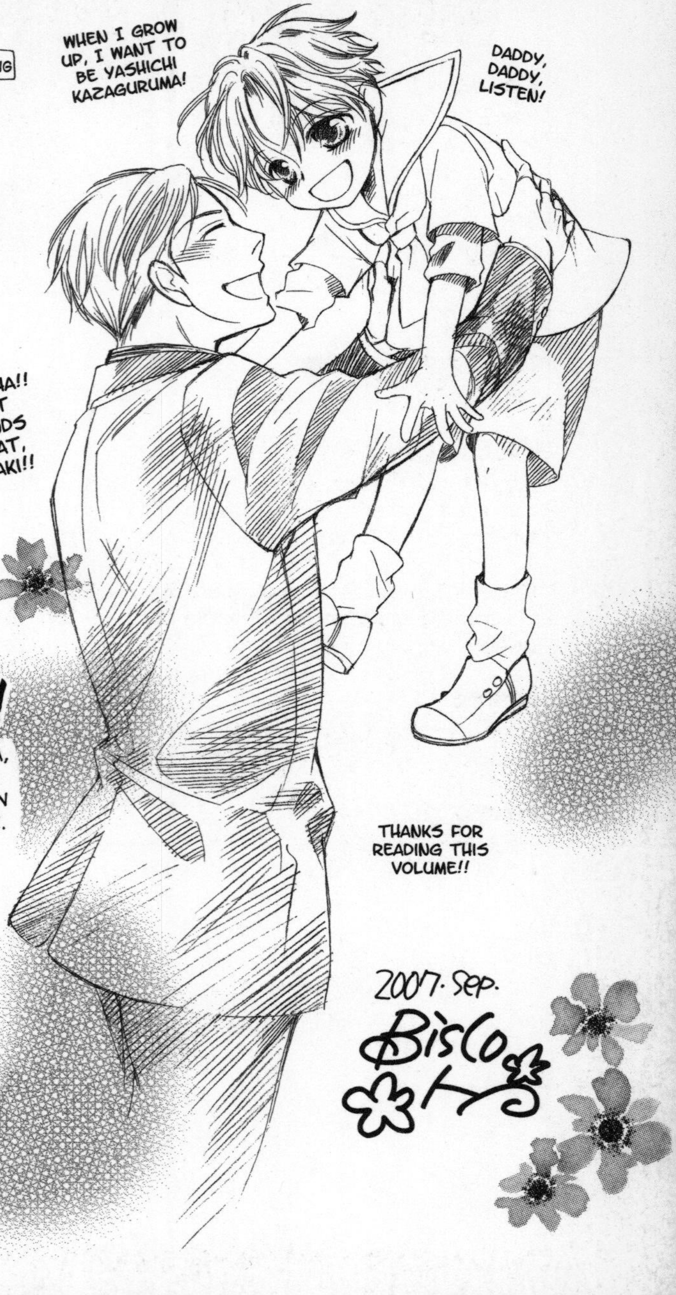
DADDY, DADDY, LISTEN!
WHEN I GROW UP, I WANT TO BE YASHICHI KAZAGURUMA!
HA HA HA!! THAT SOUNDS GREAT, TAMAKI!!

Special Thanks!!

THANKS TO YAMASHITA, ALL THE EDITORS, AND EVERYONE INVOLVED IN PUBLISHING THIS BOOK.

AKANE OGURA, MIDORI SHIINO, AKIRA HAGINO, NATSUMI SATO, WATARU HIBIKI, YOKO SANO.

STAFF

YUI NATSUKI, RIKU, AYA AOMURA, YUTORI HIZAKURA, AND MY MOM.

THANKS FOR READING THIS VOLUME!!

2007. Sep.

Bisco H

EDITOR'S NOTES

EPISODE 47
Page 25: *Tsundere* is an otaku term for female characters who tend to be rather unfriendly or prickly at first, but are gentle, loving, and kind once you get to know them. The word is a combination of *tsunsun*, or "prickly, morose" and *dere dere*, or "lovestruck."

EPISODE 48
Page 44: A charm for combating stage fright is to trace the kanji for *hito*, or "person," on your palm with your finger.

EPISODE 49
Page 85: A *fundoshi* is traditional underwear for men, similar to a loincloth.

EPISODE 50
Page 104: A *mawashi* is the belt that sumo wrestlers wear. It can also have material that hangs down in the front like an apron, similar to what Tamaki is wearing.

Page 112: The book Tamaki is holding, *Hanasaka Jiisan* (Flower Blossoming Old Man), is a folktale about a dog that repays a good deed to an old man.

EPISODE 51
Page 135: In old Chinese medicine, sleeping with one's stomach uncovered was thought to lead to digestive disorders.

EGOISTIC CLUB
Page 178: Kazaguruma no Yashichi was a character on *Mito Koumon* (see the editor's notes in volume 4).

Ouran High School

Host Club

FAN ART

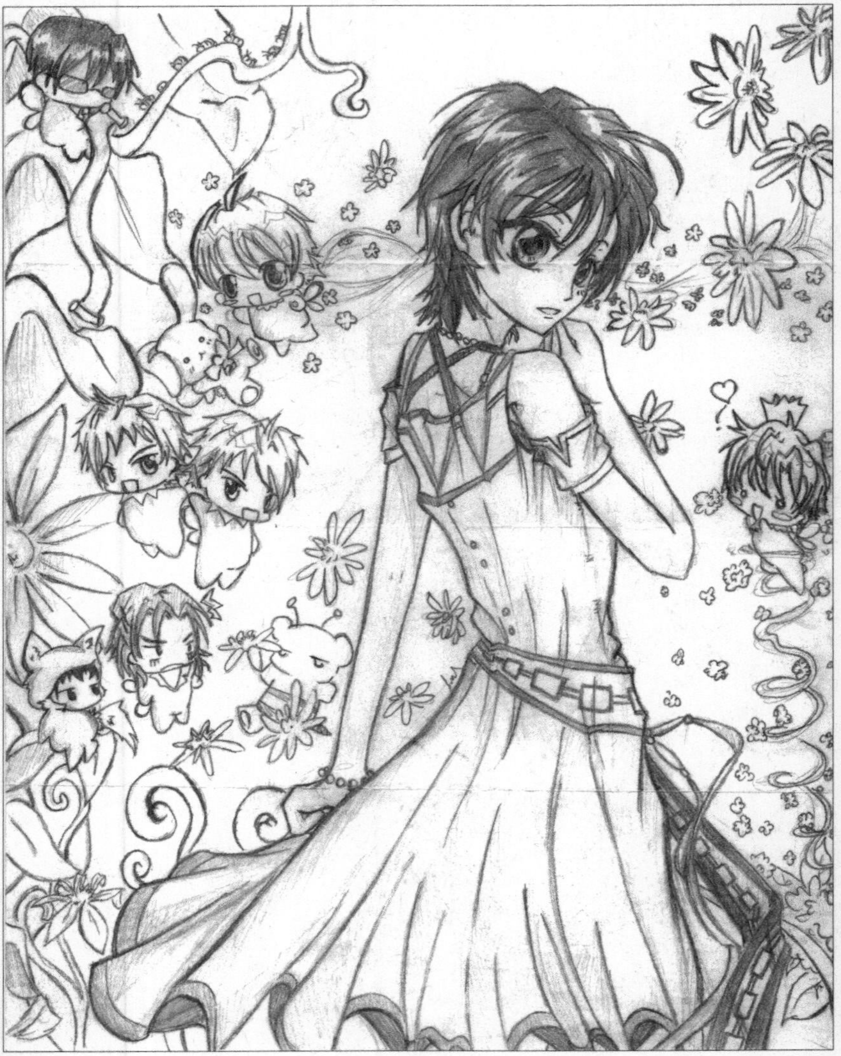

JoAnn Kang

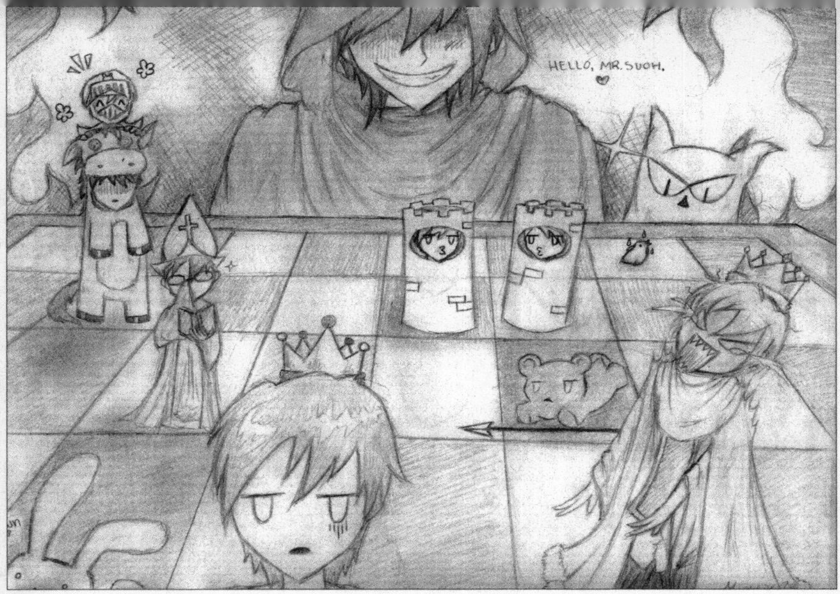
HELLO, MR. SUOH.

Michelle Zheng

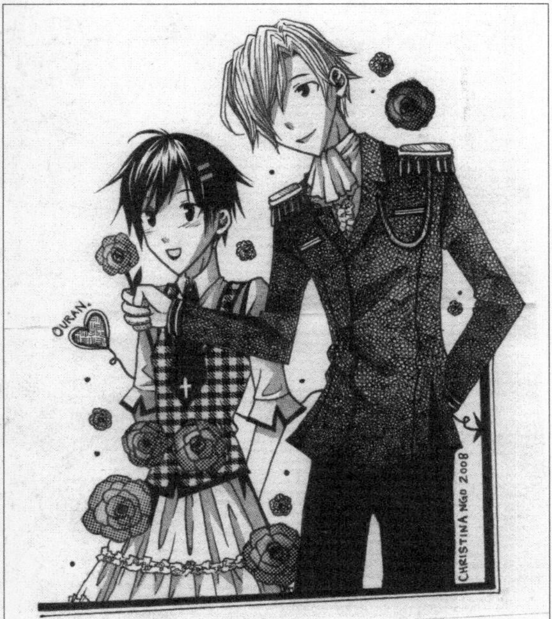
OURAN.
CHRISTINA NGO 2008

Christina Ngo

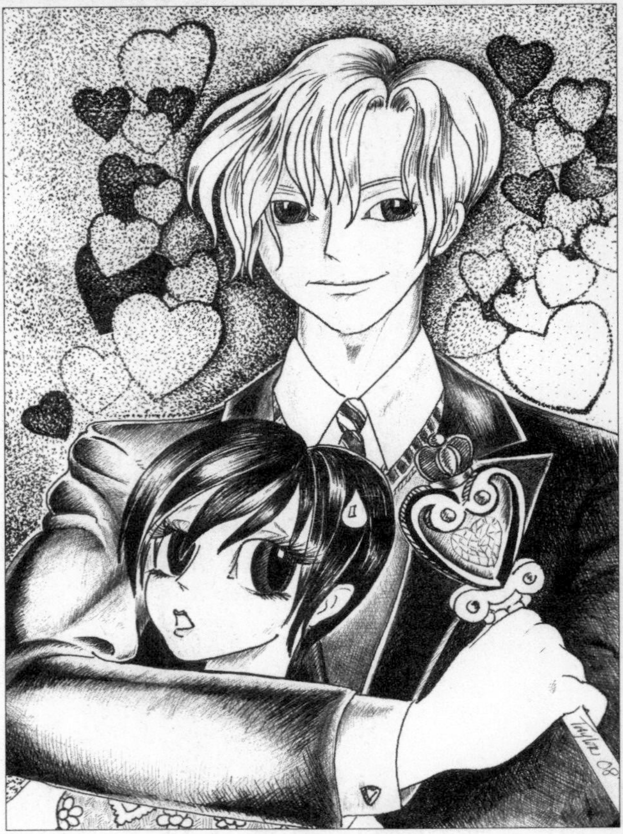

Annette Taylor

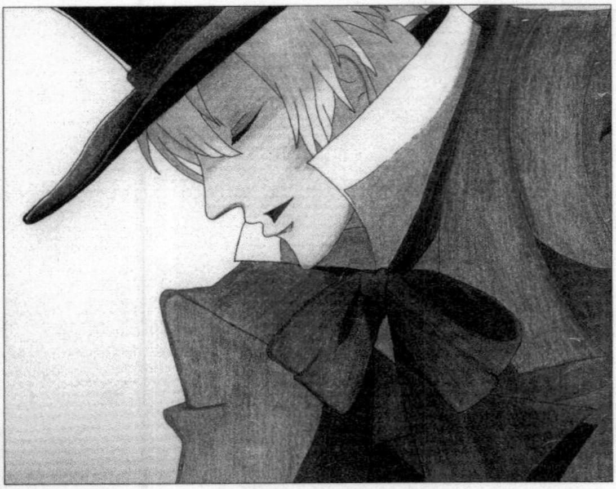

Tanya Chapman

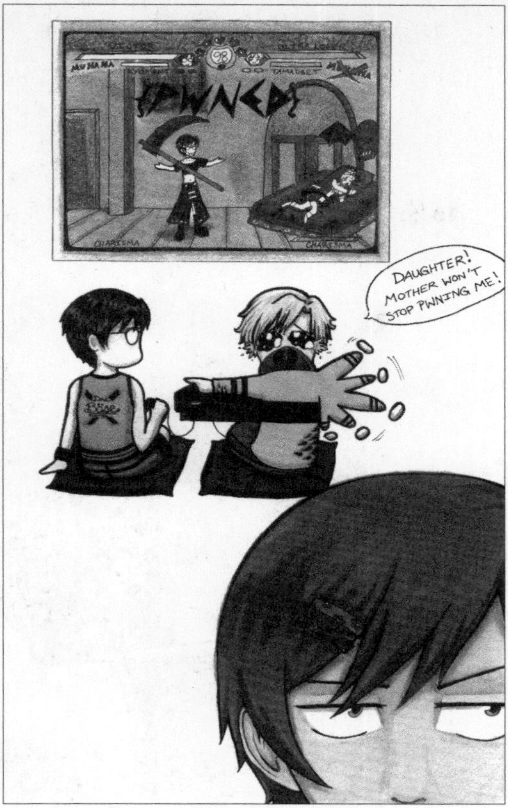
PWNED!
DAUGHTER! MOTHER WON'T STOP PWNING ME!

Shannon LaFlan

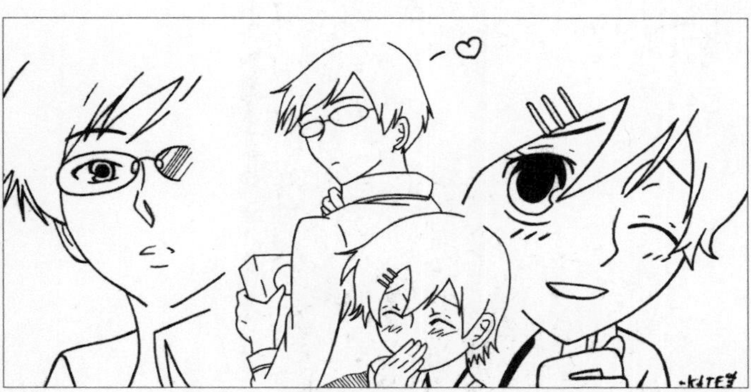

Kate Burns

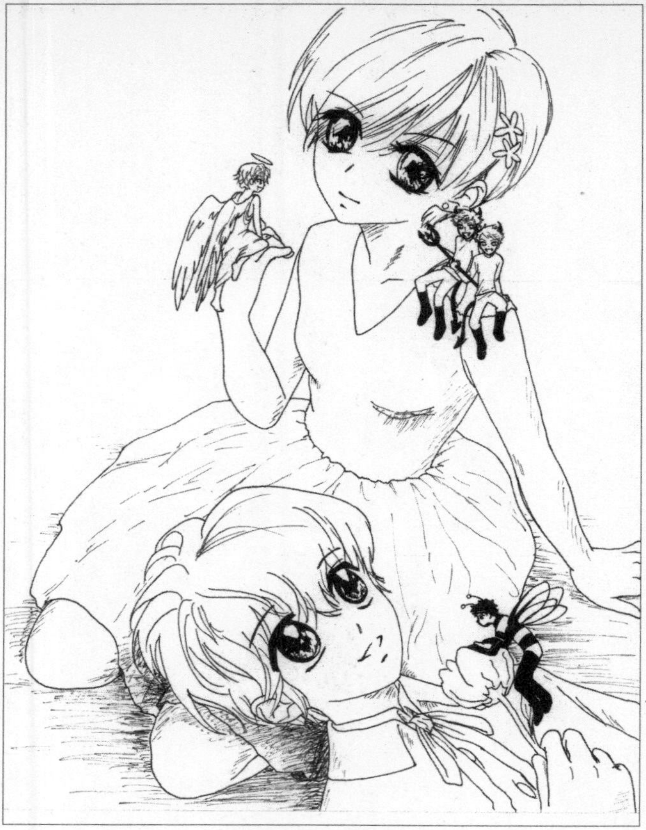

Briana De Iulio

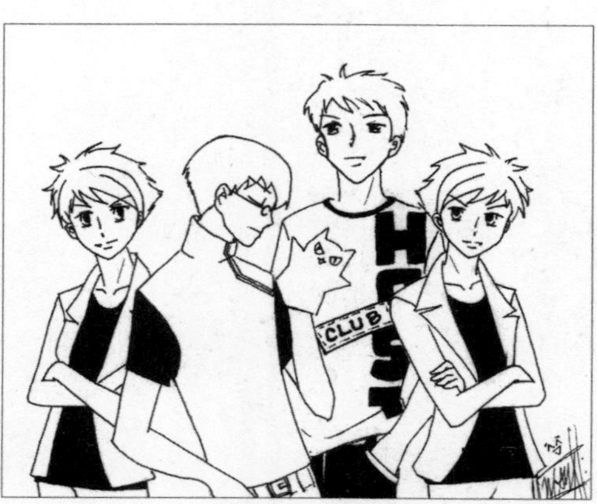
CLUB

Maritza A. Molina

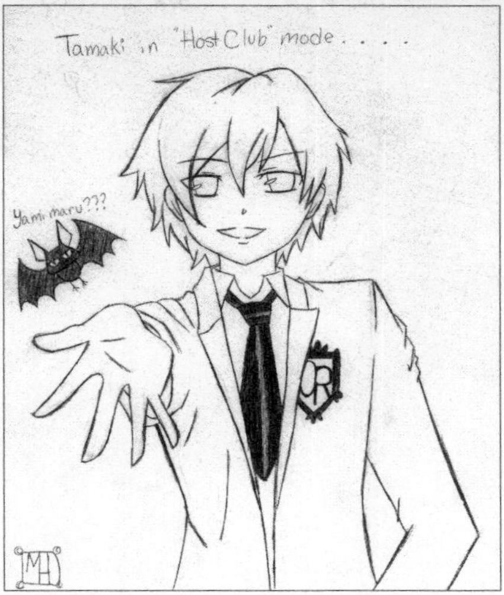
Tamaki in "Host Club" mode....
Yami-maru???
Shoon Lei Phyo

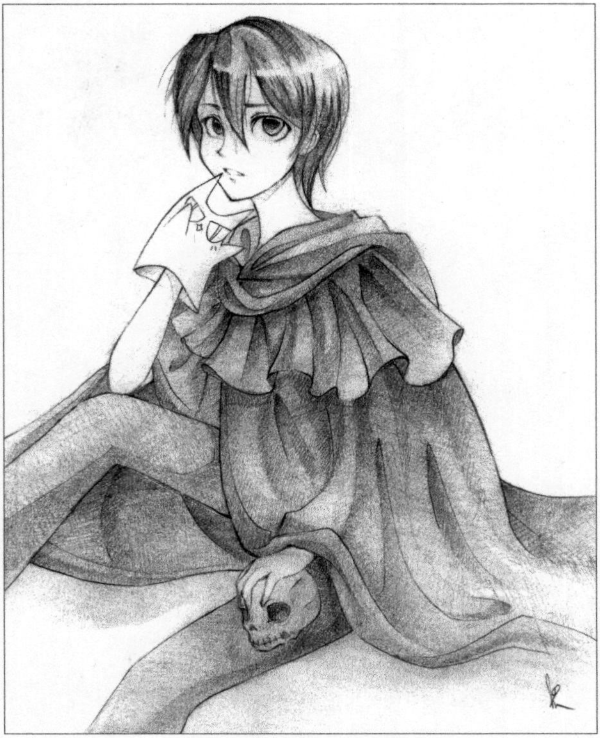
Mackenzie Heywood

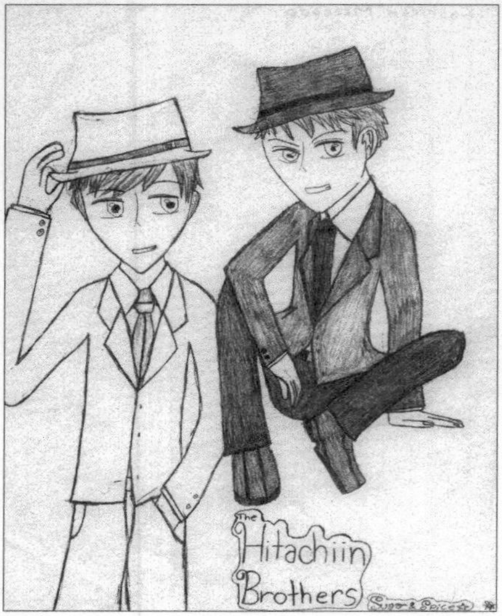
The Hitachiin Brothers

Kathleen Mercado

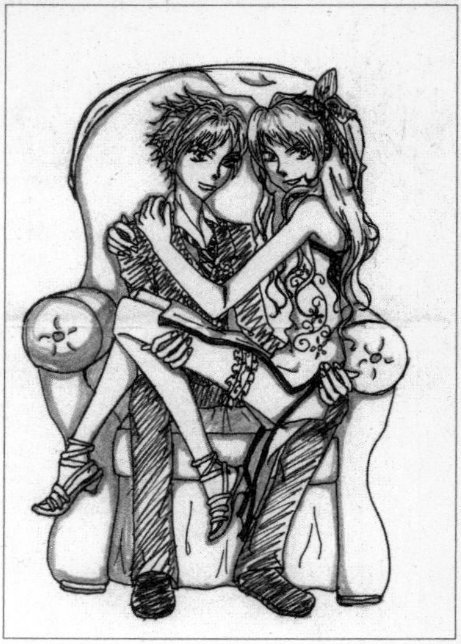

Shannon Xiong

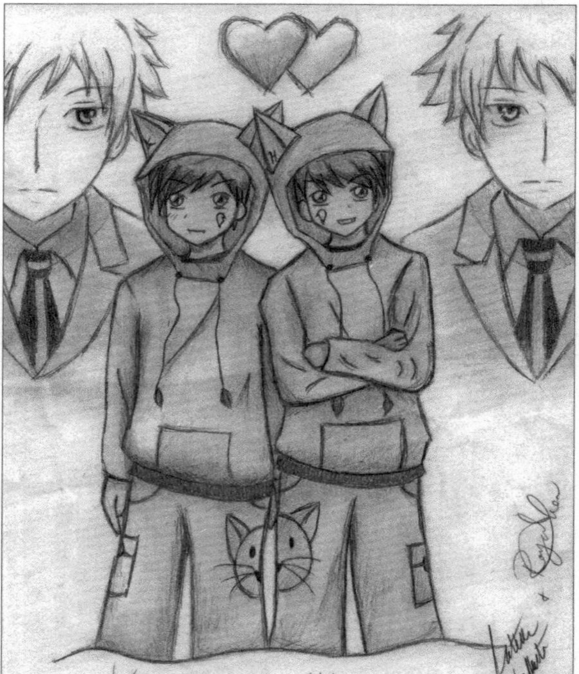
Kaoru ♥ & Hikaru ♥

Kathleen Lallanta & Royal Chen

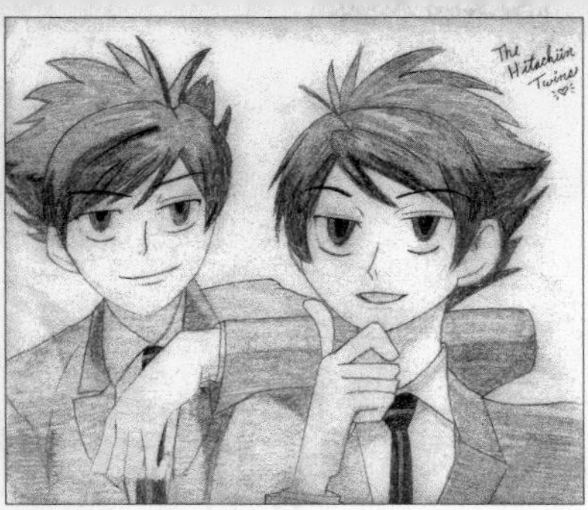
The Hitachiin Twins

Darcy Dunn

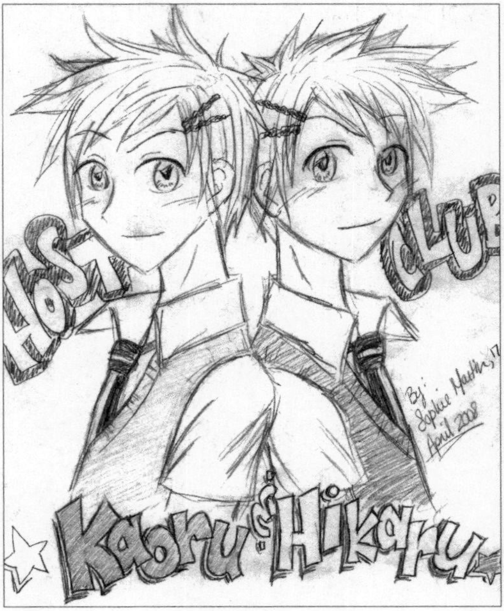
HOST
CLUB
By: Sophie Martin, 17
April 2008
Kaoru & Hikaru

Sophie Martin

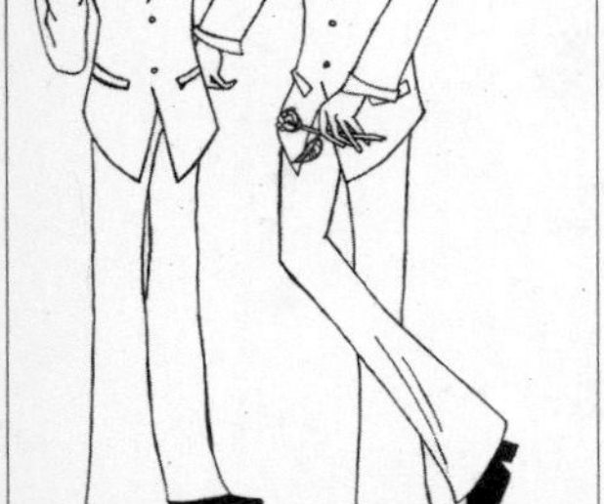
Amanda Mah

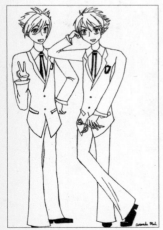

Amanda Mah

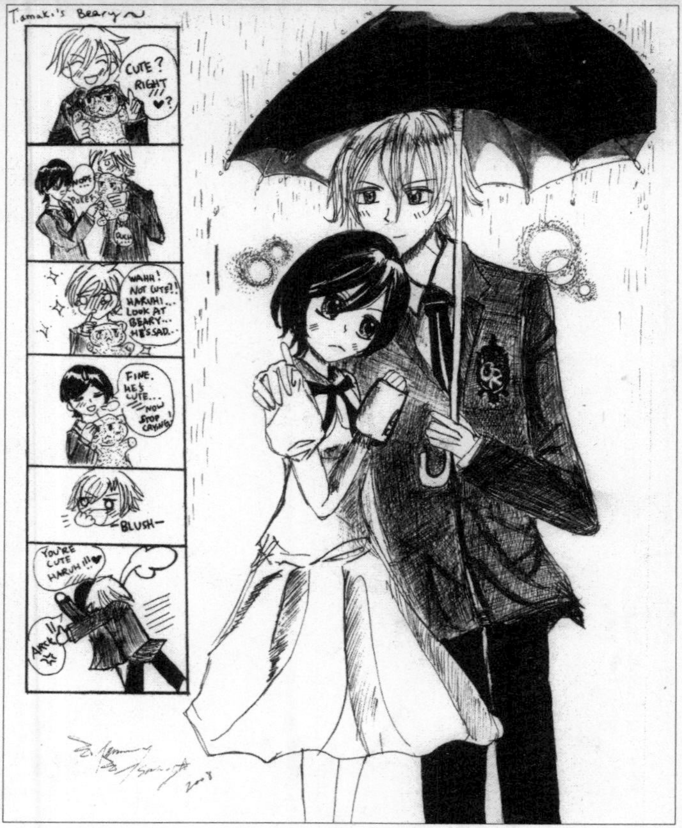
Tamaki's Beary~
CUTE? RIGHT /// ♥?
NOPE...
POKE
OUCH...
WAHH! NOT CUTE?!! HARUHI... LOOK AT BEARY... HE'S SAD...
FINE. HE'S CUTE... NOW STOP CRYING!
-BLUSH-
YOU'RE CUTE HARUHI!!!♥
ARRCK!!

Tammy Tsang

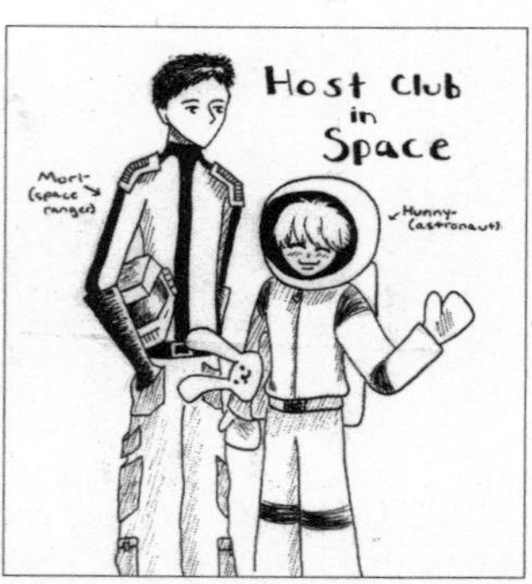
Host Club in Space
Mori- (space ranger)
Hunny- (astronaut)

Nicola Overstreet

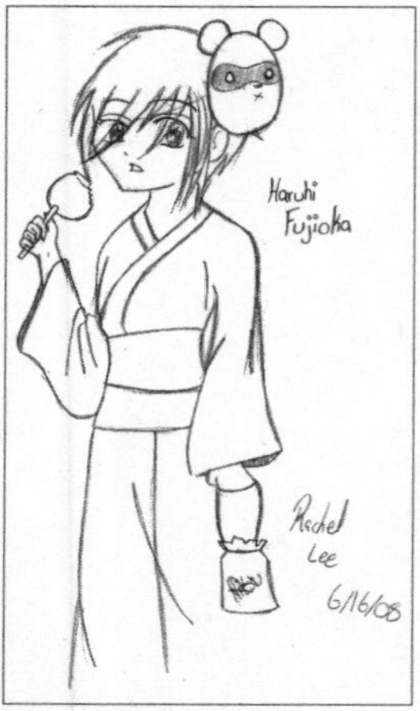
Haruhi Fujioka
Rachel Lee
6/16/08

Rachel Lee

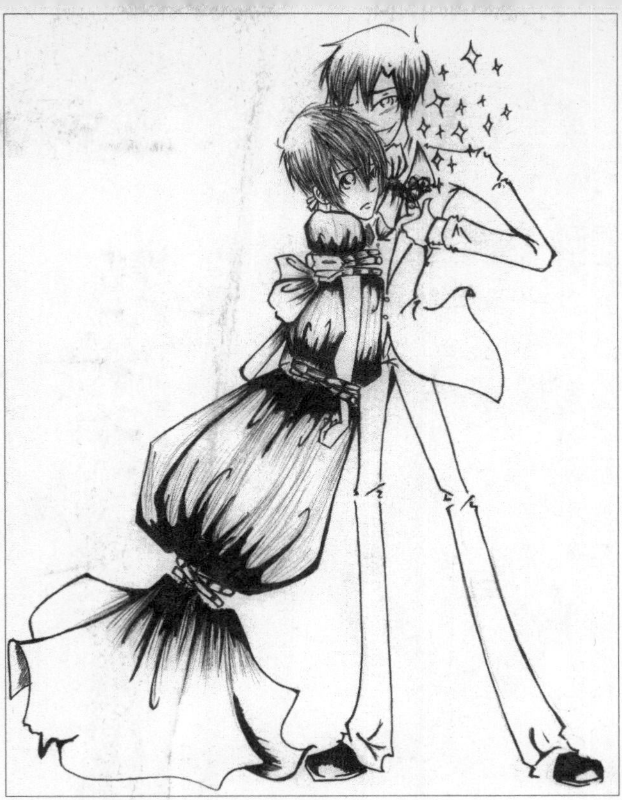

Jesse Smallman

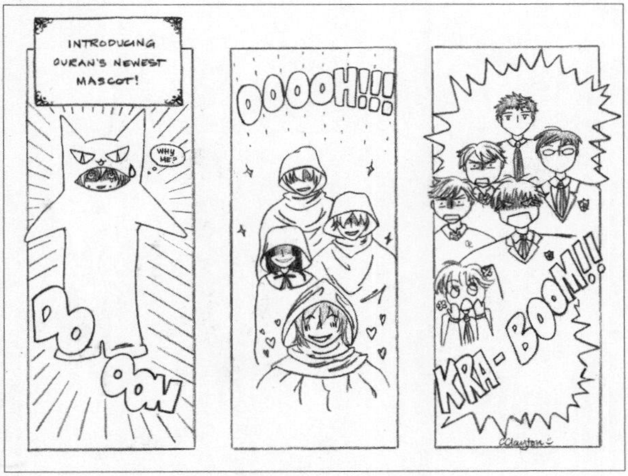
KRA-BOOM!!
OOOOH!!!
INTRODUCING OURAN'S NEWEST MASCOT!
WHY ME?
DO OON

Cheryl Clayton

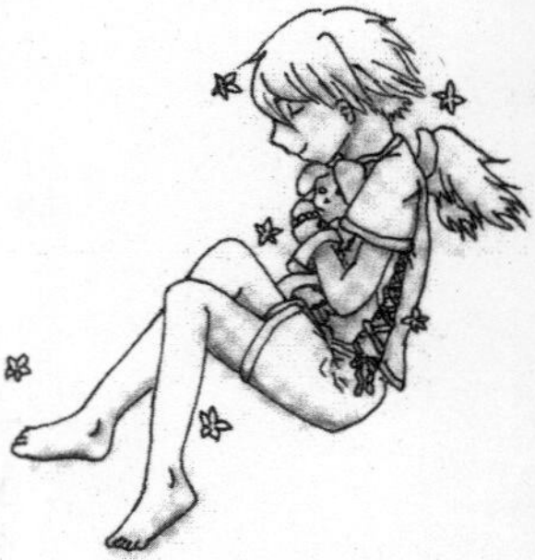

Bao Loan Nguyen

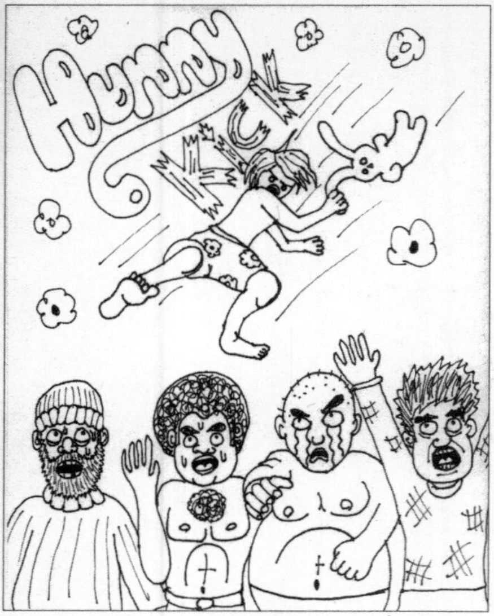
HUNNY KICK

Ryan Yu

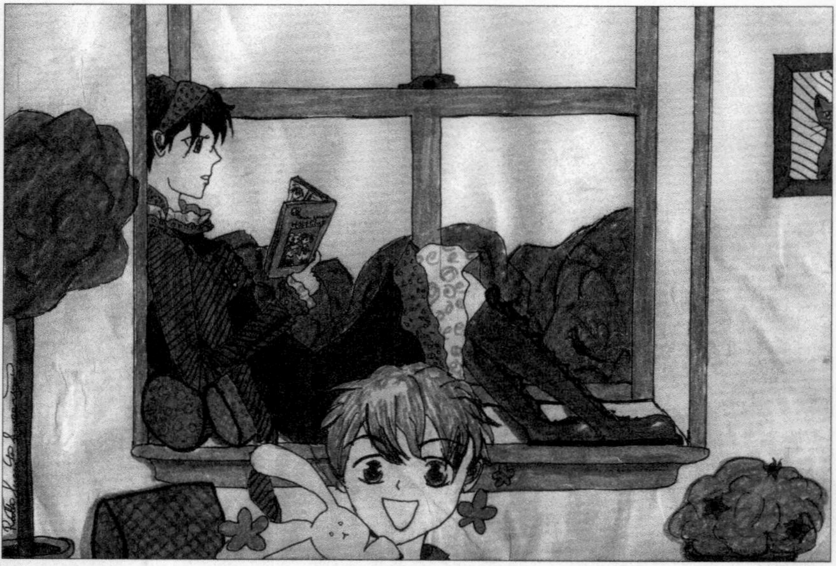

Ruth Juanita Swearingin

Author Bio

Bisco Hatori made her manga debut with *Isshun kan no Romance* (A Moment of Romance) in *LaLa DX* magazine. The comedy *Ouran High School Host Club* is her breakout hit. When she's stuck thinking up characters' names, she gets inspired by loud, upbeat music (her radio is set to NACK5 FM). She enjoys reading all kinds of manga, but she's especially fond of the sci-fi drama *Please Save My Earth* and *Slam Dunk*, a basketball classic.

OURAN HIGH SCHOOL HOST CLUB
Vol. 11
The Shojo Beat Manga Edition

STORY AND ART BY BISCO HATORI

Translation & English Adaptation/Masumi Matsumoto
Touch-up Art & Lettering/George Caltsoudas
Graphic Design/Izumi Evers
Editor/Nancy Thistlethwaite

Editor in Chief, Books/Alvin Lu
Editor in Chief, Magazines/Marc Weidenbaum
VP, Publishing Licensing/Rika Inouye
VP, Sales and Product Marketing/Gonzalo Ferreyra
VP, Creative/Linda Espinosa
Publisher/Hyoe Narita

Printed in Canada

Published by VIZ Media, LLC
P.O. Box 77010
San Francisco, CA 94107

Shojo Beat Manga Edition
10 9 8 7 6 5 4 3 2 1
First printing, November 2008

store.viz.com

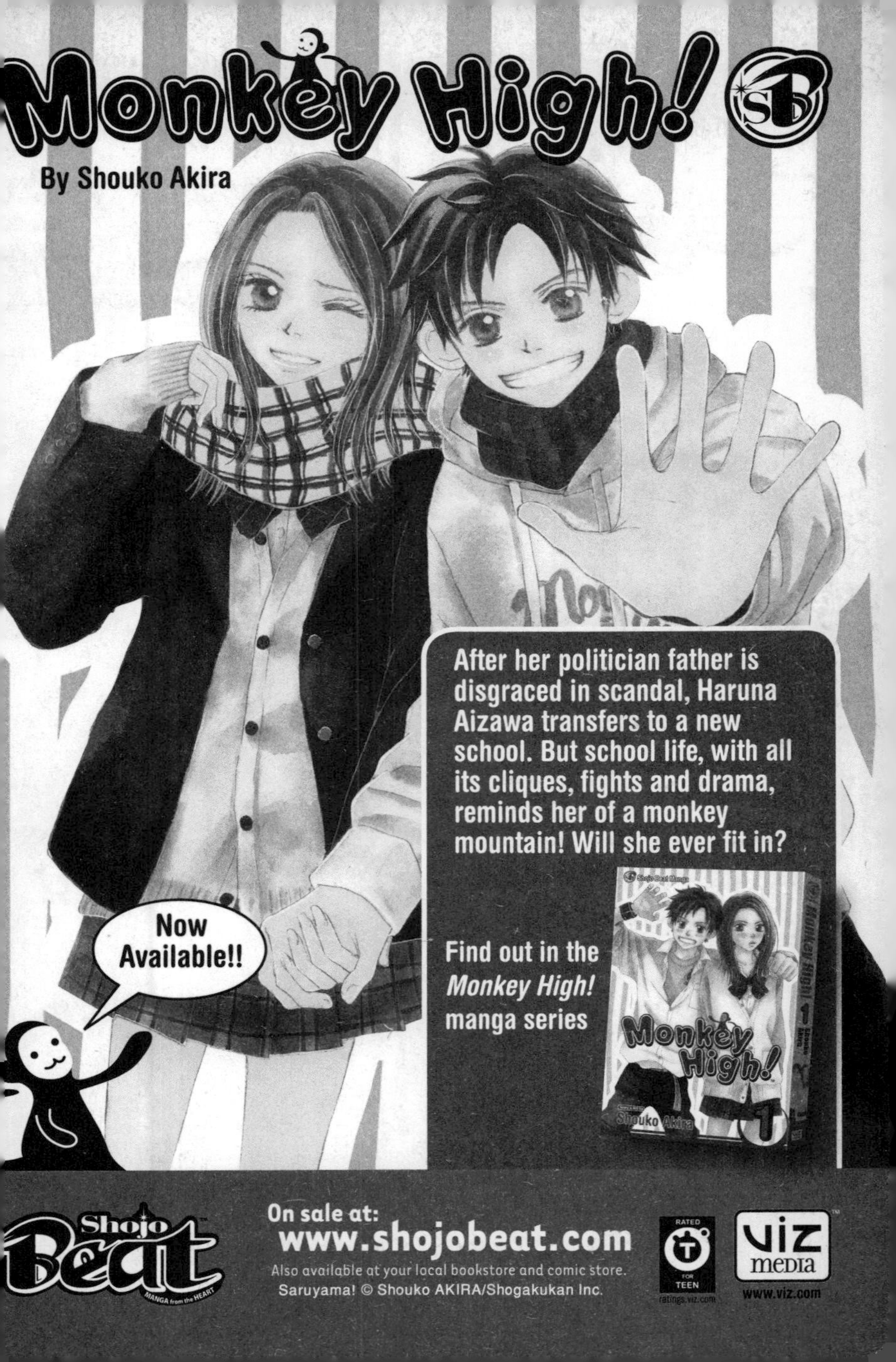
Monkey High!
By Shouko Akira
After her politician father is disgraced in scandal, Haruna Aizawa transfers to a new school. But school life, with all its cliques, fights and drama, reminds her of a monkey mountain! Will she ever fit in?
Now Available!!
Find out in the Monkey High! manga series
Monkey High!
Shouko Akira
Shojo Beat
On sale at:
www.shojobeat.com
Also available at your local bookstore and comic store.
Saruyama! © Shouko AKIRA/Shogakukan Inc.
RATED T FOR TEEN
ratings.viz.com
VIZ media
www.viz.com

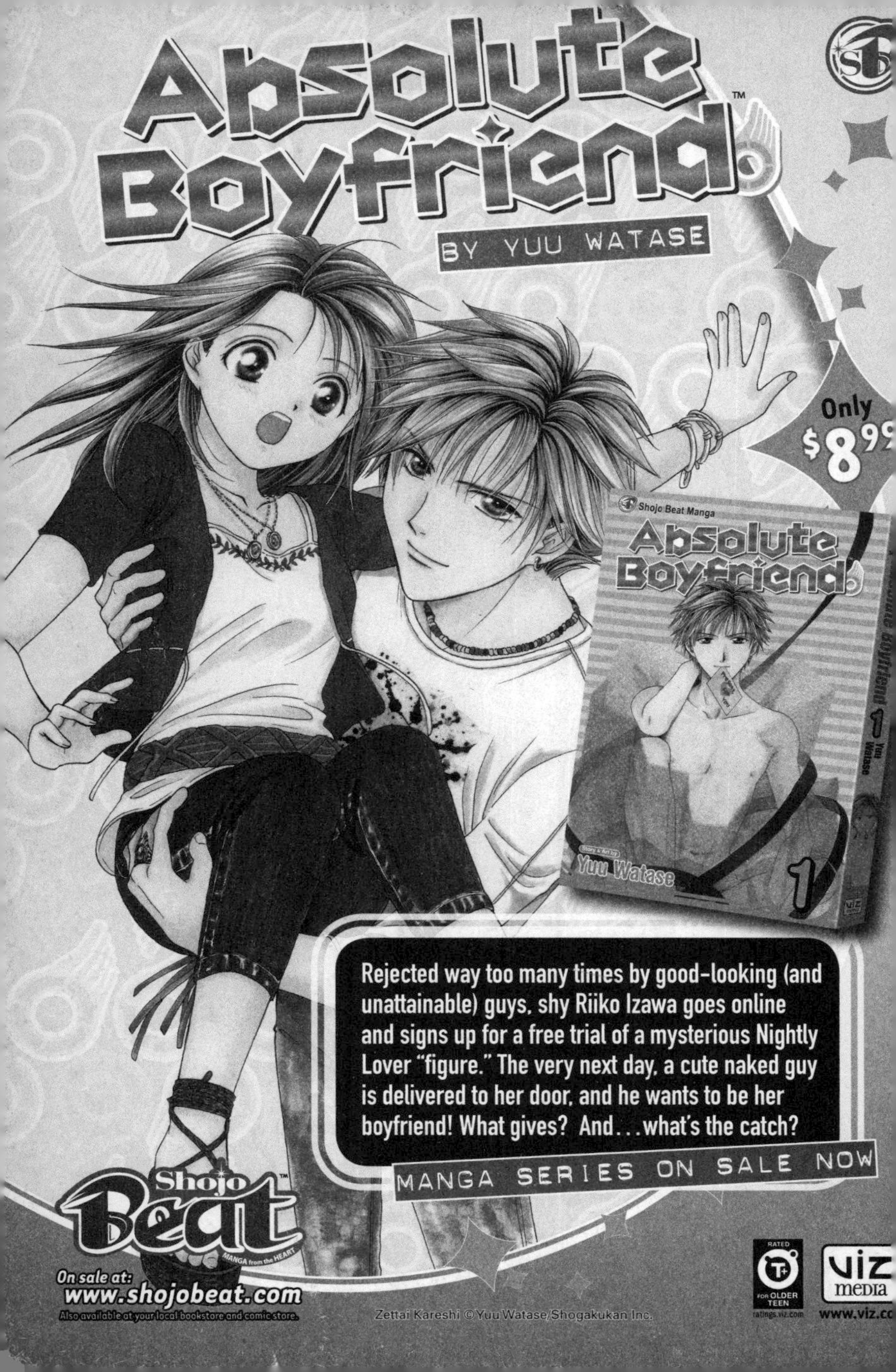
Absolute Boyfriend™
BY YUU WATASE
Only $8.99
Shojo Beat Manga
Absolute Boyfriend
Absolute Boyfriend 1 Yuu Watase
Story & Art by
Yuu Watase
1
Rejected way too many times by good-looking (and unattainable) guys, shy Riiko Izawa goes online and signs up for a free trial of a mysterious Nightly Lover "figure." The very next day, a cute naked guy is delivered to her door, and he wants to be her boyfriend! What gives? And...what's the catch?
MANGA SERIES ON SALE NOW
Shojo Beat™
MANGA from the HEART
On sale at:
www.shojobeat.com
Also available at your local bookstore and comic store.
Zettai Kareshi © Yuu Watase/Shogakukan Inc.
RATED T+ FOR OLDER TEEN
ratings.viz.com
viz media
www.viz.co

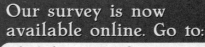